LAND USE
CONTROLS
IN THE UNITED STATES

Books by Natural Resources Defense Council, Inc.
LAND USE CONTROLS IN NEW YORK STATE
LAND USE CONTROLS IN THE UNITED STATES

LAND USE CONTROLS

IN THE UNITED STATES

A Handbook on
the Legal Rights of Citizens

BY

NATURAL RESOURCES DEFENSE COUNCIL, INC.

ELAINE MOSS, *Editor*

THE DIAL PRESS/JAMES WADE
New York
1977

Manufactured in the United States of America
Second printing, 1977

Library of Congress Cataloging in Publication Data

Natural Resources Defense Council.
  Land use controls in the United States.

  Bibliography: p.
  Includes index.
  1. Regional planning—Law and legislation—
United States. 2. Environmental law—United States.
I. Moss, Elaine. II. Title.
KF5698.N38   346′.73′044   76-41667
ISBN 0–8037–4676–8
ISBN 0–8037–4677–6 pbk.

ACKNOWLEDGMENTS

Many people have participated in the preparation of this book. Present or former NRDC staff members who have been involved are John H. Adams, Esq.; Angus Macbeth, Esq.; Sarah Chasis, Esq.; L. Cullen Phillips; Diane L. Donley; Khristine L. Hall, Esq.; Ronald Outen; David G. Hawkins, Esq.; J. G. Speth, Esq.; Edward L. Strohbehn, Jr., Esq.; Laurance Rockefeller, Esq.; Ross Sandler, Esq.; Frances G. Beinecke; Johanna H. Wald, Esq.; Roger Beers, Esq.; and John D. Leshy, Esq. Other individuals who have read various sections and offered suggestions are Richard O. Brooks, Esq.; Adrian Curtis; and Clifton Curtis, Esq.

CONTENTS

NRDC

The Natural Resources Defense Council (NRDC) is a nonprofit, tax-exempt, membership organization dedicated to protecting America's endangered natural resources and improving the quality of the human environment. With offices in New York, Washington, D.C., and Palo Alto, California, its staff of over twenty lawyers, scientists, and other specialists combine monitoring of government agencies, scientific research, litigation, and citizen education in a program of action. NRDC's major involvements have been in the areas of air pollution, water pollution, nuclear safety, land use, management of the public lands, strip mining, stream channelization, protection of fish and wildlife, transportation, noise, ozone depletion, and environmental carcinogens. Its special projects on specific issues include a Land Use Project, a Coastal Zone Project, a Catskill/Adirondack Project, a Clean Air Project, and a Clean Water Project. NRDC is supported entirely by tax-deductible contributions.

LAND USE
CONTROLS
IN THE UNITED STATES

CHAPTER 1

Purpose and Scope of the Book

L AND IS OUR most fundamental natural resource. How it is used affects

· the integrity of biological systems upon which human life depends
· the degree of water pollution, air pollution, noise pollution, and traffic congestion in our society
· the amounts and types of energy we consume
· the preservation of open space
· our customs, the character of our communities, and the kind of lives we are able to lead

When environmental protection first became a powerful force in the United States, air and water pollution were most readily identified as the problems which had to be solved. Air and water were seen as common resources shared by all the people and pollution was recognized as harmful to the general public. Land, on the other hand, has traditionally been viewed as "private property," which owners may use as they please, provided that they do not injure others. However, as major alterations of the natural state of land have become common in land development, the harm to the public caused by different kinds of land use has become much more apparent and better defined.

We now know that when wetlands are filled and covered with dwellings or concrete, not only is open space lost, but an entire ecosystem is destroyed. A biologically rich and productive natural resource which sustained plant and animal life at the bottom of the food chain, as well as provided natural flood protection and oxidation of wastes, is exchanged for a man-made creation which serves only its own ends. When pastures are carved into subdivisions, among the many problems that are likely to follow are erosion, water pollution, water supply depletion, traffic congestion, bad air, noise, and diminishing wildlife. It is now clear that the hand of man has fallen very heavily on our country, leaving behind not just aesthetic blight but severe disruptions of ecological systems and conditions detrimental to human health and welfare.

A fuller awareness of the serious harms which the general public may suffer as a result of what individuals do with their land has made it apparent that more effective and more extensive land use regulation is essential. Citizens across the country are now insisting that action be taken to stop the abuse of land that has resulted from our past approach—or lack of approach—to land use decision making. Refusing to accept destructive disregard for natural resources as inevitable and recognizing that specialists, government officials, and politicians will never solve all their problems for them, more and more people are exercising their rights to influence governmental decision making and to seek enforcement of laws. They are forming citizens' groups to work for sound land use planning and regulation, to fight proposals or projects which ignore environmental damage, and to demand that government address these problems responsibly.

In the past, regulation of land use has been carried out almost exclusively at the local level of government, in scattered and fragmented jurisdictions. Our heightened understanding of the broad and serious impact of different uses of land, along with an appreciation of the past failures of local governments to protect environmental values, has led to the realization that other levels of governments must also be involved in matters affecting land use. During the past three years national land use policy and planning assistance acts have been seriously considered by Congress. Partly in response to this proposed federal legislation, as well as to the severity of the problems faced and the degree of public concern, a number of states have established statewide land use programs and many others are carefully studying the possibility of doing so. In 1972 a Coastal Zone Management Act was passed by Congress to provide federal funds and guidance for the planning and implementation of water and land use management programs in coastal areas (including those bordering on the Great Lakes), where the impact of development is particularly destructive. In addition, land use control and management requirements are important components of the landmark federal environmental legislation passed during the early 1970s to control air and water pollution across the country. Other important federal laws, such as the National Environmental Policy Act (NEPA) and the statutes governing the National Flood Insurance Program, also have considerable bearing on land use issues. Further, there are federal laws that require the filing or registration of disclosure information on subdivided land and other types of property, that set standards and environmental restraints on the planning and construction of highways and airports, and that establish management procedures for the vast federally owned public lands, which comprise one third of the nation's land.

Most federal programs, of course, involve not only the federal government, but state and local governments as well. State and localities participate in different programs in a variety of ways: they receive grants and assistance; they develop implementation plans; they review plans, project proposals, and environmental impact statements; they issue permits on behalf of the federal government; and they enforce federal standards. All in all, as is intended in a federal system, national programs are usually intergovernmental programs.

This book sets out for citizens what means exist now for controlling or influencing the use of land. It explains laws and programs affecting land use which have been established at all levels of government. Each chapter includes a section or sections on "citizen action" which discuss how citizens can participate in the implementation and enforcement of the law. If the monumental problems of land abuse are to be squarely confronted and effective solutions sought, this kind of public involvement in governmental decision making is absolutely essential.

The book first reviews the basic constitutional issues which are involved in land use regulation. Central to this discussion is the frequently adjudicated "takings" issue, but other important constitutional questions such as due process and equal protection are also reviewed.

Attention is then turned to the task of setting out existing land use controls. The federal laws which have provisions affecting land use are discussed first, since they, of course, apply nationwide. In each case, not only are statutory requirements explained, but also agency regulations and problems of implementation which have arisen.

After a full treatment of the major federal laws with land use control implications, land use programs at the state level are then discussed. Since it is not possible to review the actions taken by all fifty states or to clarify the countless organizational variations which exist, this discussion focuses on the generic types of legislation which have been enacted, providing as many specific examples as space permits, and on the statewide land use programs which have been adopted by certain states.

The problems of regional organizations and several instances of effective regional land use programs are described next. Emphasis is placed on the need to find regional solutions to regional problems.

Finally, the book explains the various kinds of land use controls that may exist at the local level of government. Since land use control at the local level is carried out by thousands of jurisdictions across the country and varies markedly in different areas, the discussion here presents a general account of local powers. It reviews the basis of local regulation of land use and development, what the most prevalent controls and programs are and how they work, and such topics as rural unpreparedness for development, local conservation commissions, and property tax concerns.

A note on legal citations is provided as an aid for those using the notes at the end of each chapter. This note briefly and simply explains how court cases, statutes, and regulations are recorded and cited.

Every effort has been made to ensure that the material presented in this book is as up-to-date as possible. However, in a field such as land use new legislation, regulations, and court decisions appear virtually every week. Also, land use is such a broad and complex subject that it is not possible to deal with all its aspects in a single volume. The intent here is to set out the basic framework of land use legislation and regulation as it exists in the United States today.

CHAPTER 2

Basic Constitutional Issues

THE UNITED STATES Constitution sets limits on the actions which the federal government and the governments of the states may take in dealing with their citizens. For land use control, the most significant restraint is imposed by the Fifth Amendment, which bars the federal government from taking private property for public use without just compensation. The terms of the Fourteenth Amendment make this prohibition applicable to the state governments as well and, in addition, state constitutions have similar "takings" provisions. Thus both the federal and state governments are constitutionally limited in their powers over private property. Other constitutional requirements—the rights to equal protection of the law, to due process of law, and to travel—have an impact on land use as well. They will be discussed following an examination of the "takings clause."[1]

The takings clause has three major components: public use, just compensation, and taking. The concepts of public use and just compensation are comparatively straightforward. Public use refers to the requirement that the public interest be served by a governmental taking of private property. It is served where the government acts under the so-called "police power" to promote the public health, safety, morals, and welfare. In general the courts have interpreted the concept of public use very broadly, and a governmental appropriation of private property will be found to be for a public use in almost all cases. Obvious examples of permissible takings are those necessary for public roads, parks, buildings, airports, and urban renewal projects. In a case involving the taking of property for an urban renewal project, the U.S. Supreme Court has provided a wide and extensive definition of the public welfare:

> The concept of the public welfare is broad and inclusive. . . . The values it represents are spiritual as well as physical, aesthetic as well as monetary. It is within the power of the legislature to determine that the community should be beautiful as well as healthy, spacious as well as clean, well-balanced as well as carefully patrolled.[2]

Thus few challenges to governmental abridgements of private property rights will succeed solely on the grounds that they are not within the confines of "public use" or the police power. It should also be noted that a taking of property for public use may involve less than assumption by the government of full title to the land involved, as when government requires an access right-of-way across private property.

Just compensation is also an essentially straightforward requirement. It dictates that when property is taken, the government must pay the owner for the value of that which has been taken. There are, of course, frequent disputes concerning how the value of taken property should be measured, what the value actually is, and how the effect of taking part of a piece of property on that which remains can be assessed. These are important issues for those whose land is taken, but they do not go to the heart of the central problem raised by the takings clause.

The major takings issue pertains to government regulation of private property and whether or not particular regulations amount to a taking for which compensation must be paid. If government wants to build a highway through farmland, it will clearly have to compensate the landowners for the land needed for this public purpose. On the other hand, government may enact regulations pursuant to a public purpose that restrict the uses which may be made of private property but require no compensation. For example, a limitation on the height and size of buildings which assures that they will not cut off light and air from their neighbors is a regulation under the police power for which compensation need not be paid. This is true even though some uses of the property which may be of very

real economic value are thereby denied to the owner. In some locations this perfectly ordinary zoning regulation might decrease the
value of a piece of property by perhaps $100,000 or 25 percent of its
value.

The basic problem then is the determination in particular cases
of whether a given restriction on the use of property is a permissible
regulation for which compensation need not be paid or is rather a
taking for which compensation must be provided. Four basic theories have been developed by the courts to analyze this distinction. No
one of these theories is used solely or consistently by present-day
courts; instead, most cases show a mixing of theories. This makes it
difficult in any hard case to know which way a court will decide and
for what reasons. Nevertheless, an understanding of the basic theories used in analysis can provide insight into the considerations
which the courts weigh and enable one to make some judgments
regarding how particular cases will be viewed. Further information
concerning how these theories can be effectively applied to defend a
challenged law or to strengthen proposed legislation is available from
the Natural Resources Defense Council.[3]

The first theory setting out a means of distinguishing between
regulation and taking focuses on one aspect of regulation under the
police power, namely, the fact that regulation seeks to prevent private parties from harming the public. This theory holds that when
a regulation simply seeks to prevent harm from a private party, no
taking is involved and no compensation is required. It is an expression of one of the oldest precepts of the common law: No man may
use his property so as to injure his neighbor. The courts have relied
on this theory to uphold some very drastic regulations. For instance,
in *Mugler* v. *Kansas,*[4] the Supreme Court in 1887 upheld a law which
prohibited the manufacture and sale of liquor in Kansas and thereby
made Mugler's brewery worthless. The court held that no compensation was required, stating:

> The exercise of the police power by the destruction of property which
> is itself a public nuisance, or the prohibition of its use in a particular
> way, whereby its value becomes depreciated, is very different from
> taking property for public use. . . . In the one case, a nuisance only is
> abated; in the other, unoffending property is taken away from an inno-
> cent owner.[5]

Forty years later, the Supreme Court upheld a stringent Virginia law
which required the destruction of red cedar trees that were in close

proximity to apple orchards, because the cedars were hosts to a pest which destroyed apple trees.[6] No compensation was allowed for the loss of the cedars.

A final example of the use of this theory in the modern context of wetland protection is provided by the 1972 decision of the Wisconsin Supreme Court in *Just* v. *Marinette County.*[7] In that case, the court upheld a prohibition against the filling of a freshwater wetland and stated:

> An owner of land has no absolute and unlimited right to change the essential natural character of his land so as to use it for a purpose for which it was unsuited in its natural state and which injures the rights of others. . . . The changing of wetlands and swamps to the damage of the general public by upsetting the natural environment and the natural relationship is not a reasonable use of that land which is protected from police power regulation. . . . [N]othing this court has said or held in prior cases indicate [sic] that destroying the natural character of a swamp or a wetland so as to make that location available for human habitation is a reasonable use of that land when the new use, although of a more economical value to the owner, causes a harm to the general public.[8]

The second theory for distinguishing a regulation from a taking is the reverse side of the first theory. It contends that when a regulation is imposed in order to achieve a public benefit rather than simply to prevent a private harm, then a taking for which compensation must be paid has occurred. This was one of the theories used by the Supreme Court in 1922 in analyzing a Pennsylvania law which prohibited underground coal mining that would result in the subsidence or caving in of public buildings, streets, or homes.[9] The circumstance that prompted the law was the ownership by a mining company of subsurface mining rights to land upon which the town and private individuals held surface rights. The Court struck down the law:

> The rights of the public in a street purchased or laid out by eminent domain are those it has paid for. If in any case its representatives have been so short sighted as to acquire only surface rights without the right of support, we see no more authority for supplying the latter without compensation than there was for taking the right of way in the first place and refusing to pay for it because the public wanted it very much. . . . We are in danger of forgetting that a strong public desire to improve the public condition is not enough to warrant achieving the desire by a shorter cut than the constitutional way of paying for the change.[10]

The Connecticut Supreme Court in 1964 relied partially on the same type of analysis in striking down a floodplain zoning regulation which limited the uses of land in the floodplain to those which did not involve structures.[11] Permissible uses included parks, playgrounds, and "wildlife sanctuaries operated by governmental units or non-profit organizations." The court did not let the regulation stand, holding that:

> although the objective of the Fairfield flood and erosion control board is a laudable one and although we have no reason to doubt the high purpose of their action, these factors cannot overcome constitutional principles. . . . Where most of the value of a person's property has to be sacrificed so that community welfare may be served, and where the owner does not directly benefit from the evil avoided . . . , the occasion is appropriate for the exercise of eminent domain.[12]

It does not take long to perceive that the prevention of harm from private parties and the securing of a public benefit are coincident elements of regulation under the police power. The police power is exercised to promote the public health, safety, and welfare. Therefore, it typically operates simultaneously to prevent harm by private parties and to secure a benefit for the public. Although the closing of Mugler's brewery in Kansas was held to be a prevention of harm for which no compensation was available, it could also have been viewed as the achievement of a public benefit at private expense. Likewise, although the Pennsylvania coal mining law was judged to secure a public benefit for which compensation had to be paid, it could also have been considered to prevent harm to homeowners and street users. Because of this inherent interrelationship, the traditions of a court and the general feelings and perceptions of the public are of great importance in guiding judges in their decisions regarding whether a regulatory law permissibly prevents private harm or impermissibly secures a benefit for the public.

The third theory is not based on philosophical distinctions between harm and benefit, but focuses on the practical consequences of regulation: financial loss. This theory holds that where there is a diminution of value which amounts to a practical confiscation of the property or which leaves the owner no reasonable use of his land (usually meaning no economically profitable use), then a taking has occurred and compensation must be paid. In both the Pennsylvania coal mining case and the Connecticut floodplain case discussed above, the courts put heavy emphasis on the loss of value and use of the property incurred by private property owners. Generally a finding that there has been a practical confiscation of private property is closely intertwined with a finding that a law impermissibly secures a public benefit. This third theory is the basis upon which courts in Maine and Massachusetts have struck down statutes that sought to preserve wetlands but which, in so doing, destroyed the value of wetland property held by people who wished to fill and develop it.[13]

A study made in 1963 showed that a loss of two thirds of the value of property was the average point at which the courts have found a taking rather than a permissible regulation.[14] But much more drastic losses of value have survived attack. In *Hadacheck* v. *Sebastian*[15] the Supreme Court upheld a regulation where the loss in value was from $800,000 to $60,000, and diminutions of approximately 75 percent are quite frequent among statutes which have withstood constitutional challenge.[16] Not surprisingly, commentators have concluded that there is no basis for precise prediction in dollars and cents and that while financial loss is a relevant consideration, it is not always the decisive one.[17]

The fourth theory employs a balancing test, and while it is not always clear exactly what is weighed on either side of the balance, generally the importance of the governmental policy being achieved is weighed against the intrusion into the privately held property. The more important the governmental policy, the less likely the court is to find a taking; and the greater the invasion of private rights, the more likely a taking will be found. The Supreme Court first set out this rule in 1894,[18] and reaffirmed it as good law once again in 1962 in *Goldblatt* v. *Town of Hempstead:*

> To justify the State in . . . interposing its authority in behalf of the public, it must appear, first, that the interests of the public . . . require such interference; and, second, that the means are reasonably necessary for the accomplishment of the purpose, and not unduly oppressive upon individuals.[19]

The New Hampshire Supreme Court relied, in part, on such a balancing test in sustaining the denial of a permit to fill tidal wetlands:

> The validity of the state action is determined by balancing the "importance of the public benefit which is sought to be promoted against the seriousness of the restriction of a private right sought to be imposed." *Richardson* v. *Beattie,* 98 N.H. 71, 75–76, 95 A.2d 122, 125 (1953). The state action is sustained in these cases unless the public interest is so

clearly of minor importance as to make the restriction of individual rights unreasonable.[20]

This theory contains some of the basic notions of due process, the constitutional requirement that there be a reasonable relationship between a regulation imposed and the interest of the public which is protected. The due process provision, which is discussed further below, is part of the Fourteenth Amendment to the U.S. Constitution and works as a guide for court rulings under the takings clause.

In this discussion of fundamental takings theories, several examples have been drawn from decisions involving various wetlands statutes. Such statutes are a very important contemporary form of land use control, and the many court decisions which have been handed down in challenges to their constitutionality demonstrate in a striking manner that different takings theories may be employed to uphold or strike down comparatively similar types of land use legislation. This can be partially explained by differing fact patterns in the individual cases, but can equally be attributed to changing perceptions on the part of the courts and the use of different legal theories in analyzing the facts. The prevention of harm theory has received more emphasis as the courts have become aware of the importance of wetlands to biological production, flood prevention, and pollution abatement, as well as the integrity of ecological systems. Decisions upholding wetlands statutes have emphasized these elements in Wisconsin,[21] New Hampshire,[22] and Maryland.[23] Earlier decisions employed the second and third theories—the impermissible extraction of a public benefit and the loss of value or of reasonable use—to strike down wetlands protection laws in New Jersey,[24] Massachusetts,[25] Connecticut,[26] and Maine.[27] The balancing theory has been used to sustain a wetlands regulation in New Hampshire,[28] and all four theories were discussed and weighed by the Connecticut Supreme Court when it upheld a wetlands statute and a permit decision made pursuant to that statute.[29]

Thus the body of law on the takings issue has no consistent unifying rationale and cannot be regarded as a coherent whole. The Supreme Court's precept is indisputable: "There is no set formula to determine where regulation ends and taking begins."[30]

Other Constitutional Issues

In the discussion of the takings clause, it has already been pointed out that the due process clause of the U.S. Constitution comes into play by prohibiting regulations in which there is no reasonable relation between the end sought and the regulation enacted. This requirement, along with citizens' constitutional rights to equal protection of the law and to travel, is very significant in the context of land use regulation.

The courts have ruled that if a law enacted by a legislature is reasonable rather than arbitrary and bears a rational relationship to a permissible state objective, they will not strike the law down as violative of the due process or the equal protection clause.[31] In dealing with land use regulations, the courts have generally given these constitutional requirements a very liberal reading and found only the most extreme regulations impermissible.

For example, in 1974 the U.S. Supreme Court upheld an ordinance enacted by Belle Terre, a village of seven hundred people located on Long Island's North Shore, which restricted land use to one-family dwellings.[32] As used in the ordinance, "family" was defined as (1) one or more persons related by blood, adoption, or marriage, living and cooking as a single housekeeping unit; or (2) not more than two persons unrelated by blood, adoption, or marriage, living and cooking together as a single housekeeping unit.

The ordinance was challenged on the ground that by prohibiting groups consisting of more than two unrelated people from residing in the community, it deprived a household of unrelated individuals of the equal protection of the law. The Supreme Court found that the ordinance did not violate the equal protection clause, since it was reasonable and not arbitrary and bore a rational relationship to permissible governmental objectives, which were held to include low density, reduced traffic flow, clean air, and quiet:

> A quiet place where yards are wide, people few, and motor vehicles restricted are legitimate guidelines in a land-use project addressed to family needs. . . . The police power is not confined to elimination of filth, stench, and unhealthy places. It is ample to lay out zones where family values, youth values, and the blessings of quiet seclusion and clean air make the area a sanctuary for people.[33]

The plaintiffs had also claimed that the Belle Terre ordinance interfered with people's right to travel and to migrate and settle within a state. The Supreme Court, however, held that the ordinance did not infringe upon this right, observing that it was not aimed at transients.

In other cases, courts have struck down land use regulations for unlawfully excluding certain groups of people. Generally, the term "exclusionary zoning" has been applied by the courts to regulatory schemes which work to exclude housing for low income groups, and thereby also exclude racial minorities. For example, a municipal zoning ordinance struck down as exclusionary by New Jersey's highest court in *Southern Burlington County N.A.A.C.P.* v. *Township of Mount Laurel*[34] permitted only one type of housing—single-family detached dwellings. All other types of housing, including apartments, town (row) houses, and mobile homes, were prohibited. Some multi-family units had been allowed by agreement under a planned unit development ordinance, but even these units were designed for the relatively affluent. The court also found that the Mount Laurel zoning ordinance was so restrictive in its minimum lot area, lot frontage, and building size requirements that it precluded single-family housing for even moderate income families. Finally, the town had zoned almost 30 percent of its land, or over 4,100 acres, for industrial and related uses, allowing farm dwellings as the only permissible residential use. During the past ten years, however, only about one hundred acres of the town had been developed industrially and the court saw little likelihood of any extensive industrial development in the future.

Basing its judgment on the provisions of the New Jersey constitution, rather than on the U.S. Constitution or state enabling legislation, the court found Mount Laurel's zoning ordinance to be contrary to the general welfare and outside the intended scope of the zoning power. It further held that:

> As a developing municipality, Mount Laurel must, by its land use regulations, make realistically possible the opportunity for an appropriate variety and choice of housing for all categories of people who may desire to live there, of course including those of low and moderate income.[35]

Thus the court not only struck down the zoning ordinance, but in an unusual, precedent-setting step required the town to take positive action to make low income housing feasible.

The issues of exclusionary zoning, due process, and denial of the right to travel also arise in the context of the phased growth control ordinances enacted by localities in recent years. The right of government to regulate land development in the interest of controlling growth was approved by the highest court of New York State in

1972.[36] The town of Ramapo, which is within commuting distance of New York City, amended its zoning ordinance to include a special permit system for residential development. Under this system no property could be developed for residential purposes until the developer could show that certain capital improvements—whether constructed by the town or by the developer himself—would be available for a project by the time it was completed. The town had developed a comprehensive plan for its future growth and upon this had based an eighteen-year capital improvement program setting out the town's schedule for construction of municipal facilities. Thus the town's provision of services needed for residential development would not be forthcoming for some property for as long as eighteen years.

In upholding the Ramapo ordinance, the court pointed to the fact that the restrictions on development were of limited duration and concluded:

> In sum, where it is clear that the existing physical and financial resources of the community are inadequate to furnish the essential services and facilities which a substantial increase in population requires, there is a rational basis for "phased growth" and hence, the challenged ordinance is not violative of the Federal and State Constitutions.[37]

The court held that the ordinance was not exclusionary, but rather sought "to provide a balanced cohesive community dedicated to the efficient utilization of land."[38] It noted that coupled with the town's restrictions were provisions for low and moderate income housing on a large scale.

In 1974 a federal district court in California struck down growth control ordinances enacted by the city of Petaluma, which is forty miles north of San Francisco, on the grounds that they interfered with people's constitutional right to travel and live where they wish.[39] Under the "Petaluma Plan," the city sought to control growth by: (1) limiting new housing units in projects involving five or more units to five hundred units per year, and (2) creating an "urban extension line," which was intended to mark the outer limits of the city's expansion for at least five years, and probably longer. Within this perimeter, the city used density limitations and other techniques to set a maximum population of 55,000 (compared to the projection made in 1962 that the city's population would be 77,000 by 1985). The plan further directed that the five hundred building permits issued each year be allocated as evenly as feasible between single-family dwellings and multiple-unit dwellings (including rental units). Each year 8 to 12 percent of the housing units approved were required to be for low and moderate income housing.

The district court ruled that the plan amounted to an effort to avoid the problems that accompany contemporary trends in population growth by limiting the number of people henceforth permitted to move into the city. The court found that the means employed by the city violated the constitutionally protected right to travel and immigrate to the area. No compelling state interest was found to justify the abridgement of this constitutional right. The financial burden on the city of providing sewage treatment facilities and increased water supply for the greater growth was not found to be adequate justification, nor was a desire to preserve the city's present character. The court very broadly concluded:

> A zoning regulation which has as its purpose the exclusion of additional residents in any degree is not a compelling governmental interest, nor is it one within the public welfare.[40]

The U.S. Court of Appeals for the Ninth Circuit reversed the decision of the district court.[41] First, it ruled that the plaintiff in the case, the Construction Industry Association of Sonoma County, did not have standing to sue on the constitutional issue of the right to travel, since on this issue it was asserting claims not on its own behalf but "on behalf of a group of unknown third parties allegedly excluded from living in Petaluma."[42] The court then reviewed the plaintiff's claim that the Petaluma Plan violated its own due process rights.

The court found that the Petaluma Plan was not arbitrary and unreasonable. It cited two recent cases, *Belle Terre*[43] and *Ybarra* v. *City of Town of Los Altos Hills,*[44] in which the preservation of quiet family neighborhoods and the preservation of a rural environment had been found to be legitimate governmental interests falling within the concept of the public welfare. The court summarized its judgment as follows:

> We conclude therefore that under *Belle Terre* and *Los Altos Hills* the concept of the public welfare is sufficiently broad to uphold Petaluma's desire to preserve its small town character, its open spaces and low density of population, and to grow at an orderly and deliberate pace.[45]

The court also held that the Petaluma Plan was not an exclusionary zoning device, pointing out that although the plan would slow the city's overall growth rate, its requirements for multiple-unit dwellings and low and moderate income units would replace the past pattern of single-family detached homes with an assortment of housing units, varying in price and design. In the words of the court, the plan "offers new opportunities, previously unavailable, to minorities and low and moderate-income persons."[46]

The Construction Industry Association of Sonoma County petitioned the U.S. Supreme Court to review the circuit court's decision in the Petaluma case, but in February 1976 the Supreme Court denied this petition. Consequently, the adoption of plans similar to Petaluma's is expected to take place in many other communities.

In summary, just as is true with respect to the takings clause, court decisions on other constitutional issues related to land use also show considerable variation. The complexities and difficulties inherent in land use regulation, as well as current study and debate, are reflected in the decisions of the various courts. Future decisions in this controversial area may bring further clarification and greater coherence.

NOTES

1. For a book-length review of the takings issue see Fred Bosselman, David Callies, and John Banta, *The Taking Issue: An Analysis of the Constitutional Limits of Land Use Controls* (Washington, D.C.: U.S. Government Printing Office, 1973), which was prepared for the Council on Environmental Quality.

2. Berman v. Parker, 348 U.S. 26, 33 (1954).

3. A "Takings Pamphlet" is available without charge from the Natural Resources Defense Council, 15 West 44th Street, New York, N.Y. 10036.

4. 123 U.S. 623 (1887).

5. 123 U.S. at 669.

6. Miller v. Schoene, 276 U.S. 272 (1928).

7. 201 N.W.2d 761, 4 ERC 1841 (Wis. 1972).

8. 201 N.W.2d at 768.

9. Pennsylvania Coal Co. v. Mahon, 260 U.S. 393 (1922).

10. 260 U.S. at 415–416.

11. Dooley v. Town Plan and Zoning Commission of Town of Fairfield, 151 Conn. 304, 197 A.2d 770 (1964).

12. 197 A.2d at 773–774.

13. State v. Johnson, 265 A.2d 711 (Me. 1970); Commissioner of Natural Resources v. S. Volpe and Co., 349 Mass. 104, 206 N.E.2d 666 (1965).

14. Jan Krasnowiecki and Ann Louise Strong, "Compensable Regulations for Open Space," *Journal of the American Institute of Planners* 24 (1963):89.

15. 239 U.S. 394 (1915).

16. *See* Jon A. Kusler, "Open Space Zoning: Valid Regulation or Invalid Taking," 57 *Minn. L. Rev.* 1, 33 (1972).

17. Robert M. Anderson, *American Law of Zoning: Zoning, Planning, Subdivision Control* (Rochester, N.Y.: The Lawyers Co-operative Publishing Co., 1968), § 2.23.

18. Lawton v. Steele, 152 U.S. 133, 137 (1894).

19. 369 U.S. 590, 594 (1962).

20. Sibson v. State, 336 A.2d 239, 242, 5 ELR 20300, 20301 (N.H. 1975).

21. Just v. Marinette County, 201 N.W.2d 761, 4 ERC 1841 (Wisc. 1972).

22. Sibson v. State, 336 A.2d 239, 5 ELR 20300 (N.H. 1975).

23. Potomac Land and Gravel Co. v. Governor of Maryland, 266 Md. 358, 293 A.2d 241 (1972). In this case the decision also relied on the state's ownership rights in tidal waters.

24. Morris County Land Improvement Co. v. Township of Parsippany-Troy Hills, 40 N.J. 539, 193 A.2d 232 (1963).

25. Commissioner of Natural Resources v. S. Volpe and Co., 349 Mass. 104, 206 N.E.2d 666 (1965) and MacGibbon v. Board of Appeals of Duxbury, 347 Mass. 690, 200 N.E.2d 254 (1964) and 356 Mass. 635, 255 N.E.2d 347 (1970).

26. Bartlett v. Zoning Commission, 161 Conn. 24, 282 A.2d 907 (1971).

27. State v. Johnson, 265 A.2d 711 (Me. 1970).

28. Sibson v. State, 336 A.2d 239, 5 ELR 20300 (N.H. 1975).

29. Brecciaroli v. Commissioner of Environmental Protection, _____ A.2d _____, 5 ELR 20319 (Conn. 1975).

30. Goldblatt v. Town of Hempstead, 369 U.S. 590, 594 (1962).

31. *E.g.,* Village of Belle Terre v. Boraas, 416 U.S. 1, 6 ERC 1417 (1974).

32. *Ibid.*

33. *Ibid.* at 9.

34. 67 N.J. 151, 336 A.2d 713 (1975).

35. 336 A.2d at 731–732.

36. Golden v. Planning Board of Town of Ramapo, 30 N.Y.2d 359, 334 N.Y.S.2d 138, 285 N.E.2d 291 (1972), *appeal dismissed,* 409 U.S. 1003 (1972).

37. 285 N.E.2d at 304–305.

38. *Ibid.* at 302.

39. Construction Industry Association of Sonoma County v. City of Petaluma, 375 F. Supp. 574, 6 ERC 1453 (N.D. Cal. 1974).

40. 375 F. Supp. at 586.

41. 522 F.2d 897, 8 ERC 1001 (9th Cir. 1975), *cert. denied,* 96 S.Ct. 1148 (February 23, 1976).

42. 522 F.2d at 904.

43. Village of Belle Terre v. Boraas, 416 U.S. 1, 6 ERC 1417 (1974).

44. 503 F.2d 250 (9th Cir. 1974).

45. 522 F.2d at 908–909.

46. 522 F.2d at 908 n. 16.

CHAPTER 3

The National Environmental Policy Act (NEPA)

Basic Provisions of NEPA

THE NATIONAL ENVIRONMENTAL Policy Act (NEPA),[1] which was signed into law on January 1, 1970, is the bedrock of federal environmental legislation. It sets out general federal environmental policy and contains action-forcing provisions affecting federal agencies. The most important of these provisions requires that an environmental impact statement (EIS) be prepared for "major Federal actions significantly affecting the quality of the human environment."[2]

The national environmental policy established by the act is set forth with the caveat that this policy is to be carried out through means "consistent with other essential considerations of national policy." Within this constraint, it is federal policy to

(1) fulfill the responsibilities of each generation as trustee of the environment for succeeding generations;
(2) assure for all Americans safe, healthful, productive and esthetically and culturally pleasing surroundings;
(3) attain the widest range of beneficial uses of the environment without degradation, risk to health or safety, or other undesirable and unintended consequences;

(4) preserve important historic, cultural, and natural aspects of our national heritage, and maintain, wherever possible, an environment which supports diversity and variety of individual choice;

(5) achieve a balance between population and resource use which will permit high standards of living and a wide sharing of life's amenities; and

(6) enhance the quality of renewable resources and approach the maximum attainable recycling of depletable resources.[3]

The act directs that to the fullest extent possible federal agencies should carry out their programs in accordance with these broad policy aims. The required case-by-case analysis of proposed agency actions through an EIS is the act's most effective measure of ensuring that this is done. By means of this EIS process, environmental consequences must be considered *before* action is taken. Each EIS must include a detailed statement on

(i) the environmental impact of the proposed action,

(ii) any adverse environmental effects which cannot be avoided should the proposal be implemented,

(iii) alternatives to the proposed action,

(iv) the relationship between local short-term uses of man's environment and the maintenance and enhancement of long-term productivity, and

(v) any irreversible and irretrievable commitments of resources which would be involved in the proposed action should it be implemented.[4]

The EIS is first prepared in draft form and made available for comment to all government agencies with relevant expertise and jurisdiction and to the public. After full consideration of all comments and any additional information received, the agency then prepares a final EIS which accompanies the proposal for action through the decision-making process.

As has been indicated, the act specifies that the EIS requirement applies to major federal actions significantly affecting the quality of the human environment. "Major federal actions" include not only actions directly undertaken by federal agencies, but also federal decisions to approve, fund, or license activities which will be carried out by others. Thus, for example, an EIS must be prepared not only for such direct federal actions as the construction of a major Post Office development[5] or the construction by the U.S. Army Corps of Engineers of a flood control dam,[6] but also for federal-aid highway grants to state or local governments[7] and for the issuance of licenses to private parties for the construction of nuclear power plants.[8] Even federal agencies which are only indirectly involved in environmental questions have been required to file EISs on their proposed actions. For instance, the Interstate Commerce Commission has been required by the courts to prepare an EIS on the proposed abandonment of railway lines.[9] The Office of Interstate Land Sales Registration has been required to file an EIS on its acceptance of federally required disclosure statements from a land developer.[10] In December 1974, moreover, the U.S. District Court for the District of Columbia found that the Securities and Exchange Commission's implementation of NEPA failed to comply with the requirements of the law and ordered the commission to undertake further rule making to bring its corporate disclosure regulations "into full compliance with the letter and spirit of NEPA."[11] The Natural Resources Defense Council, as a plaintiff in this case, held that all reporting corporations should be required to submit to the Securities and Exchange Commission information concerning the adverse effects of their corporate activites on the environment, as well as their efforts to reduce these impacts.[12]

As originally written, NEPA applied to all federal agencies. Since its enactment, however, Congress and the courts have established a number of exceptions to this universal mandate. Congress has passed laws which exempt the federal Environmental Protection Agency (EPA) from the requirements of NEPA when it is taking action under the Clean Air Act[13] and when it is issuing pollutant discharge permits (except those for new sources) under the Federal Water Pollution Control Act Amendments of 1972.[14] The courts have ruled that EPA was not required to prepare a NEPA statement for an action under the Federal Insecticide, Fungicide, and Rodenticide Act where the procedures the agency followed were the functional equivalent of the NEPA process.[15] EPA has generally contended that it is exempt from NEPA on the grounds that the act is aimed at development agencies and not at environmental protection agencies. This contention has not been finally resolved. EPA has been preparing EISs on some of its grants for sewage treatment plants, which, as is discussed in Chapter 6, have a critical impact on land development patterns.

Congress has also passed special legislation for a few particular projects, such as the Trans-Alaska Pipeline[16] and the North Expressway in San Antonio,[17] removing these projects from the complete system of review provided by NEPA. The courts have exempted a few programs from NEPA, such as that established by parts of the

Emergency Petroleum Allocation Act of 1973,[18] where the speed with which the agency was required to act did not allow time for a full NEPA review.

Initially, federal agencies themselves were also generally required to prepare NEPA statements to assure as far as possible that a public and impartial analysis of a proposal was made rather than the self-serving critique that might be prepared by an applicant for a license or for funds.[19] Federal agencies which grant funds to state or local governments or license the activities of private parties usually relied on the applicant for the grant or license to make the initial collection of data and the preliminary environmental analysis, but the extent to which the federal agency had to rework this material was not clearly defined. Nonetheless, certainly some independent judgment and not simply a blind rubber-stamping of the work of others was required. In a division of judgment regarding how the burden of EIS preparation could be shared between the federal and state governments in the federal-aid highway program, the Second and Seventh Circuit Courts of Appeals required genuine federal participation in statement preparation,[20] while other circuits required only consultation, analysis, and formal adoption by the federal agency.[21]

In July 1975 Congress amended NEPA to permit state agencies with statewide jurisdiction to prepare EISs in programs where federal grants are made to the states.[22] Federal officials, however, retain the critical responsibilities of providing guidance and participating in EIS preparation and of independently evaluating the EIS prior to its approval. This amendment will have the greatest impact on the huge federal-aid highway program, where it authorizes state highway departments to prepare NEPA statements.

In an earlier congressional action, the Housing and Community Development Act of 1974, the Secretary of Housing and Urban Development (HUD) was given the authority to delegate his NEPA responsibilities to localities applying for federal community development grants.[23] HUD promulgated regulations implementing this section of the act in January 1975,[24] so the process of environmental review on most HUD projects is now effectively in the hands of local officials.

In general, actual preparation of NEPA statements by federal agencies and fully independent federal assessments are the best assurances that the most objective and environmentally sound decisions will be made in the long run. The efforts which have been made to authorize federal agencies to delegate their NEPA responsibilities to applicants for federal funds or approvals are essentially efforts to dilute the force of NEPA and to allow more actions to be undertaken without disinterested environmental analysis.

There has been extensive litigation on the question of whether given particular actions are major actions significantly affecting the human environment. It is impossible to define the threshold of actions that will bring NEPA into play, but the courts have generally interpreted the phrase liberally. For example, a federal loan guarantee for a sixteen-story apartment building was held to require the preparation of an EIS.[25] In this case, the court stated that the defendants had ignored the cumulative effects of the proposed project. In general, the courts have often required an EIS for projects of modest dimensions when the long-range effects of the project or its impact in conjunction with related activities have been found to be significant. Indirect as well as direct effects have been considered in making this determination. Thus, if a proposed project will have secondary effects such as increased air pollution, land development, or noise, these factors may be weighed by the courts in deciding whether or not an action significantly affects the environment. Finally, it is also important to note that the "human environment" encompasses cities, as well as areas in which the natural environment has been less disturbed.

NEPA requires more than a narrow analysis of the proposed agency action. The courts have ruled that one of the fundamental aims of the statute is to provide information on which rational decisions can be made, not only by the federal agency involved, but also by the President, the Congress, and the public.[26] Under this mandate an agency must look beyond its own jurisdiction in examining alternatives to the proposed action. For example, an agency which is considering offshore drilling must consider alternatives, such as changes in the oil-import quota system, which it cannot directly effect itself.[27] The provision for agency and public comment on draft EISs is particularly important in ensuring that this requirement is fulfilled, since this process establishes a means through which the agency writing the statement can be informed of facts and alternatives beyond its immediate expertise.

The required scope of NEPA statements has been another subject of litigation. Two important concepts have emerged from this process: segmentation and tiering. Segmentation refers to the breakdown of larger projects into segments for the purposes of EIS preparation. In general, agencies have not been allowed to obscure the total environment impact of a project by dividing it into smaller undertakings. Thus, in San Antonio the Department of Transportation was not allowed to break a larger road project into segments, thereby masking the total impact of the entire project.[28] Similarly, the Army Corps of Engineers was required to consider not just the immediate impact of executing the first steps of a navigation improvement project, but also the effects of such action on the development of the entire river basin.[29]

Various tests have been developed by the courts to determine whether a single project has been broken into segments or whether an independent entity is before the court. One test has been the determination of whether the project proposed will have a coercive effect on other federal actions or will involve an irreversible commitment to another project. If it will do so, the court is likely to require that all aspects of the project be reviewed together under NEPA.[30] Some courts have held that when a project has independent utility, this weighs heavily in establishing that it is a single project and is, on that ground alone, the proper subject of an EIS.[31] The better reasoned decisions have held that independent utility alone is not enough and that a careful review of all the facts and circumstances of the case is necessary.[32]

Tiering of NEPA statements has resulted from the need for agencies to prepare EISs both on their broad programs and on specific facilities or activities in particular geographical areas. Thus, for example, the Bureau of Land Management has prepared a "programmatic" EIS on the proposed federal increase in oil and gas leasing on the Outer Continental Shelf and is preparing "site-specific" EISs for the particular geographical areas where this leasing is proposed to occur. Similarly, the Atomic Energy Commission (now the Energy Research and Development Administration and the Nuclear Regulatory Commission) was required by the courts to prepare a programmatic EIS on its entire "fast breeder" nuclear reactor development program, as well as on individual test facilities and plants.[33] Thus while the programmatic EIS examines the large-scale and long-range environmental effects of an agency program, the site-specific EIS explores the environmental effects of carrying out that program in a particular locale.

The timing of the EIS is another question which has been frequently before the courts. The decisions which have been handed down have indicated that the EIS must be prepared at the earliest practical point in time.[34] This has been deemed necessary to assure that the comprehensive review and objective assessment intended by the act will be responsibly carried out. If the preparation of the EIS were allowed to take place after planning was well underway, desirable alternatives might have already been foreclosed, a fully objective analysis would not be possible, and opportunities to make alterations minimizing environmental costs would be lost. Essentially, an EIS must be written late enough in the development process to contain meaningful information, but it must also be written early enough so that this information can practically serve as an input in the decision-making process.[35] Some doubt, however, has been thrown on the entire question of the timing of EISs and their integration into agency review procedures by a footnote in the recent Supreme Court case of *Aberdeen and Rockfish Railroad* v. *SCRAP*.[36] This footnote indicated that the circuit courts of appeal may have misconstrued NEPA in requiring early consideration of environmental issues.

In some cases actual federal funding may come relatively late in the development of a project. For example, in the federal-aid highway program initial state qualification for future federal reimbursement may take place years before funds are granted. As a result, highway officials have argued that a federal commitment is not actually made to a highway project until a grant of federal funds is made and thus that an EIS does not have to be prepared until a state actively seeks such a grant. This position, had it been allowed, would have permitted the states to carry highway projects through advanced stages of planning, to determine the location of roads, and even to buy land, all before an EIS was prepared. The courts have not accepted this obvious flouting of the purposes of NEPA that would have allowed practically all planning decisions on a highway project to be made before an assessment of the environmental effects of alternative actions was carried out. In *La Raza Unida* v. *Volpe*,[37] the court ruled that compliance with NEPA and other environmental statutes was required for federal location approval, which occurs at an early stage of highway planning. The court held that "[t]he state should not have the considerable benefits that accompany an option to obtain federal funds without also assuming the attendant obligations. Any project that seeks even the possible protection and assistance of the federal government must fall within the statutes and regulations."[38]

In the early days of NEPA there was considerable litigation on the question of whether EISs had to be prepared on existing projects which had been initiated in some way or had received some type of federal approval prior to January 1, 1970, the effective date of NEPA.[39] This has been a particularly important issue with respect to such agencies as the Department of Transportation, the Army Corps of Engineers, and the Bureau of Reclamation, which in January 1970 had large backlogs of authorized projects, many of which had not yet reached the construction stage. In making their decisions on individual cases, the courts have weighed the nature of the project, whether a continued federal presence was involved, the stage of completion, and the severity of the environmental effects associated with the project. The results have been varied, but in one of the strongest opinions favoring the application of NEPA to uncompleted actions the U.S. Court of Appeals for the Sixth Circuit held that:

> an agency must file an impact statement whenever the agency intends to take steps that will result in a significant environmental impact, whether or not these steps were planned before January 1, 1970, and whether or not the proposed steps represent simply the last phase of an integrated operation most of which was completed before that date. [Adding in a footnote:] Although this formulation might compel the preparation of impact statements for projects that are so nearly complete that there is no reasonable prospect that the decision to proceed as planned would be reversed, that is no reason to adopt a lesser standard and thereby encourage bureaucratic evasion of responsibility.[40]

In this case an EIS was required for a dam project in which the concrete portion had been completed in 1969, two thirds of the necessary land had been acquired, and $29 million out of a budgeted $69 million had been spent.

Many states have now passed state legislation patterned in whole or in part on NEPA. These state laws require that some or all state and local agencies prepare environmental impact statements on their proposed actions. It is crucial that citizens in states with "little NEPAs" familiarize themselves with the requirements of these laws, since they may be of great consequence for land use problems. It is not possible here to review all of the individual state statutes modeled on NEPA, but the Council on Environmental Quality has provided the following brief inventory of such laws as of December 1974:

> Since 1970, 21 states and the Commonwealth of Puerto Rico have adopted environmental impact statement [EIS] requirements similar to those set forth in NEPA. Thirteen of the 21 states and the Commonwealth of Puerto Rico have legislatively adopted a comprehensive EIS

requirement: California, Connecticut, Hawaii, Indiana, Maryland, Massachusetts, Minnesota, Montana, North Carolina, South Dakota, Virginia, Washington, and Wisconsin. Three states—Michigan, New Jersey, and Texas—have administratively promulgated a comprehensive EIS requirement. In addition, five states require preparation of impact statements on specific classes of projects. Arizona requires that impact statements be prepared for proposed water-oriented projects. Georgia requires an environmental analysis for certain toll road projects. In Nevada, there is a special provision relating to utility power plant siting. Nebraska's Department of Roads prepares impact statements on State-funded highway projects. Delaware requires the preparation of statements in connection with the issuance of permits under its Coastal Zone Act and its Wetlands Law. [Footnotes omitted.][41]

Since this compilation, New York has also passed a state NEPA law requiring an EIS for actions by state or local government agencies which may have a significant effect on the environment.

Agency Implementation of NEPA

The Council on Environmental Quality (CEQ), which was established under NEPA, is responsible for the general guidelines governing EIS preparation and approval.[42] These CEQ guidelines have been supplemented by specific guidelines and regulations pertaining to compliance with NEPA that have been adopted by individual federal agencies.[43]

Under the present system an agency first makes an assessment of a proposed action to determine whether or not an EIS is required. A decision not to prepare an EIS is called a "negative declaration." If an agency decides that an EIS is required, it publishes a notice of its intent to prepare one in the *Federal Register*. If more than one agency is directly involved in the proposed action, the agencies may select a "lead agency" to assume supervisory responsibility in the preparation of the EIS.

As has been pointed out, an agency must prepare a draft EIS upon which it must seek comments both from the public and from other federal, state, and local agencies which have expertise or jurisdiction relevant to the action under consideration. The draft EIS is usually available for comment for a period of ninety days. Notice of this availability is given in the *Federal Register* and may appear in local newspapers. Citizens who want to comment on a particular draft EIS should take special care to make sure they know when it becomes available. A public hearing may be held on a draft EIS, but this usually happens only when a hearing on the proposed actions is required under the provisions of other statutes or is already an existing aspect of agency procedures.

Not only must public comment on a draft EIS be sought out; it must also be seriously weighed by the agency in the preparation of the final EIS. In a case dealing with an interstate highway, the court held that:

> The public may also raise environmental questions by way of comment to the draft impact statement. Since the final impact statement must respond to these comments, as well as to the comments of government agencies, environmental harm which might have been overlooked by highway officials may be brought to their attention. For this reason, highway officials must give more than cursory consideration to the suggestions and comments of the public in the preparation of the final impact statement. The proper response to comments which are both relevant and reasonable is to either conduct the research necessary to provide satisfactory answers, or to refer to those places in the impact statement which provide them. If the final impact statement fails substantially to do so, it will not meet the statutory requirements.[44]

The final EIS, which the agency drafts following the comment period, accompanies the proposal through the agency review process. This review process varies enormously from agency to agency. For example, when the Nuclear Regulatory Commission licenses nuclear power plants, the commission conducts a review hearing modeled on court procedures in which testimony under oath and examination and cross-examination of witnesses are required. On the other hand, hearings of the Army Corps of Engineers on permits to undertake construction in navigable waters are on a legislative hearing model. Numerous position statements are allowed, but the hearings do not follow rules of evidence or permit thorough cross-examination of the agency's experts.[45] Other agencies hold no hearings in their established review process.

On the basis of the final EIS and the agency review, a decision on a particular proposal is made and whatever environmental protection the agency imposes becomes part of the course of action adopted. The courts assure that the procedural requirements of NEPA are met, but, except in clear cases of abuse, they are unwilling to substitute their judgment on substantive matters for that of an agency deemed expert in the matters it considers. For this reason, working within the administrative process in which NEPA statements are drawn up and reviewed is critical for citizens who want to influence the environmental aspects of any proposal.

The various federal agencies have reacted with differing degrees of enthusiasm to their new responsibilities under NEPA. A number of agencies have been reluctant to comply with NEPA "to the fullest extent possible," as is required by the act, and the first half of the 1970s saw much legal action to force agencies to fulfill the procedural requirements of NEPA. Most of these battles have now been won in favor of full procedural compliance, and most agencies now prepare EISs as a matter of course. Many agencies have not, however, assumed the responsibility imposed on them by NEPA of using "all practicable means, consistent with other essential considerations of national policy," to prevent environmental damage.[46] For example, the federal Food and Drug Administration released its first draft EIS in April 1975 and in the same month promulgated a regulation stating that it could disregard adverse environmental effects in decisions governed by its own statutory mandate.[47] When the Environmental Defense Fund challenged this regulation, the federal district court held that NEPA requires the Food and Drug Administration to ensure that all environmental considerations are taken into account in its decision making, even though statutes administered by FDA may not mandate consideration of such factors.[48]

During the years from 1972 through 1974 between 1148 and 1371 NEPA statements were filed each year by federal agencies.[49] By far the largest number of these statements was prepared by the U.S. Department of Transportation (DOT), mostly on road projects. For instance, in 1972 DOT filed 674 statements and in 1973, 432. The Army Corps of Engineers prepared the next largest number of EISs. Since these are the two largest public works and development agencies in the federal government, these statistics are not surprising. On the other hand, other agencies such as the Nuclear Regulatory Commission and the Federal Power Commission do not file such large numbers of NEPA statements, but their EISs usually deal with projects that are massive in size and environmental impact.

Environmentalists today are turning much more attention toward the substantive quality of the NEPA statements which are prepared. Unfortunately, far too frequently the quality of these impact statements leaves much to be desired. For example, NEPA statements are sometimes silent on the most severe environmental effects that would be caused by a proposed project. In an EIS prepared on a stream channelization project discussed in detail below, the Soil Conservation Service did not discuss the increase in erosion which would be caused by the project, even though erosion is one of the most significant impacts of channelization.The technological and scientific data included in an EIS, moreover, should be closely scrutinized by outside experts to assure that errors in fact or faulty assumptions are not incorporated. In addition to specific omissions and errors, NEPA statements also often exhibit an overall inadequacy. For example, EISs on different types of projects in different states often contain passages of exactly the same language, indicating that they have been mechanically copied rather than thoughtfully prepared.

The quality of EISs varies a great deal from agency to agency and from project to project. This has been clearly demonstrated in the NEPA statements prepared by the Nuclear Regulatory Commission (NRC), the Federal Power Commission (FPC), and the Army Corps of Engineers on the impact of power plants on the Hudson River fishery. As the lead agency in different projects, each of these three agencies analyzed the respective effects of three proposed plants, all of which were to be reasonably close to each other and presented basically the same dangers to aquatic biota. The results of the analyses carried out varied so much that one could hardly believe the agencies were concerned with the same body of water. The NRC predicted very major damage to the striped bass fishery; the FPC predicted insignificant damage; and the Corps of Engineers only dealt with the fishery in passing, made no quantitative predictions, and treated the fish as a minor issue. The variation in these results underscores the importance of agency diligence in seeking out and thoroughly analyzing available information. In this case, the NRC had access to the extensive resources of the Holifield National Laboratory; the FPC relied primarily on the expertise of other government agencies with limited staff resources; and the Corps of Engineers relied primarily on the analysis made by utilities, a few overworked people in its own office, and an underpaid consultant. The different approaches taken toward NEPA requirements were clearly apparent in the impact statements which were written.

There is truly no substitute for thorough and diligent work by agency staffs, but this will only take place as a matter of course if agencies are properly funded and the public constantly insists on high quality work rather than reviews which only meet the minimum requirements of the act. It is doubtful that the courts, which do not view detailed review of technical matters to be their responsibility, will be of great assistance on this issue. It is something that must be won by persuading agencies of the importance of the NEPA mandate and through political action in Congress. This point was brought home emphatically by the district court which reviewed the Corps of Engineers' EIS on the Truman Dam in Missouri:

> It is simply unrealistic for plaintiffs in this case to assume that this or any other Court is going to make findings of fact which would attempt to resolve the conflicts between data contained and relied upon in the final EIS which may conflict with data which plaintiffs believe is more reliable.[50]

Thus it is not likely that disputes regarding facts will be resolved by the courts. Except in rare cases, it is the agency which determines the facts and, therefore, every effort should be made to bring full information to the attention of agency officials and to convince them of the correctness of one's position in difficult cases.

NEPA and Land Use Control

In contrast to air and water pollution problems, which are subject to federal regulation under the Clean Air Act of 1970[51] and the Federal Water Pollution Control Act Amendments of 1972,[52] there is no comprehensive federal statute dealing with land use. National land use acts have been seriously considered by the past several sessions of Congress, but have not been passed.

Nonetheless, NEPA can be a very significant statute with respect to decisions affecting land use in which there is major federal involvement. For instance, highways are a critical determinant of future land development patterns and all important federal-aid highway projects must pass through a NEPA review. Any dredging or filling within the waters of the United States requires a permit from the Army Corps of Engineers,[53] and thus may require the preparation of an EIS. Federal licensing of power plants and federal construction of flood control projects, as well as activities on the public lands such as forest management and grazing,[54] are all actions for which NEPA statements are prepared. These examples could be multiplied and detailed in great number. The important fact to remember is that an important federal presence in a development scheme will usually bring in its train the requirement of compliance with the terms of

NEPA. And, of course, state laws modeled on NEPA may be directly relevant to governmental decisions concerning land use.

For purposes of illustration, two examples of the role NEPA has played in projects with important land use impacts are provided here.

1. Highways

The impact of highway construction on land use and the way in which the federal-aid highway program operates are discussed in Chapter 10. The following discussion describes a particular case in which a citizens' group took legal action under NEPA to halt a highway project until an adequate EIS was prepared.

In 1972 the Conservation Society of Southern Vermont filed suit against the U.S. Department of Transportation (DOT) and the Vermont Department of Highways to compel the preparation of an EIS on plans to convert a twenty-mile segment of Route 7 into a four-lane, limited access expressway.[55] This segment, from Bennington to Manchester, was to be part of a continuous highway of interstate standards planned to extend from Long Island Sound to the Canadian border of northern Vermont, along the present Route 7 corridor. The federal district court ruled in favor of the plaintiff and enjoined all construction on the highway segment, pending the preparation of an EIS.

In 1973 DOT released a draft and then a final EIS, and subsequently petitioned the court to dissolve the injunction on the grounds that an adequate EIS had been prepared. The court denied this motion, holding

a. That the EIS was prepared by the Vermont Department of Highways rather than the Federal Highway Administration, with only federal rubber-stamping. Such delegation of NEPA responsibilities to a self-interested applicant for federal funds was held to be a flouting of the goal of objective decision making.

b. That an assessment had to be made of the environmental impact not just of the proposed twenty-mile project, but also of the overall plan to build a four-lane expressway from Long Island Sound to the Canadian border. Thus, the court held that an overall EIS on the entire project, as well as an EIS on the twenty-mile segment, was required before construction could begin on the twenty-mile segment.

c. That the EIS prepared did not consider a number of critical environmental factors, such as the secondary land use effects of the proposed construction.

The defendants appealed the first two of these rulings to the U.S. Court of Appeals for the Second Circuit. In December 1974 this court unanimously affirmed the decision of the district court in a strong opinion that emphasized the necessity of "genuine federal participation" in the preparation of an EIS rather than federal rubber-stamping of the work of applicants. The circuit court also upheld the ruling that an overall EIS on the entire Route 7 plan had to be prepared before construction could begin on the Bennington-Manchester segment.

Following this decision, DOT filed a petition for a writ of certiorari with the U.S. Supreme Court, requesting the Court to review both issues: (1) who had to prepare the EIS, and (2) what should the scope of the EIS be? The Conservation Society of Southern Vermont filed a brief in opposition to this petition. In October 1975 the Supreme Court granted DOT's petition and summarily disposed of the case by remanding it to the Second Circuit for further consideration in light of the recent amendment to NEPA, discussed above, which allows state agencies to prepare EISs under certain circumstances, and of the Supreme Court's decision in *Aberdeen & Rockfish Railroad* v. *SCRAP*.[56]

Upon remand, in February 1976 the Second Circuit reversed its decision, apparently interpreting the amendment to NEPA as congressional rejection of its earlier position. Quite properly, the court held that EIS preparation could now be delegated to the state highway department; however, it ignored the clear language of the amendment which retains strict standards for federal participation in EIS preparation and independent review of the EIS. On the issue of segmentation, the court found that under *SCRAP* a broad corridor EIS is not necessary in cases like this where the highway segment involved has "local utility."

This new decision seriously threatens NEPA's goals of broad and impartial environmental review. If local utility may be used to justify the narrow scope of an EIS, long-range environmental impacts will not receive adequate attention and the piecemeal approach to road building will regain much of its former vigor. If statutory requirements for meaningful federal participation and review are not enforced, then the self-interest of state highway departments and other state agencies seeking federal funds will become a much more serious factor in EISs.

2. Stream Channelization

The stream channelization and ditching program of the Soil Conservation Service (SCS) of the U.S. Department of Agriculture has widespread and serious environmental significance. Under this program, heavy earth-moving equipment cuts trench-like channels through the natural course of free-flowing streams—in the name of flood control and drainage. Among the adverse effects of such operations are deterioration of water quality, drastic reductions in fish and wildlife populations, the erosion of river banks, and the possible increase of downstream flooding as a result of the more efficient drainage of upland areas. In addition, severe aesthetic degradation is caused by the channelization process. The SCS has estimated that over 175,000 miles of the nation's streams could be altered by its channelization program, and over 400 projects, involving some 12,000 miles of channelization, are already planned.

In November 1971 the Natural Resources Defense Council (NRDC), which has a special project on streams, along with several other environmental organizations, filed a legal action against the SCS in an effort to stop the proposed stream channelization of sixty-six miles of Chicod Creek and its tributaries in North Carolina.[57] NRDC contended that the SCS project would have a devastating effect on a beautiful and highly productive stream-swamp ecosystem in the Carolina low country. The complaint alleged that the SCS had not adequately evaluated the environmental consequences of the project and that the benefits of the project did not exceed its true costs, as is required for this type of federal project.

In March 1972 the federal court granted NRDC's motion for a preliminary injunction on the project and directed the SCS to prepare and circulate a draft EIS under NEPA. The impact statement prepared by the SCS during the summer of 1972 was inadequate in many important respects. For example, the SCS had not discussed the increase in erosion that channelization of Chicod Creek and changes in land use along the stream would produce, despite the fact that erosion is one of the most serious consequences of channelization. NRDC, therefore, went back to court in the fall of 1972 to challenge the adequacy of the impact statement and to request a second injunction.

In February 1973 the court ruled that the SCS's environmental impact statement was indeed inadequate, ordered the SCS to prepare a new statement, and further enjoined commencement of the project. In May 1974 the SCS released a new draft EIS for the Chicod project.

Through its Project Streams, during the public comment period NRDC coordinated a review of this statement by twenty experts from fields such as water quality, geology, wildlife, economics, riverine ecology, and fisheries. The SCS released the final EIS in December 1974, but by the spring of 1976 had not yet requested the court to lift the injunction on the project. In addition, NRDC has raised before the court the issue of whether the proposed channelization requires a Section 404 permit under the Federal Water Pollution Control Act Amendments of 1972, which are discussed in detail in Chapter 5.

As a result of the Chicod Creek case, not only has assessment of the environmental effects of this project been achieved, but also the SCS is now preparing NEPA statements on many other channelization projects scheduled for execution in various parts of the country. In addition, a marked slowdown in the overall stream channelization program has been apparent.

Citizen Action

Citizens who are faced with a land use problem in which a federal agency or federal funding is involved or a federal permit, license, or certificate is required should seek to answer the following questions:

1. Is an EIS under NEPA required before a decision can be made on a proposed action?
2. If an EIS is required, is one being prepared?
3. If an EIS is being prepared, what agency is preparing it and when will a draft statement be available for public comment?
4. Are all procedural requirements being properly met?
5. Will the draft EIS be reviewed in a public hearing? If so, when and where?

Where a state law patterned on NEPA is applicable, the same process should be followed with respect to that law.

In an assessment of the adequacy of an EIS, the following are critical questions to raise:

1. Was the draft EIS prepared early enough in the decision-making process to allow responsible consideration of alternatives,

including the alternative of no action, and incorporation in planning of measures to reduce environmental harm?

2. Is the EIS unduly limited in scope, thereby avoiding consideration of broad policy issues, related projects, and impact on later options?

3. Have all adverse environmental impacts of the proposed action been fully discussed and fairly evaluated in the EIS?

4. Have all indirect effects, such as secondary land use impacts, been included?

5. Have alternatives to the main proposal been fully considered and have their respective environmental effects been compared?

6. If a state agency with statewide jurisdiction has prepared the EIS, has the decision-making federal agency fulfilled its statutory responsibilities to furnish guidance and participate in the EIS preparation, as well as to carry out an independent evaluation of the statement prior to its approval?

7. Does the final EIS indicate that the public comments submitted on the draft EIS have been seriously considered by the agency?

Overall, citizens should not be intimidated by the official or imposing appearance of an EIS, but should approach the document with a critical, open mind, focusing on the most important issues. A thick EIS is by no means a good EIS, nor is the detail provided necessarily the information which is needed.

It is always important to become involved in the NEPA process as early as possible, since it is at this stage that administrators are most receptive to new information and approaches. If an EIS is not being prepared in circumstances which appear to require one, citizens should investigate the reasons why no statement is being drawn up, discuss the problem with federal agency officials, and seek clarification of the issue. During the preparation of an EIS, every effort should be made to assure that agencies make use of all the relevant expertise and information available to them. It is particularly important to see that an agency does not take the easy way out of relying solely on information provided by the advocates of a project.

As has been pointed out, the commenting period on the draft EIS gives the public the opportunity to make criticisms and suggestions and to provide information which must be weighed in the agency's preparation of the final EIS. Citizens should take full advantage of this opportunity to prepare and submit comments which clarify the deficiencies of the EIS. If the draft EIS is reviewed in a public hearing, citizens should make certain that they are represented by as able a spokesman as possible. When it appears that violations of the law have occurred, competent legal advice should be sought to determine whether or not a suit could be brought.

NEPA is an environmental full disclosure law, and, as such, is a crucial instrument for public analysis of proposed actions affecting the environment. It provides a means for environmental control, modification, or abandonment of projects. Fully utilized, it can change the thinking through which government decisions are made. Given minimal consideration, it can degenerate into a paper exercise used to justify projects and proposals already decided upon. It is largely up to citizens affected by federal action to ensure that this critical federal legislation is fully and effectively enforced.

NOTES

1. 42 U.S.C. § 4321 *et seq.*

2. 42 U.S.C. § 4332 (2) (C).

3. 42 U.S.C. § 4331 (b).

4. 42 U.S.C. § 4332 (2) (C).

5. Chelsea Neighborhood Associations v. U.S. Postal Service, 516 F.2d 378, 7 ERC 1957 (2d Cir. 1975).

6. E.g., Environmental Defense Fund v. Froehlke, 368 F. Supp. 231, 6 ERC 1074 (W.D. Mo. 1973).

7. See Chapter 10 for a discussion of the federal-aid highway program.

8. Calvert Cliffs' Coordinating Committee v. Atomic Energy Commission, 449 F.2d 1109, 2 ERC 1779 (D.C. Cir. 1971).

9. City of New York v. United States, 337 F. Supp. 150, 3 ERC 1570 (E.D.N.Y. 1972); but see, Aberdeen & Rockfish Railroad v. SCRAP, 422 U.S. 289, 7 ERC 2009 (1975).

10. Scenic Rivers Association v. Lynn, 520 F.2d 240, 8 ERC 1021 (10th Cir. 1975). See Chapter 9 for a discussion of the Office of Interstate Land Sales Registration.

11. Natural Resources Defense Council v. Securities and Exchange Commission, 389 F. Supp. 689, 693, 7 ERC 1199, 1200 (D.D.C. 1974).

12. The plaintiffs also sought disclosure of statistics pertaining to equal employment practices. The court found that the importance of the plaintiffs' claims was underscored by the large number of "ethical investors" in this country—including individuals, universities, and foundations—who have large sums of money to invest and wish to make investment and voting decisions in accordance with their societal principles. See Chapter 9 for a discussion of the actions taken by the SEC as a result of the court order.

13. The Clean Air Act is found at 42 U.S.C. § 1857 *et seq.*, but the exemption

indicated was established by the Energy Supply and Environmental Coordination Act of 1974, 15 U.S.C. § 793 (c) (1).

14. 33 U.S.C. § 1371(c) (1).

15. Environmental Defense Fund v. Environmental Protection Agency, 489 F.2d 1247, 6 ERC 1112 (D.C. Cir. 1973).

16. Trans-Alaska Pipeline Authorization Act, Public Law 93–153, § 203(d); 87 Stat. 57b, § 203(d).

17. Federal-Aid Highway Act of 1973, Public Law 93–87, § 154; 87 Stat. 250, § 154.

18. Gulf Oil Company v. Simon, 373 F. Supp. 1102, 6 ERC 1565 (D.D.C. 1974).

19. Greene County Planning Board v. Federal Power Commission, 455 F.2d 412, 3 ERC 1595 (2d Cir.), *cert. denied,* 409 U.S. 849, 4 ERC 1752 (1972).

20. Conservation Society of Southern Vermont v. Secretary, 508 F.2d 927, 7 ERC 1236 (2d Cir. 1974); Swain v. Brinegar, 517 F.2d 766, 7 ERC 2046 (7th Cir. 1975).

21. E.g., FAIR v. Brinegar, 484 F.2d 638 (5th Cir. 1973); Citizens Environmental Council v. Volpe, 484 F.2d 870, 5 ERC 1989 (10th Cir. 1973), *cert. denied,* 416 U.S. 936, 6 ERC 1440 (1974); Iowa Citizens for Environmental Quality v. Volpe, 487 F.2d 849, 6 ERC 1088 (8th Cir. 1973); Life of the Land v. Brinegar, 485 F.2d 460, 5 ERC 1780 (9th Cir. 1973).

22. Public Law No. 94–83, 89 Stat. 424 (August 9, 1975); 42 U.S.C. § 4332(2) (D).

23. 42 U.S.C. § 5304 (h).

24. 40 *Federal Register* 1393 (January 7, 1975); 24 C.F.R. Part 58.

25. Goose Hollow Foothills League v. Romney, 334 F. Supp. 877, 3 ERC 1087 (D. Ore. 1971).

26. Committee for Nuclear Responsibility v. Seaborg, 463 F.2d 783, 3 ERC 1126 (D.C. Cir. 1971); Natural Resources Defense Council v. Morton, 458 F.2d 827, 3 ERC 1558 (D.C. Cir. 1972).

27. Natural Resources Defense Council v. Morton, 458 F.2d 827, 3 ERC 1558 (D.C. Cir. 1972).

28. Named Individual Members of the San Antonio Conservation Society v. Texas Highway Department, 446 F.2d 1013, 2 ERC 1871 (5th Cir. 1971).

29. Atchison, Topeka, and Santa Fe Railway Company v. Callaway, 382 F. Supp. 610, 7 ERC 1016 (D.D.C. 1974).

30. Appalachian Mountain Club v. Brinegar, 394 F. Supp. 105, 7 ERC 1076 (D.N.H. 1974).

31. Ecology Center of Louisiana v. Brinegar, _____ F. Supp. _____, 7 ERC 1254 (E.D. La. 1974).

32. Conservation Society of Southern Vermont v. Secretary, 508 F.2d 927, 7 ERC 1236 (2d Cir. 1974).

33. Scientists' Institute for Public Information v. Atomic Energy Commission, 481 F.2d 1079, 5 ERC 1418 (D.C. Cir. 1973).

34. Calvert Cliffs' Coordinating Committee v. Atomic Energy Commission, 449 F.2d 1109, 2 ERC 1779 (D.C. Cir. 1971); Natural Resources Defense Council v. Morton, 458 F.2d 827, 836, 3 ERC 1558, 1563 (D.C. Cir. 1972).

35. Scientists' Institute for Public Information v. Atomic Energy Commission, 481 F.2d 1079, 5 ERC 1418 (D.C. Cir. 1973).

36. 422 U.S. 289, 321, 7 ERC 2009, 2018 (1975). Additional troubling questions about the timing of EIS preparation have been raised by the recent Supreme Court decision in Kleppe v. Sierra Club. 44 U.S.L.W. 5104 (June 28, 1976). In this case the Court rejected the plaintiffs' request for a regional, programmatic EIS on coal development in the Northern Great Plains on the ground that the responsible federal agency had not yet put forward a formal proposal or overall plan of action for that region. This decision may allow federal agencies, in some instances, to defer comprehensive environmental review until after some major planning decisions have been made.

37. 337 F. Supp. 221, 3 ERC 1306 (N.D. Cal. 1971).

38. 337 F. Supp. at 227.

39. For a full analysis of this litigation, as well as other NEPA problems which were before the courts during the years from 1970 to 1973, see Frederick R. Anderson, *NEPA in the Courts: A Legal Analysis of the National Environmental Policy Act* (Washington, D.C.: Resources for the Future, Inc., 1973; distributed by the Johns Hopkins Press, Baltimore and London).

40. Environmental Defense Fund v. Tennessee Valley Authority, 468 F.2d 1164, 1177, 4 ERC 1850, 1857 (6th Cir. 1972).

41. Council on Environmental Quality, *Environmental Quality: The Fifth Annual Report of the Council on Environmental Quality* (1974), p. 401. Information on recent amendments and problems of implementation can be found in Council on Environmental Quality, *Environmental Quality: The Sixth Annual Report of the Council on Environmental Quality* (1975), pp. 651–653.

42. See 40 C.F.R. § 1500 *et seq.*

43. These guidelines and regulations have been published in the *Federal Register* and the regulations have been codified in appropriate volumes of the *Code of Federal Regulations* (C.F.R.).

44. Lathan v. Volpe, 350 F. Supp. 262, 265, 4 ERC 1487, 1489 (W.D. Wash. 1972).

45. See Citizens for Clean Air v. Corps of Engineers, 349 F. Supp. 696, 4 ERC 1456 (S.D.N.Y. 1972).

46. 42 U.S.C. § 4331(b).

47. The regulation in question can be found at 40 *Federal Register* 16662 (April 14, 1975); 21 C.F.R. § 6.1(a) (3). The statutory mandate cited by the Food and Drug Administration includes the Federal Food, Drug, and Cosmetic Act, 21 U.S.C. § 321 *et seq.;* the Fair Packaging and Labeling Act, 15 U.S.C. § 1451 *et seq.;* and the Public Health Service Act, 42 U.S.C. §§ 262, 263, 263b–263n.

48. Environmental Defense Fund v. Mathews, 410 F. Supp. 336, 8 ERC 1877 (D.D.C. 1976).

49. Council on Environmental Quality, *Fifth Annual Report,* p. 389.

50. Environmental Defense Fund v. Froehlke, 368 F. Supp. 231, 240, 6 ERC 1074, 1079 (W.D. Mo. 1973).

51. 42 U.S.C. § 1857 *et seq.* See Chapter 4.

52. 33 U.S.C. § 1251 *et seq.* See Chapter 5.

53. 33 U.S.C. §§ 401, 403, and 1344. See Chapter 5.

54. See Chapter 11 for a discussion of the significance of NEPA for federal agency management of the public lands.

55. Conservation Society of Southern Vermont v. Volpe, 343 F. Supp. 761, 4

ERC 1226 (D. Vt. 1972), *motion to dissolve injunction denied sub nom.* Conservation Society of Southern Vermont v. Secretary, 362 F. Supp. 627, 5 ERC 1683 (D. Vt. 1973), 508 F.2d 927, 7 ERC 1236 (2d Cir. 1974), *vacated and remanded sub nom.* Coleman v. Conservation Society, 423 U.S. 809 (1975), *rev'd on remand,* 531 F. 2d 637 (1976). The Natural Resources Defense Council filed a brief *amici curiae* on behalf of itself and eleven other environmental organizations in both the district and the circuit court.

56. 422 U.S. 289, 7 ERC 2009 (1975).

57. Natural Resources Defense Council v. Grant, 341 F. Supp. 356, 2 ELR 20185 (E.D.N.C. 1972), *motion to reduce bond denied,* 355 F. Supp. 280, 2 ELR 20647 (E.D.N.C.), *injunction withdrawn,* 2 ELR 20467 (E.D.N.C.), *remanded,* 2 ELR 20555 (4th Cir.), *motion for temporary restraining order granted and bond reduced,* 2 ELR 20648 (E.D.N.C. 1972), *motion for injunction granted,* 355 F. Supp. 280, 3 ELR 20176 (E.D.N.C. 1973).

CHAPTER 4

The Clean Air Act of 1970

THE CLEAN AIR ACT passed in 1970[1] requires the Administrator of the U.S. Environmental Protection Agency (EPA) to establish national ambient air quality standards for six major air pollutants: carbon monoxide, particulates, hydrocarbons, sulfur oxides, nitrogen dioxide, and photochemical oxidants. These standards set the maximum concentration or concentrations of each pollutant to be allowed in ambient air—that is, in the air we breathe.

Congress requires that two types of ambient standards be designated: (1) "primary standards" to establish the level of air quality necessary, with an adequate margin of safety, to protect human health; and (2) "secondary standards" to safeguard values pertaining to the public welfare, including plant and animal life, visibility, buildings, and materials. Table 1 lists the two sets of standards which have been established. The primary standards were to be attained by mid-1975 or by 1977 where extensions have been granted. The secondary standards must be attained within a "reasonable time," the exact determination of which is left to the EPA Administrator.

The act requires each state to develop implementation plans to attain and maintain the federal standards. These plans must be submitted to EPA for approval, and Congress set forth in the act itself specific requirements which each plan must meet in order to be approved. Where the EPA Administrator determines that a state

Table 1
National Primary and Secondary Ambient Air Quality Standards

Pollutant	Primary Standard	Secondary Standard
Sulfur Oxides:	(a) 80 micrograms per cubic meter (0.03 p.p.m.)—annual arithmetic mean. (b) 365 micrograms per cubic meter (0.14 p.p.m.)—maximum 24-hr. concentration not to be exceeded more than once a year.	1,300 micrograms per cubic meter (0.5 p.p.m.)—maximum 3-hr. concentration not to be exceeded more than once a year.
Particulate Matter:	(a) 75 micrograms per cubic meter—annual geometric mean. (b) 260 micrograms per cubic meter—maximum 24-hr. concentration not to be exceeded more than once a year.	(a) 60 micrograms per cubic meter—annual geometric mean, as a guide to be used in assessing implementation plans to achieve 24-hr. standard. (b) 180 micrograms per cubic meter—maximum 24-hr. concentration not to be exceeded more than once a year.
Carbon Monoxide:	(a) 10 milligrams per cubic meter (9 p.p.m.)—maximum 8-hr. concentration not to be exceeded more than once a year. (b) 40 milligrams per cubic meter (35 p.p.m.)—maximum 1-hr. concentration not to be exceeded more than once a year.	Same as Primary Standard.
Photochemical Oxidants:	160 micrograms per cubic meter (0.08 p.p.m.)—maximum 1-hr. concentration not to be exceeded more than once a year.	Same as Primary Standard.
Hydrocarbons:	160 micrograms per cubic meter (0.24 p.p.m.)—maximum 3-hr. concentration (6 to 9 a.m.) not to be exceeded more than once a year.	Same as Primary Standard.
Nitrogen Dioxide:	100 micrograms per cubic meter (0.05 p.p.m.)—annual arithmetic mean.	Same as Primary Standard.

Note: All measurements of air quality are corrected to a reference temperature of 25°C. and to a reference pressure of 760 millimeters of mercury (1,013.2 millibars).
Source of data: 40 C.F.R. §§ 50.4–50.11.

plan, or parts of a plan, is not approvable, he is required by the act to promulgate federal regulations to correct deficiencies.

The state agencies which are responsible for developing state plans vary considerably in name and structure. Some are independent agencies concerned exclusively with air pollution problems, while others are divisions of larger departments, such as environmental protection or conservation departments. The names and addresses of all state air pollution control agencies, as well as regional and local agencies and the regional offices of the federal EPA, are listed in *Directory, Governmental Air Pollution Agencies,* which is published by the Air Pollution Control Association.[2]

To assist in the development and implementation of state plans, EPA has divided each state into air quality control regions. In each of these geographical regions, a unified approach to attaining and maintaining standards can be developed. On the basis of its air quality, each region is classified as priority I, II, or III for each pollutant—with priority I indicating the most polluted air. To find out what regions have been established in a particular state and how these regions have been classified, citizens can either examine federal regulations[3] or consult their state air pollution control agency.

It must be stressed, however, that the designation of different control regions does not affect in any way the uniform applicability of all federal and state standards and regulations. For example, national primary and secondary air quality standards, emission limitations, and prohibitions against degradation of clean air are binding in all areas of the state. The potential of a proposed new pollution source for causing a violation of such standards or regulations must always be considered.[4]

Although the Clean Air Act does not define a national land use policy for protecting air quality, it does require state plans to include land use or transportation controls where they are necessary to achieve the federal ambient air quality standards.[5] This chapter discusses the following four aspects of state plans which bear on land use decision making, while transportation control plans are examined in Chapter 10:

1. Pre-construction review of major new stationary sources of pollution;
2. Pre-construction review of indirect sources;
3. Development of maintenance plans; and
4. Prevention of significant deterioration of air quality in existing "clean air" areas.

Unfortunately, there has been great delay in the development and implementation of needed and required land use controls under the

Clean Air Act. This has been a very sensitive political issue which EPA has attempted to avoid as much as possible through postponements, compromises, and hesitation. Meanwhile, opponents of such controls have introduced in Congress amendments to the Clean Air Act which would greatly alter or strike out altogether the indirect source review, transportation control, maintenance planning, and nondegradation provisions of the act. In early 1976 the House and Senate committees responsible for clean air legislation began meeting to draft the proposed amendments and bills were reported out by both committees in the spring of 1976. During the congressional debate on this proposed legislation, it is very important for citizens to work to prevent the erosion of the Clean Air Act's potential to resolve air pollution problems which are inextricably bound to land use decisions.

1. Pre-construction Review of Major New Stationary Sources

Stationary sources of air pollution are sources which emit pollutants from a stack while operating, for example, smelters, paper mills, fossil-fueled power plants, and steel mills. The Clean Air Act requires every state plan to include a procedure for pre-construction review of the location of every new stationary source (or modification of an existing stationary source) for which a new source performance standard has been established by EPA.[6] In order to insure *maintenance* of the national air quality standards, which is required by the act, EPA's regulations require pre-construction review of all new sources which might jeopardize the standards.[7] To insure the viability of state review and permit systems, moreover, the act requires that each state obtain adequate authority to prevent the construction of a source if it would prevent the attainment or maintenance of the national ambient air quality standards.[8]

The requirement that the location of proposed stationary sources be reviewed prior to construction, which obviously has very significant implications for land use, was established by the act as a complement to the requirement that stationary sources meet emission limitations established by EPA. These emission limitations prescribe the maximum amount of particulate matter or gases, such as sulfur dioxide, nitrogen dioxide, and hydrocarbons, that can be emitted from the stack. Such limitations alone, however, cannot insure the attainment and maintenance of ambient air quality standards. For instance, the location of a new stationary source such as a power plant or an incinerator in a heavily developed urban area would almost certainly jeopardize the attainment or maintenance of the ambient air quality standards in that region, even if the new source met specified emission limitations. Likewise, the location of a large source in a valley would have a substantially greater adverse impact on ambient air quality than the location of the same source on a mountain top, where pollutants are more widely dispersed. In fact, one very prevalent maneuver of the power and smelting industries has been the attempt to use tall stacks (sometimes as high as one thousand feet) rather than install available stack gas-cleaning equipment which actually removes pollutants from the emission stream. The use of tall stack dispersion techniques was ruled unlawful by the U.S. Court of Appeals for the Fifth Circuit on two grounds: (1) Congress intended that pollutant emissions be reduced, not merely diluted, and (2) such techniques violate the principle of nondegradation which is discussed below.[9] Subsequently, both the Sixth and the Ninth Circuit Courts have also ruled against tall stacks.[10]

The relationship between a single source of emissions and the total quantities of pollutants measured in the air at ground level is difficult, if not impossible, to define accurately. The development of a dispersion model involves computation of the rate of emissions, determination of the prevailing wind direction and speed, preparation of an inventory of total emissions in the region, and assessment of the effects of local topography. The ultimate determination sought is whether emissions directly attributable to a proposed new source would push ground-level concentrations of pollutants over the acceptable limits. It was precisely because of the difficulty of relating emissions from a single source to ground-level concentrations which result from many different sources that Congress, in order to insure that ambient standards are not violated, required state plans to include emission limitations applicable to each source at the stack.

It may be virtually impossible for the layman to assess the validity of a dispersion model. Citizens who are concerned that the location of a particular source will jeopardize air quality should obtain the assistance of a professional air quality planner from a private consulting firm or enlist the aid of professionals within the state or local air pollution control agency to help them develop a critique of the state's assessment of the air quality impact of the proposed source.

If a state grants a permit for the construction of a source which, as a result of its location, will cause a violation of ambient air quality standards, the only recourse for citizens under the Clean Air Act would be the filing of a citizen's suit under Section 304 of the act.[11] In such an action, the citizen-plaintiff must be prepared to show either (1) that the state did not meet procedural requirements, such as carrying out the review *before* construction began, or (2) that the pre-construction review indicated that violations would occur, yet a permit was granted anyway, or (3) in the case of a state determination that violations would not occur, that the calculations or the model was incorrect.

2. Pre-construction Review of Indirect Sources

Each state is required by the Clean Air Act and subsequent court decisions interpreting the act to prepare a plan to insure the maintenance of the national primary and secondary standards within its borders and to develop a procedure for pre-construction review of indirect sources similar to the procedure developed for review of stationary sources.

Indirect sources are those which attract mobile sources of air pollution, such as the automobile and the airplane. Examples are highways, shopping centers, sports stadiums, coliseums, and airports. During the last two decades in this country, we have experienced such a tremendous growth in automobile ownership and usage that existing data indicate that even stringent control of exhaust emissions from automobiles is not sufficient to prevent the accumulation of hazardous concentrations of carbon monoxide, hydrocarbons, nitrogen dioxide, and photochemical oxidants at facilities where large numbers of vehicles converge. Therefore, in order to fulfill Congress's mandate to maintain healthful air quality levels, the impact of facilities which will attract large numbers of automobiles must be reviewed prior to construction.

EPA required the states to submit plans for reviewing indirect sources by August 15, 1973. In February 1974 EPA promulgated a federal regulation for those states which either had failed to submit such a plan or had submitted a plan which was not approved.[12] This regulation applied to forty-eight states, since only Alabama and Florida had submitted indirect source review plans which EPA could approve. (As discussed below, Alabama has since suspended its plan.) Under the federal regulation, EPA or an agency designated by the state and approved by EPA must conduct a review of any proposed highway, airport, shopping or parking facility of the dimensions specified in the federal promulgation. Table 2 and Table 3

Table 2
Indirect Sources of Air Pollution to Be Reviewed in Urban Areas
(Standard Metropolitan Statistical Areas)

ROADS & HIGHWAYS	
NEW	20,000 vehicles per day (average)
MODIFIED	10,000 vehicles increase per day over existing traffic (average)
AIRPORTS	
NEW	50,000 operations (incoming and outgoing flights) or 1.6 million passengers per year
MODIFIED	50,000 operations per year increase over existing level, or 1.6 million passenger increase per year
OTHER INDIRECT SOURCES	
NEW	Parking for 1,000 cars or more
MODIFIED	Parking for 500 cars over existing number

Source of data: 40 C.F.R. § 52.22 (b) (2).

Table 3
Indirect Sources of Air Pollution to Be Reviewed in Nonurban Areas

ROADS & HIGHWAYS	No review
AIRPORTS	Same as in urban areas
OTHER INDIRECT SOURCES	
NEW	Parking for 2,000 cars or more
MODIFIED	Parking for 1,000 cars or more over existing number

Source of data: 40 C.F.R. § 52.22 (b) (2).

define the categories of proposed indirect sources which must be reviewed in urban and nonurban areas, respectively.

Originally, the EPA regulation required that a permit be obtained for such facilities if construction was to begin on or after January 1, 1975. On December 30, 1974, however, EPA amended the regulation, suspending implementation of federal indirect source review procedures until at least July 1, 1975.[13] EPA announced this suspension after passage by Congress of an appropriations bill that prohibited EPA from spending any money to regulate parking programs through June 30, 1975. On July 3, 1975, EPA suspended parking-related indirect source review indefinitely.[14] It did so in deference to Congress's consideration of proposed amendments to the Clean Air Act, one of which would require the states to adopt and implement an indirect source review regulation and would deny EPA any authority to review parking-related facilities. Since Congress's concern about indirect source review has focused on parking facilities, EPA stated that it intended to supply additional guidelines on evaluating the impact of airports and highways "in the near future," so that federal review of these types of indirect sources could commence. As of spring 1976, EPA had not yet published these promised guidelines and no provision had been made for the initiation of airport and highway indirect source review.

When it announced the indefinite suspension of parking-related indirect source review, EPA stated that it did not believe the Clean Air Act's goal of maintaining ambient air quality standards could be achieved without indirect source review. It went on, however, to indicate a preference for state and local execution of this controversial review. Nonetheless, EPA stated that if there was no congressional action "for a substantial time period," it might reinstate the current federal indirect source review regulation.

The federal suspension has no effect on existing or future state laws or regulations on indirect source review. The following states have adopted their own indirect source review programs: Connecticut, Florida, Idaho, Kentucky, Maine, Minnesota, Nebraska, New Hampshire, New York, Nevada, North Carolina, Oregon, Vermont, Virginia, West Virginia, and Wisconsin. Of these, the plans of Florida, Idaho, Kentucky, and North Carolina have been approved by EPA. Alabama and Washington also enacted indirect source review regulations, but after the federal suspension, Alabama suspended its regulation and Washington formally repealed its regulation. States may, of course, adopt an indirect source review regulation at any time. If the federal regulation is reinstated, a state regulation approved by EPA rather than the federal promulgation would govern indirect source review in that state.

The federal regulation is described and analyzed here, since, if reinstated, it will apply to almost all the states, and also because it serves as a guide to approvable state plans. The provisions of the federal regulation require that within thirty days of the receipt of an application for the construction of an indirect source, the reviewing agency must notify the public of its preliminary determination to approve or disapprove construction; must make available to the public a copy of the application and other related materials, as well as the agency's determination; and must advertise in the area's newspaper(s) the opportunity for written public comment (for at least a thirty-day period after the date of the advertisement). The federal regulation also specifies the type of information which must be considered in the agency's determination of whether a proposed indirect source is to be approved or disapproved.

From the environmentalist's point of view, the EPA regulation on the review of indirect sources is wholly inadequate to protect air quality against mounting pollutant levels caused by automobile exhaust gases.[15] EPA's decision to confine review to sources of a gargantuan character is one of the greatest failures of the regulation. In order to provide adequate coverage, the regulation should apply to sources small enough so that no one source or any collection of sources would interfere with the attainment or maintenance of the standards or result in any significant deterioration of air quality. The preamble to the regulation does not even imply that the selected size parameters are adequate to prevent such effects. In fact, according to the preamble, the "cutoff levels" are justified only in terms of some unspecified "nationwide context."

Not only are the cutoff levels not justified, but on their face they are demonstrably inadequate to prevent interference with attainment and maintenance of the standards and significant deterioration. First, the cutoff levels ignore the fact that many areas of the country have existing high levels of pollution, at or in excess of the standards. In such areas, construction of facilities exempt from review will violate or will increase violations of standards. Second, the cutoff levels ignore the cumulative impact of a number of unreviewed sources on air quality. There is nothing in the regulations to prevent the accumulation of sources that have a total associated activity greater than the cutoff level but which are each below that level when considered separately. For example, four parking lots around a single intersection or on a single block, each with a parking capacity of 600 cars, would have a total capacity of 2,400 cars. Thus, although each individual lot would fall below the 1,000 car cutoff level and consequently would not be subject to review, the total number of cars served by the four lots would be almost two-and-one-half times the cutoff level.

Existing conditions demonstrate that these cutoff levels will not provide protection against violations of standards. For example, most of the intersections in midtown Manhattan or downtown Washington, D.C., do not contain a single source large enough to be subject to review under the established cutoff. Yet, at many of these same intersections the eight-hour carbon monoxide standard is being exceeded regularly by large margins. If the present EPA regulation had been in effect since the time the sites of these intersections were virgin countryside, the regulation would have done nothing to prevent the present violations from occurring. Similarly, the regulation does nothing to protect present virgin areas from such pollution.

The use of an approach which distinguishes between "urban areas" and "nonurban areas," moreover, directly violates the principle of preventing significant deterioration which EPA is under court order to implement.[16] By exempting from review in nonurban areas, the construction of highways of any size and of other sources twice the size allowed in urban areas, EPA is adopting measures which allow at least twice as much pollution impact to occur in clean air areas as in dirty air areas. The Supreme Court has affirmed lower court holdings that the Clean Air Act does not permit this, and EPA has a legal duty to obey these court rulings.

Another controversial aspect of the federal regulation is the definition of "construction," which determines which proposed sources must apply for a permit. A permit is required only for projects which *begin* construction after a certain date (originally January 1, 1975, but now unspecified as a result of the suspension discussed above), but EPA has defined construction so broadly that even the clearing of land—which could have taken place years before the developer even determined what to build on the site—might qualify as "commencing construction" and allow the owner or developer to escape review. The definition states that construction includes land preparation "specifically designed for an indirect source." However, this vague requirement may not be difficult for a developer to skirt in the case of a site which was cleared before building plans were made. Nevertheless, if the developer has not been steadily at work on the site since clearing the land, it may be successfully argued that his construction has not been "continuous" and that the source must therefore be reviewed.

In view of the serious shortcomings of the federal regulation, as well as the indefinite postponement of its implementation, citizens would do well to urge their own states to adopt strong indirect source review plans. Persuading a state to take a forceful stand on indirect source review would not be an easy task. While adequate review of indirect sources is extremely important to the quality of the air we breathe and thus to public health, it is a very controversial issue.

Across the country a number of organizations and influential interest groups such as chambers of commerce, merchants' associations, and real estate developers have resisted—on both national and local levels—proposals for indirect source review. Most opponents of indirect source review insist that it is a "no-growth" policy that would have a devastating impact on local and regional economies. It is important that citizens who recognize the importance of indirect source review counter this gross exaggeration. Review and regulation of indirect sources should be developed to provide for planned growth that does not sacrifice healthful air quality, but they are not intended to prevent growth altogether. There is no reason why large shopping centers or stadiums cannot be constructed, as long as adequate mass transportation service, either public or private, is made available so that the number of automobiles traveling to the facilities can be kept to a minimum. Further, private developers can use their influence to help strengthen mass transit systems; they can urge local governments to extend or improve transit service and seek new federal money to do so, or they can themselves apply to the Urban Mass Transportation Administration for federal funding to sponsor particularly innovative transit proposals. Developers also have the option of considering construction in central business districts, where public transportation is usually already available.

An additional problem that citizens working for effective indirect source review should expect to run into is the fact that firm data do not exist for predicting with great accuracy the air quality impact of particular types of indirect sources. EPA's guidelines for analyzing the air quality impact of projected growth[17] offer some insights and guidance on this problem, but their methodology is not infallible. The very lack of firm data, however, means the layman may be in as sound a position as the technician to evaluate the adequacy of a proposed plan or to prepare a critique of the reviewing agency's assessment of the air quality impact of a particular proposed source. The most effective approach for the layman is to determine—either through his or her own reading of the EPA guidelines and the agency's analysis or by questioning agency officials—what assumptions were used in calculating the projected air quality impact of a proposed source. The following are very important questions which should be asked:

1. *Where did the reviewing agency assume the monitor would be located?* One hundred feet from the curb, sixty feet, or at curbside? Twenty feet off the ground, twelve feet, or five to six feet? In short,

would the monitor measure the concentrations to which drivers, cyclists, and pedestrians would be exposed?

2. *Did the agency use emission factors which take into account the vehicle age mix and vehicle operating temperatures that are representative for the area?* Old cars have considerably higher emission rates than new cars. Further, during motor warm-up (which, of course, takes longer in periods of cold weather) cars have much higher emissions than they do when fully warmed up.

3. *Did the state assume that new cars would meet the federal vehicle emission standards?* Originally, stringent emission standards for automobiles were to take effect in 1975. This deadline was extended by EPA until 1976 for hydrocarbon (HC) and carbon monoxide (CO) emissions and until 1977 for nitrogen dioxide (NO_2) emissions. Then Congress passed legislation extending the deadline for HC and CO standards until 1977 and the deadline for the NO_2 standard until 1978. Congress also gave EPA the authority to extend the deadline for HC and CO standards until 1978, which EPA did in March 1975. In addition, proposals to extend the effective dates of all three standards even further are included in the proposed amendments to the Clean Air Act under consideration by Congress.

Furthermore, there is considerable evidence available now that new cars are not meeting the interim emission standards they were designed to achieve. In actual on-the-road use, these cars are emitting much higher levels of pollutants than the prototype models emitted in certification tests conducted at the factory.[18]

4. *Do the traffic volumes used in the model reflect the worst situations?* For example, in a shopping center the peak volumes probably occur during the Christmas shopping season at the close of business. The model for a sports stadium should reflect the traffic volume leaving the stadium—when everyone cranks up and attempts to leave at the same time. In the case of a proposed highway, the model should not rely on the design capacity of the highway, since our existing highways are daily clogged with traffic levels which exceed their design capacity.

5. *Does the model reflect the impact a proposed source may have on other "hot spots" in the area?* While a single source may not cause violations at the site, the traffic it generates may lead to increased congestion or violations at prominent intersections in the region. Under EPA's present regulation the review must consider the projected traffic volumes at intersections in the immediate vicinity of the source; but depending on the roadway network in a region, a single source such as a coliseum, stadium, or elaborate shopping mall may

generate trips from great distances which cause bottlenecks at intersections which are not in the immediate vicinity of the source.

Faulty assumptions such as those revealed by questions like these should be identified and, ideally, corrected as soon as possible both in models for indirect source review and in the review of particular proposed sources.

3. Development of Maintenance Plans

The Clean Air Act and the court decision in *Natural Resources Defense Council* v. *Environmental Protection Agency*[19] require EPA to review state implementation plans to make certain they insure that the national air quality standards will be not only attained, but also maintained. EPA regulations implementing this requirement[20] call for submission of specific maintenance plans by the states for those areas in which study indicates the national standards will be violated by 1985 as a result of growth and development. The purpose of these plans is to prevent such violations from occurring, and they must include whatever measures are necessary "to insure that projected growth and development will be compatible with maintenance of the national standards. . . ."[21]

The EPA regulations, which were promulgated in June 1973, required each state by March 10, 1974 (a deadline that was later extended to May 10, 1974), to submit preliminary designations of areas in which national standards could be violated during the next decade. EPA was then supposed to publish in the *Federal Register* by August 16, 1974, its determinations of which of these areas would be subject to further study. For such identified areas, each state was then to prepare a more detailed air quality analysis of the impact of growth and development. Where this analysis indicated that standards would in fact be exceeded by 1985, the states were required by June 18, 1975, to submit ten-year maintenance plans to prevent such violations.

According to a tentative timetable developed by EPA on the basis of this deadline, the agency hoped by September 1974 to have published guidelines for analyzing the air quality impact of projected growth and for developing an approvable maintenance plan.[22] The states were then to complete their draft plans by February 1975, announce public hearings in April, hold these hearings in May, and submit final plans to EPA by the June 1975 deadline.

Unfortunately, despite the ruling federal statute, court order, and regulations, this entire time frame has now been abandoned. First, the states were very late in submitting their preliminary designations. Then, EPA failed to identify by August 1974 which of these proposed designated areas would require further air quality analysis and planning by the states and did not complete these determinations until September 1975. Further, EPA fell badly behind in the publication of its guidelines, which grew into a thirteen-volume set, the last volume of which was released in the summer of 1975.[23] On June 19, 1975, EPA rescinded the June 18, 1975, deadline for submission by the states of full analyses and actual ten-year maintenance plans for problem areas.[24] Instead, it stated that the EPA Administrator would specify individual schedules for each area identified for study. This step was taken despite the statutory framework of deadlines set out in the Clean Air Act[25] and the mandate of the U.S. Court of Appeals for the District of Columbia.[26] The Natural Resources Defense Council has initiated discussions with EPA regarding the unlawful nature of this administrative discretion.

On May 3, 1976, EPA promulgated in the *Federal Register* new regulations on maintenance plans, amending and expanding the existing regulations.[27] These regulatory changes not only include the provision that individual submission dates are to be set for the different areas being studied, but also authorize the EPA Administrator to delegate the responsibility for establishing these schedules to the regional EPA administrators. These regional officials, moreover, are now also responsible for deciding whether maintenance plans will be required in particular areas, the periods of time the plans must cover, and the portion of the plan provisions which the state must have the legal authority to implement. In effect, under the new regulations, EPA is improperly allowing discretionary interpretations of the basic requirements of the Clean Air Act, i.e., (1) that all states must submit air quality implementation plans by a specified date, (2) that all plans must be adequate to insure the attainment and maintenance of ambient standards, and (3) that all states must have adequate legal authority to carry out their plans. These and other significant failings result in a markedly inadequate program for assuring the maintenance of ambient air quality standards as required by the Clean Air Act.

In May 1975 the National Resources Defense Council filed suit against EPA on the grounds that the regulations promulgated for maintenance plans did not fulfill the dictates of the law.[28] This suit has been postponed, pending congressional action on the proposed amendments to the Clean Air Act now under consideration.

The broken deadlines, the extensions, and the attempts to establish unlawful administrative discretion regarding maintenance plans reflect the great reluctance EPA has shown to move forcefully ahead with those aspects of the Clean Air Act which involve land use controls. Perhaps fearful of opposing forces which have now proposed amendments to the Clean Air Act that would greatly weaken or delete the transportation and land use controls provision of the act, EPA has not been willing to assume strong leadership in this area. Support and pressure from citizens who are well informed about the Clean Air Act and the regulations promulgated under it are badly needed to see that EPA and the states carry out their legal obligations to assure that national air quality standards are attained and maintained.

The following are the initial criteria established by EPA for the preliminary designations of areas to be analyzed for possible violations of standards by 1985:[29]

1. Particulate matter
   a. Areas where national standards will not be achieved by 1985.
   b. Areas now in compliance with national standards, but where growth by 1985 may increase particulate emissions to the degree that standards will not be maintained.
   c. Areas where state plans may not be sufficient to achieve or maintain standards.
2. Sulfur oxides (SO_x)
   Areas where national primary standards will not be maintained through 1985 because of increases in the use of fossil fuels. For the preliminary analysis it was assumed that this potential was not exacerbated by the energy crisis.
3. Carbon monoxide (CO)
   Areas where a recent maximum eight-hour average exceeds 25 parts per million (p.p.m.).
4. Photochemical oxidants (O_x)
   Areas where a transportation implementation plan for photochemical oxidants is needed.
5. Nitrogen dioxide (NO_2)
   The following five particular Standard Metropolitan Statistical Areas were specified: Chicago, Denver, Los Angeles, New York City, and Salt Lake City.

Both these criteria and the preliminary designations actually made leave much to be desired. For instance, the criterion for carbon monoxide pollutants covers only those areas where the existing eight-hour average for carbon monoxide exceeds twenty-five p.p.m., a level almost three times the primary eight-hour standard (nine p.p.m.) established to protect human health. The presumption that maintenance plans are necessary only for those areas where present carbon monoxide levels are above twenty-five p.p.m. relies heavily on the capability of still unperfected automobile exhaust emission control devices to reduce carbon monoxide emissions drastically. It assumes that these devices will not only cut existing concentrations by two-thirds, but will also offset the increased emissions resulting from increased automobile usage expected in the next ten years.[30] Unfortunately, it is much more likely that automobile pollutant concentrations actually will increase in urban areas because of increased automobile travel and the fact that emission control devices perform less effectively on the road than under design conditions.

The chief constraint to an accurate determination of which areas of a state may violate national standards by 1985 is limited monitoring by state agencies. For example, many states do not meet even the minimum federal requirements for monitoring carbon monoxide, which call for monitors only in regions which have an urban area with a population over 200,000. Regions with a population of 600,000 or more are required to have only two monitoring sites for carbon monoxide.

In contrast to monitoring for pollutants caused by automobiles, monitoring for sulfur oxides and particulate matter, which are primarily caused by stationary sources, has been conducted for a longer period of time and at more sites. In determining whether a state is monitoring in enough locations and in the proper places in an area to define the pollution problems caused by these two contaminants, citizens will need to call upon their own knowledge of the area and of the number of pollution sources (especially large ones), as well as their firsthand experience with pollution problems, such as poor visibility on bad days.

Monitors for sulfur oxides and particulate matter should be located so that they measure the worst conditions in the area and should be stationed at proper heights to reflect the concentrations to which the public is exposed. In addition, prevailing meteorological conditions which affect the dispersion of pollutants are a very important factor in the proper location of monitors for pollution caused by stationary sources. Many stationary sources also have "fugitive emissions" of gases and particulates which escape from the building through windows, vents, and doors, as well as emissions from the stacks. Such fugitive emissions can result in seriously high ground concentrations of pollutants in the vicinity of a plant, but very frequently the state's monitors are located too far away to measure them.

In actuality, virtually every state in the nation suffers from an inadequate network for the monitoring of air pollution. Lack of data, however, cannot legally serve as a justification for failing to consider whether a maintenance plan will be necessary in an area.

The preliminary designations made by the states of areas in which violations of national standards may occur by 1985 were published in the *Federal Register* by EPA in the summer of 1974.[31] A list of areas designated within a particular state, as well as maps or descriptions of monitoring sites, should be available from that state's air pollution control agency. EPA's determinations of which of these areas will be subject to further analysis and planning, overdue since August 1974, were published in the *Federal Register* in three groups, on April 29, 1975, June 2, 1975, and September 9, 1975.[32]

If citizens find that an area of particular concern is not among the areas designated by their state, they should make inquiries regarding how monitoring is carried out in this area and what measurements have been recorded. It is quite possible that an area was not included on the list of designated areas simply because no data existed to indicate that standards were being violated or that violations were very likely in the future.

4. Prevention of Significant Deterioration

Another aspect of air quality maintenance which has important implications for land use is the development by EPA and the states of measures to prevent significant deterioration. Simply stated, nondegradation is the principle that areas where air quality is presently better than the national standards should be protected. Although this specific language was not used in the Clean Air Act, the legislative history of the act demonstrates Congress's intent to prevent further degradation of air quality. In fact, such a policy had already been adopted by the National Air Pollution Control Agency (NAPCA), a branch of the U.S. Department of Health, Education, and Welfare (HEW), even before the passage of the 1970 Clean Air Act.

Just on the face of the matter it is clear that while conducting a major federal-state effort to clean up the air in areas of the country we have polluted to unhealthful levels, we should not at the same time allow existing clean air areas to be sacrificed. But even more conclusive reasons exist for protecting our clean air areas. The national standards were established on the basis of existing scientific evidence to protect human health and to prevent damage to animal life and vegetation. As research continues, however, and as measuring instrumentation grows more sophisticated, it is presumed by leading scientists in the field that we will discover adverse effects at lower and lower levels of pollution. Congress acknowledged this likelihood when it provided that the national standards should be reevaluated and revised when necessary to reflect new evidence.[33] Strong evidence of adverse effects on human health from sulfur dioxide at levels below the present primary standards has already been uncovered.[34] Thus the potential for finding adverse health effects and vegetation damage at levels lower than the existing standards is a very strong argument for protecting our existing clean air areas. An additional consideration is that if these areas are diminished and high levels of pollutants are allowed to hang in the air nationwide, it will become more and more difficult to conduct the kinds of scientific testing necessary to determine threshold levels of damage to health and vegetation.[35]

When federal EPA officials balked at applying the principle of nondegradation in the early 1970s, the Sierra Club initiated a suit to force the agency to protect existing clean air areas. In May 1973 the Supreme Court affirmed the lower court decisions requiring EPA to prevent significant deterioration.[36]

In July 1973 EPA proposed alternative plans for the prevention of significant deterioration, but final regulations were not promulgated until December 5, 1974.[37] These regulations set out a regulatory scheme for sulfur oxides and particulate matter in which areas that have air quality better than national standards for these pollutants are to be designated as class I, class II, or class III, depending on the amount of pollution to be allowed in each. The greatest degree of deterioration is permitted in class III areas, where air pollution can be increased up to the national secondary standards. Thus no protection from degradation is provided in these areas. In class II areas, the allowable increase in sulfur oxides and particulate emissions is compatible with what EPA terms "moderate well-controlled growth." For instance, in a class II area, a controlled one thousand-megawatt utility plant could be accommodated within the allowable increment. The best protected areas are those designated class I, where the permitted increment in sulfur oxides and particulate emissions is the smallest. In all classes, "increment" refers to the allowable increase in ground level concentrations of pollutants, not to an increase in pounds of total emissions. No attempt is made in this scheme to prevent degradation caused by increases in pollutants associated with automobiles—that is, carbon monoxide, hydrocarbons, nitrogen dioxide, and photochemical oxidants. The two pollutants affected here, sulfur oxides and particulate matter, are caused primarily by stationary sources, including power plants and manufacturing installations.

Unless or until a state decides to classify its regions, all of its areas which have air quality that is better than the national secondary standards will be considered class II areas. If the state does wish to redesignate a clean air area as class I or class III, it must conduct a public hearing, and must make a discussion of the reasons for the redesignation available for public inspection at least thirty days before the hearing.

The major drawback of this three-class approach is that unless designations of class II and III areas are carefully limited, substantial deterioration of air quality will result in vast areas of the country. It is estimated that in over 80 percent of the nation air quality is presently cleaner than required by the secondary standards. Under the three-class plan, it is likely that only a few areas, akin to wilderness areas, will enjoy full protection from gradually deteriorating air quality. In addition, the system of reclassification is so designed that if a particular site in a class I or II area is desired for a large power plant installation, the state can, after a public hearing, reclassify this site as a class III area. Thus the system sanctions action similar to "spot zoning," a means of catering to special interests which has traditionally been held unlawful by the courts.

EPA's response to the nondegradation issue thus has been less than wholehearted and eager. It is especially important to note that the regulations which EPA has promulgated limit the increase of pollutant concentrations in ambient air, but do not limit the total amount of emissions allowed from the stack. Depending on particular meteorological conditions, this could permit stack emissions to despoil clean air over large regions, contributing further to the problem of suspended sulfates and acid rainfall.[38] Furthermore, although three federal courts of appeals have ruled that using tall stacks to disperse pollutants in lieu of reducing emissions is unlawful, in part because this violates the principle of nondegradation,[39] on January 13, 1976, EPA issued a policy guidance memorandum for its regional administrators which would allow new sources in clean air areas to use tall stacks.

Concerned citizens should try to determine the practical implications for their state of EPA's regulations on prevention of significant deterioration. EPA regional officials or state air pollution control agency officials should be pressed to equate the allowable increases of pollutants to actual projects—to numbers of steel plants, smelters, incinerators, and electric power plants—and to establish the total amount of pollution that will be allowed in a given area.

Since the states are not required to redesignate any area as class I or class III, they are not required to hold public hearings on which areas should be protected and to what extent. It is likely, however, that most states will conduct a hearing or hearings to consider redesignation. Any hearing held must be conducted "in or near" the area affected. Since, however, the preservation of clean air areas is a matter of statewide and national concern rather than a strictly local issue, individuals or organizations should not hesitate to participate in hearings held in other localities or even in other states, particularly in neighboring states where decisions regarding allowable increases in pollution may mean more pollution in one's own state.

The Sierra Club, which won the original court decision mandating EPA to take action to prevent significant deterioration, is now challenging EPA's regulatory scheme in the courts on the grounds that it does not adequately protect clean air areas.[40] However, citizens should proceed on the assumption that the EPA regulations are finally binding and should consult their state air pollution control agency regarding its plans for public hearings. Wherever possible, citizens should urge state officials, politicians, and other influential people to see that hearings are held in all clean air areas and that preliminary determinations—which must be made by the state air pollution control agency prior to the public hearings—are made to redesignate as many areas as possible as class I areas, where the smallest increment in pollution is permitted.

Citizen Action

The kinds of citizen action needed to ensure responsible implementation of those aspects of the Clean Air Act which pertain to land use decisions have been indicated in the course of this chapter. Repeated emphasis has been given to the need for concerned and informed citizens to press EPA and the states to develop and implement land use controls when they are needed for the attainment and maintenance of national air quality standards. The following additional information and suggestions are provided as aids for those who wish to pursue such citizen action in the fight for environmentally sound land use decision making in this country.

In order to participate effectively in the implementation of the Clean Air Act, citizens should first familiarize themselves with the act itself, with the regulations promulgated by EPA under the act, and with related state regulations. While some of the information included in these materials is quite technical, it is not extremely difficult to pinpoint crucial procedural requirements and basic standards. Federal procedural requirements for new stationary source review and indirect source review are found at 40 *Code of Federal Regulations* (C.F.R.) § 51.18 and also at 38 *Federal Register* 15836 (June 18, 1973). These regulations contain the requirements for public notice, advertisement of the state air pollution control agency's approval or disapproval, and provision of a thirty-day period for written public comments. Specific requirements which must be met by state air pollution control agencies and by applicants in the review of indirect sources are found at 40 C.F.R. § 52.22 and also at 38 *Federal Register* 7276 (February 25, 1974). Regulations which specify the categories of stationary sources that are subject to new source performance standards and these standards themselves are included in 40 C.F.R. Part 60 and were promulgated and amended in the *Federal Register* on several different dates. EPA's regulations for designating areas in which national standards may be violated before 1985 and for developing maintenance plans are found at 40 C.F.R. § 51.12 and also at 38 *Federal Register* 15836 (June 18, 1973). New proposed regulations on the maintenance of national air quality standards were published by EPA in the *Federal Register* on October 20, 1975 (40 *Federal Register* 49048). EPA's thirteen volumes of *Guidelines for Air Quality Maintenance Planning and Analysis,* listed in Table 4, are available free of charge to nonprofit organizations from:

Table 4
EPA's Guidelines for Air Quality Maintenance Planning and Analysis*

Volume 1:   Designation of Air Quality Maintenance Areas
Volume 2:   Plan Preparation
Volume 3:   Control Strategies
Volume 4:   Land Use and Transportation Considerations
Volume 5:   Case Studies in Plan Development
Volume 6:   Overview of Air Quality Maintenance Area Analysis
Volume 7:   Projecting County Emissions
Volume 8:   Computer-Assisted Area Source Emissions Gridding Procedure (CAASE)
Volume 9:   Evaluating Indirect Sources
Volume 10: Reviewing New Stationary Sources
Volume 11: Air Quality Monitoring and Data Analysis
Volume 12: Applying Atmospheric Simulation Models to Air Quality Maintenance Areas
Volume 13: Allocating Projected Emissions to Sub-County Areas

*A brief description of the contents of each of these volumes can be found at 40 *Federal Register* 49049 (October 20, 1975).

Air Pollution Technical Information Center
U.S. Environmental Protection Agency
Research Triangle Park, North Carolina 27711

They are available at a nominal cost to anyone from:

National Technical Information Service
5285 Port Royal Road
Springfield, Virginia 22151

Federal regulations on prevention of significant deterioration are found at 39 *Federal Register* 42509 (December 5, 1974). Copies of all of the above regulations published in the *Federal Register* and a copy of the 1970 Clean Air Act itself can be obtained from:

Office of Public Affairs
U.S. Environmental Protection Agency
Waterside Mall
401 M Street, S.W.
Washington, D.C. 20460

Despite the importance of regulations, however, it is important to remember that they are merely intended to implement a state or federal statute and are not inviolate. When a state or federal regulation is inadequate to meet the requirements of the 1970 Clean Air

Act, it can be challenged. For example, whenever a state submits a new state regulation to EPA and EPA approves it, citizens may file a court challenge within thirty days of the EPA approval.[41] Furthermore, citizens who are concerned about a particular proposed project which developers or the state asserts meets regulatory requirements should be quick to point out that the project must also meet statutory requirements—that is, it must not lead to the violation of any national standard.

Twice a year EPA publishes a document entitled *State Air Pollution Implementation Plan Progress Report,* which reviews what the states have done during the past six months. For each state it includes a summary, as well as a breakdown by air quality control regions, of compliance status; monitoring requirements and actual monitors; charts pertaining to air quality maintenance areas; and enforcement actions. The quality of these progress reports has improved significantly since EPA began publishing them, and they now serve as a very helpful resource. Copies are available from both the Air Pollution Technical Information Center and the National Technical Information Service, whose addresses are given above.

For information regarding the status of an application or the review of a particular proposed source, inquiries should be made with state air pollution control officials. If staff members of a regional or branch office cannot answer questions raised, they should refer one to appropriate officials in the state agency's central office.

In general, contacts should be made with state air pollution control officials and with federal officials in EPA's regional offices, so that one can keep abreast of the state's compliance with federal requirements, the flow of EPA guidelines and technical documents, and any changes in regulations or deadlines. Moreover, agency officials can be invaluable in explaining technical reports, describing the data available, or suggesting other sources of information. In all their contacts with agencies, citizens should try to be as specific as possible in their inquiries and should press for specific responses.

Citizens should not be timid about requesting information or assistance from air pollution control officials. The Clean Air Act of 1970 was exemplary in requiring assurances that the state planning process would be open to citizen participation. The debate on the bill at the time of its passage reflected the strong congressional intent that citizens be represented in the planning process and be provided with tools to assist in the enforcement of the act. Moreover, Congress took an unprecedented stand in requiring that the confidentiality of "process" data from private companies must be waived when it pertains to pollutant emissions and thus conflicts with the public's need to know.

"Politics" and "social and economic impact" are phrases citizens may often encounter in responses to their inquiries or suggestions for strict review procedures or enforcement provisions in the state plan. In writing the Clean Air Act of 1970, however, Congress pointedly rejected language which would require consideration of social and economic costs in plans to abate air pollution. The U.S. Court of Appeals for the Fifth Circuit has reaffirmed this reading of the act in a forceful decision which struck economic considerations from enforcement provisions in the Georgia state implementation plan:

> First, Congress made it clear that considerations of economic cost or technical feasibility were *always* to be subordinate to considerations of public health. Second, and as a corollary to this, Congress made it clear that cost and feasibility were not to be considered in meeting the three-year deadlines for attaining national primary standards. Those standards are set in terms of what is required for the protection of public health.[42]

Thus citizens should press agency officials and elected representatives to commit their state to adequate plans for reviewing stationary and indirect sources, for maintaining standards, and for preventing significant deterioration of existing air quality. Educating members of the public who are not already concerned about environmental issues can greatly contribute to the success of this effort. Strong public opinion combined with the threat of citizen suits to challenge inadequate plans offer considerable leverage for influencing state proposals.

A very important point which should be stressed is that public hearings held on state proposals should represent the culmination of citizen efforts, not the beginning. By the time a public hearing is held, it is probably too late to effect major changes in a state proposal. In the past, public hearings have often been scheduled only a week to ten days before the deadline for the submission of plans to EPA, and only major changes, if any, have been made after the hearing. This does not mean that efforts should not be made to prepare strong testimony, to arrange for witnesses, and to encourage a large number of people to attend. The public hearing is the citizens' first opportunity to "build a record"—to introduce formal evidence, present pertinent statistics, and express public opinion. Under the act, the transcript of the hearing must be considered by EPA in its review of a state plan. Moreover, this record is vital when a legal challenge is made to an inadequate plan under the Clean Air Act's provision for citizen suits, which is discussed below.

After a plan has been submitted to EPA, there is still opportunity to influence EPA's review and to press EPA to correct any deficiencies in state proposals through promulgation of federal regulations. Citizens should find out which EPA regional office is primarily responsible for review of their state plan and who in that office is heading up the review. Criticisms of the plan should then be communicated directly to this person. He or she should be alerted to important statistics which may jeopardize the plan's adequacy or to invalid assumptions the state might have used in projecting growth rates, emissions, or future air quality.

The EPA review offers another opportunity to "go on record." The EPA Administrator publishes in the *Federal Register* his proposed approval or disapproval of each state plan and allows a thirty-day written comment period before making the final determination.[43] Even if citizens' comments do not reverse EPA's position, detailed and specific examples of the inadequacy of a state plan can be very helpful in the preparation of a legal case against EPA or the state to remedy a weak plan. Not only do written comments and hearing transcripts formally introduce important facts which can then be taken before the court, they also serve notice to the court that these facts or issues were brought to the attention of the state or EPA officials *prior* to the submission or approval of the plan. This strengthens the citizens' position that they turned to the courts for remedy only as a last resort.

As has been indicated, the Clean Air Act of 1970 includes a special provision for citizen suits.[44] Under this provision, any person has the right to sue in federal district court to enjoin violations of the act or state implementation plans. This broad right is limited in the following ways: (1) A citizen may not sue for damages, but only to enjoin an illegal act or to force the performance of a nondiscretionary duty. (2) If the Administrator of EPA or the state is diligently prosecuting a suit in the federal courts, a citizen may not institute a separate suit, but he may intervene and become a party to the suit. The act also provides for the payment of litigation costs, including attorney and expert witness fees, at the discretion of the court.

NOTES

1. 42 U.S.C. § 1857 *et seq.*

2. The Air Pollution Control Association's address is: 4400 Fifth Avenue, Pittsburgh, Pa. 15213.

3. 40 C.F.R. Part 52.

4. The state must apply a margin of error in approving or disapproving the construction of new sources, because the 1970 Clean Air Act requires the state to *insure* the attainment and maintenance of national standards. (§ 110[a] [2] [B]; 42 U.S.C. § 1857c–5[a] [2] [B].) Any construction which might jeopardize attainment and maintenance should be prohibited.

5. § 110(a) (2) (B); 42 U.S.C. § 1857c–5(a) (2) (B).

6. § 110(a) (2) (D); 42 U.S.C. § 1857c–5(a) (2) (D). The Administrator of EPA has established new source performance standards for the following categories: fossil-fuel-fired steam generators, incinerators, Portland cement plants, nitric acid plants, sulfuric acid plants, asphalt concrete plants, petroleum refineries, storage vessels for petroleum liquids, secondary lead smelters, secondary brass and bronze ingot production plants, iron and steel plants, and sewage treatment plants.

7. 40 C.F.R. § 51.18.

8. § 110(a) (4); 42 U.S.C. § 1857c–5(a) (4).

9. Natural Resources Defense Council v. Environmental Protection Agency, 489 F.2d 390, 6 ERC 1248 (5th Cir. 1974).

10. Big Rivers Electric Corporation v. Environmental Protection Agency, 523 F.2d 16, 8 ERC 1092 (6th Cir. 1975); Kennecott Copper Corporation v. Train, 526 F.2d 1149, 8 ERC 1497 (9th Cir. 1975).

11. 42 U.S.C. § 1857h–2. See Richard E. Ayres and James F. Miller, "Citizen Suits Under the Clean Air Act Amendments of 1970," *Natural Resources Defense Council Newsletter,* vol. 1, no. 4 (Winter 1971). Copies are available at $.50 per copy from the Natural Resources Defense Council, 15 West 44th Street, New York, New York 10036.

12. 39 *Federal Register* 7270 (February 25, 1974); 40 C.F.R. § 52.22.

13. 39 *Federal Register* 45014 (December 30, 1974).

14. 40 *Federal Register* 28064 (July 3, 1975).

15. A suit challenging EPA's indirect source review regulation has been brought by the Natural Resources Defense Council in conjunction with other organizations, but is now pending until congressional action is taken on the proposed amendments to the Clean Air Act. Natural Resources Defense Council v. Environmental Protection Agency, Civil No. 74–1235 (D.C. Cir., filed February 14, 1974).

16. See the discussion of significant deterioration later in this chapter.

17. U.S. Environmental Protection Agency, *Guidelines for Air Quality Maintenance Planning and Analysis, Volume 9: Evaluating Indirect Sources,* Draft (Research Triangle Park, N.C.: Office of Air Quality Planning and Standards, 1975).

18. U.S. Environmental Protection Agency, *Computation of Emission Factors* (2d ed.; Research Triangle Park, N.C.: Office of Air Quality Planning and Standards, March 1975), Supplement 5 and Appendix D.

19. 475 F.2d 968, 4 ERC 1945 (D.C. Cir. 1973).

20. 38 *Federal Register* 15836 (June 18, 1973); 39 *Federal Register* 16344 (May 8, 1974); 40 C.F.R. § 51.12.

21. 40 C.F.R. § 51.12 (g) (2).

22. *See* U.S. Environmental Protection Agency, *Guidelines for Air Quality Maintenance Planning and Analysis, Volume 1: Designation of Air Quality Maintenance Areas* (Research Triangle Park, N.C.: Office of Air Quality Planning and Standards, January 1974): OAQPS No. 1.2–016:I–7.

23. U.S. Environmental Protection Agency, *Guidelines for Air Quality Maintenance Planning and Analysis* (Research Triangle Park, N.C.: Office of Air Quality Planning and Standards, 1974–1975). The volumes of this series are listed in Table 4 and addresses from which they can be obtained are provided in the citizen action section of this chapter.

24. 40 *Federal Register* 25814 (June 19, 1975).

25. § 110; 42 U.S.C. § 1857c–5.

26. Natural Resources Defense Council v. Environmental Protection Agency, 475 F.2d 968, 4 ERC 1945 (D.C. Cir. 1973).

27. 41 *Federal Register* 18382 (May 3, 1976).

28. Natural Resources Defense Council v. Environmental Protection Agency, Civil No. 75–1530 (D.C. Cir., filed May 28, 1975).

29. U.S. Environmental Protection Agency, *Guidelines for Air Quality Maintenance, Volume 1: Designation of Maintenance Areas,* pp. 23–26.

30. The number of vehicle miles traveled (VMT) by automobiles across the nation increased by 5 percent, 6 percent, and 8 percent in 1970, 1971, and 1972, respectively. The gasoline shortage in the winter of 1973–1974 curbed this increase temporarily, but, with increased supplies at hand, the VMT is on the rise again. For more information on trends in automobile travel and the inaccuracies in EPA's predictions regarding mechanical exhaust control devices, see Natural Resources Defense Council, *Transportation Controls for Clean Air,* available from the Natural Resources Defense Council, 917 15th Street, N.W., Washington, D.C. 20005; Calspan Corporation, *Automobile Exhaust Emission Surveillance* (Summary) (March 1973), available from EPA; and H. A. Ashby, R. C. Stahman, B. H. Eccleston, and R. W. Hurn, "Vehicle Emissions—Summer to Winter," Society of Automotive Engineers, Paper 741053 (1974), available from the Society of Automotive Engineers, 400 Commonwealth Drive, Warrendale, Pa. 15096.

31. 39 *Federal Register* 25330 (July 10, 1974) and 39 *Federal Register* 28906 (August 12, 1974).

32. 39 *Federal Register* 18726 (April 29, 1975); 40 *Federal Register* 23746 (June 2, 1975); and 40 *Federal Register* 41941 (September 9, 1975).

33. At hearings held on the 1970 Clean Air Act, Dr. John T. Middleton, commissioner of the National Air Pollution Control Administration, testified that: "We know from the criteria published for sulfur oxides, that at certain levels definite adverse effects occur in the lung. We also know that at a little lower level there are more subtle effects on the action of the lung, and that below that some enzyme system begins to fail or to function improperly.

"The no-effect level would have to be somewhere below that, but as science progresses, it is very likely we are going to find still other body chemical systems that are being affected, so the no-effect level always corresponds, you might say, to the limitations of scientific knowledge in this area.

"It is because our knowledge is, hopefully, improving with time that . . . there is a need to revise the air quality criteria periodically . . . which . . . in turn may require different air quality standards." (U.S., Congress, Senate, Subcommittee on Air and Water Pollution of the Committee on Public Works, *Hearings on S. 3229, S. 3466, S. 3546,* 91st Cong., 2d Sess., 1970, p. 1490.)

34. The EPA CHESS study, released in 1973, reported: "Our data indicate that adverse effects on elderly subjects with heart and lung disease, and on panels of asthmatics, are being experienced even on days below the national primary standard for 24-hour levels of SO_2 and total suspended particulates." (U.S. Environmental Protection Agency, *Health Consequences of Sulfur Oxides: Summary and Conclusions Based Upon CHESS Studies of 1970–1971,* Draft, [August 15, 1973], p. 22.)

35. Unlike sulfur dioxide, sulfates (SO_4, which forms when SO_2 that is released into the atmosphere oxidizes) are distributed in dangerous concentrations over wide areas, not just at the points where plumes from specific sources touch down. An EPA memorandum has indicated that high sulfate levels are being recorded even in rural areas of the country, hundreds of miles from large sulfur dioxide sources. This memorandum urged that unless study and control are initiated at once, uniform levels of sulfate concentrations will make it impossible to conduct valid studies of the potential adverse effects of various concentrations and exposures.

36. Sierra Club v. Ruckelshaus, 344 F. Supp. 253, 4 ERC 1205 (D.D.C. 1972), *aff'd per curiam,* 4 ERC 1815 (D.C. Cir. 1972), *aff'd by an equally divided Court sub nom.* Fri v. Sierra Club, 412 U.S. 541, 5 ERC 1417 (1973). As previously pointed out, the U.S. Court of Appeals for the Fifth Circuit has subsequently held that the use of tall smokestacks and other means of dispersing pollutants violated the principle of nondegradation. Natural Resources Defense Council v. Environmental Protection Agency, 489 F. 2d 390, 6 ERC 1248 (5th Cir. 1974).

37. 38 *Federal Register* 18986 (July 16, 1973) and 39 *Federal Register* 42509 (December 5, 1974).

38. When sulfur dioxide (SO_2) is released into the atmosphere, it can oxidize to form sulfates (SO_4) which then combine with water molecules to form sulfuric acid (H_2SO_4), resulting in what is known as sulfuric acid mist or acid rainfall.

39. Natural Resources Defense Council v. Environmental Protection Agency, 489 F.2d 390, 6 ERC 1248 (5th Cir. 1974); Big Rivers Electric Corporation v. Environmental Protection Agency, 523 F.2d 16, 8 ERC 1092 (6th Cir. 1975); Kennecott Copper Corporation v. Train, 526 F.2d 1149, 8 ERC 1497 (9th Cir. 1975).

40. Sierra Club v. Environmental Protection Agency, Civil Nos. 74–2063 and 74–2079 (D.C. Cir. 1974).

41. § 307; 42 U.S.C. § 1857h–5.

42. Natural Resources Defense Council v. Environmental Protection Agency, 489 F.2d 390, 411–412, 6 ERC 1248, 1263 (5th Cir. 1974).

43. The EPA Administrator is not required by the act to provide a thirty-day comment period; however, this has become an established practice of EPA in recognition of its responsibilities to provide for citizen participation.

44. § 304; 42 U.S.C. § 1857h–2. See Note 11 above.

CHAPTER 5

The Federal Water Pollution Control Act Amendments of 1972

THE PASSAGE OF the Federal Water Pollution Control Act Amendments of 1972[1] marked a turning point in the approach taken toward the problem of water pollution control in this country. Whereas past legislation had endorsed the practice of allowing certain waters to remain severely degraded to permit industrial and other uses, the 1972 amendments rejected this concept and adopted the view that "no one has the right to pollute—that pollution continues because of technological limits, not because of any inherent right to use the nation's waterways for the purpose of disposing wastes."[2] The new law rejected traditional reliance on the "assimilative capacity" of our waterways and made it clear, as Senator Muskie stated on the floor of the Senate, that our "streams and rivers are no longer to be considered part of the waste treatment process."[3]

In implementing these new principles, the 1972 amendments recognized and came to grips with economic and technological constraints in such a way as to produce a regulatory program that is strong, but workable. Also, they recognized that if water quality is to be protected, there must be not only effective regulation of existing sources of water pollution, but also land use planning and controls to regulate the location of new sources. Before discussing in more detail the sections of the amendments which deal most directly with land use, a brief overview of this new act's most important provisions will be presented to outline the overall attack on water pollution, of which land use planning and control are an essential component part.

The New Act: An Overview

The key goal of the 1972 amendments is "to restore and maintain the chemical, physical, and biological integrity of the Nation's waters."[4] Six national policies are set out as means by which this goal can be achieved. These policies are that:

(1) . . . the discharge of pollutants into the navigable waters be eliminated by 1985;

(2) . . . wherever attainable, an interim goal of water quality which provides for the protection and propagation of fish, shellfish, and wildlife and provides for recreation in and on the water be achieved by July 1, 1983;

(3) . . . the discharge of toxic pollutants in toxic amounts be prohibited;

(4) . . . Federal financial assistance be provided to construct publicly owned waste treatment works;

(5) . . . areawide waste treatment management planning processes be developed and implemented to assure adequate control of sources of pollutants in each State; and

(6) . . . that a major research and demonstration effort be made to develop technology necessary to eliminate the discharge of pollutants into the navigable waters, waters of the contiguous zone, and the oceans.[5]

The regulatory and grant-in-aid programs established by the 1972 amendments to implement these new national policies are innovative and far-reaching. Primary responsibility for implementation resides with the U.S. Environmental Protection Agency (EPA), but state-federal cooperation is an essential aspect of the total effort.

The regulatory program created is divided into two complementary parts as a result of the basic distinction made by the act between point sources and nonpoint sources of pollution. A point source is any confined, discrete conveyance such as a pipe, ditch, or even a floating craft.[6] Typical point sources include discharges via a pipe of effluent from industrial works or municipal sewage treatment plants. Uncollected runoff from an agricultural area or a mining operation is a typical example of a nonpoint source of pollution.[7] The water pollution caused by such nonpoint sources is extremely serious, and has been estimated to account for perhaps half of our total water pollution problem.[8]

For point sources, the act provides the following regulatory scheme:

1. By July 1977 all dischargers other than municipal sewage treatment plants must have achieved effluent limitations based upon the "best practicable" pollution control technology currently available, and public treatment works must have achieved limitations based upon secondary treatment.[9]

2. By July 1983 nonmunicipal point sources must have the "best available technology economically achieveable" in operation, and municipal sewage treatment plants must have installed the "best practicable waste treatment technology."[10]

3. Special effluent standards for toxic water pollutants must be based solely on environmental and safety considerations and must be met substantially before the 1977 deadline.[11]

4. New source performance standards based upon the "best available demonstrated control technology" must be met by all new facilities or installations.[12]

5. Special effluent restrictions for particular dischargers based upon existing water quality standards must be employed whenever it is apparent that application of the toxic and technologically based standards described above will not achieve water quality standards in a given basin.[13]

6. These effluent restrictions must be applied to point sources through a permit program—the National Pollutant Discharge Elimination System (NPDES)—administered either by EPA or the states.[14] The 1972 amendments contain strong monitoring and enforcement provisions, including provisions for citizen suits, for ensuring that permit conditions are actually met.[15]

The act's regulatory program for controlling nonpoint source pollution is set out primarily in Section 208.[16] The provisions of this section, which are discussed in more detail below, must be carried out either by designated areawide agencies or by the state. Comprehensive plans must be prepared which provide, among other things, for (1) the control of nonpoint source pollution, (2) the protection of groundwaters, and (3) the regulation of the location and construction of any facilities which may result in pollution. These plans must be submitted to the Administrator of EPA for his approval and, once approved, must be implemented by appropriate regulatory agencies. The overall purpose of Section 208 planning is to ensure that the act's goal of "water quality which provides for the protection and propagation of fish, shellfish, and wildlife and provides for recreation in and on the water" is achieved by 1983.

Along with this regulatory program, the act also establishes a grant-in-aid and planning program for the construction of municipal sewage treatment plants,[17] and requires that each state develop a continuing planning process.[18] Both of these aspects of the act are discussed more fully below.

Problems of Implementation

EPA's implementation of the 1972 amendments has brought a number of disappointments. The following are important examples of failings which have led to legal action by the Natural Resources Defense Council (NRDC) and other environmental organizations:

1. Under stern directives from the Office of Management and Budget, EPA initially refused to allot $9 billion authorized by the act for the construction of municipal sewage treatment plants. Allotment of these funds began only after the U.S. Supreme Court ruled in February 1975 that this impoundment was illegal.[19] As a consequence of the impoundment, a substantial number of municipalities will not meet the 1977 requirements of the act pertaining to sewage treatment works.[20]

2. EPA has not met more than a score of rule-making deadlines set by the act. These failures have been extremely troublesome because the act is structured around a series of interdependent deadlines applicable to the states, to polluters, and to EPA itself. If EPA had been allowed to let these deadlines—particularly the early ones —pass completely unheeded, the entire scheme of the act would have unraveled. To prevent this, NRDC and others have challenged EPA's failure to meet statutory deadlines in three separate law suits.[21]

3. In preparing its required list of toxic pollutants for which very strict effluent standards must be developed, EPA omitted many extremely toxic and carcinogenic substances, such as arsenic, lead, and asbestos. In fact, EPA failed to include on this totally inadequate list most of the substances regulated because of their toxicity in the 1962 Public Health Service drinking water standards. Subsequent NRDC

legal action led to an out-of-court settlement that now requires EPA to develop effluent standards for sixty-five additional toxic pollutants.[22] These standards may, however, take into account the economic feasibility of their implementation.

4. In developing permit programs for discharges of pollutants intended by statute to apply to all point sources, EPA excluded from regulation a wide range of nonindustrial point sources. NRDC took EPA to court to establish the important principle that discharging pollutants from point sources without obtaining an appropriate discharge permit is unlawful.[23]

In large part EPA's shortcomings can be attributed to a lack of adequate resources. Sent out by Congress to do battle with almost the entirety of American industry and agriculture, as well as with other federal agencies which speak for powerful commercial interests, EPA has been armed in a woefully inadequate manner. This weakness has often led to overcautious, hesitant, and intimidated behavior by EPA in implementing the act.

It is important that citizens who are concerned about the problems of water pollution and the land use considerations which cannot be separated from these problems recognize both (1) that Congress has passed strong legislation which mandates the cleaning-up of the country's waters and (2) that implementation of this legislation often falls short of the legal requirements established. In whatever ways possible, citizens should support the provision of adequate resources for EPA and press for conscientious and legally responsible implementation of environmental legislation by this agency.

Land Use Planning Provisions of the 1972 Amendments

1. Section 208

At least six sections of the 1972 amendments are concerned with planning.[24] Of these, Section 208 is by far the most important, since it (1) provides the means of harnessing the resources and developing the programs needed to achieve the act's 1983 water quality goal; (2) requires control of pollution from point and nonpoint sources by means of land use and land management controls and other regulatory programs; and (3) requires broad regional analysis of pollution problems, of the implications of growth for water quality, and of the long-term need for new sewage treatment plant capacity. In the words of EPA, the plans developed under Section 208 "will ultimately serve as the basis for implementation of essentially all programs under the Act."[25]

Section 208 provides that "water quality management plans," designed to achieve the act's 1983 goal of "fishable and swimmable" water, must be developed and implemented for all areas of each state. The purpose of "208" planning, which must be carried out with full public participation, is to develop and then implement new management and regulatory programs both to clean up the waters in polluted areas and basins and to prevent pollution from spoiling relatively unpolluted areas. The 208 planning process should result in:

a. Management programs which are capable of handling the long-term (twenty-year) sewage treatment needs of an area, including sewage treatment plant construction, sludge management, and land treatment;

b. Regulatory programs (including land use requirements) to control runoff and other pollution associated with agriculture, mining, forestry, construction, and urban stormwater;

c. Regulatory programs to control the location, modification, and construction of any facilities that can result in water pollution;

d. Regulatory programs to protect groundwaters and prevent saltwater intrusion; and

e. Other programs needed to achieve and maintain high-quality waters.

Once a 208 plan has been approved by EPA and the agencies responsible for its implementation have been designated by the governor, all grants for the construction of municipal sewage treatment plants under Section 201 (discussed below) must be in conformity with the approved 208 plan. Also, no permit may be issued under the National Pollution Discharge Elimination System (NPDES) established under Section 402 if the permit conflicts with an approved 208 plan.

The requirements of Section 208 apply throughout each state, but they may be carried out either by local areawide agencies or by the state. The act provides that the governor of each state may designate for areawide planning particular areas which have severe water quality control problems.[26] In all areas of the state which are not so designated, the state itself must carry out the required 208 planning. Special federal funds are made available for planning under Section 208.[27]

EPA's implementation of Section 208 began with a false start. The agency initially attempted through its regulations to limit the scope of Section 208 almost entirely to the specific metropolitan areas designated for areawide planning. It gave no directions to the states regarding planning in other areas, thus giving the misleading impression that 208 planning was only required in the designated areas. This problem was exacerbated by the fact that the governors of several key states chose to exercise their right to prohibit the creation of any 208 designated areas within their states and it appeared likely that other states would follow this lead. Under EPA's interpretation of the act, this would have meant that in these states only nonpoint source planning would have been required and the most serious urban-industrial problems would have been ignored.

In October 1974 the Natural Resources Defense Council (NRDC) filed suit to compel EPA to carry out its statutory responsibility to implement full Section 208 planning on a statewide basis and to do so in a timely manner.[28] In June 1975 the federal district court handed down a lengthy decision upholding NRDC's position and requiring EPA promptly to promulgate regulations mandating the states to carry out 208 planning in all areas not designated for areawide programs. The court also ordered that completed 208 plans must be submitted to EPA by state and areawide agencies no later than November 1, 1978. This deadline was established to assure that 208 plans are implemented in time to make possible the achievement of the 1983 goal of fishable and swimmable water set by the act. Under the statutory time frame, 208 plans should have been completed by the middle of 1977, but EPA's failure to require statewide planning, as well as its sluggishness in implementing areawide planning, led to the abandonment of this schedule. In setting a new definite date for 208 plan submission, the court sought to hold EPA to responsible implementation of the purposes of the act.

On November 28, 1975, EPA promulgated final regulations for 208 planning by both state and areawide agencies.[29] These regulations combine implementation of Section 208 requirements with that of Section 303(e), which requires each state to have a "continuing planning process."[30] This means that the 208 plans will be combined with the basic plans EPA has required the states to prepare as part of the continuing planning process. The new regulations also include provisions for state revisions of water quality standards and establishment and implementation of an antidegradation policy, both of which are discussed in the next section of this chapter.

The EPA regulations are not without serious faults, as the discussion of water quality standards will demonstrate, but basically they do provide a fairly good framework for the development and implementation of Section 208 plans. For example, the regulations recognize the critical importance of long-range planning, and require water quality management planning that will guide decision making over at least a twenty-year period. On the other hand, the regulations also relate planning to the need for action in the short-run by requiring the preparation of a state strategy, which must be updated annually, to prevent and control water pollution over a five-year period.

Not only are the states required to implement all Section 208 requirements in areas not designated for areawide planning, they must also assume a strong coordinating role and are ultimately responsible for all 208 planning within their boundaries. Each governor is required to designate a state planning agency to coordinate all 208 planning within the state.

As has been pointed out, the primary objective of the 208 plans must be to establish the management and regulatory programs necessary to achieve the 1983 national water quality goal established by the act, and all of these plans must be submitted to EPA no later than November 1, 1978. Within these constraints, however, the level of detail and timing of the plans for various state planning areas will depend on the "water quality problems of the area and the water quality decisions to be made" and will be established by agreement between the state and the appropriate EPA regional administrator, after full opportunity for public participation.[31] Where a state asserts that certain types of planning and implementation will not be carried out, it must formally certify with supporting data that "particular water quality and/or source control problems do not exist or are not likely to develop within the time-frame of the plan."[32]

A critical aspect of the planning process is the determination of what regulatory programs will be necessary to carry out the purposes of the act. The planning agencies must both (1) assess existing state and local regulations to ascertain how they are or will be used to implement the water quality management plans, and (2) set out what additional regulatory programs must be established. The plans must also identify the agencies recommended for designation by the governor as the management agencies responsible for implementing the provisions of the 208 plan.

Public participation is required throughout all stages of the development of the water quality management plans. According to the regulations:

> The goal of the public participation is to involve the public in the formulation of the plan, including the determination of the planning goals, and to develop public support that will ultimately lead to acceptance and implementation of the plans.[33]

Specific suggestions regarding public involvement in the 208 planning process are discussed in the "citizen action" section at the end of this chapter.

2. Water Quality Standards and Antidegradation

a. *Water Quality Standards.* The states were first required to adopt federally approved interstate water quality standards by 1965 water pollution legislation.[34] The Federal Water Pollution Control Act Amendments of 1972 continued these standards and also required the states to adopt standards for intrastate waters. The states must review and revise their water quality standards at least once every three years, and all revisions must be approved by EPA.

Water quality standards are the combination of designated uses of a stream segment (such as fishing or drinking water) and the pollutant criteria necessary to achieve these uses. They (1) serve as a planning objective for the states; (2) define effluent limitations more stringent than the 1983 "best available technology" requirement where such limitations are needed to meet the goals of the act; and (3) provide a basis for controlling nonpoint sources of pollution. Good water quality standards are essential if the act's 1983 fishable and swimmable water quality goal is to be achieved.

The EPA regulations promulgated on November 28, 1975, set out EPA's policy for required state review and revision of water quality standards.[35] In brief, the new regulations provide that

1. The states must review their water quality standards every three years and revise them where appropriate.

2. Water quality standards must protect public health and welfare and provide protection for downstream water quality standards.

3. The states must upgrade existing water quality standards where current water quality supports higher uses than those presently designated.

4. The states must upgrade existing water quality standards to achieve the act's 1983 goal of fishable and swimmable waters where attainable. Attainability is to be determined on the basis of environmental, technological, social, economic, and institutional factors.

5. The states may downgrade existing water quality standards upon a demonstration that

a. Existing standards are not attainable because of natural conditions (such as leaching from natural heavy metal deposits);

b. Existing standards are not attainable because of irretrievable man-induced conditions (as when known methods are incapable of restoring the water to the designated use); or

c. The application of existing standards would result in *substantial* and *widespread* adverse economic and social impact (such as a large increase in unemployment not due to other factors in a large area for over one year).

The preamble to the regulations contains a strong statement on upgrading water quality standards to the level of the 1983 goal:

> EPA strongly supports the establishment of water quality standards which will support the protection and propagation of fish, shellfish, and wildlife and recreation in and on the water. In furtherance of this objective, EPA believes that water quality standards should be established at levels consistent with the [1983] goal of section 101(a) (2) of the Act for every stream segment wherever those levels are attainable.[36]

This strong statement is modified in the body of the regulations, where attainability is defined in an overly broad manner to include considerations of environmental, technological, social, economic, and institutional factors.[37] Industry can be expected to attempt to exploit this weakness by arguing that water quality standards should not be upgraded—claiming, for instance, that upgrading would have an adverse social or economic impact. Citizen action is needed to bolster each state's position by insisting that water quality standards be set at the level needed to protect both aquatic life and human health (the fishable/swimmable standard).

The provision allowing downgrading of water quality standards is another weakness in the regulations. The criteria for downgrading outlined above should be applied very infrequently. Essentially these same criteria were applied in developing the existing water quality standards only three years ago.[38] Accordingly, except in those very unusual circumstances where no new information has been brought to light, there is no justification for downgrading standards.

The time frame for the 1976 state review of water quality standards established by the EPA regulations required each state to include in its "state continuing planning process," due for submission to EPA for approval in April 1976, a schedule for state review of water quality standards. This schedule was required to include milestones, including public hearings, for the revision process and to ensure that standards are revised in ample time to be used in 1977–83 management and regulatory decisions. Between April and December 1976, each state must carry out its review and revision of water quality standards. This process must provide for meaningful public participation, including public hearings. Revisions of standards must be submitted to EPA for approval no later than December 31, 1976.

b. *Antidegradation.* The nondegradation principle has been discussed in Chapter 4 in the context of air pollution control. The same type of problem exists in water pollution control, where water bodies whose actual water quality is better than that required by water quality standards must be protected from degradation down to standards.

The November 28 EPA regulations established a strong, new national policy against further degradation of the nation's waters.[39] These antidegradation regulations, if *properly implemented,* can protect high-quality waters from becoming polluted, and can halt further pollution where it already occurs. The regulations carry out the basic objective of the 1972 amendments, which is to restore *and maintain* the chemical, physical, and biological integrity of the nation's waters. Strong citizen action is essential to translate this new policy into reality in the face of efforts by utilities and other industry groups to weaken it.

The new national antidegradation policy has several important elements. First, the new EPA regulations provide without qualification that "[n]o further water quality degradation which would interfere with or become injurious to existing instream water uses is allowable."[40] Thus, if a particular body of water in its existing condition could be used for sport fishing, it cannot be degraded in any way which would reduce its quality as a sport fishery. Similarly, if the waters are suitable for the propagation of fish, shellfish, or wildlife or for swimming or for drinking water supply, then they must remain suitable for these possible uses and for any others for which they are now suited. This does not mean that water quality cannot go down at all, since small increases in pollutant loads *may* be consistent with protecting the uses to which a water body could now be put.

Second, with one exception, the new regulations do not permit *any* increase in pollutant loads in those high-quality waters which are currently better than the levels needed to support the propagation of fish, shellfish, and wildlife, and recreation in and on the water. The one exception allows a state to decide, after public participation, "to allow lower water quality as a result of necessary and justifiable economic or social development."[41] This loophole is narrowed in two very important respects. One is that the exception cannot be applied *at all* to "high quality waters which constitute an outstanding National resource, such as waters of National and State parks and wildlife refuges and waters of exceptional recreational or ecological significance."[42] Another is that the exception cannot be applied in any way that allows water quality to fall below the levels needed to protect fish and wildlife and recreation in and on the waters.

The provisions of the new antidegradation policy protect waters not only from industrial expansions and sewage treatment plants, but also from commercial, agricultural, construction, and forestry sources.

The EPA regulations provide for implementation of the national antidegradation policy in three stages:

1. By April 26, 1976, each state was required to have developed and submitted to EPA for approval a "state continuing planning process" containing a schedule for the development and adoption of a statewide policy on antidegradation.

2. Between April and December 1976, each state must, after public hearings, adopt the new statewide policy on antidegradation. This policy must be submitted to EPA for approval and must be at least as protective as the national policy.

3. On July 1, 1977, the new statewide antidegradation policy must go into effect. After that date, all proposed activities resulting in increased water pollution will have to be screened for consistency with federal-state antidegradation requirements.

Both the act itself and the EPA regulations require the states to provide meaningful opportunities for public participation at each of these three stages of implementation.

3. Construction of Municipal Sewage Treatment Plants

Section 201 authorizes the Administrator of EPA to make grants for the planning and construction of publicly owned sewage treatment plants. While the purpose of Section 201 is to improve water quality, construction grants awarded under this section can have enormous implications for land development, since in large measure the size and location of sewage treatment facilities, along with the size and placement of connecting interceptor sewer lines, determine the extent and shape of community growth. Past experience has indicated that where facilities are built for a population considerably larger than that existing in an area, growth to the capacity of the system is often generated. Thus, great care should be taken before new sewerage facilities are constructed to assess their land use impacts, to consider alternative dimensions, and to provide for needed land use planning and regulation.

Unfortunately, it appears that very little attention has been paid to the land use implications of Section 201 grants. In 1974 a study of the impact of sewerage construction grants on residential land use was published by the Council on Environmental Quality (CEQ).[43] This study, which analyzed fifty-two EPA grants for sewerage construction,[44] showed that the grants had provided for substantial excess sewerage capacity and that either the land use impacts of the grants had not been assessed or negative secondary effects of residential development had not been considered. In eight detailed case studies that were prepared on areas as diverse as Tulsa, Oklahoma, and Ocean County, New Jersey, urban planners and local officials expressed the belief that nothing could halt development in their respective areas and that sewage treatment systems had to be provided.

In fact, according to the CEQ study, procedures used in the physical design of interceptors, local planning and review procedures for project plans, and methods of project financing may encourage the "inevitability" of development. With regard to financing, the summary of the report stated that:

> Study findings indicate that current financing procedures—on both the local and federal level—may encourage the construction of sewerage systems tailored to the needs of future developers rather than the control of pollution problems.[45]

For example, some communities intend to finance the local share of project costs by assessing connection fees on new development, an approach which will create pressure for rapid growth. Finally, since the federal program is viewed as a one-time-only opportunity, communities are encouraged to seek as much excess capacity as possible.

One of the most disturbing findings of the CEQ study was that over half of the land to be served by the projects studied was vacant at the time the projects were proposed. Thus it appears that many localities were seeking not only to improve water quality, but also to obtain a federal subsidy for suburban growth on vacant land. This appears to run counter to the intent of the act which requires the EPA Administrator to encourage sewerage schemes which combine open space and recreational considerations with waste management.[46]

The 1972 amendments to the Federal Water Pollution Control Act provide some safeguards for the construction grant program to assure that it is focused on improving water quality and that the land use effects of the program are adequately assessed. Unfortunately, these safeguards are either not working properly or their implementation is too new to be evaluated.

First, before a treatment plant or sewerage system is constructed, federal funding is available for required facilities planning which assesses the effects of the proposed construction.[47] However, prior to fiscal year 1976, many projects received design funding after simply producing documents supporting compliance with minimal facilities planning requirements. Moreover, even when the full facility planning process is carried out, there is no assurance that environmental effects, including land use impacts, are assessed adequately, since EPA does not appear to be implementing the regulations governing this planning very aggressively.

In addition, the act requires integration of Section 201 grants with the planning provisions of Section 208. As has been pointed out above, once a Section 208 plan has been approved by EPA, all grants for the construction of sewage treatment works must be in conformity with this plan. This provision reflects Congress's intent that the construction of waste treatment facilities be coordinated with the land use planning and regulation required under Section 208. However, this requirement does not affect construction grants that are made before an approved 208 plan is in existence, and, as has been discussed, EPA's implementation of Section 208 has proceeded at a very slow pace.

Grants for sewerage construction must also be in conformity with state planning under Section 303, through which statewide construction priorities must be established. However, the continuing planning process program under Section 303 has been significantly altered by the EPA regulations promulgated on November 28, 1975, and it is too early to assess the effect of these revisions.

Another safeguard is the National Environmental Policy Act (NEPA).[48] Although EPA is excused by the act from preparing environmental impact statements under NEPA for permits (except those for new sources) granted under the National Pollutant Discharge Elimination System (NPDES) established by Section 402, EPA is not excused from preparing such impact statements in the construction grant area. Initially, EPA was not preparing NEPA statements for construction grants, but under pressure from Congress and from citizens in particular areas where construction of sewerage facilities was proposed, the agency has altered its position somewhat. As of December 1974, EPA had prepared environmental impact statements for about sixty-five out of a total of approximately four thousand project grants. The prospects for fuller environmental review by EPA in the future are no more promising. For fiscal 1976, EPA set as a *goal,* preparation of environmental impact statements for 5 percent of the construction grants awarded.

In general, the movement toward the preparation of NEPA statements, which must consider alternative possibilities, land use implications, and other environmental consequences, exists in tension with EPA's desire to expedite the granting of funds available for waste treatment facilities. The latter motivation has in a number of cases led EPA to overlook important land use considerations, while environmental impact statements have often been prepared on a "squeaky wheel" basis. The present administrative trend in EPA suggests that environmental impact statements are more likely to be filed for large projects. EPA officials believe that while the percentage of impact statements prepared is small compared to the large number of grants, the statements cover a larger percentage of the total number of grant dollars.

In essence, then, the sewerage construction grant program established under Section 201 is extremely important in terms of land use. Concerned citizens should be aware of its potential impact on their communities and ready to monitor its implementation.

Another important provision of the 1972 amendments with

which citizens who are concerned about land use problems should be familiar is Section 402(h),[49] which authorizes EPA to stop any new sewer hookups where treatment plants are in violation of an NPDES permit condition. EPA actually has the right to seek a court order prohibiting such connections, and should be pressed to do so, if necessary.

Further, on January 15, 1974, EPA released a policy memorandum authorizing the inclusion of special growth related planning conditions in NPDES permits issued for municipal sewerage facilities that are threatened by rapid growth.[50] A municipality seeking an NPDES permit for such a facility can be required, as an enforceable permit condition, to anticipate and regulate new sewer hookups which would overload the treatment plant. Although EPA permit writers are not required to impose such conditions, they are required to consider doing so when dealing with sewerage systems which are already utilized to 85 percent of capacity and are experiencing or anticipate growth at 3 percent or more per year. Unfortunately, EPA permit writers have largely ignored this policy memorandum. A municipal permit that contains a growth related condition is a rarity.

Army Corps of Engineers Permits and the Federal Water Pollution Control Act Amendments of 1972

Prior to the passage of the 1972 amendments to the Federal Water Pollution Control Act, it was unlawful to put any refuse matter (except liquid municipal sewage effluent and runoff from streets) into any navigable water or tributary thereof without a permit from the U.S. Army Corps of Engineers. This permit program, which was authorized under the so-called "Refuse Act,"[51] was replaced by the permit programs established under Sections 402 and 404 of the 1972 amendments. Although the Refuse Act itself is still on the books, it has been almost completely superseded by the Federal Water Pollution Control Act, as amended in 1972.

The Army Corps of Engineers is still responsible under legislation enacted prior to the 1972 amendments for issuing permits for dredging and filling operations and construction activities in navigable waters. The following activities, variations of which are often involved in land development projects, are unlawful without a permit from the Corps of Engineers:

1. Construction of a dam, dike, bridge, or causeway over or in any navigable water.[52]

2. Excavation, filling, or in any manner modifying any lake or channel of any navigable water.[53]

It should be noted that the Army Corps of Engineers is subject to the requirement of the National Environmental Policy Act (NEPA)[54] that federal agencies must prepare an environmental impact statement before taking any action that significantly affects the environment. Thus, for example, before issuing a permit for the construction of a dam, the Corps of Engineers must prepare an environmental impact statement which must be available for public comment.

Section 404[55] of the 1972 amendments gave new responsibilities to the Army Corps of Engineers in the regulation of dredging and filling operations. It established that no dredged or fill material can be discharged into the waters of the United States unless a Section 404 permit has been obtained from the Corps of Engineers. While earlier statutory provisions pertaining to dredging or filling in navigable waters focused on the possible interference of such operations with navigation, the focus of Section 404 is on the discharge of materials into receiving waters or surrounding wetlands and on the biological effects of such discharges. In some respects the new Section 404 permits overlap dredge and fill permits required by earlier legislation, but they differ in their prime concern with water quality and their applicability to wetlands. Thus the Section 404 program does not supplant the older permit program, but is in addition to it.

A very significant difference between the older Corps of Engineers permit programs and the provisions of Section 404 is that the former are subject to traditional concepts of navigability, while the latter are not. Some explanation is needed to clarify this distinction. In a number of respects the concept of navigability that has been developed over the years by the Corps of Engineers is quite broad.[56] For example, the fact that in the past hunters and trappers who were engaged in interstate or foreign commerce used canoes on a waterway would be sufficient to establish it as navigable water. Also, once a determination of navigability is made, it is not extinguished by later actions or events which impede or destroy navigable capacity. Further, a waterway may be deemed navigable water even if it possesses falls, rapids, sand bars, or similar obstructions. This principle of navigability has always been central to the Corps of Engineers' work.

One very important resulting limitation has been the restriction of Corps jurisdiction in tidal areas to below mean high tide. In other cases, feeder streams and waters have been excluded from Corps jurisdiction because they were not classified as navigable.

The 1972 amendments go beyond traditional concepts of navigability by very broadly defining "navigable waters" as "the waters of the United States, including the territorial seas."[57] EPA correctly concluded that this new definition eliminated the requirement of navigability, leaving only the requirement that the pollution of waters covered by the act be capable of affecting interstate commerce.[58] In its programs, the agency held that federal jurisdiction extended to point source discharges not only into interstate waters and their tributaries, but also into intrastate waters from which fish or shellfish are taken for sale in interstate commerce, intrastate waters used by industries engaged in interstate commerce, and intrastate waters utilized by interstate travelers for recreational or other purposes.

Unfortunately, despite three federal court decisions upholding aspects of EPA's position,[59] the Army Corps of Engineers initially refused to incorporate the broader federal jurisdiction of the 1972 amendments into its administration of the Section 404 permit program. Relying on historical concepts of navigability, the Corps stated in the regulations for Section 404, which it promulgated in April 1974, that it did not have the authority to regulate activities above mean high tide.[60] It took this stand despite the fact that two of the courts which had ruled on the broader jurisdiction of the 1972 amendments had quoted the following statement made in Congress just before the amendments were passed: "No longer are the old, narrow definitions of navigability, as determined by the Corps of Engineers, going to govern matters covered by this bill."[61] The environmental implications of the Corps's recalcitrant position were very serious, since it excluded from regulation important coastal and estuarine wetlands which are flooded periodically, but lie above mean high tide.

Consequently, in August 1974 the Natural Resources Defense Council, along with the National Wildlife Federation, brought suit seeking a ruling that the Corps of Engineers' regulations governing the Section 404 permit program were unlawfully restrictive.[62] In March 1975 the U.S. District Court for the District of Columbia upheld this suit, ruling that federal jurisdiction under the Federal Water Pollution Control Act is not limited by the traditional tests of navigability and that the Army Corps of Engineers had acted unlawfully and in derogation of its responsibilities when it adopted regulations incorporating such limitations for Section 404. The court ordered the Corps of Engineers to exercise its jurisdiction over dredging and filling operations in "the waters of the United States," which include all wetland areas. To assure that this was done promptly, it established deadlines for publication by the Corps of proposed and then final 404 regulations recognizing the full regulatory mandate of the act.

The Corps of Engineers issued proposed regulations for the Section 404 permit program in accordance with the court order on May 6, 1975.[63] On the same day EPA published proposed guidelines for the issuance of these permits,[64] in keeping with the joint character of this program specified by the act. The Corps of Engineers also put out an inflammatory press release advising the public that under some of its proposed regulations the farmer who wanted to plow a field or the mountaineer who wanted to protect his land against stream erosion might have to obtain a federal permit. The press release went on to state that under the broad interpretation of the 1972 amendments, millions of people might be presently violating the law, and that convicted offenders might be subject to fines of up to $25,000 a day or one year imprisonment. Not surprisingly, this press release prompted a great public outcry and led to congressional hearings on the Section 404 program.

With time and the intercession of the Secretary of the Army, the Corps of Engineers came to accept its new responsibilities to protect water quality and wetlands much more realistically. On July 25, 1975, it promulgated a very acceptable interim final regulation for Section 404 that properly excluded normal farming, silvicultural and ranching activities, but set out a workable framework for the protection of water resources.[65] This interim regulation was effective immediately, but a ninety-day period for comments on its provisions was set (and later extended another forty days[66]) and a final regulation responsive to suggestions made in these comments and in public hearings and meetings held by the Corps of Engineers is expected to be promulgated in the late spring of 1976. On September 5, 1975, EPA promulgated interim final guidelines, for which a ninety-day comment period was specified.[67] Final guidelines are also expected in 1976.

The 404 program developed by the Corps of Engineers and EPA will be implemented in three phases. In phase I, which began when the Corps regulation was promulgated, 404 requirements are operative for all coastal waters and all navigable waters already regulated by the Corps, as well as for all wetlands contiguous or adjacent to these waters. In phase II, which will begin on July 1, 1976, regulation will be extended to all primary tributaries and their contiguous or adjacent wetlands and to all lakes. With phase III, on July 1, 1977, will come full regulation of discharges of dredged or fill materials into the waters of the United States. This phasing in of the 404 permit program was necessitated by manpower and budgetary constraints, but, unfortunately, it places many controversial projects in the later stages of implementation. The regulation does, however, authorize the application of permit procedures for particular discharges ahead of schedule if the appropriate district engineer of the Corps of Engineers determines on the basis of the water quality concerns expressed in the EPA guidelines that such action should be taken.

Certain activities, such as the construction of minor bulkheads for property protection, are excluded from the permit program altogether, but again the district engineers are granted the discretion to exercise jurisdiction over cases where they determine that the discharges involved would have a significant impact on the environment. The Corps of Engineers stated in the preamble to the 404 regulation that it intended to rely very heavily on the public to bring to the attention of the district engineers activities of this type which should be regulated on a case-by-case basis.

An important mechanism established by the 404 regulation in addition to individual permits for particular discharges is the general permit. The latter permit may be issued for certain clearly described categories of structures or work and must prescribe the conditions to be followed in the construction of such structures or the performance of such work. Once a general permit is issued, those wishing to carry out activities which it covers would not have to obtain an individual permit. Only activities that have minimal environmental effects, either singularly or cumulatively, may be authorized by a general permit. While this device is an effective means of making the 404 program workable, the regulation should have required that all those operating under a general permit register their activities with the Corps of Engineers. Instead, except for mandatory registration when a general permit does not designate a specific body or bodies of water, the interim regulation leaves this type of reporting to the discretion of the district engineer.

The standard procedures for the processing of applications for 404 permits require the district engineers to issue a full public notice and provide the opportunity for public comment on the application. If anyone who has an interest which may be affected by the issuance of a permit for a discharge requests a hearing, or if another state objects to the issuance of a permit on the basis of water quality and requests a hearing, the district engineer must arrange a public hearing in accordance with Corps of Engineer regulations. If no hearing is to be held, the district engineer may still decide to hold a public meeting to discuss the application. The appropriate district engineer must also determine at the earliest possible time whether an environmental impact statement must be prepared on a proposed activity for which a permit is requested.

In the late spring of 1976 some of the controversy which had surrounded Section 404 in 1975 reemerged. An amendment which would restrict the scope of the 404 permit program was introduced in Congress and is being debated as this book goes to press. Citizens concerned about wetlands and water pollution should keep abreast of these developments.

Citizen Action

Vigorous public participation is absolutely essential if the land use planning and regulatory provisions of the 1972 amendments are to be effectively carried out. Through active involvement in the implementation of the act and EPA regulations, citizens who are concerned about water quality and related land use problems can influence conditions in their state for many years to come.

The specific requirements for public participation which have been mentioned in the course of this chapter are all expressions of the act's mandate that:

> Public participation in the development, revision, and enforcement of any regulation, standard, effluent limitation, plan, or program established by the Administrator [of EPA] or any State under this Act shall be provided for, encouraged, and assisted by the Administrator and the States.[68]

General regulations providing for public participation in decision making under the act have been promulgated by EPA and should be read by concerned citizens.[69] These regulations require each agency carrying out activities under the act to conduct a program for public involvement which, among other things, must include:

1. Provision of technical information to interested persons and organizations;

2. Public access to agency records;

3. Procedures for receiving information and evidence submitted by citizens; and

4. Invitation, reception, and consideration of written comments from interested persons or organizations regarding proposed rule making.

In addition, whenever applications are made for certain kinds of grants (including construction grants under Section 201 and planning grants under Section 208) a "summary of public participation" must be included. This summary must "describe the measures taken by the agency to provide for, encourage, and assist public participation in relation to the matter; the public response to such measures; and the disposition of significant points raised."[70]

Citizens should take full advantage of the rights granted to them under the Federal Water Pollution Control Act Amendments of 1972 in their efforts to stop water pollution and land abuse. The following discussion summarizes critical areas in which forceful citizen involvement is essential.

1. *208 Planning.* The states and local areawide agencies must develop adequate 208 plans by November 1, 1978. The following are three big issues which citizens should be prepared to confront as 208 planning goes forward:

a. When the 208 plan is submitted to EPA, it must include the necessary regulatory authority to implement the plan. Opposition to the necessary controls will be strong and effective citizen support will be needed to ensure their enactment.

b. One of the crucial elements of the 208 plan will be the development of what EPA calls "Best Management Practices" (BMPs) for certain sources of pollution, including nonpoint sources. The 208 plan is to set forth BMPs, including land use requirements, to control such sources as runoff from construction, forestry practices, agriculture, mining, and urban streets. Citizens will need to work actively to develop the best possible management practices in their area, and to assure that regulatory controls are developed to enforce them. Existing laws should be reviewed to determine whether they have sufficient force to implement the BMPs.

c. Another critical element of the 208 plan is the development of a growth factor or allotment upon which total maximum daily loads for point and nonpoint sources and for municipal waste treatment needs will be based. Citizens should insist on meaningful public participation in the development of this important plan component.

Clearly the tasks facing 208 planning agencies are politically difficult ones. The land use implications of an effective 208 plan may be distasteful to land developers, industries, and local governments. Constant public scrutiny and effort will be required to minimize or counter political pressures brought to bear during the development of the plan.

In letters to their governor and state water pollution control administrator, citizens should:

a. Request to receive all materials and notices regarding 208 activities in their area.

b. Urge that citizen advisory committees be set up for various planning areas.

c. Ask to be on a list to be informed about meetings with municipalities and industries concerning their individual waste load allocations and the growth allotments each is to receive, and ask that an effective process be established to enable the public to participate in this crucial aspect of 208 planning.

Letters should also be written to the EPA Administrator (401 M Street, S.W., Washington, D.C. 20460) and the EPA regional administrator responsible for one's state, stressing public support for a strong 208 program and requesting a copy of EPA's *208 Guidelines for State Water Quality Management Planning,* January 1976.

2. *Water Quality Standards.* Citizens should immediately write their governor and their state water pollution control administrator and

a. Urge them to upgrade the state's water quality standards to provide for the protection and propagation of fish, shellfish, and wildlife, and recreation in and on the water. Citizens should insist that the state adopt a strong policy requiring dischargers to document in detail claims of adverse economic or social impact or technological or institutional difficulties in meeting upgraded standards.

b. State their opposition to any downgrading of water quality standards and insist that the criteria for downgrading be narrowly construed and applied.

c. Ask how they can participate in the review and revision of the state's water quality standards. Citizens should be given a full and meaningful role that is not limited to appearance at public hearings.

d. Request a copy of the state's present water quality standards and the 1976 schedule for reviewing and revising these standards.

e. Ask to receive all notices of meetings and public hearings concerning water quality standards and antidegradation.

Letters should also be written to the EPA Administrator and the appropriate EPA regional administrator, expressing support for water quality standards which will achieve the 1983 fishable/swimmable goal and for a strong federal role in reviewing state water quality revisions. In these letters, citizens should ask for a copy of EPA's latest edition of *Water Quality Criteria,* the basic document for defining the water quality needed to achieve the 1983 goal.

Finally, citizens should join with other environmentalists to write letters, attend state and local meetings, and participate in all public hearings regarding revisions of state water quality standards. They should be prepared—at public hearings and meetings and in written comments—to make the case that water quality standards in their state should be upgraded to meet the 1983 goal; to refute polluters' claims that environmental, technological, economic, social, or institutional factors prevent an upgrading; and to fight any attempts to downgrade existing standards. EPA's own strong policy statement in the preamble to its November 1975 regulations can be used to bolster one's position.

3. *Antidegradation.* As soon as possible, citizens should write to their governor and state water pollution control administrator to call for a state antidegradation policy that is at least as strong as the national policy set out in EPA's regulations; to ask to receive a copy of the state's current antidegradation policies (which are typically much weaker than the new federal requirements); and to ask to receive notice of all public meetings and hearings concerning antidegradation and water quality standards revision. At the public hearings, citizens should join together in insisting that the statewide antidegradation policy to be submitted to EPA contain an identification of those high-quality waters in the state which are of "exceptional recreational or ecological significance" or which for some other reason are an "outstanding National resource." As has

been indicated, waters in this category cannot be degraded *at all*. Citizens should also press their state to develop and submit to EPA not only an antidegradation *policy*, but also a *program* to implement this policy. Since the National Pollutant Discharge Elimination System (NPDES) permit program already identifies most point source dischargers, citizens should focus particular attention on ensuring that their state has a program to control nonpoint sources of pollution.

4. *Construction of Municipal Sewage Treatment Plants.* Careful planning must be carried out before sewage treatment facilities are constructed or expanded. Citizens should be aware of the profound effect which additional plant and sewer line capacity has on the dimensions and location of future growth; should make certain that the entire community is aware of these consequences; should ensure that the excess capacity of the plant, as well as the size and location of interceptor lines, is carefully scrutinized and evaluated by the public; and should take whatever local action is necessary to assure that necessary land use planning provisions and regulations are established to anticipate and control the impact of new facilities.

Citizens should also demand that EPA prepare an environmental impact statement before federal funds are granted to build a new sewage treatment plant. This impact statement must consider the land use implications of the new construction, as well as other environmental effects. Citizens should study the draft impact statement very carefully and submit strong and specific comments on it to EPA.

Citizens should also be aware that EPA is authorized by Section 402(h) of the 1972 amendments to stop additional hookups to a sewage treatment plant that is violating a condition of its NPDES permit to discharge pollutants. Such proposed hookups should be reported to EPA and pressure should be brought to bear to assure that EPA takes action to prevent any further overloading of the plant in question.

5. *The 404 Permit Program.* Citizens should actively monitor the implementation of this important permit program by the Army Corps of Engineers. They should write to the district engineer within whose jurisdiction they fall, requesting that they be placed on a mailing list to be notified of proposed issuances of permits. Particular types of permits or geographical areas of concern could be specified in this request for notices. If the Corps of Engineers proposes to issue a permit which citizens believe should not be issued, all pertinent

information should be brought to the attention of the district engineer. Furthermore, as has been pointed out, whenever a district engineer issues the required public notice regarding a proposed permit, if anyone who has an interest which may be affected by the issuance of the permit requests a public hearing, one must be held. When hearings are held, the public should attend in numbers and should be well prepared to debate the issues at stake. If a hearing is not held, citizens can urge the district engineer to call a public meeting to discuss the application. Efforts may also be made to demonstrate to the district engineer that an environmental impact statement should be prepared on a permit application.

Citizens should carefully monitor the general permit mechanism developed by the Corps of Engineers. Specifically, they should make certain that general permits, which are to be issued on a district basis, are developed *only* for activities which have minimal environmental effects, either singularly or cumulatively, and that the permits contain the conditions needed to protect water quality.

The Corps of Engineers encourages the public to assist the district engineers in identifying particular activities which should be regulated on a case-by-case basis even though they are covered by a general permit or are otherwise exempt from individual permit procedures. Care should be taken to notify the appropriate district engineer of such activities and to provide him with as much relevant information as possible. Citizens should also report to the district engineer any activities requiring an individual permit that are initiated without a proper permit. Finally, citizens should make sure that the Corps of Engineers itself is carrying its 404 responsibilities to the full extent of its jurisdiction as set forth by the federal district court and in accordance with the phased implementation scheme established in the Corps's regulations.

NOTES

1. 33 U.S.C. § 1251 *et seq.* These amendments were passed by Congress on October 18, 1972, as Public Law 92–500. The citations to particular sections of the act (i.e., the Federal Water Pollution Control Act Amendments of 1972) in the text of this chapter refer to the section numbers of Public Law 92–500, a copy of which can be obtained from the Office of Public Affairs, U.S. Environmental Protection Agency, Washington, D.C. 20460.

The discussion in the first part of this chapter draws heavily from an article by

94 /   LAND USE CONTROLS IN THE UNITED STATES

Natural Resources Defense Council attorney J. G. Speth, "The 1972 Federal Water Pollution Control Act: Problems and Prospects After One Year," *Natural Resources Lawyer,* VII, no. 2 (Spring 1974): 249–256.

2. U.S. Senate, Committee on Public Works, *A Legislative History of the Federal Water Pollution Control Act Amendments of 1972,* 93d Cong., 1st Sess., 1973, p. 1460 (hereafter *Legislative History*).

3. *Legislative History,* p. 165. For an informative discussion of these concepts, see Walter E. Westman, "Some Basic Issues in Water Pollution Control Legislation," *American Scientist* 60 (1972): 767.

4. § 101 (a); 33 U.S.C. § 1251 (a).

5. *Ibid.*

6. § 502 (14); 33 U.S.C. § 1362 (14).

7. There is a gray area between clear examples of point sources and nonpoint sources. Determinations of whether particular types of "conveyances" are to be considered point sources or nonpoint sources can be expected to come both from administrative clarifications by EPA and from litigation.

8. The contribution of pollutants from nonpoint agricultural sources (such as fertilizer and pesticide runoff) has been recognized for years. See, for example, Council on Environmental Quality, *Environmental Quality: The Third Annual Report of the Council on Environmental Quality* (1972), pp. 11–16.

Only recently, however, has attention been focused on runoff from city streets. A report prepared in 1974 for the Council on Environmental Quality concluded that only about 20 to 60 percent of the total annual oxygen-demanding material entering receiving waters from a city comes from the sewage treatment plant; the remainder comes from runoff and discharges into storm sewers which do not feed into the treatment plant. During a single storm event, 94 to 99 percent of the oxygen-demanding material entering receiving waters is from runoff and sewer overflows. The street runoff from a typical moderate size city, moreover, will contain up to 250,000 pounds of lead and 30,000 pounds of mercury per year. See Enviro Control, Inc., *Total Urban Water Pollution Loads: The Impact of Storm Water* (1974), available from National Technical Information Service (NTIS #PB231730), 5285 Port Royal Road, Springfield, Virginia 22151

9. § 301 (b) (1); 33 U.S.C. § 1311 (b) (1).

10. § 301 (b) (2); 33 U.S.C. § 1311 (b) (2).

11. § 307 (a); 33 U.S.C. § 1317 (a).

12. § 306; 33 U.S.C. § 1316.

13. §§ 301 (b) (1) and 303(d); 33 U.S.C. §§ 1311 (b) (1) and 1313 (d).

14. § 402; 33 U.S.C. § 1342.

15. §§ 308, 309, and 505; 33 U.S.C. §§ 1318, 1319, and 1365. Citizen suits are authorized by the 1972 amendments on essentially the same terms as those provided by the Clean Air Act, discussed at the end of Chapter 4, except that suits under the water act are limited to persons "having an interest which is or may be adversely affected." Thus a general, but unaffected interest in water pollution control would not be a sufficient basis for a lawsuit.

16. 33 U.S.C. § 1288.

17. §§ 201–207; 33 U.S.C. §§ 1281–1287.

18. § 303 (e); 33 U.S.C. § 1313 (e)

19. Train v. City of New York, 420 U.S. 35, 7 ERC 1497 (1975).

20. The state of Virginia unsuccessfully sought a declaration from the federal district court relieving the state and its municipalities from compliance with the secondary treatment requirements of the act except where EPA has made sewerage grants available. Virginia State Water Control Board v. Train, _____ F. Supp._____, 8 ERC 1609 (E.D. Va. 1976). NRDC filed an amicus curiae brief opposing the state's position.

21. Natural Resources Defense Council v. Fri, Civil No. 849–73 (D.D.C., June 19, 1973) (consent decree); Natural Resources Defense Council v. Train, 6 ERC 1033 (D.D.C. 1973), *aff'd*, 510 F.2d 692, 7 ERC 1209 (D.C. Cir. 1974); and Environmental Defense Fund v. Train, Civil No. 0172–75 (D.D.C., February 6, 1975).

22. NRDC's suit was dismissed by the district court, but appeal to the circuit court led to the out-of-court settlement. Natural Resources Defense Council v. Train, 6 ERC 1702 (D.D.C. 1974), Civil No. 74–1538 (D.C. Cir. 1974).

23. Natural Resources Defense Council v. Train, 396 F. Supp. 1393, 7 ERC 1881 (D.D.C. 1975).

24. §§ 102, 106, 201, 208, 209, and 303; 33 U.S.C. §§ 1252, 1256, 1281, 1288, 1289, and 1313.

25. 40 *Federal Register* 55335 (November 28, 1975).

26. § 208 (a); 33 U.S.C. § 1288 (a). Regulations governing identification of areas with water quality control problems and designation of responsible areawide planning agencies were promulgated by EPA in September 1973. 38 *Federal Register* 25681 (September 14, 1973); 40 C.F.R. Part 126. Further regulations requiring the reopening of the designation process, except where the EPA regional administrator determined that the initial process resulted in the designation of all eligible areas and agencies within the state, were promulgated in November 1975. 40 *Federal Register* 55339 (November 28, 1975); 40 C.F.R. § 130.13.

27. § 208 (f) (2); 33 U.S.C. § 1288 (f) (2). Under this provision, grants covering 100 percent of the costs of developing and carrying out 208 planning were available through June 30, 1975, and grants for up to 75 percent of costs are available thereafter.

28. Natural Resources Defense Council v. Train, 396 F. Supp. 1386, 7 ERC 2066 (D.D.C. 1975).

29. 40 *Federal Register* 55321 (November 28, 1975); 40 C.F.R. Parts 35, 130, and 131.

30. 33 U.S.C. § 1313 (e).

31. 40 *Federal Register* 55338 (November 28, 1975); 40 C.F.R. § 130.11 (a).

32. *Ibid.,* § 130.11 (b).

33. 40 *Federal Register* 55347 (November 28, 1975); 40 C.F.R. § 131.20 (a) (1).

34. 33 U.S.C. § 1160 (c).

35. 40 *Federal Register* 55340 (November 28, 1975); 40 C.F.R. § 130.17.

36. 40 *Federal Register* 55336 (November 28, 1975).

37. *Ibid.,* § 130.17 (c) (1).

38. U. S. Environmental Protection Agency, *Guidelines for Developing and Revising Water Quality Standards* (Washington, D.C.: U. S. Government Printing Office, April 1973).

39. 40 *Federal Register* 55341 (November 28, 1975); 40 C.F.R. § 130.17 (e).

40. *Ibid.,* § 130.17 (e) (1).

41. *Ibid.,* § 130.17 (e) (2).

42. *Ibid.*

43. Council on Environmental Quality, *Interceptor Sewers and Suburban Sprawl,* September 10, 1974. This two-volume study was prepared by Urban Systems Research and Engineering, Inc., and is available in paperback and microfiche form from: Ordering Department, National Technical Information Service, 5285 Port Royal Road, Springfield, Virginia 22151. Volume I (Analysis; NTIS #PB236477) costs $7.00 in paperback and $2.25 in microfiche; volume II (Case Studies; NTIS #PB236871) is $8.70 in paperback and $2.25 in microfiche. The first section of volume I is a summary of the entire study.

44. The fifty-two grants studied were chosen from a list of one hundred sixty projects (in three EPA regions) that had reached the stage of construction. The grants selected were those which appeared most likely to have been used to finance excess sewer capacity. As a result of errors in original estimates of excess capacity, however, the fifty-two projects studied now appear to be more representative of all EPA sewerage construction grants than they were at first thought to be.

45. Council on Environmental Quality, *Interceptor Sewers and Suburban Sprawl,* 1:5.

46. § 201 (f); 33 U.S.C. § 1281 (f).

47. 39 *Federal Register* 5252 (February 11, 1974); 40 C.F.R. § 35.900 *et seq.*

48. 42 U.S.C. § 4321 *et seq.* See Chapter 3 for a discussion of NEPA.

49. 33 U.S.C. § 1342 (h).

50. U.S. Environmental Protection Agency, "Guidance for Conditioning of Municipal Permits in High-Growth Areas," January 15, 1974. This memorandum is public information and may be obtained from EPA.

51. 33 U.S.C. § 407.

52. 33 U.S.C. § 401.

53. 33 U.S.C. § 403.

54. 42 U.S.C. § 4321 *et seq.* See Chapter 3.

55. 33 U.S.C. § 1344.

56. The regulation of the Army Corps of Engineers which discusses the traditional meaning of "navigable waters" most fully can be found at 33 C.F.R. § 209.260.

57. § 502 (7); 33 U.S.C. § 1362 (7).

58. *Environmental Reporter: Current Developments,* 3:41 (February 9, 1973): 1240. Published by the Bureau of National Affairs, Washington, D.C. 20037.

59. United States v. American Beef Packers, Inc., Crim. No. 74–0–30 (D.Neb. 1974); United States v. Holland, 373 F. Supp. 665, 6 ERC 1388 (M.D. Fla. 1974); United States v. Ashland Oil & Transportation Co., 504 F.2d 1317, 7 ERC 1114 (6th Cir. 1974).

60. 39 *Federal Register* 12118 (April 3, 1974); 33 C.F.R. § 209.120.

61. 118 *Congressional Record* 33756–57 (1972), as quoted in United States v. Holland, 6 ERC at 1392, and United States v. Ashland Oil & Transportation Co., 7 ERC at 1119.

62. Natural Resources Defense Council v. Callaway, 392 F. Supp. 685, 7 ERC 1784 (D.D.C. 1975).

63. 40 *Federal Register* 19765 (May 6, 1975).

64. *Ibid.* at 19794.

65. 40 *Federal Register* 31320 (July 25, 1975); 33 C.F.R. § 209.120.
66. 40 *Federal Register* 50720 (October 31, 1975).
67. 40 *Federal Register* 41292 (September 5, 1975); 40 C.F.R. Part 230.
68. § 101 (e); 33 U.S.C. § 1251 (e).
69. 38 *Federal Register* 22757 (August 23, 1973); 40 C.F.R. Part 105.
70. *Ibid.,* § 105.5 (d).

CHAPTER 6

The Coastal Zone
Management Act

THE COASTAL ZONE Management Act of 1972[1] was passed by
Congress to encourage the coastal states to preserve and protect the resources of the coastal zone. Basically, it makes federal
funds available to the states for the development and implementation
of comprehensive land and water use controls and management
plans for their coastal areas.

The Problem

Passage of the act was spurred by the recognition that unplanned
and uncontrolled exploitation of coastal resources was resulting in
the destruction of "[i]mportant ecological, cultural, historic, and
esthetic values in the coastal zone which are essential to the well-
being of all citizens. . . ."[2] Specifically, Congress found that:

> The increasing and competing demands upon the lands and waters
> of our coastal zone occasioned by population growth and economic
> development . . . have resulted in the loss of living marine re-
> sources, wildlife, nutrient-rich areas, permanent and adverse changes
> to ecological systems, decreasing open space for public use, and
> shoreline erosion. . . .[3]

Further, existing state and local planning and regulation were doing little if anything to check these losses and to come to grips with the urgent need to protect the remaining natural systems of the coastal zone. Consequently, in passing the Coastal Zone Management Act, Congress established that henceforth it would be national policy "to preserve, protect, develop, and where possible, to restore or enhance, the resources of the Nation's coastal zone for this and succeeding generations. . . ."[4]

It is not difficult to account for the problems which beset coastal areas.[5] Man has long concentrated his activities in these attractive, productive, and convenient regions. In the United States over half the population lives in areas adjacent to the coasts, including those of the Great Lakes. Recreation has been a booming coastal industry, and industrial plants and commercial activities have flourished. Considerable mineral and petroleum resources are located offshore. In 1972 domestic production of offshore oil and gas accounted for over 12 percent of total national production, and present estimates of total recoverable offshore petroleum resources are very high.[6] In addition, half of the total biological productivity of the world's oceans takes place near the coasts. Indeed, coastal estuaries and wetlands are the most productive natural areas in the world, nuturing the aquatic organisms that form the basis of the food chain. For example, estimates indicate that a single acre of tidal wetlands yields 535 pounds of fish a year in catches in coastal waters or at sea.[7]

In the face of such bounty, public recognition of the ecological fragility and resource limitations of coastal areas has been very late in coming and has been preceded by substantial overcrowding, overdevelopment, and destruction of valuable resources. The concentration of large urban centers along the coast has generated immense amounts of domestic and industrial wastes which, in turn, have been dumped into the oceans. Along the California coastline alone, 130 waste disposal outfalls annually dump 444 billion gallons of domestic and industrial sewage (which has received varying degrees of treatment) into bays, estuaries, lagoons, and inshore waters which reach the sea.[8] Offshore activities associated with the extraction of minerals and oil have resulted in serious pollution of marine environments, and billions of gallons of seawater that are used to cool power plants are discharged back into the water at very high temperatures. Many highly productive estuaries and wetlands have also been dredged for ports and marinas, filled to provide more land for development, and polluted by soil from upland erosion as well as by solid and liquid wastes. In the nation as a whole, one-fourth of all salt marshes have now been destroyed. Both New York and California have lost well over half of their tidal wetlands. Public access to coastal beaches and lands has also diminished rapidly as open spaces have been converted into recreational subdivisions, coastal highways, and sites for power plants and water-related industries. In California the general public may legally use only 263 miles of the 1,072-mile mainland coast.

The energy crisis has even further exacerbated the pressures being placed on the coastal zone, since in its wake has come an extensive federal program for greatly increased exploitation of off-shore oil reserves. Such drilling will not only affect the ecological systems of the Outer Continental Shelf (OCS), where the oil reserves are located, but will also have a tremendous onshore impact in terms of supporting facilities and related industries such as harbors, refineries, petrochemical plants, distribution facilities, and accompanying residential and commercial development. A discussion of the federal OCS leasing program appears in Chapter 11, which deals with the public lands of the United States.

Major Provisions of the Act

The severity of the problems existing in the coastal zone and the absence of adequate state and local initiatives to combat these problems led in 1972 to the enactment of the federal Coastal Zone Management Act. Its major provisions establish the following two-stage process through which the states may obtain federal financial assistance for the protection of coastal areas:

1. Development of a comprehensive, long-range coastal management plan which meets broad statutory criteria; and
2. Federal approval of the plan developed, followed by state implementation of the plan.

Federal grants covering up to two-thirds of costs are available to coastal states for both the program development stage and the implementation stage. The program development grants are commonly known as Section 305 grants and the implementation or administrative grants as Section 306 grants, since these were the sections of the act which established the grant programs.[9]

As an incentive to relatively prompt development of coastal zone management plans, the act provides that no more than three annual program development grants may be awarded to any one state and no awards of this type may be made after June 30, 1977. An additional nonfinancial incentive provides that once a state's management program receives federal approval, all federal actions which directly affect the coastal zone must "to the maximum extent practicable" be consistent with the state's approved plan. Application for all grants under the Coastal Zone Management Act are optional for the states.

Under the act the coastal states include not only those states which border on the oceans or other saltwater bodies, but also those bordering on the Great Lakes. Further, for the purposes of the act, the term "coastal state" also applies to the four territories of Puerto Rico, the Virgin Islands, Guam, and American Samoa. In all, thirty states plus the four territories are eligible for grants under the act.

"Coastal zone" is defined by the act to mean the coastal waters and adjacent shorelands of the coastal states, including "transitional and intertidal areas, salt marshes, wetlands, and beaches." The exact inland limits of the coastal zone are left to the discretion of the states, but the zone must extend inland "to the extent necessary to control shorelands, the uses of which have a direct and significant impact on the coastal waters."[10]

The "coastal waters" themselves are defined to include (1) the Great Lakes and their connecting waters and estuary-type areas such as bays, shallows, and marshes, and (2) the oceans and other waters adjacent to the shorelines which contain a measurable quantity of seawater, including, but not limited to, sounds, bays, lagoons, bayous, ponds, and estuaries.

The act assigns the responsibility of administering its provisions to the U.S. Secretary of Commerce, who, in turn, has delegated this authority to the National Oceanic and Atmospheric Administration (NOAA), one of the agencies of the U.S. Department of Commerce. Within NOAA, an Office of Coastal Zone Management has been created to implement the act.

Requirements which each state must meet in the development of a coastal zone management plan in order to receive federal funds are set out in the statute. Each such plan must include the following:

(1) an identification of the boundaries of the coastal zone subject to the management program;
(2) a definition of what shall constitute permissible land and water uses within the coastal zone which have a direct and significant impact on the coastal waters;

(3) an inventory and designation of areas of particular concern within the coastal zone;

(4) an identification of the means by which the state proposes to exert control over the land and water uses referred to in paragraph (2) of this subsection, including a listing of relevant constitutional provisions, legislative enactments, regulations, and judicial decisions;

(5) broad guidelines on priority of uses in particular areas, including specifically those uses of lowest priority;

(6) a description of the organizational structure proposed to implement the management program, including the responsibility and interrelationships of local, areawide, state, regional, and interstate agencies in the management process.[11]

The management program must also provide for "adequate consideration of the national interest involved in the siting of facilities necessary to meet requirements which are other than local in nature."[12] This provision is discussed in more detail below.

The statute further requires that state management programs be developed in accordance with regulations promulgated by NOAA, and that opportunity be provided for full participation "by relevant Federal agencies, state agencies, local governments, regional organizations, port authorities, and other interested parties, public and private. . . ."[13]

The state must also show that it is organized to implement the management program and that it has the authority necessary to do so. This authority must include the power:

(1) to administer land and water use regulations, control development in order to ensure compliance with the management program, and to resolve conflicts among competing uses; and

(2) to acquire fee simple and less than fee simple interests in lands, waters, and other property through condemnation or other means when necessary to achieve conformance with the management program.[14]

The act directs that the management program must provide for a means of administrative regulation or review at the state level. A state must adopt one or a combination of the following three techniques for controlling land and water uses: (1) direct regulation by the state; (2) local regulation in accordance with state standards, subject to administrative review; and (3) local regulation, subject to state review for consistency with the management program. In addition, the state must develop a method of assuring that local regulations within the coastal zone "do not unreasonably restrict or exclude land and water uses of regional benefit."[15]

Each state must coordinate its management program with existing local, areawide, and interstate plans. It must also establish a mechanism through which there will be continued coordination and consultation between the state agency administering the management program and local governments, interstate agencies, regional agencies, and areawide agencies within the coastal zone. NOAA regulations encourage the extension of such cooperation between state and regional agencies into the actual establishment of interstate and regional agreements and joint action.[16] This approach is particularly recommended for environmental problems and resource development in the national or regional interest.

Another provision of the act specifies that it does not in any way affect any requirement which is established by the Federal Water Pollution Control Act, as amended,[17] or by the Clean Air Act, as amended,[18] or any requirement which is established pursuant to either of these acts by federal, state, or local government. Moreover, the act goes on to mandate that such requirements must be incorporated in the coastal zone management programs developed and must serve as the water pollution control and air pollution control requirements applicable to such programs.

The state management program must make provision for procedures through which specific areas may be designated for preservation or restoration for their conservation, recreational, ecological, or aesthetic values. The Coastal Zone Management Act itself makes federal grants available to aid the coastal states in acquiring, developing, and operating estuarine sanctuaries for research and educational purposes.[19] Federal grants of up to 50 percent of such costs are authorized, to a maximum of $2 million for any one sanctuary. The Office of Coastal Zone Management of NOAA also administers the marine sanctuaries program which was established under the Marine Protection, Research, and Sanctuaries Act of 1972.[20] The purpose of this program is to preserve or restore marine areas for their conservation, recreational, ecological, or aesthetic values.

The act permits a state, subject to the approval of NOAA, to develop and adopt its management program in segments so that immediate attention can be focused on those areas which have the most serious problems. If it does this, the state must adequately provide for the ultimate coordination of the different segments of its management program into a single unified program and must do this as soon as is reasonably practicable.

One of the basic policies of the act is "to encourage the participation of the public," as well as of federal, state, and local governments and regional agencies in the development of coastal zone management programs. A state management program cannot obtain federal approval unless the state has provided opportunity for full participation in the development of the program by all interested parties, public and private, and unless public hearings have been held during the process of development. At least thirty days' notice must be given for such hearings, and all agency materials pertinent to the hearing must be made available to the public for review and study.

As part of its review of each state management program that is submitted for federal approval, NOAA will be preparing an environmental impact statement under NEPA.[21] The draft impact statement and the state program will be available for comment from government officials and the public for a forty-five day period. After receiving and considering these comments, NOAA will prepare a final impact statement which will be available for a thirty day comment period. These comments must be considered by NOAA before it decides to approve or disapprove the state program. The first environmental impact statement prepared by NOAA on a state management program submitted for approval was for the state of Washington.

Features of Particular Importance

The following aspects of the Coastal Zone Management Act merit further clarification and discussion: (1) the natural interest provisions, and (2) the "areas of particular concern."

1. The National Interest Provisions

As pointed out above the act requires that state management programs provide for "adequate consideration of the national interest involved in the siting of facilities necessary to meet requirements which are other than local in nature." NOAA regulations elaborate on the meaning of this provision.[22] They state that this requirement should not be construed as compelling the states actually to include accommodations for certain types of facilities in their management programs. It is intended, rather, to make sure that such national concerns are considered at an early stage of state planning and that such facilities are not arbitrarily excluded or unreasonably restricted in the management program.

NOAA considers "requirements which are other than local in nature" to be those which lead to facilities designed to serve more than one locality. To guide the states, it has identified requirements of this type which also have siting characteristics the Secretary of Commerce believes may involve a clear national interest. This information is set forth in Table 5. Associated facilities and relevant federal agencies are also indicated. This list is not intended to be all-inclusive, but the states are expected at least to consider each of the requirements cited in their determination of permissible uses and priorities in the coastal zone.

In ascertaining local, regional, and national needs for facility sitings, the state must consult with appropriate federal agencies and agencies of other states in the region. This coordination must begin at an early stage of planning, so that national and regional needs will receive full consideration during the process of program development. The regulations emphasize that the states should *actively* seek the advice of concerned federal agencies. They also heavily underline the importance of consultations with adjacent and nearby states which share similar or common coastal resources and with regional interstate bodies.

Several other provisions of the act grant a privileged position to national security. One of these allows federal agencies to approve applications for a federal license or permit for an activity which a state finds inconsistent with its management program if the Secretary of Commerce finds that activity to be "necessary in the interest of national security." Federal agencies may also approve applications for federal assistance which are inconsistent with a state's management program if the Secretary of Commerce finds that the project proposed is necessary in the interest of national security.

The high national priority placed on greatly increased exploitation of oil resources in the Outer Continental Shelf brings the question of the national interest in the coastal zone into sharp focus. The federal leasing program for offshore oil rights has proceeded at a highly accelerated pace, and in many areas actual leasing will already have been carried out long before state coastal zone management programs are completed. To help alleviate this problem, Congress has authorized the appropriation of additional funds for program development grants during each of the three fiscal years from 1975

Table 5
Facilities Whose Siting May Involve a Clear National Interest

Requirements	Associated facilities	Cognizant Federal Agencies
1. Energy production and transmission	Oil and gas wells; storage and distribution facilities; refineries; nuclear, conventional, and hydroelectric powerplants; deepwater ports	Federal Energy Administration, Federal Power Commission, Bureau of Land Management, Atomic Energy Commission,* Maritime Administration, Geological Survey, Department of Transportation, Corps of Engineers
2. Recreation (of an interstate nature)	National seashores, parks, forests; large and outstanding beaches and recreational waterfronts; wildlife reserves	National Park Service, Forest Service, Bureau of Outdoor Recreation
3. Interstate transportation	Interstate highways, airports, aids to navigation; ports and harbors, railroads	Federal Highway Administration, Federal Aviation Administration, Coast Guard, Corps of Engineers, Maritime Administration, Interstate Commerce Commission
4. Production of food and fiber	Prime agricultural land and facilities; forests; mariculture facilities; fisheries	Soil Conservation Service, Forest Service, Fish and Wildlife Service, National Marine Fisheries Service
5. Preservation of life and property	Flood and storm protection facilities; disaster warning facilities	Corps of Engineers, Federal Insurance Administration, NOAA, Soil Conservation Service

6. National defense and aerospace	Military installations; defense manufacturing facilities; aerospace launching and tracking facilities	Department of Defense, NASA
7. Historic, cultural, aesthetic, and conservation values	Historic sites; natural areas; areas of unique cultural significance; wildlife refuges; areas of species and habitat preservation	National Register of Historic Places, National Park Service, Fish and Wildlife Service, National Marine Fisheries Service
8. Mineral resources	Mineral extraction facilities needed to directly support activity	Bureau of Mines, Geological Survey

Source: 40 *Federal Register* 1688 (January 9, 1975); 15 C.F.R. § 923.15.
*Editor's note: The Atomic Energy Commission has now been replaced by the Nuclear Regulatory Commission and the Energy Research and Development Administration.

through 1977. These funds are to be used specifically to help affected coastal states plan for impending offshore drilling and accompanying onshore impacts.

2. Areas of Particular Concern

Another important feature which management programs must include is "an inventory and designation of areas of particular concern within the coastal zone." These are areas of special statewide concern which the states are expected to emphasize in their development of coastal zone policies and controls.

NOAA regulations state that:

geographic areas of particular concern are likely to encompass not only the more-often cited areas of significant natural value or importance, but also: (a) Transitional or intensely developed areas where reclamation, restoration, public access and other actions are especially needed; and (b) those areas especially suited for intensive use or development.[23]

They advise further that immediacy of need should be a major consideration in determining "particular concern."

The regulations also provide criteria to assist the states in making the required designations. These designations must be based on a review of both natural and man-made coastal zone resources and uses, and must at a minimum consider the following:

(1) Areas of unique, scarce, fragile or vulnerable natural habitat, physical feature, historical significance, cultural value and scenic importance;

(2) Areas of high natural productivity or essential habitat for living resources, including fish, wildlife and the various trophic levels in the food web critical to their well-being;

(3) Areas of substantial recreational value and/or opportunity;

(4) Areas where developments and facilities are dependent upon the utilization of, or access to, coastal waters;

(5) Areas of unique geologic or topographic significance to industrial or commercial development;

(6) Areas of urban concentration where shoreline utilization and other water uses are highly competitive;

(7) Areas of significant hazard if developed, due to storms, slides, floods, erosion, settlement, etc.; and

(8) Areas needed to protect, maintain or replenish coastal lands or resources, including coastal flood plains, aquifer recharge areas, sand dunes, coral and other reefs, beaches, offshore sand deposits and mangrove stands.[24]

Finally, the regulations point out that the inventory and designation of areas of particular concern should be of assistance to the states in meeting the statutory requirement that management programs make provision for procedures through which specific areas can be designated for preservation or restoration for their conservation, recreational, ecological, or aesthetic values.

Implementation of the Act

The actions taken by NOAA to implement the Coastal Zone Management Act include (1) publication of regulations for various aspects of the act; (2) supervision of the grant programs established by the act; (3) preparation of studies and technical assistance materials; and (4) sponsorship of formal and informal conferences on the problems of coastal zone management.

The following are the regulations for the Coastal Zone Management Act which NOAA has published in the *Federal Register*:

1. Final regulations setting forth procedures for state applications for program development grants, promulgated on November 29, 1973.[25]

2. Final regulations for the estuarine sanctuary grant program, promulgated on June 4, 1974.[26]

3. Final regulations setting forth criteria and procedures for ap-

proval of state coastal zone management programs, promulgated on January 9, 1975.[27]

4. Interim regulations to govern the coordination required between state and federal agencies during the states' development of management programs, promulgated on February 28, 1975.[28]

In addition, on June 27, 1974, NOAA promulgated final regulations on the related marine sanctuaries program established under the Marine Protection Research and Sanctuaries Act of 1972.[29]

The progress made by the states under the grant programs is periodically summarized by NOAA in reports which are available to the public.[30] These reports provide information on each participating state, such as what funds have been committed, what particular problems are faced, what goals and objectives have been set, what overall program design has been developed, and what type of public participation has occurred. All thirty-four of the eligible coastal states and territories have applied for program development grants under the act.

The studies undertaken or contracted out by NOAA include a National Interest Study to clarify what constitutes the national interest in the coastal zone and a Sanctuaries Study to provide guidance for NOAA in the administration of the estuarine and marine sanctuaries program. Technical assistance materials developed for NOAA include *Coastal Zone Management: The Process of Program Development,* a handbook prepared by the Coastal Zone Management Institute which sets out for the states the requirements of the act and various ways in which they can be met, and *Coastal Ecosystems,* a manual by John Clark which describes ecological factors which should be taken into account when proposals for development in coastal areas are considered.[31] In addition, a citizen's handbook on coastal zone management, designed to encourage citizen participation under the act, is being prepared by the Natural Resources Defense Council and will be published in 1976.[32]

Beginning in 1973 NOAA sponsored a number of formal and informal conferences on the problems of coastal zone management. Local briefings by federal officials, regional discussions with state representatives, and national conferences are all an ongoing part of NOAA's program. The third annual national coastal zone management conference was held in Monterey, California, in May 1975.[33]

Since the conditions and the work that is being done vary widely in the different coastal states, it is not possible here to provide a complete assessment of the implementation of the act. It is possible, however, to discuss briefly some of the major problems which have developed in this implementation.

One serious problem has been the fact that federal funding for the coastal zone management program has not been of the same order as the problems faced. With only limited federal funding as an incentive, it has been difficult to get the states to do an adequate job of program development. In addition, the criteria set out in the act for coastal zone plans are very broadly worded, and the regulations promulgated by NOAA generally do not provide more specific, concrete guidance to the states. In consequence, the policies developed by the states for coastal zone management are often overly general and may not deal adequately or at all with some of the more environmentally destructive types of development. Citizens' groups, moreover, have often lacked the expertise or resources necessary for meaningful participation in their state's coastal zone planning, and have often not been able to counter the pressures exerted by development interests.

The act does not provide for sanctions against states which fail to prepare adequate coastal zone plans (or which withdraw from the program entirely). Consequently, the only leverage afforded is the possibility that federal grants will not be renewed. Since, however, those who are concerned about the protection of their state's coast are likely to view poor planning as better than no planning at all, it is doubtful that they will urge that federal funds be withdrawn.

Finally, the act does not encourage the states to establish a means for interim control of development while the coastal zone plan is being prepared. Unfortunately, the specter of increased development controls, as a state plans its management program, may in itself induce development during the planning period that would not occur otherwise.

Citizen Action

There is no environmental magic in the mere fact that a state is developing a coastal zone management program. A number of states are approaching this task with far less than wholehearted enthusiasm and imagination or with little dedication to the goal of protecting environmental values; moreover, powerful real estate and industrial interests are opposed to strict controls over development in the coastal zone. Further, the accelerated federal offshore oil leasing program poses many new serious problems.

Whatever the circumstances are in their state, citizens should press for maximum public participation in the development of a coastal zone management plan and make sure that there is full consideration of public interests. They should ensure (1) that the location, timing, and frequency of formal public hearings are sufficient to allow broad citizen participation; and (2) that there is a requirement that all decisions be made after public meetings, along with a prohibition against decision making behind closed doors.

In most states federal funds for program development have been granted to either the state planning agency or the department of natural resources. In many cases, however, some of these funds have then been subcontracted out to regional, county, or local agencies, which are given the responsibilities of collecting data and proposing boundaries. Where such work is being done locally, citizens should seek to establish a dialogue with the responsible officials and, where possible, contribute relevant environmental information.

Concerned citizens should also review all grant applications made by their state under the Coastal Zone Management Act. The names and addresses of the state agencies which have prime responsibility for program development in the various coastal states are available from NOAA. Copies of all grant applications made under the act should be available for public inspection and copying at these agencies.

Citizens will also want to review and comment on the environmental impact statement that NOAA will prepare on their state's management program when it is submitted for federal approval. As mentioned above, the draft impact statement must be available for public comment for at least forty-five days and the final impact statement for at least thirty days. Copies of both statements will be available from NOAA.

Since the program development process is already well underway in most coastal states, citizens who are not already involved should move very quickly to maximize their impact on the planning process. Early involvement in program development is always the most desirable, but tenth or eleventh hour efforts can also lead to environmental protection that might not have been provided for otherwise. Furthermore, citizen support for the enactment of new state legislation to guide program development and/or to establish a basis for proper implementation may well be needed.

Two important considerations should also not be forgotten. First, the states are authorized by the act to amend their management programs, subject to federal approval, and should be pressed to do so when serious mistakes have been made. Second, citizen participation and monitoring are needed not only during program development, but also to assure that implementation is carried out responsibly and that planned environmental safeguards actually become a reality.

Key issues in the development and implementation of a coastal zone management program include the designation of the coastal boundaries, the determination of permitted uses and their priority, the inventory and designation of areas of particular concern, and the establishment of final land and water use controls.

The designation of the coastal zone boundaries is the crucial first step in the development of a management program. It determines the location and extent of territory subject to planning and controls and, equally important, which areas are not subject to controls under the program. The act recognizes that land and water uses in areas a considerable distance inland from the land/sea interface may have significant effects on the coastal environment and that protection of this environment requires control of all areas whose uses will have "direct and significant impact on the coastal waters." In the individual states, the precise landward boundary of the coastal zone depends on actual geographic, ecological, and other conditions, but citizens should ensure that this boundary, where established, does in fact include all areas the uses of which will have a direct and significant impact on the coastal environment.

With respect to land and water uses permitted within the coastal zone, citizens should work for a management program that provides for the following:

1. Public physical and visual use of and access to beaches and coastal areas. Provisions for physical use should include not only plans for strictly water-related activities such as swimming and fishing, but also for other recreational uses such as hiking, biking and riding trails, and parks. Care must be taken, however, to assure that the carrying capacity of coastal areas (that is, their ability to withstand such use without sustaining damage) is not exceeded.

2. A comprehensive transportation program which emphasizes public transportation and mass transit.

3. Adequate protection for areas of particular concern which are

identified through the inventory. This objective should not, however, be allowed to obscure the fact that the entire coastal zone, from a broader perspective, is an "area of particular concern." Citizens should work to ensure that areas which are not specifically designated for special protection still receive planning for orderly and balanced use and development.

4. Establishment of maximum desirable population densities, zones of industrial use, areas of permitted mineral and petroleum extraction, and water quality standards.

5. Requirements that coastal zone developments and facilities approved in the future employ measures necessary to mitigate their adverse impact on the environment and resources of the coastal zone.

The inventory and designation of areas of particular concern have been discussed above. It is particularly important that citizens be aware that NOAA regulations have established a wide range of categories into which such areas may fall.[34] For example, they may be environmentally unique or fragile, historically significant, scenically important, or naturally highly productive; or they may have substantial recreational value or be subject to significant natural hazards. In addition, citizens should not forget that there are provisions for federal grants to assist in the establishment of estuarine and marine sanctuaries.

The establishment of a strong organizational framework and effective controls for coastal zone management are essential to the success of the program. As the act itself emphasizes, fragmented authority and inadequate controls have been major reasons why such widespread destruction of coastal resources has already occurred. Thus the new programs which are being developed must incorporate a sound structure for administration and enforcement and well-defined, strict controls. As discussed above, the act requires either direct regulation by the state of land and water uses or local regulation in accordance with state standards or subject to general state review. No state management program can receive federal approval unless the state has developed such controls and also has the legal authority to impose them.

In some of the states which are developing management programs, there is an apparent preference for placing virtually all controls in the hands of localities and for understating the state review role. In view of the past failures of local governments to protect environmental values and to consider regional and statewide interests, citizens should carefully scrutinize all approaches of this type. They should raise for serious consideration the question of whether localities should be allowed to approve or issue permits for developments which have regional or statewide impact.

At least one model coastal zone management statute, which outlines a system of state planning and regulation for the protection of coastal resources, has been prepared.[35] Such model legislation can assist state governments and citizens in the preparation of strong management plans and can help ensure that innovative methods of exercising needed controls are not overlooked. In addition, a number of coastal states, such as California and Washington, have coastal protection statutes which have been on the books for several years. These statutes, and the coastal management plans which the states have developed under them, may provide similar guidance.

The following are important points to consider in assessing the adequacy of proposed controls:

1. Are adequate funds and staff provided to implement the controls?

2. Are there significant opportunities for citizen participation in enforcement? May private citizens sue to secure compliance with a management program? Can they recover reasonable attorney's fees and witness fees if they bring such suits? Prospective commercial and industrial developers should not be allowed to recover legal fees, since their assets should enable them to assume the expense of suits and such a provision would discourage citizen suits in the public interest.

3. Does the management plan adequately consider and integrate other federal laws which have an impact on coastal zone management? The most important of these laws are the Federal Water Pollution Control Act, as amended, and the Clean Air Act, as amended.

4. Are all guidelines and standards as clearly worded as possible?

5. Does the plan require that both individual and cumulative effects of proposed developments be fully explored, understood, and considered.

With regard to the organizational structure through which a management program will be implemented, citizens should make certain that there is a single, strong agency that is responsible for the ultimate enforcement of the plan or the review of its implementation.

In addition, the relationships between all involved federal, state, and local agencies should be as clear and straightforward as possible.[36]

There are two further issues which are not discussed in the act itself, but which are very important to coastal zone management. These are interim land use controls and environmental impact assessments of major land use decisions. Interim land use controls are essential, since it takes time to develop a management program, hold hearings, and secure final approval. The predictable response by developers to prospective land and water use controls will be a rush to begin projects prior to the institution of the controls in order to avoid their requirements. Such development may influence the character of the eventual management program, may foreclose desirable options, and may continue the heedless destruction of coastal resources which the Coastal Zone Management Act was intended to prevent.

Although interim controls are not required by the act, citizens should press for some mechanism through which development in the coastal zone can be controlled prior to federal approval and state implementation of the final coastal zone management plan. Such a mechanism may require new state legislation. Possible techniques that might be employed include (1) an absolute moratorium on development; (2) selected moratoria on particular kinds of development, such as second-home subdivisions, because of their severe environmental effects; and (3) an interim permit system.

The last alternative, an interim permit system, was established in California by that state's landmark Coastal Zone Conservation Act, which was enacted through an initiative and referendum process in November 1972.[37] Under the California act, until the completion of a coastal zone plan to guide development there may be no development within that portion of the California coastal zone which lies one thousand yards inland from mean high tide unless a permit is obtained from one of the coastal commissions established by the act. A variety of provisions govern the granting of permits, but the basic standard requires that no interim permit may be granted unless the commission finds "that the development will not have any substantial adverse environmental or ecological effect."[38]

The California experience indicates, however, that even with interim controls, citizens should expect and prepare for enormous pressures to develop coastal areas. One year after the California act was passed, 5,636 applications for interim development had been filed. Of this number, 4,736 applications had been granted; 755 were still being processed or had been withdrawn by the applicant; and only 145 permit applications had been denied.[39]

A central aspect of both an interim control program and a final management program should be environmental impact assessments of major land use decisions. Experience with the National Environmental Policy Act (NEPA)[40] and several of the state NEPA programs patterned after it has shown that this step, which is taken before irrevocable decisions are made, may provide the key to environmentally sound decision making.

Accordingly, citizens should work for the requirement that environmental impact assessments must be made of particular projects prior to any substantial development both during the interim period of program development and after the management program has been adopted. A typical environmental impact assessment might consist of the following:

1. A description of the probable environmental consequences of the proposed project.
2. The relationship of the project to the management program, if the latter has been adopted.
3. A discussion of alternatives to the project. For example, why was the particular location for the project chosen? Are there any other possible locations where there would be less environmental impact?
4. A discussion of the need for the project.

Additionally, states should establish conditions with respect to environmental impact which must be met prior to approval of a proposed project. In the period prior to completion of the management plan, no project should be approved unless the environmental impact assessment shows, as stated in the California coastal act, that "the development will not have any substantial adverse environmental or ecological effect." After the coastal zone management plan is adopted, there should be a requirement that projects must conform to the plan and have no undue significant adverse environmental effect.

Finally, the opportunity for public participation should be an established part of the environmental impact assessment process. This should include public hearings on the advisability and impact of proposed projects.

In some parts of the country citizen participation in the development of coastal zone programs has already been underway for several years. The most notable example of this has been in California, where a citizens' campaign actually achieved enactment of the state's Coastal Zone Conservation Act[41] in November 1972, only days after the federal Coastal Zone Management Act was passed. The experience in California has demonstrated the degree of commitment which citizens are willing to make for the protection of a natural resource which they value. The statute that resulted has served as a model for other states in the development of coastal zone management programs and other land use planning. The remainder of this chapter is devoted to a discussion of this important example of citizen action and state legislation to protect the coastal zone.

The citizens' effort in California has been spearheaded by the California Coastal Alliance, which is a statewide alliance of individuals and organizations committed to saving the California coast from destructive overdevelopment. In 1972, after bills seeking to establish protective coastal measures and increased public access to the beach had died in two successive sessions of the state legislature, the alliance decided to take the issue directly to the people via the initiative and referendum process authorized by the California state constitution.[42] In a truly Herculean effort volunteer workers across the state gathered and qualified the 418,000 signatures needed to place the coastal initiative on the ballot. A spirited campaign then ensued in which the alliance met with intensive, heavily financed opposition from oil companies, land development corporations, and other special interests. Yet the bipartisan citizen effort prevailed, sustained by the enthusiasm and hard work of people of all ages and backgrounds. When the vote was finally counted on November 7, 1972, a majority of 55 percent had voted for "Proposition 20," the California Coastal Zone Conservation Act.[43]

The new act declared "that the California coastal zone is a distinct and valuable natural resource" and "that the permanent protection of the remaining natural and scenic resources of the coastal zone is a paramount concern to present and future residents of the state and nation. . . ."[44] To achieve these objectives the act established six regional commissions and one state commission charged with the responsibilities of preparing a coastal zone plan and of controlling development within the coastal zone prior to the completion of that plan. The intended scope of the ultimate coastal zone plan can be seen in the list of components which it must contain: land use, transportation, conservation, public access, recreation, power plant and other public facility siting, ocean minerals and living resources, maximum population densities, and educational or scientific use. The plan must be completed and submitted to the state legislature by 1976, when the act terminates.

The California coastal act contemplates that its policies will be achieved in large measure through the efforts of an informed and concerned populous. All meetings of the commissions must be open to the public. Public hearings are required in connection with the issuance of regulations by the commissions, the preparation of the coastal zone plan, and decisions on permit applications. In addition, "any person aggrieved" by the approval of a permit may appeal to the state commission and if the state commission also grants approval, may petition for judicial review of that decision.

Finally, stiff monetary penalties are imposed for violations of the act, and private citizens are encouraged to take legal action to enforce its provisions. The act grants standing to "any person" to maintain an action to restrain violations or recover civil penalties. It also dispenses with certain procedural requirements which would otherwise apply to such actions, and provides for awards of attorney's fees.

The passage of this strong act did not, however, spell the end of coastal problems in California. The same interests that spent $3 million trying to defeat the passage of the California coastal act have used their resources to make successful applications for permits for development and to bring lawsuits challenging denials of permits as well as basic provisions of the state act. The coastal commissions are substantially underfunded and understaffed. The broad public focus which developed during the campaign for passage of the act has, naturally enough, diminished over time. Nonetheless, the California Coastal Alliance is still a very active and effective organization, and committed citizens across the state are still working to realize the goals established by the state's hard-won coastal act.

NOTES

1. 16 U.S.C. § 1451 *et seq.*
2. 16 U.S.C. § 1451 (e).
3. 16 U.S.C. § 1451 (c).
4. 16 U.S.C. § 1452.

5. See Bostwick H. Ketchum, *The Water's Edge: Critical Problems of the Coastal Zone* (Cambridge, Mass.: The M.I.T. Press, 1972).

6. Council on Environmental Quality, *OCS Oil and Gas: An Environmental Assessment,* a report to the President (Washington, D.C.: Government Printing Office, April 1974), 1:20 *et seq.*

7. R. H. Stroud and P. A. Douglas, eds., "Introduction," *A Symposium on the Biological Significance of Estuaries* (Washington, D.C.: Sports Fishing Institute, 1971).

8. California Coastal Zone Conservation Commission, *Preliminary Coastal Plan* (March 1975), p. 24.

9. These two sections are codified as § 1454 and § 1455, respectively, in 16 U.S.C.

10. 16 U.S.C. § 1453 (a).

11. 16 U.S.C. § 1454 (b).

12. 16 U.S.C. § 1455 (c) (8).

13. 16 U.S.C. § 1455 (c) (1).

14. 16 U.S.C. § 1455 (d).

15. 16 U.S.C. § 1455 (e) (2).

16. 38 *Federal Register* 33048 (November 29, 1973); 15 C.F.R. § 920.16.

17. 33 U.S.C. § 1251 *et seq.* See Chapter 5.

18. 42 U.S.C. § 1857 *et seq.* See Chapter 4.

19. 16 U.S.C. § 1461.

20. 16 U.S.C. § 1431 *et seq.*

21. 40 *Federal Register* 8547; 15 C.F.R. § 925.5. See Chapter 3 for a discussion of NEPA.

22. 40 *Federal Register* 1688 (January 9, 1975); 15 C.F.R. § 923.15.

23. 38 *Federal Register* 33046 (November 29, 1973); 15 C.F.R. § 920.13. Additional regulations dealing with areas of particular concern are found at 40 *Federal Register* 1687 (January 9, 1975); 15 C.F.R. § 923.13.

24. 40 *Federal Register* 1687 (January 9, 1975); 15 C.F.R. § 923.13.

25. 38 *Federal Register* 33044; 15 C.F.R. Part 920.

26. 39 *Federal Register* 19922; 15 C.F.R. Part 921.

27. 40 *Federal Register* 1683; 15 C.F.R. Part 923.

28. 40 *Federal Register* 8546; 15 C.F.R. Part 925.

29. 39 *Federal Register* 23254; 15 C.F.R. Part 922.

30. The following is NOAA's address:

Office of Coastal Zone Management
National Oceanic and Atmospheric Administration (NOAA)
U.S. Department of Commerce
3300 Whitehaven Street, N.W.
Washington, D.C. 20285
Attention: Public Affairs Officer

Another source of current information on coastal zone management is the weekly newsletter entitled *Coastal Zone Management,* which is published by Nautilus Press, 1056 National Press Building, Washington, D.C. 20004. The cost of this newsletter is $135 per year.

31. Coastal Zone Management Institute, *Coastal Zone Management: The Pro-*

cess of Program Development (Sandwich, Mass.: 1974), available to the public for $7.50 prepaid or $9 if billed from: Coastal Zone Management Institute, P.O. Box 221, Sandwich, Massachusetts 02563; John Clark, Coastal Ecosystems: Ecological Considerations for Management of the Coastal Zone (Washington, D.C.: The Conservation Foundation, 1974), available for $4 in paperback (plus $.25 for postage and handling) and $7.95 in hardback (plus $.50 for postage and handling) from: Publications Department, The Conservation Foundation, 1717 Massachusetts Avenue, N.W., Washington, D.C. 20036.

32. Information regarding the availability of this handbook can be obtained from the Natural Resources Defense Council, 664 Hamilton Avenue, Palo Alto, California 94301.

33. The proceedings of this conference are available in pamphlet form from NOAA.

34. 40 Federal Register 1687 (January 9, 1975); 15 C.F.R. § 923.13.

35. Nancy Smith, Peter Ratner, and Angus Macbeth, "Model Coastal Zone Statute," Coastal Zone Management Journal, vol. 1, no. 2 (Winter 1974), p. 209.

36. Interim regulations governing the required coordination between state and federal agencies during program development by the state were promulgated by NOAA on February 28, 1975. 40 Federal Register 8546; 15 C.F.R. Part 925.

37. This act is set forth in the California Public Resources Code § 27000 et seq.

38. Cal. Public Resources Code § 27402 (a).

39. The Natural Resources Defense Council has a California Coastal Advocacy Project which monitors and participates in the implementation of the California Coastal Zone Conservation Act.

40. 42 U.S.C. § 4321 et seq. See Chapter 3.

41. A very readable and informative account of this accomplishment is Janet Adams, "Proposition 20—A Citizens' Campaign," 24 Syracuse L. Rev. 1019 (1973).

42. Cal. Const. art. IV, §§ 1 and 22.

43. Cal. Public Resources Code § 27000 et seq.

44. Ibid., § 27001.

CHAPTER 7

The National Flood Insurance Program

THE NATIONAL FLOOD Insurance Program contains requirements of great significance for land use control in floodplain areas. The program was established by the National Flood Insurance Act of 1968,[1] under which federally subsidized flood insurance was made available to residents of communities which participate in the program. Previously, due to the high-risk factors involved, flood insurance had not been available from the private sector. The prime requirement for community participation is the establishment of satisfactory land use controls to regulate development within areas identified as having special flood hazards. The act provided that the federal government would first identify flood-prone communities and then delineate special flood hazard areas and provide more specific flood data. As more data are supplied, communities must adopt more stringent land use regulations.

This legislation marked an important reorientation in federal flood policy, which in the past had concentrated almost entirely on the construction of public works such as dams and levees for flood prevention. By 1968 it had become apparent that while such works could not prevent *all* floods, the illusion of full protection which they conveyed was resulting in rapidly increasing development in flood-risk areas. When floods defied control, the federal government was then obliged to provide millions of dollars of disaster relief funds. Thus with one hand the federal government was expending huge sums of money for flood control measures which encouraged settlement in floodplain areas and with the other was paying out enormous sums in disaster relief to floodplain residents. In addition to these direct economic costs, by 1968 an awareness of the great environmental costs associated with projects such as dams and channelization had also developed. Consequently, in that year Congress established the National Flood Insurance Program to encourage flood protection through local regulation of land uses and to provide a system of subsidized flood insurance.

When in 1973 Congress saw that only a small percentage of eligible flood-prone communities were participating in the National Flood Insurance Program, it passed new and stronger legislation, increasing both the benefits and sanctions of the program. The Flood Disaster Protection Act of 1973[2] established the following sanctions:

1. On and after July 1, 1975, no *federal assistance* can be granted for the acquisition or construction of property within any area identified by the federal government as having special flood hazards, *unless the community in which such area is located is then participating in the National Flood Insurance Program.*[3] In order to participate in the program, a community must adopt land use regulations which are consistent with federal criteria.

2. The federal agencies which supervise, approve, regulate, or insure banks, savings and loan associations, or similar institutions must by regulation prohibit such institutions from making, increasing, extending, or renewing, on or after July 1, 1975, any *loans* secured by improved real estate in an area identified as having special flood hazards, *unless the community in which the area is located is then participating in the National Flood Insurance Program.*[4]

In addition, in special flood hazard areas no individual property owner may obtain such federal assistance or loans unless the property in question is also covered by flood insurance.[5]

These are powerful sanctions, requiring communities and individuals to take positive action to avoid the loss in flood hazard areas of (1) federal assistance for acquisition or construction, and (2) loans from any financial institution subject to any kind of federal supervision, regulation, or insurance—which include virtually all banks and savings and loan associations. These financial restrictions would apply to all loans and mortgages from the Small Business Administration, the Federal Housing Administration, and the Veterans Administration, as well as all federally related banks and other lending institutions. They apply to any flood-prone community which did not adopt adequate land use controls to qualify for participation in the National Flood Insurance Program before July 1, 1975 (or one year after the community is identified as flood-prone, whichever is later), or does not adopt the more stringent controls required where more specific flood data is supplied.

The Flood Disaster Protection Act of 1973 also increased the benefits of the National Flood Insurance Program. The limits of available coverage for both structures and contents were greatly increased, while rates were substantially reduced. In addition, the act increased from $250 million to $500 million the amount that the Secretary of Housing and Urban Development can borrow from the U.S. Treasury to finance the program. Moreover, whereas the 1968 act had established a monetary limit on the total amount of claims that could be outstanding at any one time, the 1973 act replaced this dollar restraint with a time limitation on the issuance of flood insurance contracts. No such contracts may be written after July 30, 1977, at which time a federal review of the program will be conducted.

Administration of the Program

The National Flood Insurance Program is administered by the Federal Insurance Administration of the U.S. Department of Housing and Urban Development (HUD). The private insurance industry, which is represented by the National Flood Insurers' Association, cooperates with the federal government in this subsidized program and writes all flood insurance policies. The National Flood Insurers' Association appoints servicing companies, generally on a statewide basis, to disseminate information both to the public and to insurance agents, to process all flood insurance policies, and to handle the adjustment of claims. Policies may be purchased by property owners in eligible communities from any licensed property and casualty insurance agent or broker.

Information and assistance regarding qualification for the program are available to communities directly from the Federal Insurance Administration. In addition, the governor of each state has appointed a state coordinating agency to assist communities in qualifying for the program, especially in developing acceptable land use control measures. A list of these state agencies and their addresses can be obtained from the Federal Insurance Administration, whose address is given on page 131.

The Federal Insurance Administration is responsible for identifying all flood-prone communities and for delineating the boundaries of floodplain areas which have special flood hazards. It may consult and enter into contracts with other federal departments and agencies (such as the Army Corps of Engineers, the U.S. Geological Survey, and the Soil Conservation Service), as well as with state and local agencies to obtain the information needed to make these determinations. A provision of the 1973 act established that the identification of special flood hazard areas and determination of the degree of hazard in each area must be completed at the earliest date possible.

By June 30, 1974, the Federal Insurance Administration was required to have notified all known flood-prone communities which were not participating in the program of their tentative identification as a community containing one or more areas having special flood hazards. After this notification, each community was required either (1) to apply promptly for participation in the program, or (2) within six months to submit technical data to the Federal Insurance Administration establishing that the community either was not seriously flood prone or had corrected flood hazards by flood works or other flood control measures. The Federal Insurance Administrator may grant a public hearing to any community when there is conflicting data on the nature and extent of a flood hazard; or, alternatively, the community may be given the opportunity to submit written evidence. In either case, the Administrator's determination is conclusive, if supported by substantial evidence.

As further information on flood hazards becomes available, the Federal Insurance Administration may identify additional flood-prone communities.

The standard which has been adopted by the Federal Insurance Administration for the identification of special flood hazard areas and the determination of flood elevation data to guide local land use controls is the so-called "100-year flood." This standard represents the flood level that on the average has a 1 percent chance of being equaled or exceeded in any given year. Thus special flood hazard areas are those areas in which there is a 1 percent chance of such flooding in any given year. Determination of this probability is not based on historical data alone, but takes into consideration such factors as topography, tidal surge, and man-made devices such as levees and dams.

Once a community has been identified as flood prone (that is, as a community which contains one or more areas which have special flood hazards), it must have qualified for participation in the National Flood Insurance Program by July 1, 1975 or within one year after notification, whichever is later, to avoid the sanctions discussed above.

In order to qualify for the program, a flood-prone community must adopt adequate land use control measures which are consistent with federal criteria set out in HUD regulations.[6] These regulations provide that "the minimum requirements governing the adequacy of the land use and control measures for flood-prone areas adopted by a particular community depend on the amount of technical data formally provided to the community by the [Federal Insurance] Administrator."[7] The Federal Insurance Administration is to provide data which

1. Define the special flood hazard areas within the community;

2. Identify water surface elevations, setting forth the heights which would be reached by the "100-year flood" at points within the floodplain; and

3. In riverine floodplains, identify the "floodway," which includes the stream channel and immediately adjacent areas which during the 100-year flood would carry the major portion of flood waters moving at great velocity; or

4. In coastal floodplains, identify the "coastal high hazard area" which is subject to high velocity waters.

The following minimum standards for flood-prone communities apply according to the amount of data provided to a given community by the Federal Insurance Administration. A community must meet the respective minimum requirements of (2) through (5) below within six months after it receives the specified data from the Federal Insurance Administration. A participating community which does not adopt land use control measures in accordance with these minimum standards within six months will lose its eligibility. A community can also have its eligibility suspended if it allows development which violates the measures it has enacted, thereby violating its agreement with the Federal Insurance Administration. Although some participating communities have been suspended for such actions, monitoring efforts need to be strengthened. When a community's eligibility is suspended, no flood insurance policies may be sold or renewed until it is formally reinstated by the Federal Insurance Administration; and as a nonparticipant in the program, the community incurs the federal sanctions.

1. When the Federal Insurance Administration has not defined the special flood hazard areas within a community, has not provided water surface elevation data, and/or has not provided sufficient data to identify the floodway or coastal high hazard area, the community must:

a. Require building permits for all proposed construction or other improvements in the community;

b. Review all building permit applications for new construction or substantial improvements to determine whether proposed building sites will be reasonably safe from flooding;

c. Review subdivision and development proposals to assure that they are consistent with the need to minimize flood damage; that all public utilities and facilities are located, elevated, and constructed to minimize or eliminate flood damage; and that adequate drainage is provided; and

d. Require new or replacement water supply systems and/or sanitary sewage systems to be designed to minimize or eliminate infiltration of flood waters into the systems and discharges from the systems into flood waters, and require on-site waste disposal systems to be located in a manner that will avoid impairment and contamination during flooding.

2. When the Federal Insurance Administration has identified special flood hazard areas, but has not provided data on water surface elevations, the floodway, or the coastal high hazard area, the minimum land use control measures adopted by a community for the floodplain must:

a. Take into account floodplain management programs, if any, already in effect in neighboring areas;

b. Apply at a minimum to all areas identified as having special flood hazards;

c. Provide that within special flood hazard areas, the laws and ordinances concerning land use and control and other measures designed to reduce flood losses will take precedence over any conflicting laws, ordinances, or codes;

d. Require building permits for all proposed construction or other improvements in special flood hazard areas;

e. Review building permit applications for major repairs in special flood hazard areas to determine that the proposed repair uses materials that are resistant to flood damage and methods that will minimize such damage;

f. Review building permit applications for new construction or substantial improvements within special flood hazard areas to assure that the proposed construction (including prefabricated and mobile homes) is protected against flood damage; is designed and anchored to prevent flotation, collapse, or lateral movement; and uses construction materials that are resistant to flood damage and methods that will minimize such damage; and

g. Meet all the requirements of (c) and (d) listed above under (1).

3. When the Federal Insurance Administration has identified special flood hazard areas, and has provided water surface elevations for the 100-year flood, but has not provided data sufficient to identify the floodway or coastal high hazard area, the minimum land use control measures adopted by a community for the floodplain must:

a. Meet all the requirements listed above under (2);

b. Require new construction or substantial improvements of residential structures within special flood hazard areas to have the lowest floor (including the basement) elevated to or above the level of the 100-year flood;

c. Require new construction or substantial improvements of nonresidential structures within special flood hazard areas to have the lowest floor (including the basement) elevated to or above the level of the 100-year flood or, along with utility and sanitary facilities, to be flood-proofed up to this level; and

d. In riverine situations, provide that until a floodway has been designated, no use, including landfill, may be permitted within special flood hazard areas unless the applicant for the use has demonstrated that the proposed use, when combined with all other existing and anticipated uses, will not increase the water surface elevation of the 100-year flood more than one foot at any point.

4. When the Federal Insurance Administration has identified special flood hazard areas in a riverine floodplain, has provided water surface elevation data for the 100-year flood, and has provided floodway data, the land use control measures adopted by the community for the floodplain must:

a. Meet all the requirements listed above under (2);

b. Meet the requirements of (b) and (c) listed above under (3);

c. Designate a floodway for passage of the water of the 100-year flood. Selection must be based on the principle that the area chosen must be designed to carry the waters of the 100-year flood without increasing the water surface elevation of the flood more than one foot at any point;

d. Provide that existing nonconforming uses in the floodway will not be expanded but may be modified, altered, or repaired to incorporate flood-proofing measures, provided that such measures do not raise the level of the 100-year flood; and

e. Prohibit fill or encroachments within the designated floodway that would impair its ability to carry and discharge the waters resulting from the 100-year flood, except where the effect on flood heights is fully offset by stream improvements.

5. When the Federal Insurance Administration has identified special flood hazard areas in a coastal floodplain, has provided water surface elevation data for the 100-year flood, and has identified the coastal high hazard area, the land use control measures adopted by the local government for the floodplain must:

a. Meet all the requirements listed above under (2);

b. Meet the requirements of (b) and (c) listed above under (3);

c. Provide that existing uses located on land below the elevation of the 100-year flood in the coastal high hazard area will not be expanded; and

d. Provide that no land below the level of the 100-year flood in the coastal high hazard area may be developed unless the new construction or substantial improvement (i) is located landward of the reach of the mean high tide, (ii) is elevated on adequately anchored piles or columns to a lowest floor level at or above the 100-year flood level and securely anchored to such piles or columns, and (iii) has no basement and has the space below the lowest floor free of obstructions.

In addition to setting out these minimum standards, the HUD regulations make recommendations for the development of overall comprehensive management plans for flood-prone areas. Central to these considerations is the need to divert unwise development from flood-prone areas and to encourage land uses there which are consistent with the flood damage potential of such areas.

On March 26, 1975, the Federal Insurance Administration of HUD published in the *Federal Register* proposed amendments to the existing regulations for the National Flood Insurance Program.[8] The public comment period for these proposals extended through May 1975 and public hearings were scheduled to be held across the country after that time. Promulgation of the final regulations is expected in the summer of 1976. The proposed amendments contain a number of very important provisions. For example, after the Federal Insurance Administration has identified the floodplain area having special flood hazards, the flood-prone community:

> Must in riverine situations, submit to the Administrator evidence of coordination with upstream, downstream or adjacent communities adversely affected by any development, fill, encroachment, or alteration or relocation of a watercourse.[9]

Moreover, once special flood hazard areas have been identified, communities may not simply sit back and wait for the Federal Insurance Administration to supply further flood data, but must take "reasonable measures to consider and use" any available 100-year flood data as criteria for administering the required floodplain regulations adopted by the community.

Where 100-year flood elevation data have been supplied, the proposed regulations require that flood proofing of all new construction and substantial improvements of nonresidential structures be carried out in accordance with the standards for completely flood-proofed structures contained in the U.S. Army Corps of Engineers publication "Flood-Proofing Regulations." A registered professional engineer or architect must also certify that all flood-proofing measures used for a structure are reasonably adequate to enable it to withstand the various impacts and effects of the 100-year flood.

Special new provisions are also proposed for mobile homes. These distinguish between new and existing mobile home parks within special flood hazard areas. Elevation to the 100-year flood level is required for mobile homes in new parks, while mobile homes moving into existing parks where facilities are already in place do not have to be elevated. In the latter case, however, full disclosure must be made to every new mobile home purchaser that the mobile home is being located in a special flood hazard area. In addition, within a designated floodway or coastal high hazard area, no new mobile home park, expansion of an existing park, or location of new mobile homes is permitted.

Once a floodway is designated, the proposed regulations would prohibit all new construction and substantial improvements which would result in an increase in flood heights during the 100-year flood. The existing regulations permit fill and encroachments where the effect on flood heights is fully offset by stream improvements, but the proposed amendments do not include this exception.

In the case of designated coastal high hazard areas, it is proposed that the use of fill for structural support be prohibited.

Since it is not possible to predict exactly what form the final regulations for the National Flood Insurance Program will take, citizens who are aware of the significance of this important program should take special care to obtain copies of the final regulations when they are published in the *Federal Register.*

One of the most serious problems of the National Flood Insurance Program is that while identification of flood-prone communities has been essentially completed, data on water surface elevations, floodways, and coastal high hazard areas may not be supplied to some communities for a number of years. As is manifest in the federal criteria spelled out above, communities are not required to institute more stringent land use control measures until such specific flood data are supplied. Consequently, since the land use control measures required for initial qualification in the program can be a rather vague building permit system, effective regulation of land uses in flood hazard areas may be postponed in some areas for at least several years, and perhaps longer.

It should be noted that the existing HUD regulations provide that prior to the provision of data by the Federal Insurance Administration, a community may use data obtained from other federal or state agencies or from consulting services as a basis for land use control measures in flood hazard areas. As has been pointed out, the proposed amendments to these regulations would make serious consideration of such action mandatory. Some states have made arrangements for state agencies to provide technical assistance to local communities in developing floodplain programs.

Citizen Action

Citizens should be aware that the strong provisions of the National Flood Insurance Program may not be strictly and smoothly implemented. In many quarters the required land use control measures may be politically unwelcome. While a vague resolution supporting the principle of land use regulation in flood hazard areas may not meet much opposition, more specific and stringent requirements pertaining to elevation precautions, flood proofing, or prohibition of new residential uses in a floodway are likely to be resisted by those planning or supporting construction in flood hazard areas. Thus various local political and administrative maneuvers to avoid full compliance with laws and regulations can be expected.

In some areas, there may be extended delays in the provision of needed data by the federal government. When this occurs, flood-prone communities can retain their eligibility in the National Flood Insurance Program with loose and unsophisticated land use control measures, since they are not required to comply with stricter standards until data are received on water surface elevations, the floodway, and coastal high hazard areas. Thus a distorted picture of what is required of participating communities with regard to land use regulation may be fostered.

The implementation of the National Flood Insurance Program, therefore, needs to be monitored by concerned citizens who have familiarized themselves with the provisions of federal and state laws and regulations, and who make sure that officials in their community are conscientiously carrying out the requirements of the program. Any efforts that are made to thwart such implementation should be subjected to full public scrutiny and reported to the Federal Insurance Administration, whose address is as follows:

> Federal Insurance Administration
> U.S. Department of Housing and
> Urban Development (HUD)
> Washington, D.C. 20410

Once a flood-prone community has qualified for participation in the program, citizens should make sure that developments approved for special flood hazard areas by such local bodies as the planning board or the zoning board of appeals comply with the land use requirements of the flood insurance program. The likelihood that a community will lose its eligibility under the program if it approves developments in violation of its agreement with the Federal Insurance Administration should be stressed. Any such violations should be reported to the Federal Insurance Administration and investigation should be requested. Citizens who report the violations of their own local government, of course, run the risk that if the community is suspended, their own individual flood insurance policies cannot be renewed; but the entire community's need to retain flood insurance coverage can also serve as pressure to bring about speedy compliance.

NOTES

1. 42 U.S.C. § 4001 *et seq.*
2. *Ibid.*
3. § 202 (a); 42 U.S.C. § 4106 (a).
4. § 202 (b); 42 U.S.C. § 4106 (b).
5. § 102 (a); 42 U.S.C. § 4012 (a).
6. 24 C.F.R. Part 1910.
7. 24 C.F.R. § 1910.3.
8. 42 *Federal Register* 13420 (March 26, 1975).
9. *Ibid.* at 134278; 24 C.F.R. § 1910.3 (b) (5) (proposed).

CHAPTER 8

The Wild and Scenic Rivers Act

I N 1968 CONGRESS passed a Wild and Scenic Rivers Act establishing the national policy:

> that certain selected rivers of the Nation which, with their immediate
> environments, possess outstandingly remarkable scenic, recreational,
> geologic, fish and wildlife, historic, cultural, or other similar values
> shall be preserved in free-flowing condition, and that they and their
> immediate environments shall be protected for the benefit and enjoy-
> ment of present and future generations.[1]

The act implemented this policy by instituting a National Wild
and Scenic Rivers System (hereafter the system), by designating all
or portions of eight rivers and adjacent lands as the original components of this system, by setting out methods and standards for future
additions to the system, and by designating twenty-seven other rivers
to be studied for possible inclusion in the system.

As of May 1, 1976, eight additional rivers have been added to the
system, four by congressional action[2] and four by state action.[3]
Thirty new rivers have been added by Congress to the list of rivers
to be studied for possible inclusion.[4] Table 6 lists the component
rivers of the system and Table 7 lists the rivers designated by Congress as potential additions.

Table 6
Component Rivers of the National Wild and Scenic Rivers System*

Original components, designated in October 1968:

1. Clearwater, Middle Fork, Idaho
2. Eleven Point, Missouri
3. Feather, California
4. Rio Grande, New Mexico
5. Rogue, Oregon
6. Saint Croix, Minnesota and Wisconsin
7. Salmon, Middle Fork, Idaho
8. Wolf, Wisconsin

Later additions:

9. Lower Saint Croix, Minnesota (added by Congress in 1972)
10. Chattooga, North Carolina, South Carolina, and Georgia (added by Congress in 1974)
11. Rapid, Idaho (added by Congress in 1975)
12. Upper Middle Snake, Idaho and Oregon (added by Congress in 1975)
13. Allagash Wilderness Waterway, Maine (added by state action in 1970)
14. Little Miami, Ohio (added by state action in 1973)
15. Little Beaver, Ohio (added by state action in 1975)
16. New River, North Carolina (added by state action in 1976)

*Only the names of the rivers, forks, and states are given here; the particular segment or segments designated by Congress are specified in 16 U.S.C. § 1274, as amended (see Note 2). Sources of further information about the rivers added by state action are indicated in Note 3.

Table 7
Rivers Designated as Potential Additions to the National Wild and Scenic Rivers System*

Designations made in October 1968:

1. Allegheny, Pennsylvania
2. Bruneau, Idaho
3. Buffalo, Tennessee
4. Chattooga, North Carolina, South Carolina, and Georgia
5. Clarion, Pennsylvania
6. Delaware, Pennsylvania and New York
7. Flathead, Montana
8. Gasconade, Missouri
9. Illinois, Oregon
10. Little Beaver, Ohio
11. Little Miami, Ohio
12. Maumee, Ohio and Indiana
13. Missouri, Montana
14. Moyie, Idaho
15. Obed, Tennessee
16. Penobscot, Maine
17. Père Marquette, Michigan
18. Pine Creek, Pennsylvania
19. Priest, Idaho
20. Rio Grande, Texas
21. Saint Croix, Minnesota and Wisconsin
22. Saint Joe, Idaho
23. Salmon, Idaho
24. Skagit, Washington
25. Suwannee, Georgia and Florida
26. Upper Iowa, Iowa
27. Youghiogheny, Maryland and Pennsylvania

Designations made in January 1975:

28. American, California	44. Manistee, Michigan
29. Au Sable, Michigan	45. Nolichuckey, Tennessee and
30. Big Thompson, Colorado	North Carolina
31. Cache la Poudre, Colorado	46. Owyhee, South Fork, Oregon
32. Cahaba, Alabama	47. Piedra, Colorado
33. Clark's Fork, Wyoming	48. Shepaug, Connecticut
34. Colorado, Colorado and Utah	49. Sipsey Fork, West Fork, Alabama
35. Conejos, Colorado	bama
36. Elk, Colorado	50. Snake, Wyoming
37. Encampment, Colorado	51. Sweetwater, Wyoming
38. Green, Colorado	52. Tuolumne, California
39. Gunnison, Colorado	53. Upper Mississippi, Minnesota
40. Illinois, Oklahoma	54. Wisconsin, Wisconsin
41. John Day, Oregon	55. Yampa, Colorado
42. Kettle, Minnesota	56. Dolores, Colorado
43. Los Pinos, Colorado	

Designation made in December 1975:

57. Lower Middle Snake, Idaho,
Oregon, and Washington

---

*Only the names of the rivers, forks, and states are given here; the particular segment or segments designated for study are specified in 16 U.S.C. § 1276, as amended (see Note 4).

The system is administered by the Secretary of the Interior and, where national forest lands are involved, by the Secretary of Agriculture.

Several different kinds of protection are afforded the river areas in the system. First of all, the act authorizes the appropriation of funds for the acquisition of land in designated river areas. Originally the act authorized the appropriation of up to $17 million for such acquisitions, but Congress has now amended this provision, authorizing over $40 million for land acquisition and specifying the amount authorized for each river.

Secondly, the act places restrictions on water resources projects which directly affect river areas of the system. The Federal Power Commission is prohibited from licensing "the construction of any dam, water conduit, reservoir, powerhouse, transmission line, or other project works" on or directly affecting a river in the system.[5] Also, no department or agency of the United States may "assist by loan, grant, license, or otherwise in the construction of any water resources project that would have a direct and adverse effect on the values for which such river was established. . . ."[6] This does not preclude licensing of or assistance to developments below or above a designated river area or on a tributary stream which "will not invade the area or unreasonably diminish the scenic, recreational, and fish and wildlife values" which were present in the area on October 2, 1968, the date the act was passed.[7]

Moreover, no federal department or agency may recommend authorization of any water resources project that would have a direct and adverse effect on the protected values of a river in the system or request appropriations to begin the construction of such a project, unless:

1. It advises in writing either the Secretary of the Interior or the Secretary of Agriculture (whichever is responsible for the administration of the river area in question) of its intention to do so at least sixty days in advance; and

2. It specifically reports to Congress in writing at the time it makes its recommendation or request, how construction of this project might affect the river area and its protected values.

The same protective measures also apply for a limited time to rivers which are designated as potential additions to the system. These rivers are so protected until 1978 or three years after they are added to the list of potential additions, whichever is later, unless during this time the river is found not to qualify for addition and proper notification of this determination is made. Additional time may be allowed for consideration of a river report by Congress or, in the case of state submissions, by the Secretary of the Interior.

In general, each river area of the National Wild and Scenic Rivers System must be administered in a manner that protects and enhances the values which led to its inclusion in the system. Primary emphasis in this administration must be given to protecting aesthetic, scenic, historic, archeological, and scientific features.

The land acquisition provisions established by the act authorize the Secretaries of the Interior and of Agriculture to acquire lands and interests in land, such as scenic easements, within the authorized boundaries of any component of the system.[8] Neither secretary may, however, acquire fee title to an average of more than one hundred acres per mile on both sides of the river. State-owned lands may be acquired only by donation. If 50 percent or more of the entire acreage within a river area is owned by the federal, state, or local government, the secretaries are prohibited from acquiring fee title to any lands by condemnation under the authority of the act. However, they are permitted in such circumstances to use condemnation to clear a title or to acquire scenic easements or other easements which are "reasonably necessary" to give the public access to the river.[9]

Land cannot be acquired by condemnation if it is located within any incorporated city, village, or borough which has a "duly adopted, valid zoning ordinance that conforms to the purposes of [the act]."[10] To establish the terms of such conformity, the appropriate secretary must issue guidelines specifying standards for local zoning ordinances. These standards must have the object of (1) prohibiting new commercial or industrial uses that are not consistent with the purposes of the act, and (2) protecting bank lands by means of acreage, frontage, and setback requirements on development. Both the Department of the Interior and the Department of Agriculture have approached this task on a river-by-river basis, preparing guidelines suited to the particular circumstances of each river.

Authorization is also established by the act for exchanges of property in which a person may trade land within a river area for federally owned land that (1) is located in the same state, and (2) is under the jurisdiction of the appropriate secretary. Further, other federal agencies and departments which have administrative jurisdiction over lands within a river area may transfer this jurisdiction to the appropriate secretary. The secretaries are also empowered to accept donations of lands and interests in land, as well as funds and other property which can be used in the administration of the system.

Owners of detached, one-family dwellings acquired under the act may retain rights of use and occupancy for noncommercial residential purposes for a term of up to twenty-five years. These rights may be terminated if the appropriate secretary is given reasonable cause to find that use and occupancy are being exercised in a manner that conflicts with the purposes of the act. In such a case, a fair market price for the unexpired portion of the rights must be paid to the holder.

As has been pointed out, the act not only designates the original component river areas of the system, it also provides for future additions to the system. A river area can become part of the system in two ways:

1. If, like the original components, it is authorized for inclusion by an act of Congress; or
2. If it (a) is designated as a wild, scenic, or recreational river by an act of the legislature of the state or states through which it flows, (b) is permanently administered as such a river by an agency or

political subdivision of the state without expense to the federal government, and (c) is approved by the Secretary of the Interior for inclusion in the system.

To be eligible for inclusion in the system, a river area must include a free-flowing stream and adjacent land areas that possess one or more of the values set out by Congress—that is, scenic, recreational, geologic, fish and wildlife, historic, cultural, and other similar values. A river that is not presently free-flowing can, if restored to this condition, become eligible for inclusion. "Free-flowing" as defined by the act means "existing or flowing in natural condition without impoundment, diversion, straightening, rip-rapping, or other modification of the waterway."[11] The act further states that the existence of "low dams, diversion works, and other minor structures at the time any river is proposed for inclusion . . . shall not automatically bar its consideration for such inclusion: *Provided,* that this shall not be construed to authorize, intend, or encourage future construction of such structures within components of the national wild and scenic rivers system."[12] Under the act, a river is "a flowing body of water or estuary or a section, portion, or tributary thereof, including rivers, streams, creeks, runs, kills, rills, and small lakes."[13]

Each river area included in the system must be classified and administered as one of the following types of areas:

(1) Wild river areas—Those rivers or sections of rivers that are free of impoundments and generally inaccessible except by trail, with watersheds or shorelines essentially primitive and waters unpolluted. These represent the vestiges of primitive America.
(2) Scenic river areas—Those rivers or sections of rivers that are free of impoundments, with shorelines or watersheds still largely primitive and shorelines largely undeveloped, but accessible in places by roads.
(3) Recreational river areas—Those rivers or sections of rivers that are readily accessible by road or railroad, that may have undergone some development along their shorelines, and that may have undergone some impoundment or diversion in the past.[14]

Different segments of the same river can be classified in different categories. For example, a section of a river which is otherwise designated as "scenic" may be too developed to warrant this classification, but may qualify for a "recreational" designation.

The Secretary of the Interior and the Secretary of Agriculture are responsible for seeing that studies are carried out of all rivers designated by Congress as potential additions to the system. Studies of the twenty-seven rivers designated for study when the act was originally passed in 1968 must be completed by October 1978. Those for the twenty-nine rivers designated in 1975 must, with several specified exceptions, be completed by October 1979. In the execution of these studies priority must be given to those river areas (1) where there is the greatest likelihood of development which would render them unsuitable for inclusion, and (2) which possess the greatest proportion of private lands. In all cases, the cooperation of appropriate state and local government agencies must be sought in the preparation of river studies. If a state so requests, a study must be carried out jointly with state and/or local agencies. Finally, every river study must include a determination of the degree to which state or local governments could participate in the protection of the river if it were added to the system.

When a river study is completed, a report must be submitted to the President on the suitability or nonsuitability of the river for addition to the system. The President then must report his recommendations to Congress, which makes the final determination of whether or not a particular river or river segment is added.

The report on each river, including maps and illustrations, must give an account of the following:

1. The characteristics which do or do not make the river area worthy of inclusion;

2. The current status of land ownership and use in the area;

3. The effects inclusion of the area in the system would have on potential uses of land and water;

4. The federal agency proposed to administer the area, if it is added to the system;

5. The extent to which it is proposed that administration, including the costs involved, be shared by state and local agencies; and

6. The estimated federal costs of acquiring necessary land and interests in land, as well as administering the area, if it is added.

Each completed river report must be printed as a Senate or House document.

Before a report is submitted to the President and to Congress, copies must be circulated among the Secretaries of the Interior,

Agriculture, and the Army, the Chairman of the Federal Power Commission, the heads of other affected federal agencies, and, unless the lands proposed for inclusion are already owned by the federal government or have been authorized for acquisition by Congress, the governor of the state or states in which the river area is located. A ninety-day comment period must be allowed and all comments received must be included in the submission made to the President and Congress.

Rivers recommended for inclusion in the National Wild and Scenic Rivers System by state action must be approved by the Secretary of the Interior, after comment from the Secretaries of Agriculture and the Army, the Chairman of the Federal Power Commission, and the heads of other affected federal agencies.

Of the fifty-seven river studies mandated by Congress, thirty-two are being carried out by the Department of the Interior and twenty-two by the Department of Agriculture, while three studies are the joint responsibility of the two departments. Administratively, the Bureau of Outdoor Recreation is coordinating the Department of the Interior's river studies and the Forest Service is coordinating those of the Department of Agriculture. Other appropriate federal, state, and local agencies are also consulted during the study process.

As of May 1, 1976, four of the original twenty-seven rivers designated for study by Congress have been added to the system. The Lower Saint Croix and a segment of the Chattooga were added by Congress, and the Little Miami and the Little Beaver were added by state action approved by the Secretary of the Interior. In addition, the Allagash Wilderness Waterway in Maine has also been added to the system as a result of state action and the Upper Middle Snake and the Rapid River have been added by direct congressional action. Five other river studies and reports have been completed. Of these, negative reports which found that the river did not qualify for inclusion in the system resulted in the cases of three rivers: the Clarion and Allegheny in Pennsylvania and the Maumee in Ohio and Indiana. Action has not yet been taken on the positive reports prepared on the Upper Iowa River in Iowa and the Suwannee River in Georgia and Florida. The studies and reports on other designated rivers are in various stages of preparation. A number of these are nearing completion and may be considered for inclusion by Congress in 1976.

In addition to the National Wild and Scenic Rivers System, over half of the states have adopted their own wild and scenic rivers programs or systems. Patterned on the federal legislation, these programs provide state protection for rivers and adjacent lands selected according to state criteria and procedures. Citizens who are concerned about the protection of rivers should determine whether their state has its own wild and scenic rivers program, and, if so, how it operates.

Citizen Action

Winning protection for a river is a difficult but not impossible task for citizens to undertake. In essence, there is no magic way in which river protection can be achieved and it is usually accomplished through the unrelenting efforts of people who are willing to work very hard, to organize their efforts, to marshal local support, to work through the political process, and to explore all alternatives. These alternatives may include local action, state action, federal action, or some combination of these. State river protection laws, laws protecting wetlands, floodplain regulations, and local zoning should all be explored, as well as the National Wild and Scenic Rivers System.

In addition to determining what possibilities exist, citizens working to save a river should also assess the political forces which are at work. In some areas there may be little enthusiasm or outright antagonism toward the idea of seeking state or federal protection for a local river. In others, trying to safeguard a river through local measures may be clearly impossible. Sometimes local attitudes can be changed through a concerted public education effort. Whatever the particular circumstances, citizens will need to determine what forces they have working for them, what avenues of action are open, and what obstacles should be expected.

The federal Wild and Scenic Rivers Act established a very important means of protecting some of our rivers. As has been discussed, those rivers that are part of the system and, for a limited time, those designated for study as potential additions are protected from impoundment and other projects that would have a direct, adverse effect on them. Rivers in the system must receive protective management, and the federal government is authorized to acquire land and interests in land within the boundaries of the river corridors. Furthermore, appropriations of federal funds have been authorized for the acquisition of such land, and states have taken action to protect some of the rivers in the system.

New rivers are added to the system either by congressional action or by state action subject to the approval of the Secretary of the Interior; new rivers are added to the study list of potential additions only by congressional action. Entrance into the program is dependent not only on the qualifications of the river, but also on the strength of the political support behind it.

Local organizations which are actively involved in an attempt to win protection for a particular river can contact the following organizations for advice:

American Rivers Conservation Council
324 C Street, S.E.
Washington, D.C. 20003
(202) 547–6500

Some printed materials describing the National Wild and Scenic Rivers System are available from:

U.S. Department of the Interior
Bureau of Outdoor Recreation
18th and C Streets, N.W.
Room 4256
Washington, D.C. 20240

NOTES

1. 16 U.S.C. § 1271.

2. Public Law 92–560, § 2 (October 25, 1972); Public Law 93–279, § 1 (a) (May 10, 1974); and Public Law 94–199, § 3 (a) (December 31, 1975).

3. Two of these rivers, the Little Miami and the Little Beaver, are in Ohio, and information pertaining to them can be obtained from: Department of Natural Resources, Division of Natural Areas and Preserves, Scenic Rivers Section, Fountain Square, Columbus, Ohio 43224. Information regarding the Allagash Wilderness Waterway in Maine, can be obtained from: Bureau of Parks and Recreation, State House, Augusta, Maine 04333. Information on the New River can be obtained from: Department of Natural and Economic Resources, P.O. Box 27687, Raleigh, N.C. 27611.

4. Public Law 93–621, § 1 (a) (January 3, 1975) and Public Law 94–199, § 5 (a) (December 31, 1975).

5. 16 U.S.C. § 1278 (a).

6. *Ibid.*

7. *Ibid.*

8. The act specified that the boundaries of each of the original components of the system could include an average of not more than 320 acres per mile on both sides of the river.

9. 16 U.S.C. § 1277 (b).

10. 16 U.S.C. § 1277 (c).

11. 16 U.S.C. § 1286 (b).

12. *Ibid.*

13. 16 U.S.C. § 1286 (a).

14. 16 U.S.C. § 1273 (b).

CHAPTER 9

Consumer and Investor Protection

IMPORTANT LAWS AND programs designed to protect purchasers of real estate, or which serve to protect such purchasers, have been established at the federal level of government. The following federal protective measures are discussed in this chapter:

1. The Interstate Land Sales Full Disclosure Act
2. Required registration with the U.S. Securities and Exchange Commission (SEC) of condominiums and co-ops sold primarily as managed investment opportunities
3. Laws prohibiting mail fraud

Vital provisions of the above require full disclosure of information about real estate offerings both to government agencies and to prospective purchasers; prohibit fraudulent practices, such as false or misleading advertising; forbid the omission of material facts in required documents; and establish penalties for violations.

These provisions are important to those concerned about land use for several reasons:

1. Certain types of real estate projects and practices must comply with their requirements. If this compliance does not take place, then

development which is carried out is unlawful and the developer is subject to the legal sanctions set out for violations. Depending on the circumstances and the statute involved, these remedies may include administrative enforcement proceedings, civil actions for injunctions or damages, and criminal prosecutions.

2. The preparation and filing of registration or "offering" statements involve both time and money. Irresponsible or highly speculative developers may be deterred from attempting shaky projects by these expenses, as well as by the legal obligation to disclose information.

3. The more that is publicly known about real estate projects, the better. The necessity of full disclosure can prevent secret deals which lead to windfall profits for developers and unexpected costs for both purchasers and communities. The requirement that developers reveal information—such as facts about their financial stability, the terms of sales or leases, the physical layout of the project and its relationship to other facilities and services—not only offers the prospective purchaser the opportunity to detect flaws in the offering, it also serves a similar disclosure purpose as far as the community is concerned. If misrepresentations of truth, omissions of material facts, or fraudulent schemes occur, there are existing mechanisms through which complaints can be made and pressure for corrective action can be brought to bear. In addition, access to detailed information about particular projects is provided by disclosure statements for citizens who are monitoring land development projects in their area. This information can be helpful in assessing whether a project is in compliance with all other federal, state, and local laws and regulations.

4. In filings such as those required under the Interstate Land Sales Full Disclosure Act information on environmental factors such as water supply and sewage disposal is specifically required. The intent of these requirements is to protect purchasers, not the environment, but environmental protection may nonetheless be a by-product. For example, a land sales corporation in the Pocono Mountains of Pennsylvania has been convicted of falsely representing to purchasers that sewage could be disposed via conventional septic tanks which would be approved by local officials, while actually soil conditions were not suitable for this method of sewage disposal and local officials had not granted such approval.[1]

5. In July 1975 the U.S. Court of Appeals for the Tenth Circuit upheld a lower court decision requiring the Department of Housing

and Urban Development to prepare an environmental impact statement under the National Environmental Policy Act (NEPA)[2] before accepting a private developer's disclosure filing under the Interstate Land Sales Full Disclosure Act.[3] The Supreme Court reversed the circuit court's decision; but observed that under NEPA HUD might need to revise its regulations to require the disclosure of more environmental information.

The distinction between what is a fair deal for an individual purchaser of property and what is a fair deal for a community and its natural resources is, in fact, quickly disappearing. Even though he may not be a committed environmentalist, the individual who buys land for a second home does not want to find himself faced with an inadequate water supply, sewage problems, bad air quality, noise, and traffic congestion. The soundness of an investment, moreover, is directly affected by these factors. Thus as land becomes more and more scarce and as scientific evidence of the interrelationships of land uses accumulates, the needs of consumer and investor protection can be expected to draw closer and closer together.

It should also be pointed out that NEPA has very broad import in the realm of investor decision making since it applies across the board to federal disclosure requirements administered by the SEC. In December 1974 the U.S. District Court for the District of Columbia ordered the SEC to bring its corporate disclosure requirements "into full compliance with the letter and spirit of NEPA"[4]— a mandate which should lead, among other things, to the required disclosure of the environmental impacts, including land use impacts, of corporate activities. As discussed below, the plaintiffs in this case consider the SEC's response to the court order to be inadequate; consequently, debate and legal action on this critical issue can be expected to continue.

THE INTERSTATE LAND SALES FULL DISCLOSURE ACT

In 1969 the U.S. Congress, recognizing the tremendous growth of the land sales industry and the corresponding need for consumer protection, passed the Interstate Land Sales Full Disclosure Act.[5] Under this act it is unlawful for any developer or agent, directly or indirectly, to make use of any means of interstate commerce or the mails to sell or lease subdivision lots unless:

1. A "statement of record" has been filed with the Office of Interstate Land Sales Registration (OILSR) of the U.S. Department of Housing and Urban Development (HUD);[6] and

2. A printed "property report" which meets all OILSR requirements is furnished to every purchaser before he or she signs any contract or agreement for sale or lease.

It is also unlawful for such a developer or agent in selling or leasing, or offering to sell or lease, subdivision lots:

(A) to employ any device, scheme, or artifice to defraud, or
(B) to obtain money or property by means of a material misrepresentation with respect to any information included in the statement of record or the property report or with respect to any other information pertinent to the lot or the subdivision and upon which the purchaser relies, or
(C) to engage in any transaction, practice, or course of business which operates or would operate as a fraud or deceit upon a purchaser.[7]

Full and detailed disclosure of information about the subdivision must be made in the statement of record. The property report is a shorter document, intended to be read in full by all purchasers, which includes some of the same material as the statement of record, as well as other information required by OILSR regulations.[8] A copy of the property report must be registered with OILSR along with the statement of record. The OILSR regulations explain the requirements for the preparation and filing of both documents, setting out a specified format and detailed instructions.

Exemptions

The act exempts certain types of sales and leases from its provisions, unless the method of disposition is adopted for the purpose of evading the act.[9] In any administrative proceeding or litigation, the burden of proof rests with the developer to show that he is not attempting to evade the act.

Subject to this condition, the provisions of the act do not apply to:

1. The sale or lease of land in subdivisions which have fewer than fifty lots (there is no requirement that lots be contiguous, but only

that they be offered or sold as part of a "common promotional plan");

2. The sale or lease of lots in subdivisions where *every* lot is five acres or larger in size;

3. The sale or lease of any improved land on which there is a residential, commercial, or industrial building, or to the sale or lease of land under a contract that obliges the seller to construct such a building on the land within two years;

4. The sale or lease of real estate under or pursuant to court order;

5. The sale of evidence of indebtedness secured by a mortgage or deed of trust on real estate;

6. The sale of securities issued by a real estate investment trust;

7. The sale or lease of real estate by any government or government agency;

8. The sale or lease of cemetery lots;

9. The sale or lease of lots to any person who acquires the lots for the purpose of engaging in the business of constructing residential, commercial, or industrial buildings or for the purpose of resale or lease of such lots to persons engaged in such business; or

10. The sale or lease of real estate which is zoned by the appropriate government authority for industrial or commercial development, as long as certain other stringent requirements are met.[10]

While none of the above require a written determination of eligibility from OILSR, there is one special statutory exemption for which such a decision is necessary. Under this exemption, a subdivider does not have to register with OILSR if this office determines that *all* of the following criteria are met:

1. At the time of the sale or lease, the real estate is free and clear of all liens, encumbrances, and adverse claims;

2. Each and every purchaser or his or her spouse had made a personal on-site inspection of the land before signing a contract, and the developer submits a written affirmation of this to OILSR;

3. The developer has filed a proper claim of exemption with OILSR;

4. The developer has obtained OILSR approval of a statement detailing all reservations, restrictions, taxes, and assessments applicable to the land; and

5. This statement has been furnished to every purchaser prior to

the signing of a contract and the developer has obtained in writing the purchaser's acknowledgment of the receipt of the statement.

All of these statements, filings, and agreements in effect waive the prospective buyer's right to examine a property report containing detailed information about land for which he or she might pay thousands of dollars. The inclusion of this complicated exemption in the act stemmed from pressure to provide "on-site" exemptions, on the grounds that Congress's original intent was to regulate sight unseen sales. As has been reported in the *Federal Register,* however, "it has been OILSR's experience from the outset of the Act that a purchaser's presence on-site does not in itself afford him adequate information and protection in making a decision to purchase or not to purchase a lot."[11] In keeping with this finding, Congress in 1974 abolished another provision, discussed below, which allowed on-site purchasers to waive their revocation rights.

In all cases, prospective purchasers of lots should seek to learn as much as possible about the land. When a developer has gone to considerable trouble to avoid filing disclosure information with OILSR and furnishing property reports, prospective buyers should seek to determine why.

In addition to statutory exemptions, there are also several other exemptions which have been established by OILSR regulations, as is authorized by the act.[12] Under these, the provisions of the act do not apply to the following:

1. The sale or lease of lots when every lot will be sold for less than one hundred dollars, including closing costs, provided that the purchaser is not required to buy more than one lot.

2. The lease of lots for less than five years, provided that the lessee is not obligated to renew the lease.

3. The sale or lease of subdivision lots, numbering less than fifty and constituting 5 percent or less of the total number of lots in the subdivision, when the other lot sales or leases are exempt under other provisions (such as those exempting sales or leases of lots on which there is a residential, commercial, or industrial building).

It is also possible for a developer to file a request for an exemption order with OILSR for a subdivision of fewer than three hundred lots which are offered "entirely or almost entirely" to residents of the state in which the land is located. All advertising over which the developer has control must also be confined to that state. (An example of interstate advertising which is beyond a developer's control is the reception by television sets in New Jersey of advertising transmitted by New York City stations.) Finally, no more than 5 percent of all annual lot sales may be made to nonresidents of the state in which the subdivision is located.

OILSR also allows developers to accept what it terms "reservations" from prospective purchasers of lots or condominiums prior to filing a statement of record or property report.[13] In this permissible pre-sale activity, a purchaser may express an interest in buying or leasing property at some time in the future and may make a deposit, provided that it is placed in escrow and is fully refundable. No document purporting to be a HUD property report can be supplied to a potential purchaser when a reservation is made.

State Filings

Prior to January 1, 1975, OILSR accepted as meeting federal requirements materials initially filed under state subdivision disclosure laws in California, Florida, Hawaii, and New York. In November 1974 the agency amended the regulations which permitted this and established that after January 1, 1975, it would no longer accept state filings from these states, except in cases where subdividers already had an effective registration with state authorities by that date.[14] This change was made on the grounds that the extent of disclosure and consumer protection provided through the OILSR statement of record and property report is much greater than that mandated under the state laws. OILSR indicated that only if the states strengthened their provisions to correspond with the more demanding federal regulations, would acceptance of state filings be resumed.

Florida, and also initially California, contested OILSR's decision to cease accepting their state filings, and obtained an injunction against the OILSR action.[15] California subsequently dropped out of this suit and worked closely with OILSR to improve its state requirements. As a result of the latter effort, in December 1975 OILSR ruled that, subject to certain conditions, it would once again accept California filings as meeting federal requirements.[16] Land subdividers in Hawaii and New York are not affected by either the Florida injunction or the California reinstatement, and must prepare separate materials for state and federal filings.

OILSR's basic position on this issue is that the states should adopt the OILSR statement of record and property report for their disclosure purposes and thereby "free the State personnel to take up the important functions of substantive regulation and the day-to-day scrutiny of developer operations."[17]

The Statement of Record

The statement of record required by the act is a detailed document in which information on various physical and financial aspects of the land offerings must be disclosed. While statements of record are available for public inspection at the OILSR office in Washington, D.C., developers are not obligated to furnish copies to prospective buyers.

After receipt of a statement of record from a developer, the OILSR reviews its contents for completeness and accuracy. No lots in the subdivision may be sold or leased until the statement of record becomes effective, which occurs on the thirtieth day after the filing date, unless the developer receives prior notice either that this effective date has been suspended or that an earlier effective date has been set.

The statement of record includes comprehensive disclosure information about the subdivision. Information on all of the following must be included: the dimensions of the subdivision; its ownership; the financial and legal background and relationships of its owners; topography and climate; nuisances; permits, filings and licenses required by other authorities; the condition of the title and the conditions of the offer, including terms and selling prices; roads and access to neighboring communities; utilities; drainage and flood control; recreational and common facilities; taxes and assessments; occupancy status; shopping facilities; and the availability of all municipal services.

Property Report

Developers must also register with OILSR a copy of the printed property report. The law requires that a copy of this property report be furnished to every purchaser before a sale or lease agreement is signed. If a property report is not so furnished, the purchaser may void the agreement. The statute of limitations requires that such action to void an agreement be taken within two years of the date on which it was signed. The act further provides that if a purchaser was given a copy of the property report less than forty-eight hours before he signed a purchase or lease agreement, he has until midnight of the third business day following the transaction to revoke the agreement if he so chooses. In the original act, this "cooling-off period" extended only for forty-eight hours following signing, but it was extended by Congress to three business days in 1974.[18] Also, it was previously possible for a purchaser who had personally inspected the property to waive his revocation rights, but this provision was stricken from the law by the same congressional action.

The requirements which the property report must meet are set out in detail in the OILSR regulations. These disclosure requirements were significantly broadened and strengthened by new regulations promulgated in 1973 and 1974.[19] Developers must now report whether the subdivision or any of the parties involved in its development have been or are parties to any disciplinary proceedings, bankruptcies, or litigation "which may materially affect lot purchasers in [the] subdivision." Statements must be made regarding the availability and cost to the purchaser of roads, utilities (including water supply and sewage disposal), and municipal services. It must be stated whether or not the developer has a program in effect to control soil erosion, sedimentation, and flooding throughout the entire subdivision. If there is such a program, it must be described. "Unusual conditions" affecting the subdivision must also be listed and fully explained. These include factors which affect the environment and safety of the subdivision, such as flooding and other natural hazards, as well as air pollution, traffic hazards, and unusual noises. The developer's obligations regarding proposed recreational facilities must be clearly stated and estimated completion dates must be given.

An audited and certified financial statement must now be furnished to buyers as an exhibit to the property report if the subdivision has three hundred or more lots or if the aggregate price of all lots is more than $500,000. This statement must also be registered with OILSR. After the first filing, however, the developer is required to submit annual audited statements "only if they disclose a material adverse effect on the developer's financial position." The financial strength of the developer is of concern to the lot purchaser since the price paid for a subdivision lot typically includes costs of proposed improvements to be made by the developer. In view of this, audited and certified financial statements should be required of all subdivisions, regardless of their size.

What must not be forgotten, however, is that all the disclosures in the world are worthless unless they are read and understood. Developers routinely reveal to OILSR that the land they wish to sell is remote, or submerged, or covered with stumps which the buyer must clear at his own expense. Such negative information is reported in compliance with the law by developers who are confident that not many buyers will be able to pick out flaws which are embedded in a long, intimidating document.

OILSR believes that people should recognize that the purchase of land is usually an expensive and complex undertaking, and that those who are prepared to invest thousands of dollars in a parcel of land should also be prepared to seek assistance in interpreting a property report, even if such consultation costs money. It is, to be sure, much less expensive to refuse an offer on the basis of a clear understanding of detailed information than to seek legal remedies after a contract has been signed.

Advertising Standards

In 1973 OILSR promulgated regulations governing advertising of subdivisions covered by the act.[20] These regulations are described by OILSR as an effort to define for developers the kind of advertising which it considers unlawful under the act and capable of triggering its authority to seek injunctions or restraining orders. The detail of the thirty-five advertising guidelines provided reflect the ingenuity with which some developers have misled consumers in the past.

The OILSR regulations forbid advertisements containing false or misleading statements, pictures, or sketches, as well as misleading omissions. It is also illegal for advertisements to contradict statements made in the statement of record, the property report, or any required financial statements. The front page of all printed advertisements must bear a statement (1) advising potential buyers to obtain a property report from the developer and to read it before signing anything, and (2) stating that HUD has not approved the offer in any way.

Specific examples are given of the kind of misleading or vague advertising that is prohibited. Maps must be drawn to scale, and terms like "minutes away" cannot be used unless actual road distances are also indicated. Advertising which refers to roads and streets, lot sizes, improvements, predevelopment price bargains, public facilities, property exchange privileges, water supply, sewage disposal, and resale schemes must be accompanied by detailed clarifying information.

An inference which can be reasonably drawn from advertising material is considered by OILSR to be a positive assertion of fact, unless the inference is negated in clear and unmistakable terms in the same material. If, for example, lots are advertised, OILSR considers that it can be inferred that these lots can be used immediately, that all major subsurface improvements necessary for the construction of dwellings have been made, and that roads, potable water, and sewage disposal facilities are available.

Condominiums

In recent years, condominiums have become an increasingly common type of property ownership. In this type of development, individual dwelling units are purchased outright and common property and facilities (such as hallways, swimming pools, and grounds) are owned collectively by all residents. As is discussed later in this chapter, condominiums which are sold primarily as managed investments must be registered with the U.S. Securities and Exchange Commission.

In the *Federal Register* of September 4, 1973, OILSR clarified its policy regarding the application of the Interstate Land Sales Full Disclosure Act to condominiums.[21] As explained there, OILSR views a condominium as "equivalent to a subdivision, each unit being a lot." Thus for the sale of a condominium unit to be exempted from the act "either it must be completed before it is sold, or it must be sold under a contract obligating the seller to erect the unit within two years from the date the purchaser signs the contract of sale." In February 1974 OILSR published additional guidelines specifying that in the case of "primary residence condominiums in metropolitan areas," a unit must be ready for occupancy within two years to qualify for exemption; in the case of "condominiums in which the promotion of the common facilities is the primary inducement to purchase" (such as those in recreational developments), such facilities as well as the individual unit sold must be completed within two years.[22] Any delays in construction must be legally supportable as beyond the control of the developer.

Penalties and Enforcement

The Interstate Land Sales Full Disclosure Act has a three-pronged enforcement scheme:

1. *Civil liability.* Under the act, a buyer can void a sales or lease agreement if he was not given a property report before signing the agreement. If he received the property report within forty-eight hours before signing, he may revoke the agreement at any time up until midnight of the third business day following the transaction.[23] A purchaser may also sue the developer for damages if the latter makes an untrue statement or fails to state a material fact in the statement of record or the property report.[24]

2. *Administrative remedies.* The Administrator of OILSR may suspend a subdivider's statement of record, if any untrue statement or omission of a material fact occurs in this document.[25] If the developer corrects the statement of record, it can be reinstated, but no sales or leases can be made while the suspension is in effect. OILSR is authorized to make investigations concerning possible violations of the act or OILSR regulations and to publish findings.[26]

3. *Injunctions and prosecution of offenses.* The Administrator of OILSR may bring an action in a federal district court for a temporary or permanent injunction or restraining order whenever it appears that a subdivider is engaged in or is about to engage in acts or practices in violation of the act or OILSR regulations. OILSR is empowered to transmit evidence of alleged violations to the U.S. Attorney's office for criminal prosecution under the act.[27] The penalty for willfully violating any provision of the act or OILSR regulations is a fine of up to five thousand dollars and imprisonment for up to five years, or both.[28]

Enforcement action by OILSR under the act has been sporadic in the past, but examples of effective enforcement which demonstrate the potential of the act can be cited. In June 1973 the U.S. Attorney for the Southern District of New York brought a forty-two count indictment against the Pocono International Corporation and its principal stockholder that was based in large part on violations of the act.[29] This indictment alleged that Pocono International had used several means of interstate commerce and the mails to offer and sell subdivided lands in the Pocono Mountains of Pennsylvania for which no statement of record had been filed with OILSR, as required by the act. It also alleged that the developers had falsely represented to prospective lot purchasers that sewage could be disposed of by means of conventional septic tanks which would be approved by local officials, while in fact soil conditions were not suitable for this method of sewage disposal and town officials had not granted such approval. In June 1974 the defendants were convicted on twenty counts of the indictment, and the second circuit court of appeals affirmed this conviction in November 1975.

In June 1974 OILSR added field representatives to its staff for the first time. These thirty new employees of the Land Sales Enforcement Division are stationed in offices throughout the country and are responsible both for seeking out unregistered subdivisions and for uncovering fraudulent practices by registered subdivisions. Presently, OILSR has approximately ten thousand statements of record on file, and relies heavily on citizen complaints for the initiation of investigative and enforcement actions.

Compliance with NEPA

As has been mentioned, the federal appeals court for the tenth circuit has affirmed a district court decision requiring HUD to prepare an environmental impact statement under NEPA prior to approving the statement of record and property report submitted by a private developer.[30] In the case under litigation, OILSR accepted a disclosure filing from the Flint Ridge Development Company for a three thousand lot subdivision in eastern Oklahoma. This subdivision is located along the banks of the Illinois River, which has been designated as a "scenic river" by the state of Oklahoma. The district court found that the river possesses substantial aesthetic qualities, pointing out that it was these very qualities which led the subdividers to undertake development in this location. However, the courts saw that when septic tanks were installed in the very porous soil of the area, contamination of the river would result. In the words of the district court, this pollution would "destroy forever the environmental quality of the Illinois River Basin."[31]

The circuit court held that OILSR can prevent this environmental damage from occurring, since it is authorized to suspend a statement of record and thereby prevent the developer from raising funds in interstate commerce. Consequently, the court ruled that OILSR's approval of the developer's statement of record and property report was a major federal action significantly affecting the quality of the human environment, and enjoined HUD and OILSR from approving the Flint Ridge filing until an EIS is prepared.

In June 1976 the Supreme Court reversed the circuit court's decision, ruling that NEPA's impact statement requirement was inapplicable here since it would conflict with the statutory requirement that statements of record go into effect thirty days after they are filed, absent inaccurate or incomplete disclosure. The Court observed, however, that this does not foreclose the possibility that under NEPA the regulations of OILSR might have to be revised to require the disclosure of more environmental information.

Citizen Action

The Interstate Land Sales Full Disclosure Act was drafted primarily to protect the interests of purchasers of land. Still, it has indirect value as a tool for environmental protection. The act does not generate land use planning, but specific disclosure information about environmental factors is required in statements of record and property reports, and misrepresentations or omissions can lead to the suspension of statements of record and injunctions, as well as to criminal prosecutions.

Concerned citizens should be aware of the act's requirements and of procedures for enforcement so that they can detect violations, report them to the proper authorities, and press for enforcement action. Although OILSR has greatly increased its enforcement staff, citizen complaints will continue to play a vital role in triggering investigations. Anyone who has reason to believe that a subdivider who is selling fifty lots or more, any one of which is less than five acres, has not registered with OILSR and is not providing a property report to purchasers should notify the nearest office of the U.S. Attorney and OILSR at the following address:

Land Sales Enforcement Division
Office of Interstate Land Sales Registration
U.S. Department of Housing and Urban Development (HUD)
451 Seventh Street, S.W.
Washington, D.C. 20410

Material misrepresentations and/or omissions in a property report or in advertising, as well as any fraudulent practices, should also be reported. For a fee of $2.50, OILSR will send a copy of the property report for a specific subdivision to anyone who requests it. Statements of record are available for public examination only at the OILSR office in Washington.

Violations or suspected violations can be reported to OILSR or an office of the U.S. Attorney by means of a personal letter or telephone call, but it is more effective to write or call on behalf of a citizens' group, a committee, or a homeowners' association.

Finally, all prospective property buyers should make sure that they receive a property report when one is required and that they follow the advice which must now be overprinted in large capital letters on the front page of every property report: "PURCHASER SHOULD READ THIS DOCUMENT BEFORE SIGNING ANYTHING." Professional help in interpreting this document should be sought if necessary. OILSR further advises against purchasing land under pressure from real estate salesmen or without actually having seen the land.

SEC DISCLOSURE REQUIREMENTS

1. Registration of Condominiums and Co-ops Sold Primarily as Managed Investment Opportunities

Each year an increasing number of condominiums are being offered for sale throughout the country. While at one time condominiums were built almost exclusively in urban and resort areas, they are now becoming more and more common in suburban and rural areas.[32] Some of these condominiums, as well as some cooperative apartment projects, fall within the scope of federal securities legislation[33] and are thus subject to disclosure requirements which are administered by the U.S. Securities and Exchange Commission (SEC).

In the condominium form of ownership the owner of each condominium unit usually has an undivided interest in or title to his individual unit and also a part interest or share in common facilities and areas such as lounges, pools, or grounds. Some condominium developers simply wish to sell each unit in a project to purchasers who will be owner-occupiers. Other developers or promoters, especially in vacation areas, offer special rental arrangements such as a "rental pool" agreement in which unit owners place their units in an "inventory" of condominiums which are rented out on a revolving basis by a managing agent.[34] Typically, under such agreements the rents received on all units and the expenses incurred are pooled, and individual owners receive ratable shares of the proceeds whether or not their own units were actually rented. Arrangements of this type are obviously designed for those who do not want to use their units full-time. The condominium's managing agent takes on the day-to-day chores of attracting, servicing, and supervising transient, short-term rentals. The pooling of available units assures each participant of a fair share of the project's overall renting potential, avoids competition among unit owners, and spreads the risk of vacancies.

The SEC holds that the offer of a condominium unit together with the offer of an opportunity to participate in such a rental pool, designed to be used by unit owners for investment purposes and dependent on the services of a specified agent, involves the offer of an investment contract which must be registered with the SEC, unless exempted on other grounds.

The SEC describes the kind of condominiums the offering of which would constitute the offering of a security in a release entitled *Guidelines as to the Applicability of the Federal Securities Laws to Offers and Sales of Condominiums or Units in a Real Estate Development.*[35] As stated in this release, if any one of the following elements is involved in a condominium offering, it will be viewed as the offering of an investment contract which must be registered with the SEC:

a. Offering participation in a rental pool arrangement to the unit owner;

b. Offering a condominium which has any rental arrangement or similar service with emphasis on the economic benefits that the purchaser will derive from the managerial efforts of the promoter or a third party chosen by the promoter;

c. Offering a rental arrangement in which the purchaser must hold his unit available for rental for any part of the year, must use an exclusive rental agent, or is otherwise materially restricted in the occupancy or rental of his unit; or

d. Offering participation in a condominium project in which there are commercial facilities in the common holdings which (1) provide income which is not used simply to offset common area expenses, and (2) are more than incidental to the project as a whole and are established as a primary income source for unit owners.

The SEC does not consider a continuing affiliation between developers or promoters and unit owners in the form of maintenance arrangements for the upkeep of buildings and grounds to bring a project under its jurisdiction.

The SEC guidelines point out that it is very difficult to anticipate the wide variety of arrangements that may be involved in a condominium offering. There may, in fact, be other situations not covered by the guidelines where a condominium offer would constitute an offering of securities. The guidelines conclude with the following statements: "Whether an offering of securities is involved necessarily depends on the facts and circumstances of each particular case. The staff of the [Securities and Exchange] Commission will be available to respond to written inquiries on such mattes."

Some cooperative apartment projects are also subject to SEC registration. In the cooperative housing form of ownership, a corporation owns an apartment building or buildings and sells shares, coupled with proprietary leases for individual units, to residents or prospective residents. Such offerings are exempt from the requirements of federal securities legislation if they meet exacting standards set forth in SEC regulations.[36] Basically the units exempted under these regulations are those sold for owner-occupancy. More complex co-op offerings which have "investment contract" features, involving rental pool arrangements, exclusive rental agent provisions, or other investment management services, are subject to SEC registration requirements.

Under the Securities Act of 1933[37] it is unlawful for any person "directly or indirectly" to sell or to offer to sell any security "by means of instruments of transportation or communication in interstate commerce or of the mails," unless a registration statement is filed with the SEC and a prospectus which meets the disclosure requirements of the act is given to each offeree or purchaser before or during an offer or sale. In other words, before a condominium involving an investment contract can be offered for sale, a comprehensive disclosure statement must be filed with the SEC and a prospectus which discloses material information for prospective purchasers must be provided before or during the offer or sale of each condominum unit. The penalties for failure to comply with these provisions include civil sanctions (suits by purchasers for restitution or damages),[38] criminal penalties ($5,000 fines and/or five years' imprisonment for willful violations of the act),[39] and administrative remedies (suspension of the registration statement by the SEC).[40]

Prohibitions applicable to advertising and sales practices used in the sale of condominiums which must be registered with the SEC are discussed in the SEC release *Advertising and Sales Practices in Connection with Offers and Sales of Securities Involving Condominium Units and Other Units in Real Estate Developments.*[41] The following restrictions are of prime importance:

a. Disseminating sales literature or advertising prior to the required registration of a condominium would constitute an illegal offer. (Certain notices by the seller that he intends to make an offering which will be registered with the SEC are not covered by this restriction if they are made in accordance with SEC regulations.[42])

b. No purchase price payments, deposits, or purchase commitments may be accepted, nor may indications of interest be solicited prior to the filing of the registration statement.

c. Once the registration statement is filed but before it becomes effective: (1) offers may be made, but no *written offer* may be made except by means of a proper preliminary prospectus; and (2) indications of interest may be taken, but no payments, deposits, or purchase commitments may be accepted, even if they are placed in escrow or are fully refundable.

d. After the effective date of the registration statement, *sales* may be made only if a proper final prospectus is provided to every offeree before or during every written offer. Supplemental sales literature may be sent to a prospective investor only if it is accompanied by a prospectus and if the literature is not false or misleading.

Federal securities laws exempt certain types of offerings from registration. The SEC and the courts generally view these exemptions narrowly, however, and most condominiums which are offered for sale as managed investments will not be exempt. The following are two notable exemptions:

a. *The intrastate exemption.* The Securities Act of 1933 exempts from registration those securities which are offered for sale and sold entirely within one state.[43] To qualify for this exemption, the offeror, all purchasers, and all offerees must be residents of the same state. If an *offer* is made to only one person who is not a resident of that state, the exemption is lost.

b. *The private offering exemption.* The act also exempts "transactions by an issuer not involving any public offering."[44] In other words, offers are exempt which are so limited as to be private in character. This exemption is of little consequence with respect to condominium sales, since it is virtually impossible under the usual marketing and advertising techniques of developers to sell condominium units in this way.

It should be noted, however, that since 1933 there have been many suits and much debate on the issue of exactly what constitutes a private offering. The courts have consistently held that the private offering exemption cannot be mechanically based on the fact that only a given number of offerees are involved in a particular project. The ultimate test of the exemption has been held to be whether the offerees' associations with, or knowledge of, the offeror is such that they have available to them the information which would otherwise be provided by the registration requirements and thus do not need the protection necessary in public offerings.[45] More exact guidelines have been established by a new SEC regulation, "rule 146," which became effective on June 10, 1974.[46] This rule established that a *sale* of securities to thirty-five people or less will be considered a private offering if certain investor tests are met, notably if all purchasers are adequately informed or have access to adequate information about the issuer.

Citizen Action

Citizens who are concerned about particular condominium developments should seek answers to the following questions:

a. Does the condominium offering have any of the investment contract features (rental pool, mandatory rental arrangements, extensive commercial facilities) described above?

b. If so, has the condominium been registered with the SEC and is a formal prospectus being supplied before or with every written offer?

c. Are there any misleading statements or serious omissions in the prospectus?

If a condominium appears to be subject to SEC jurisdiction and (a) it has not been registered, or (b) a proper prospectus is not being provided before or with every written offer, or (c) misleading statements or omissions exist in the prospectus, a full written report should be filed with the SEC and the advice of SEC officials should be sought. Registration of investment contract condominiums is handled in the Washington office of the SEC by the following division:

Division of Corporation Finance
U.S. Securities and Exchange Commission (SEC)
500 North Capitol Street
Washington, D.C. 20549

Because of the many possible complexities, citizens may wish to consult a securities attorney. If it turns out that a violation of federal securities laws or regulations has occurred, the SEC should be pressed to take appropriate enforcement action.

2. SEC Compliance with NEPA

In December 1974 the U.S. District Court for the District of Columbia held that the SEC's promulgation of regulations implementing its obligations under NEPA failed to meet the requirements of the Administrative Procedure Act and ordered the commission to undertake further rule making to bring its corporate disclosure regulations "into full compliance with the letter and spirit of NEPA."[47] In the legal action which led to this decision the Natural Resources Defense Council (NRDC), as a plaintiff in the case, contended that all reporting corporations should be required to submit to the SEC meaningful information concerning the environmental impacts of their corporate activities and what actions they are taking to reduce adverse effects.[48] The court found that the importance of NRDC's position was underscored by the large number of "ethical investors" in the country who have large sums of money to invest and need this type of information to make investment and voting decisions in accordance with their principles.

NRDC maintains that in order to comply fully with NEPA, the SEC must require substantive environmental disclosures. Among the environmental effects which NRDC believes corporations should be required to disclose are land use impacts associated with such activities as strip mining, clear-cutting, the development of second-home or suburban subdivisions or resort complexes, the construction of transportation facilities, the sale of off-road vehicles, the development of shopping centers and other complexes, and the disposal of solid wastes. For example, corporations constructing "investment contract" condominiums, discussed in the preceding section, should be required to disclose the impact of their projects on water pollution, water supply, critical areas such as wetlands or dunes, parking-related air pollution, and solid waste disposal.

During the first half of 1975 the SEC conducted a three-month public proceeding, including public hearings, during which substantial investor interest in environmental disclosures was demonstrated. Nonetheless, in November 1975 the commission published proposed regulations which did not provide for the disclosure of any substantive environmental information.[49] These proposed regulations would have required a registrant only to submit a list of its most recently filed "environmental compliance reports" indicating that the registrant had failed to satisfy, at any time within the previous twelve months, environmental standards established pursuant to federal statutes.[50] In its final regulations, promulgated in May 1976,[51] the SEC dropped even the requirement for such a list. It decided to respond to the court order not by expanding its disclosure requirements but simply by specifying more explicitly the types of capital expenditures for environmental control facilities that registrants are required to disclose.

Consequently, although the SEC has now fulfilled certain procedural rule-making requirements, NRDC does not consider that the commission has met its responsibilities under NEPA and will seek further judicial review. Citizen support will continue to be needed in this effort to compel the SEC to bring its corporate disclosure requirements "into full compliance with the letter and spirit of NEPA," as required by the federal district court.

LAWS PROHIBITING MAIL FRAUD

Under federal law it is a crime to use the mails for the purpose of carrying out fraud, a prime example of which would be the intentional misrepresentation of truth to induce sales of land, homes, or condominiums.[52] Sending promotional materials through the mails which use "false or fraudulent pretenses, representations, or promises" to sell land or dwellings would constitute mail fraud, as would the use of the mails to receive checks or transmit deeds in a fraudulent scheme. Further, it is a crime for a developer or promoter to use "a fictitious, false, or assumed title, name, or address or name other than his own proper name" in connection with a fraudulent sales scheme conducted through the mails.[53]

The use of interstate or foreign communication via radio, television, telephone, or telegraph to perpetrate fraud is also unlawful. Anyone who "transmits or causes to be transmitted by means of wire [telephone or telegraph], radio, or television communication in interstate or foreign commerce any writings, signs, signals, pictures or sounds" for the purpose of fraud commits a federal crime.[54]

The penalty for each of these crimes is a fine of not more than one thousand dollars or imprisonment for not more than five years, or both.

Citizen Action

A concerned citizen who has good reason to believe that a developer or promoter may be violating any of the above provisions of federal law in the promotion of land, homes, or condominiums should notify the nearest office of the U.S. Attorney.

NOTES

1. United States v. Goldberg, 527 F.2d 165 (2d Cir. 1975).

2. 42 U.S.C. § 4321 *et seq.* See Chapter 3 for a full discussion of NEPA.

3. Scenic Rivers Association v. Lynn, 382 F. Supp. 69, 7 ERC 1172 (E.D. Okla. 1974), *aff'd*, 520 F.2d 240, 8 ERC 1021 (10th Cir. 1975), *rev'd sub nom.* Hills v. Scenic Rivers Association, 44 U.S.L.W. 4954 (June 24, 1976).

4. Natural Resources Defense Council v. Securities and Exchange Commission, 389 F. Supp. 689, 693, 7 ERC 1199, 1200 (D.D.C. 1974).

5. 15 U.S.C. § 1701 *et seq.*

6. The Secretary of HUD was authorized by the act to establish the OILSR to administer the act's provisions.

7. 15 U.S.C. § 1703 (a) (2).

8. The OILSR regulations are found at 24 C.F.R. § 1700 *et seq.*

9. 15 U.S.C. § 1702; 24 C.F.R. § 1710.10 *et seq.* OILSR issued guidelines on statutory and regulatory exemptions to the act in October 1975. 40 *Federal Register* 47166 (October 8, 1975).

10. This exemption was added by the Housing and Community Development Act of 1974 (Public Law No. 93–383 [August 22, 1974], which included amendments to the Interstate Land Sales Full Disclosure Act. Regulations implementing these new amendments were promulgated at 39 *Federal Register* 38098 (October 29, 1974); 24 C.F.R. Part 1710.

11. 38 *Federal Register* 23873 (September 4, 1973).

12. 24 C.F.R. § 1710.13 *et seq.*

13. 40 *Federal Register* 47167 (October 8, 1975).

14. 39 *Federal Register* 39719 (November 11, 1974).

15. Florida v. Hills, Civil No. 74–790 (M.D. Fla., filed December 20, 1974).

16. 40 *Federal Register* 56907 (December 5, 1975).

17. 39 *Federal Register* 39719 (November 11, 1974).

18. 15 U.S.C. § 1703 (b).

19. See 38 *Federal Register* 23866 (September 4, 1973), 24 C.F.R. Parts 1700, 1710, 1715, and 1720; 39 *Federal Register* 7824 (February 28, 1974); 39 *Federal Register* 9431 (March 11, 1974); 24 C.F.R. §§ 1710.13 and 1710.26; and 39 *Federal Register* 38098 (October 29, 1974), 24 C.F.R. Part 1710.

20. 38 *Federal Register* 23897 (September 4, 1973); 24 C.F.R. Part 1715.

21. 38 *Federal Register* 23866 (September 4, 1973).

22. 39 *Federal Register* 7825 (February 28, 1974).

23. 15 U.S.C. § 1703 (b).

24. 15 U.S.C. § 1709.

25. 15 U.S.C. § 1706.

26. 15 U.S.C. § 1714 (b).

27. 15 U.S.C. § 1714 (a).

28. 15 U.S.C. § 1717.

29. United States v. Goldberg, 527 F.2d 165 (2d Cir. 1975).

30. Scenic Rivers Association v. Lynn, 382 F. Supp. 69, 7 ERC 1172 (E.D. Okla. 1974), *aff'd*, 520 F.2d 240, 8 ERC 1021 (10th Cir. 1975), *rev'd sub nom,* Hills v. Scenic Rivers Association, 44 U.S.L.W. 4954 (June 24, 1976).

31. 382 F. Supp. at 73.

32. On July 4, 1974, the Federal Trade Commission announced that it would undertake a nationwide investigation of the development and management of residential condominiums. The intent of this investigation was to determine whether companies that build, sell, or operate condominiums "have been or are engaging in unfair or deceptive practices in connection with these activites." This investigation, which might have led to broad new federal rules governing activities of the industry and legal actions on specific issues, was abruptly terminated by the commission without explanation in March 1975.

33. 15 U.S.C. § 77a *et seq.*

34. A number of hotels are now being converted to "rental pool" condominiums.

35. SEC Securities Act Release No. 33–5347, issued January 4, 1973; 38 *Federal Register* 1735 (January 18, 1973).

36. 17 C.F.R. § 230.235.

37. 15 U.S.C. § 77a *et seq.*

38. 15 U.S.C. § 77h and § 771.

39. 15 U.S.C. § 77q and § 77x.

40. 15 U.S.C. § 77h.

41. SEC Securities Act Release No. 33–5382, issued April 9, 1973; 38 *Federal Register* 9587 (April 18, 1973).

42. 17 C.F.R. § 230.135.

43. 15 U.S.C. § 77c (a) (11).

44. 15 U.S.C. § 77d (2).

45. Securities and Exchange Commission v. Ralston Purina Co., 346 U.S. 119 (1953).

46. 17 C.F.R. § 230.146; 39 *Federal Register* 15266 (May 2, 1974); 40 *Federal Register* 21709 (May 19, 1975).

47. Natural Resources Defense Council v. Securities and Exchange Commission, 389 F. Supp. 689, 693, 7 ERC 1199, 1200 (D.D.C. 1974).

48. The plaintiffs also argued that the SEC should require corporations to disclose statistics pertaining to their equal employment practices. The SEC chose not to propose regulations for this kind of disclosure. 40 *Federal Register* 51656–51657 (November 6, 1975).

49. 40 *Federal Register* 51656 (November 6, 1975).

50. See 40 *Federal Register* 58155 (December 15, 1975) for a vague discussion by the SEC of environmental compliance reports, concerning which the SEC had little knowledge when it issued its proposed environmental disclosure regulations.

51. 41 *Federal Register* 21632 (May 27, 1976).

52. 18 U.S.C. § 1341.

53. 18 U.S.C. § 1342.

54. 18 U.S.C. § 1343.

CHAPTER 10

Transportation Facilities

TRANSPORTATION FACILITIES HAVE a profound effect on land use, since they are prime determinants of where people choose to live and where businesses and industries locate. This chapter will discuss the basic federal statutes governing federal aid for and regulation of the planning and construction of highways, mass transit, railroads, and airports. Primary emphasis will be placed on the federal-aid highway program, since in the last fifty years the highway and the automobile have had the most significant impact on patterns of land use and development and have involved the most serious and widespread environmental problems.

HIGHWAYS

At one time roads and automobile use were widely and enthusiastically viewed as manifestations of progress. The initiation of the interstate system in 1956, for example, was greeted as a significant technological advance. As complex road systems have been built, however, their many negative effects have become increasingly apparent to the public.

Highways have been one of the major stimulants of growth in the metropolitan areas of this country. By opening up hitherto inaccessible rural areas, they have drawn residential, commercial, and industrial development out of existing developed areas onto vacant land. The results have been sprawl residential development, strip commercial development, and outlying industrial parks—a pattern which has involved very high environmental, economic, and social costs.[1] Rapid, uncontrolled growth in rural areas has been accompanied by prodigal destruction or waste of limited natural resources, severe disruption of ecological systems, and destruction of the way of life of rural communities. Sprawl has led to high levels of energy consumption, not only because it necessitates increased automobile usage, but also because widely dispersed development entails great wastes of energy. The movement of businesses and industries out into the suburbs and beyond has, moreover, pulled jobs and services out of the range of public transportation and thus away from those people who are most dependent on mass transit—namely, the poor, the old, and the handicapped.

Highway and road systems also directly use large areas of land. For example, one mile of interstate highway requires up to forty-eight acres; some 26 million acres of rural land in the United States are devoted to transportation systems; and in some cities, over two-thirds of the land area is consumed by streets and parking facilities.[2] In their demands for land, roads displace families, businesses, and farms; divide or dislocate neighborhoods and communities; destroy housing; and claim historic sites, parks, and critical natural areas.

The environmental effects of providing and sustaining road systems are considerable. Highway construction, with the earth disruption it involves, is a major cause of soil erosion and increased sediment loads in rivers and streams. The paved surfaces produced are nonabsorbent and create increased storm water runoff, often laden with oil and other pollutants, that contributes both to flooding and to water pollution.[3] Furthermore, motor vehicle traffic is a primary source of both air and noise pollution. The U.S. Environmental Protection Agency's estimated emissions of air pollutants in 1969 indicated that, nationwide, transportation contributed 73 percent of the carbon monoxide, 52 percent of the hydrocarbons, and 47 percent of the nitrogen oxides in the ambient air.[4] In major urban areas where motor vehicle use is most intense, transportation is responsible for a substantially greater share of our air pollution problems. In our most congested cities air pollutant concentrations are at levels damaging to human health a large percentage of the time. Noise pollution is another very serious impact. In 1972 an EPA study found that "[o]f all the irritant noise sources in both urban and rural settings, traffic noise has been isolated as the most significant."[5]

The automobile is also our least efficient means of transport in terms of energy consumption. For example, studies have shown that an ordinary bus in urban travel is almost six times as efficient as the automobile, traveling the equivalent of forty passenger miles per gallon of gasoline compared to the automobile's seven passenger miles per gallon.[6]

Finally, millions of people are killed or injured in highway accidents each year. The National Safety Council reported that in 1974 a total of 3,646,200 people were killed or injured in motor vehicle accidents.[7]

In summary, highways and motor vehicle transportation impose a very heavy toll on the environment, on energy consumption, and on public health and well-being. The automobile has played a central role in our society, but its demands and costs have now become so great that we must consider alternatives. The momentum and complexity which the federal-aid highway program has developed over time are major forces working against this critically needed reorientation.

The Federal Role in Highway Construction

Each year the federal government distributes billions of dollars for highway planning and construction through the federal-aid highway program, which is administered by the Federal Highway Administration (FHWA) of the U.S. Department of Transportation (DOT). Under this program, state highway departments receive reimbursement from the federal government for a percentage of the costs of planning, designing, and constructing highways in the interstate, primary, secondary, and urban systems. Ninety percent federal reimbursement is available for roads in the interstate system, and 70 percent is available for those in other systems. Routes in the urban system are selected by appropriate local officials, with the concurrence of the state highway department.

The federal funds expended for highways come primarily from the Highway Trust Fund, which was established in 1956. The revenues of this fund are derived from highway-related excise taxes, such as those on gasoline, oil, trucks, buses, and tires, and have in the past been spent exclusively on highways. As will be discussed in the next section on mass transit, more recent legislation has authorized the use of monies from the Highway Trust Fund for certain kinds of public transportation projects.

The workings of the federal-aid highway program are very complex and have for many years been shrouded in the further obscurity of unpublished, often obtainable memoranda. In the past few years, DOT has begun to promulgate FHWA directives and policies as official regulations in the *Code of Federal Regulations* and has been required by court order to publish other materials in the *Federal Register*.[8] Nonetheless, despite the increased availability and more regularized format of federal highway regulations, this is still a very complicated field in which there is procedural complexity, lack of clarity on a number of issues, and much litigation, as well as variation among the states and the different FHWA regional offices. In addition, during the past several years new mechanisms—such as "action plans" and "certification acceptance," which are explained below—have been developed as means of delegating increased responsibilities to the states. Since these measures are in the early stages of implementation, it is not yet clear exactly how they will work. Further, the states themselves are at different stages of implementation; thus the degree to which state procedures have replaced certain federal procedures varies from state to state. This discussion seeks to identify major aspects of the federal-aid highway program and to explain critical statutory and regulatory requirements which must be met. Every effort is made to clarify as much as possible, within the constraints of limited space, the many overlays of complexity which exist in the federal-aid highway program.

The following types of federal approvals are required by statute and may be encountered by citizens in disputes regarding particular federal-aid highways:

1. System approval: Federal approval of the state highway department's designation or redesignation of a general highway route (not a *specific* corridor) to one of the four federal systems—interstate, primary, secondary, and urban.[9]

2. Program approval: Federal approval of projects submitted by state highway departments in annual programs of projects under Section 105 of Title 23 of the U.S. Code (hereafter, the Federal-Aid Highway Act). These annual submissions are composed of projects which have emerged from the state or metropolitan planning pro-

cesses, and each project included must receive individual approval. A "project" may refer to all work on a particular segment or segments of a highway or it may refer to different types or items of work such as planning studies, surveying, right-of-way acquisition, demolition, grading, or paving. Thus, for example, a state may propose a project for all work needed to complete a highway twenty miles in length or it may divide this work into a series of projects, such as a planning project for the entire highway, a right-of-way acquisition project for ten miles, a grading and paving project for three miles, and so on.

The states have been required by FHWA to identify all projects submitted for program approval as falling within one or more of the following categories: preliminary engineering, acquisition of rights-of-way, and actual construction.[10] Preliminary engineering includes such critical activities as route studies to determine the most desirable location among alternative possibilities. Studies of the acquisition of rights-of-way at alternative locations might be identified as either preliminary engineering or acquisition of rights-of-way. More recent FHWA regulations speak in terms of the following stages of highway development: the system planning stage, the location stage, the design stage, and the actual construction stage. For example, they provide the following definitions of pre-construction stages:

(1) *System planning stage.* Regional analysis of transportation needs and the identification of transportation corridors.
(2) *Location stage.* From the end of system planning through the selection of a particular location.
(3) *Design stage.* From the selection of a particular location to the start of construction.[11]

3. Plans, specifications, and estimates (PS&E) approval: Federal approval of surveys, plans, specifications, and estimates which describe location and design features and construction requirements.[12] This approval is required for all federal-aid highway projects (including those falling under preliminary engineering, right-of-way acquisition, and actual construction). It contractually obligates the federal government to reimburse a state highway department for the federal share of the project's costs, if the state completes all work in accordance with the plans and specifications and complies with all other federal laws and regulations. Under an alternative procedure called "certification acceptance," the states are not required to obtain

PS&E and other regulatory federal approvals if they meet certain other conditions.

Several additional types of federal approvals are required by FHWA regulations. Two of these, location approval and design approval, were established by FHWA as part of the implementation of legislation, discussed below, requiring public hearings and consideration of economic, social, and environmental impacts.[13] Another regulatory provision states that no work may be undertaken on a project until FHWA grants authorization to proceed.[14] In fact, unless a state has opted for certification acceptance, federal authorizations to proceed with various stages of work and actually to spend money are required throughout the highway construction process. For example, no project may be advertised for bids until so authorized by the FHWA division engineer, who must also concur in the award of contracts.[15]

The planning and construction of a highway is a lengthy process, usually extending over a period of from seven to ten years. The manner in which federal money from the Highway Trust Fund is made available to the states has, however, strongly encouraged a piecemeal approach to highway construction.[16] Briefly stated, Congress periodically authorizes the Secretary of Transportation to apportion monies from this fund among the states for the interstate, primary, secondary, and urban systems—reflecting the system designations which have been made by the states and approved by FHWA. At the time of this apportionment, funds are not designated for particular highways, but are available to the states for projects which they propose for federal approval in their annual programs of projects under Section 105. When a state receives the required program approval for a particular project, then FHWA designates the federal share of the costs involved as available only for that project. Therefore, if a state proposed a large-scale project, FHWA would designate all the federal funds needed for it as available for that project alone, even though considerable time might be required to complete the project.

In addition, by statute, sums apportioned to a state are available for expenditure in that state for only two years after the end of the fiscal year in which they were apportioned.[17] This does not mean that all funds actually have to be spent during this period, but that the federal government must become contractually obligated to pay out the federal share of the project costs. Thus, if there were delays in a state's obtainment of PS&E approval or authorizations to proceed with work, the state could lose the part of its apportionment reserved for the project in question.[18]

These conditions have led the states to divide the work required to complete a highway into many smaller projects rather than tie up their apportionments with large-scale undertakings, plus run the risk of losing the authority to spend apportioned funds if delays are encountered. Consequently, during the period of time required to plan and construct a section of highway between two points, many different projects each of which must receive program approval, PS&E approval, and a series of FHWA authorizations to proceed, are likely to be involved.

This fragmented approach to highway construction has made it very difficult to establish and enforce needed federal environmental restraints. In 1969 when FHWA introduced location and design approvals as major features of its implementation of new statutory requirements regarding public hearings and review of environmental impact, there was considerable confusion, as well as litigation, concerning how these approvals related to existing FHWA procedures.[19] For example, design approval was defined as "that action or series of actions by which FHWA indicates to the State highway department that the essential elements of a highway as set out in [FHWA regulations] are satisfactory or acceptable for preparation of plans, specifications and estimates (PS&E) for actual construction."[20] It was not clear, however, exactly what action or actions conveyed such an indication. Location approval was established as approval by the FHWA division engineer, after a required public hearing, of an exact location for a highway; but it was not clarified how this new requirement would relate to the existing mesh of federal approvals on small-scale projects.[21]

This confusion resulted primarily because FHWA was superimposing a new approval system involving long-term considerations on an existing system of piecemeal decision making that focused largely on more immediate technical matters. With the passage of time, formal location and design approvals became established aspects of FHWA's program, but the tension between the continued practice of carrying out small-scale projects and the need for long-term consideration of environmental impacts still exists. For example, the piecemeal orientation has constantly been an issue in litigation regarding how broad the scope of environmental impact statements (EISs) prepared on federal-aid highways must be.[22]

With the institution of state action plans, reviewed below, in which the states are required to develop their own procedures to assure that environmental impacts of proposed highways are fully considered, location and design approvals have now changed complexion. Where a state has amended its action plan to include public hearing requirements in accordance with federal requirements, final clearance of an EIS or adoption of a negative declaration constitutes location approval and there is no formal requirement for federal design approval.[23]

While action plans with approved public hearing requirements directly affect location and design approvals, certification acceptance affects PS&E approval and federal authorizations to proceed at various stages of development. Under certification acceptance, which is an alternative procedure applicable to all systems except the interstate system, state certification that specified types of projects will meet state standards which are at least equivalent to federal requirements serves in lieu of PS&E approval and the step-by-step federal authorizations to proceed.[24] Certification acceptance does not, however, relieve the state highway department from the requirements of federal system approval and program approval, nor does an approved certification contractually obligate the FHWA to reimburse the states for the federal share of project costs. It is not clear at the present time whether this contractual obligation will be made by FHWA concurrently with program approval or at a later stage of development. As of February 1976 the following seven states had adopted certification acceptance and had received FHWA approval of their state certifications: Georgia, Pennsylvania, Virginia, Kentucky, Maryland, Nevada, and Tennessee.[25]

Finally, neither the adoption of action plans nor of certification acceptance affects the FHWA's responsibilities under the National Environmental Policy Act (NEPA) and the required compliance of state highway departments with the FHWA's regulations regarding the preparation of EISs on proposed highways, subjects which are discussed in the following section.

Federal Environmental, Public Hearing, and Comprehensive Planning Requirements

In attempts to mitigate some of the environmental harm caused by highways, to promote comprehensive transportation planning, and to provide for public hearings a number of federal statutes have been enacted which place significant restraints on the planning and construction of federal-aid highways. The most important of these statutes are explained in the sections which follow. The discussion of urban transportation planning necessarily refers to mass transit as well as highway planning in urban areas, since coordination of different modes of transportation is a prime goal of the statutes and regulations involved.

1. Environmental Impact Statements

Chapter 3 has explained the provision of NEPA which requires the preparation of an EIS for "major Federal actions significantly affecting the quality of the human environment."[26] Many references are made there to the federal-aid highway program and one example of a NEPA case involving a highway project is reviewed at some length. In fact, the federal-aid highway program was one of the main programs Congress had in mind when it enacted NEPA, and many of the issues which have been litigated under the act have arisen in the context of highway planning and construction.

On December 2, 1974, FHWA promulgated regulations on the preparation of EISs in the federal-aid highway program.[27] These regulations state that a highway section for which an EIS is prepared should be as long as practicable "to permit consideration of environmental matters on a broad scope and meaningful evaluation of alternatives."[28] Further, they specify that "piecemealing" of highway improvements in separate EISs must be avoided.

When an EIS is prepared on a highway section, it must be completed during the location stage, *prior to the selection of a particular location* for this section.[29] Although a public hearing is not required on the draft EIS, if a hearing or hearings are to be held on the highway section, the draft EIS must be prepared and made available at least thirty days before the first hearing. A minimum of forty-five days must be allowed for comments. In the preparation of the final EIS, consideration must be given to all substantive comments made on the draft EIS.

The regulations provide for the preparation of EISs by state highway departments, in consultation with FHWA. As originally enacted, NEPA required that EISs be prepared by the federal decision-making agency. This requirement was the subject of several court cases, in which conflicting judgments were handed down.[30] In the summer of 1975 Congress amended NEPA, authorizing state agencies to prepare EISs in federal grant programs.[31] Federal agencies, nonetheless, still must furnish guidance and participate in the preparation of each EIS and must carry out an independent evaluation before granting approval.

In the federal-aid highway program the state highway department, after consultation with the appropriate FHWA division engineer, also makes the initial determination of whether an EIS should be prepared on a particular project. The FHWA division engineer must review these determinations, and may either concur or return the determination to the state for further information and consideration.

An EIS must be prepared for every action deemed to be *both* a major action *and* an action which significantly affects environmental quality. Specific examples are provided in the regulations of (1) those actions which are ordinarily considered to be "major actions," (2) those ordinarily considered to be "non-major actions," and (3) those which ordinarily have a significant effect on the quality of the human environment. In general, the regulations state that:

> Any action that is likely to precipitate significant foreseeable alterations in land use; planned growth; development patterns; traffic patterns; transportation services, including public transportation; and natural and man-made resources would be considered a major action.[32]

Actions which ordinarily have a significant effect on the quality of the human environment include those which are likely to be controversial on environmental grounds and those which are likely to have a significantly adverse impact on "natural, ecological, cultural or scenic resources of national, state or local significance."[33]

For each major federal action that is judged *not* to have a significant impact on the quality of the human environment, a "negative declaration" must be prepared by the state highway department. This document must include pertinent information, such as a description of the proposed action, the need for the action, the alternatives considered, and the reasons why no significant environmental impact is anticipated; an account of the social, economic, environmental, and other effects considered; maps showing alternatives; other comparative data; and a discussion of the issues and comments received from other agencies and the public during the developmental period.

Negative declarations are prepared in both draft and final form, suggesting that complicated environmental questions may still be involved even though no EIS is being prepared. The draft negative declaration does not have to be circulated for comment, but its public availability must be included in any notice of a public hearing or opportunity for such a hearing. If no hearing notice is required, a special notice must be placed in a local newspaper(s) advising the public of the availability of the draft negative declaration and specifying where further information may be obtained.

The final negative declaration must contain a summary and disposition of public hearing comments regarding the environmental effects of the proposed action, as well as alternatives raised at the hearing. The FHWA division engineer must review this final declaration and examine the economic, social, and environmental issues involved before granting FHWA approval.

The state highway department and FHWA must periodically, and in all cases prior to proceeding with major project activities, reevaluate each negative declaration to determine whether there have been substantial changes which would significantly affect the quality of the human environment. If such changes have occurred, then an EIS must be prepared.

The FHWA regulations set forth the required format and contents of EISs. In addition to a summary, each EIS must include the following sections, each of which is explained further in the regulations:

a. A description of the proposed action and alternatives considered, as well as the social, economic, and environmental context.

b. The scope and status of existing land use planning.

c. The probable impact of the proposed action on the environment, including secondary effects—such as impact on growth and development—and direct effects such as the following:

(1) Natural, ecological, or scenic resources impacts.

(2) Relocation of individuals and families impacts.

(3) Social impacts.

(4) Air quality impacts.

(5) Noise impacts.

(6) Water quality impacts.

(7) Wetlands and coastal zone impacts.

(8) Stream modification or impoundment impacts.

(9) Flood hazard impacts.

(10) Construction impacts.

d. Alternatives.

e. Probable adverse environmental effects which cannot be avoided.

f. The relationship between local short-term uses of man's environment and the maintenance and enhancement of long-term productivity.

g. Irreversible and irretrievable commitments of resources.

h. The impact on properties and sites of historic and cultural significance.

i. Comments and coordination.

2. Preservation of Parklands Under Section 4(f) of the Department of Transportation Act of 1966

This statute, commonly referred to as Section 4(f), established the national policy that special efforts must be made "to preserve the natural beauty of the countryside and public park and recreation lands, wildlife and waterfowl refuges, and historic sites."[34] It prohibits the Secretary of Transportation, after August 23, 1968, from approving any program or project which requires the use of any publicly owned land from a public park, recreation area, wildlife and waterfowl refuge, or historic site of national, state, or local significance as determined by the government officials having jurisdiction over these lands:

> unless (1) there is no feasible and prudent alternative to the use of such land, and (2) such program includes all possible planning to minimize harm to such park, recreational area, wildlife and waterfowl refuge, or historic site resulting from such use.[35]

Since parks and other open spaces have often been considered convenient and less expensive locations for highway routes, the provisions of this statute have prompted much litigation. In a number of cases, Section 4(f) charges have been made in conjunction with allegations of noncompliance with NEPA.[36]

The U.S. Supreme Court has held that Section 4(f) imposes clear and specific directives on the Secretary of Transportation and constitutes "a plain and explicit bar to the use of federal funds for construction of highways through parks—only the most unusual situations are exempted."[37] In order for the Secretary to find that there were no "feasible" alternatives, the Court held that he had to determine "that as a matter of sound engineering it would not be feasible to build the highway along any other route."[38] Regarding possible "prudent" alternatives, the Court ruled that the Secretary could not reject alternatives as not being prudent unless:

> there were truly unusual factors present in a particular case or the cost or community disruption resulting from alternative routes reached extraordinary magnitudes. If the statutes are to have any meaning, the Secretary cannot approve the destruction of parkland unless he finds that alternative routes present unique problems.[39]

Since the construction of a highway through open space normally is less expensive and requires less displacement of homes and businesses, such consequences are not in and of themselves sufficient to justify the use of areas protected by Section 4(f). Truly extraordinary disruption or costs must be involved for alternative routes to be ruled out.

The FHWA regulations promulgated on December 2, 1974, set out requirements regarding Section 4(f) statements which must be prepared by the state highway departments to document compliance with the provisions of Section 4(f).[40] The Section 4(f) statement, which usually accompanies the final EIS through the FHWA review process, must be prepared either as a separate statement or as a special, self-contained section of the EIS. It must be reviewed by the Washington headquarters office of FHWA prior to approval by the regional federal highway administrator.

If the federal, state, or local official having jurisdiction over a park, recreation area, refuge, or historic site determines that it is not significant, no Section 4(f) statement is required, but the FHWA division engineer must review this determination to assure himself that it is reasonable. Special provisions and procedures are set out for historic sites. Section 4(f) does not apply to publicly owned lands, such as the national forests, which are administered for multiple uses, if the portion of land to be taken for the highway project is not itself being used for park, recreation, wildlife, waterfowl, or historic site purposes. The FHWA regulations state that if a park or other area is determined to be significant later in the development of a highway project, a Section 4(f) statement does not have to be prepared if the right-of-way from the land was acquired prior to the designation or change in significance.

3. Public Hearings

Section 128 of the Federal-Aid Highway Act requires state highway departments to hold public hearings or afford the opportunity for such hearings on federal-aid highway projects. It also requires these departments to consider the economic, social, and environmental impacts of each project and to submit a report on this consideration to FHWA along with the transcript of each hearing.

In 1969 FHWA established procedures to implement this statute that required the states to hold two public hearings, a location or corridor hearing and a design hearing, for each federal-aid highway project.[41] Prior to this time, only one hearing had been required.

On December 2, 1974, the FHWA promulgated regulations adding public participation and hearing requirements to its guidelines for state development of what are called "environmental action plans," or simply "action plans."[42] FHWA's primary purpose in providing for such action plans was to delegate to the states the responsibility for compliance with Section 109(h) of the Federal-Aid Highway Act, which requires that possible adverse economic, social, and environmental effects of proposed projects be fully considered. Once a state highway department has amended its action plan (which originally was required to be submitted to FHWA by November 1, 1974) in accordance with the new requirements set forth in December 1974 and has received FHWA approval, then the action plan rather than the older FHWA regulations requiring location and design hearings will govern public hearings on highway projects in that state. The new provisions require the states to hold only one rather than two public hearings, but it appears that a number of states will retain a two-hearing process. No deadline is set for the states to revise their action plans to include hearing procedures, but the opportunity for them to develop their own state program for federal projects is expected to be an effective impetus.

FHWA anticipates that eventually its location and design hearing regulations will be revoked, but until all the states have properly amended their action plans, two sets of federal regulations pertaining to public hearings will be in effect and citizens will need to determine which are applicable in their own state. The essentials of both sets will be outlined here, though further detail should be sought in the regulations themselves.

The older regulations require first that a location or corridor public hearing be held before an exact route for the road has been selected and before the state highway department is committed to a specific proposal. Full opportunity must be given for public participation in determining the need for the project in question, its actual location, and what the environmental effects of various alternative locations would be. As has been pointed out, if an EIS is required on a highway section, the draft EIS must be completed and made available at least thirty days before the first public hearing on the section. This first hearing is, of course, the best time for citizens to question whether there is a need for the road at all and to explore the alternative of not building it. Later, when more resources have been committed to the project, it will be much more difficult to raise these considerations.

The second, or design, hearing must be held after route location has been approved, but before the state highway department is committed to a specific design proposal. The courts have indicated that during design hearings, highway officials should be expected to give precise information about parcels of property to be taken, exact design of access ramps, interchanges, relocation programs or replacement housing, and environmental effects.[43]

Both the location and design hearings must be held "at those stages of a proposal's development when the flexibility to respond to [the public's] views still exist."[44] Both must consider the environmental and social impacts of the proposed project in such areas as regional and community growth; natural resources; community cohesion; displacement of people, businesses, and farms; air, noise, and water pollution; and aesthetic or scenic values. Specific requirements regarding notice and conduct of the hearings are spelled out in the regulations.

The new regulations setting forth public participation requirements for state action plans, which apply to pre-construction activities in the state, are much less specific. In deference to what is termed "the unique situation of each state," the guidelines do not prescribe specific organizations or procedures which states must adopt, but leave such matters to the discretion of state highway departments.[45] Essentially, the guidelines simply require the states to describe the organization to be used, the process to be followed, and the manner in which responsibility is to be delegated in the development of federal-aid highway projects.

Except in the case of public hearing requirements, the guidelines advise the states of what they *should* do. For example, they indicate that potential adverse environmental effects should be identified as early as possible in the study process, that information regarding all studies undertaken should be made available to the public, and that the public should have the opportunity to participate in an open exchange of views throughout all stages of the project's development.

The alternatives to the proposed action should include, where appropriate, other transportation modes. Procedures should also be established for the reconsideration of earlier decisions which might be occasioned by the results of further study, the availability of additional information, or the passage of time between decisions. It should be pointed out, however, that in areas with a population of more than fifty thousand, the substantive and procedural requirements of FHWA and the Urban Mass Transportation Administration (UMTA)'s joint regulations on urban transportation planning, discussed below, make actions such as these mandatory.

The public hearing requirements of FHWA's action plan guidelines specify actions which the state highway department *must* take. These agencies must include in their amended action plans provisions for one or more public hearings, or the opportunity for such hearings, to be held at a convenient time and place on any federal-aid project which:

> requires the acquisition of significant amounts of right-of-way, substantially changes the layout or function of connecting roadways or of the facility being improved, has a significant adverse impact on abutting real property, or otherwise has a significant social, economic, environmental or other effect.[46]

Each hearing conducted must be held before the highway department becomes committed to any of the alternatives presented at the hearing.

The action plans must also include public notification procedures that will be used to inform the public of hearing opportunities. These procedures must include newspaper publication of hearing notices, press releases, and other means that are likely to reach those interested in or affected by proposed projects. Initial hearing notices must be published at least thirty days in advance of hearings. Procedures must also be included for additional hearing opportunities when there have been substantial changes or an unusually long period of time since the last hearing.

The states are also encouraged by the guidelines to make greater use of small, informal meetings and other such approaches to public involvement which will stimulate effective two-way communication. In effect, the states are expected to develop broader and more diversified programs of public participation than have been the rule in the past.

FHWA must not only grant initial approval to a state's action plan, it must also approve all revisions and must periodically review the states' implementation of their action plans. The federal agency may rescind its approval of a plan or take whatever other action it deems appropriate if it determines that the action plan is not being implemented or is not achieving the objectives of the FHWA regulations. The regulations include the sanction that FHWA will not give location approvals unless the highway agency has an approved action plan.

4. Urban Transportation Planning

a. *Section 134 of the Federal-Aid Highway Act.* This statute requires that comprehensive transportation planning be carried out in urban areas. It declares that it is "in the national interest to encourage and promote the development of transportation systems, embracing various modes of transport. . . ." and provides that after July 1, 1965, the Secretary of Transportation:

> shall not approve under section 105 of this [act] any program for projects in any urban area of more than fifty thousand population unless he finds that such projects are based on a continuing comprehensive planning process carried on cooperatively by States and local communities.[47]

This required planning process, commonly known as the 3–C process, must be certified annually by FHWA and UMTA, which is discussed below. If the administrators of these two agencies, acting jointly, determine that the transportation planning process of an urbanized area substantially meets the requirements of the statute and the regulations promulgated under it, they can either (1) certify the process, or (2) certify the process subject to certain conditions.[48] These conditions may provide either (1) that specified corrective actions must be taken, or (2) that the certification applies to only some categories of programs or projects and that specified corrective actions must be taken. Annual certification or partial certification, as the case may be, is extremely important to urbanized areas since programs or projects cannot be approved unless it is granted. This certification takes place in late June, at the end of each fiscal year, though an existing certification remains in effect until a new certification or a negative determination is issued. In fact, FHWA often conditionally certifies planning processes, allowing highway projects to go ahead even though all statutory and regulatory requirements have not been met.

In regulations promulgated on September 17, 1975, FHWA and UMTA set forth the procedural and substantive requirements which must henceforth be met in urban transportation planning under Section 134 and the Urban Mass Transportation Act.[49] Included in these regulations are guidelines for the preparation of "transportation improvement programs" (TIPs), which are multiyear programs of transportation improvements containing an annual element. Projects in the annual element for which assistance is sought under Sections 3 and 5 of the Urban Mass Transportation Act are submitted directly to UMTA by the metropolitan planning organization (MPO), which is the organization designated by the governor to be responsible, along with the state, for transportation planning in a particular urbanized area.[50] In the case of projects for which assistance is to be sought under the Federal-Aid Highway Act, the entire annual element is submitted to the state highway department, which then includes those projects with which it concurs in the annual statewide program of projects submitted to FHWA under Section 105. In any case where the state does not include in its annual program a *nonhighway* public mass transportation project (discussed below under mass transit) contained in the annual element, it must also submit a statement describing the reasons why it has not done so.

In the urban system portion of the program of projects required by Section 105, federal-aid highway projects must be approved by FHWA, whereas the nonhighway public mass transportation projects included must be approved by UMTA. Joint approval is necessary in any case where the statewide program of projects does not include all nonhighway projects contained in the annual element of the transportation improvement program.

Very significant in the September 17, 1975, regulations are provisions dealing with the "transportation systems management" (TSM) element of the required urban transportation plan. This element must address the short-range transportation needs of the urbanized area by setting out means of making efficient use of *existing* transportation resources and by providing for efficient movement of people. The establishment of bus lanes and other ways of giving priority on roads to high-occupancy vehicles are emphasized as desirable actions. Other recommended measures include traffic operations improvements, provisions for bicycles, management and control of parking, changes in tolls and fare structures, encouragement of car pooling, and improvements in transit service. In order to receive funds from UMTA, MPOs must include projects recommended in the TSM element in the annual element of their transportation improvement program.

It is encouraging to see closer cooperation developing between FHWA and UMTA regarding urban transportation planning. Some friction, however, does exist between these two DOT agencies. For example, FHWA has traditionally dealt with state highway departments, while UMTA has worked with local urban agencies. Consequently, the opposition of state highway officials to strengthening the role of MPOs in the urban transportation planning process has been expressed through FHWA. Progress has already been made in resolving such differences, and hopefully cooperation will not only continue but increase in the future.

The new emphasis on public transportation projects and improvements in 3–C planning presents a faint hope that the 3–C program will become something more than the highway-justifying boondoggle it has been in the past. In 1970 the Acting Director of Environmental and Urban Research at DOT observed that the plans developed under Section 134 were "surprisingly consistent with plans that most highway departments had developed twenty or so years ago . . ."[51]

The public has also previously had little influence on Section 134 planning. The new regulations include the requirement that the 3–C process must "[i]nclude provisions to ensure involvement of the public. . . ."[52] The participation of well-informed citizens in 3–C planning is extremely important, since the possibility of substantial change in highway proposals is much more likely at this stage of development than, for example, at a public hearing on a particular highway for which planning has been underway for a period of years.

b. *Transportation Control Plans Under the Clean Air Act.* As discussed in Chapter 4, the Clean Air Act of 1970[53] requires the states to develop implementation plans to achieve the national ambient air quality standards established by the U.S. Environmental Protection Agency (EPA) under the act. The implementation plans must set forth the measures which will be taken in each of the state's air quality control regions to assure that the region's air quality conforms to the national standards. These measures must include emission limitations and other steps necessary to ensure attainment and maintenance of the standards, including, though not limited to, land use and transportation controls.[54] Since automobile exhaust emis-

Table 8
Summary of Transportation Control Plan Development, January 1976

I. TCPs have been developed for the following areas:

1. Boston	10. Washington,	20. Phoenix-Tucson
2. Springfield, Mass.	D.C.	21. Fresno
3. New York	11. Cincinnati	22. San Francisco
4. Rochester, N. Y.	12. Indianapolis	23. San Diego
5. Northern New	13. Chicago	24. Los Angeles
Jersey (Newark)	14. Minneapolis	25. Sacramento
6. Southern New	15. San Antonio	26. Seattle
Jersey (Camden-	16. Houston-Galves-	27. Spokane
Trenton)	ton	28. Fairbanks
7. Philadelphia	17. Dallas-Ft. Worth	29. Portland, Ore.
8. Pittsburgh	18. Denver	
9. Baltimore	19. Salt Lake City	

II. The following areas are in some stage of TCP development:

1. Hartford	6. Beaumont, Texas
2. Providence	7. Corpus Christi
3. New Haven	8. Albuquerque
4. St. Louis	9. Las Vegas
5. Tampa	

III. In the following areas of over 200,000 population, there are violations of automobile-related air quality standards, but no TCPs are being developed:

1. Birmingham	10. Wichita	18. Oklahoma City
2. Mobile	11. New Orleans	19. Tulsa
3. Memphis	12. Detroit	20. Nashville
4. Miami	13. Buffalo	21. Norfolk
5. Atlanta	14. Charlotte	22. Richmond
6. Honolulu	15. Dayton	23. Milwaukee
7. Louisville	16. Cleveland-	24. Toledo
8. Omaha	Akron	25. Kansas City
9. Des Moines	17. Columbus	

Sources: I and II: Document entitled "Transportation Controls" (January 1976), submitted by the U.S. Environmental Protection Agency to Senator Edmund Muskie, at his request
III: Natural Resources Defense Council, Project on Clean Air

sions are chiefly responsible for four of the six pollutants for which standards were set, EPA determined that in certain areas transportation control plans (TCPs) would be necessary to reduce concentrations of carbon monoxide, hydrocarbons, nitrogen dioxide, and photochemical oxidants to acceptable levels. Table 8 summarizes the development of TCPs across the country as of January 1976.

After repeated delays and extensions were allowed by EPA, the states were required by court order to submit their transportation control plans by April 15, 1973.[55] Under the terms of the Clean Air Act, when a state does not submit an implementation plan or submits a plan, or portion thereof, which does not meet federal requirements, EPA must promulgate regulations to serve in place of the required state plan. Since many of the TCPs submitted to EPA were inadequate, it has been necessary for EPA to promulgate regulations setting out transportation strategies for a number of air quality control regions in the various states.

The TCPs, as developed by the states or promulgated by EPA, include in their control strategies various means of reducing the air pollution caused by transportation. For example, the following are measures which have been proposed in TCPs: improved mass transit facilities and service, special bus lanes, parking disincentives in congested areas, fringe-area parking facilities, prohibition of free employee parking, encouragement of car pooling, increased tolls on highways and bridges, emission inspection programs, vehicle retrofit for older model cars, bans on truck deliveries during certain hours, and aircraft-taxing emissions reductions.

The implementation of TCPs has been subject to many difficulties. The use of the automobile is so much a part of the American way of life that efforts to restrict its use, even to protect public health, are extremely controversial. In New York State, for example, the TCP for New York City was approved by EPA in 1973, but neither the state nor the city took any action to implement the plan. In the fall of 1974 the Friends of the Earth, the Natural Resources Defense Council, and other organizations and individuals initiated an action for a preliminary injunction to compel the state and city to implement the TCP.[56] The district court ruled that the plaintiffs would prevail on the test for an injunction, but denied the motion because the TCP was in the process of being revised. The state, however, failed to complete its application for revision, and in January 1975 EPA issued administrative notices that the state and city, by failing to meet their own timetables, were in violation of twelve of the thirty-two strategies of the TCP.[57] During the next eight months EPA, refusing to begin a judicial enforcement proceeding, sought to negotiate a solution with the state and city.

By July 1975 the state and the city had agreed to move ahead on eight relatively uncontroversial strategies, but refused to take any action on four others: after-hours goods delivery, bridge tolls on the free Harlem and East River bridges, a selective ban on taxi cruising, and parking reductions. Meanwhile, the state remained in violation of all the control strategies in the plan, and EPA had taken no administrative action at all regarding twenty of the strategies. During the period of time from the plan's adoption to July 1975, moreover, carbon monoxide levels in New York City had risen by 25 percent—to over five times the federal standard.

In the midst of these delaying tactics and prolonged negotiations the Transit Authority announced without prior warning that, at the request of the city government, it was going to raise the transit fare from $.35 to $.50. The environmental groups sought court orders to enjoin the fare increase pending implementation of the TCP and to require the city and state to enforce the TCP.[58] These motions were denied by the district court and the fare was raised to $.50. In April 1976, however, the U.S. Court of Appeals for the Second Circuit, while upholding the district court on the fare increase issue, ruled unanimously that the city and state must enforce the four controversial strategies of the TCP discussed above. It further ordered the district court to conduct hearings on the remaining TCP strategies and to issue orders requiring enforcement if the city and state are found to be in default. In handing down this highly significant opinion, the court stated that "Congress [has] made clear that citizen groups are not to be treated as nuisances or troublemakers but rather as welcomed participants in the vindication of environmental interests."[59]

Other problems have arisen in air quality control regions where the state did not propose and adopt an acceptable plan. The issue there, based on constitutional arguments, is whether state officials can be compelled to implement a TCP that has been promulgated by EPA. This question has been the subject of litigation before several of the federal circuit courts of appeals. The Third Circuit held that under the commerce power Congress could compel a state to implement abatement strategies even when such strategies required a state to use its legislative, administrative, and financial powers.[60] The Ninth Circuit, however, held that the Clean Air Act only authorizes federal sanctions against a state that pollutes the air and does not authorize sanctions against a state that chooses not to govern polluters under an implementation plan imposed upon it by the federal government.[61] In a more complex decision which reviewed the various component parts of the TCP promulgated by EPA for the National Capital Region, the D.C. Circuit Court affirmed the power of the federal government to require the states to manage their road systems in a manner that reduces air pollution, but held that the Clean Air Act does not authorize EPA to require the states to enact specific legislation to carry out transportation controls.[62]

5. Consistency of Highway Planning and Construction with State Implementation Plans Under the Clean Air Act

Section 109(j) of the Federal-Aid Highway Act requires the Secretary of Transportation, after consultation with the Administrator of EPA, to promulgate guidelines to assure that highways constructed under the federal-aid highway program "are consistent with any approved plan for the implementation of any ambient air quality standard for any air quality control region designated pursuant to the Clean Air Act, as amended."

State implementation plans have been discussed both in Chapter 4 and in the preceding section of this chapter. Those parts of the state implementation plan which pertain most directly to transportation are the TCPs required for areas with critical air pollution problems; indirect source review regulations for control of sources such as highways, airports, and shopping centers, which attract large numbers of automobiles; and maintenance plans to assure that national air quality standards are not only achieved but also maintained. The difficulties which have been encountered in the implementation of each of these aspects of air pollution control have already been discussed in some detail.

FHWA promulgated the required guidelines for assuring consistency of the federal-aid highway program with the state implementation plans adopted under the Clean Air Act on December 24, 1974.[63] These guidelines require that consistency determinations be made in the following three areas:

a. *Urban Transportation Plans and Programs.* The 3–C planning required in urban areas by Section 134 of the Federal-Aid Highway Act must be annually found to be consistent with the state implementation plans under the Clean Air Act. This means that the current highway plan and program developed under the 3–C process must be consistent with the TCP developed for the air quality control region and also with any existing indirect source review or air quality maintenance regulations. The regional federal highway administrator, in consultation with the regional administrator of EPA, is responsible for reviewing the consistency determination submitted by the highway department. If the regional federal highway administrator finds significant deficiencies, such as major instances of inconsistency, he may withhold the planning certification of the 3–C planning agency, which is a necessary prerequisite for FHWA approval of highway projects for the urban area involved. To be found consistent, the 3–C highway plan and program (which include short-term and long-term components) should not only be free of provisions which would hinder any air pollution control strategy, but should also include affirmative provisions to support such strategies.

b. *Highway Sections.* In highway planning air quality must be given "appropriate consideration." According to the regulatory guidelines, when high volume facilities are proposed for areas with critical air quality problems, on-site data gathering and a high level of analysis will usually be required during the planning period.

For highway sections on which a draft EIS is prepared, this draft must contain:

(1) An identification of the air quality impact of the highway section;

(2) An identification of the analysis methodology utilized;

(3) A brief summary of early consultations held with the air pollution control agency and, where appropriate, with the indirect source review agency; and

(4) The highway department's determination regarding the consistency of each alternative under consideration with the approved state implementation plan.

Before the final EIS may be adopted by FHWA, the appropriate regional federal highway administrator must determine that the proposed highway section is consistent with the approved state implementation plan.

c. *Construction of Highways.* The highway department must also take steps to assure that its construction specifications, as well as the use of specific equipment and materials, are consistent with the approved state implementation plan. This must be done in cooperation with the air pollution control agency.

Citizen Action

In approaching highway or transportation problems, citizens need to assess the political and administrative realities which they face. An essential aspect of this task is determining the strength and responsibilities of the government agencies involved in the planning and construction of transportation projects. Circumstances vary widely among and within the different states, but the following general observations may still be helpful.

State highway departments are generally very strong agencies. In the past four or five years many states have placed their highway agencies within the framework of newly established state departments of transportation, which also have responsibilities for other modes of transportation such as mass transit. The availability of increased funds from the Urban Mass Transportation Administration, discussed below, has been a major stimulus for such reorganization. Nonetheless, the strength of the highway orientation, which has been sustained by so many years of massive federal highway funding, has been little diluted, and most state departments of transportation are dominated by highway officials. With the interstate system nearing completion, there has been a growing trend for FHWA to delegate more and more responsibilities to the states. This movement is clearly evident in the development of procedures for state action plans, certification acceptance, and delegation of EIS preparation to state highway departments.

Another factor to be noted is the delegation of greater responsibilities in transportation matters to metropolitan planning organizations (MPOs) in urban areas. MPOs, which are discussed in more detail in Chapter 13, have traditionally been rather weak and ineffective advisory bodies which sometimes possess a veneer of planning virtuosity, but usually have no means of implementing their plans, little political strength, and no assured base of financial support. Environmental concerns, moreover, have often not been high priorities with MPOs. These organizations do, however, have a regional perspective, which is so clearly needed in transportation planning, and they are perhaps more open to multidisciplinary approaches and to the use of different modes of transportation than are state transportation or highway departments, which generally have no better record on environmental issues.

Both increased public opposition to highway projects on environmental grounds and the downturn of the economy have led state highway departments to scale down their plans for new construction. In some areas, such as the state of California, actual moratoriums on new highway construction have been imposed. Focus has now shifted largely to upgrading of existing facilities, including such actions as widening of roads and replacement of bridges. Much emphasis is being placed on highway safety as a rationale for work to be done.

The actions which citizens should take to influence transportation planning in their own area or to deal with a specific problem, of course, depend a great deal on particular circumstances. A firm grasp of statutory and regulatory requirements and a realistic understanding of agency strengths, weaknesses, and responsibilities are essential, but further efforts must also be made to determine the peculiarities of individual situations and to decide what strategies citizens should adopt. The following are suggestions regarding some of the basic aspects of informed and effective citizen action:

1. Citizens should find out which government agency is responsible for transportation planning in their area and get themselves keyed into the planning process. This means finding out when meetings and hearings are to be held, making a strong and well-prepared showing at these meetings or hearings, getting on any mailing lists which the agency may have for dissemination of information or hearing notices, and finding out what the agency's plans are for the three basic planning periods: the next year, the next five years, and, with respect to major new facilities, the next twenty years. Copies of the state's action plan should be obtained and carefully studied to determine what procedures govern preconstruction highway activities within the state. Citizens should find out whether or not the state has amended its action plan to include requirements for public hearings and whether these amendments have been approved by FHWA.

2. In urban transportation planning citizens should push for the development and implementation of plans for the short-range, low capital improvements emphasized in the FHWA/UMTA regulations promulgated on September 17, 1975. Agency officials with a strong commitment to highway construction may be reluctant to develop programs involving such measures as the establishment of preferential bus lanes or car-pooling incentives, but citizens should press for responsible implementation of the federal requirements and maximization of opportunities to obtain funds to carry out needed innovations.

3. Annual federal certifications of the 3–C planning process required by Section 134 and federal consistency determinations under Section 109(j) should be carefully monitored by citizens. It should be determined whether all needed technical studies are completed for

both short- and long-term plans. A lack of data is not an excuse for failure to prepare these studies, which are essential for meaningful determinations. For example, the required consistency judgments simply cannot be made without technical basis.

4. With regard to specific highway projects that are proposed, citizens should watch carefully for notices regarding public hearings or meetings and the availability for public comment of draft EISs and negative declarations. Effective criticisms of EISs and negative declarations should be prepared during the specified comment periods, and as strong a showing as possible should be made at all public hearings or meetings which are held. Prior to any hearing, citizens should find out what standards exist for the conduct of the hearing, what rights and obligations they will have, and what will be expected of them.

5. In projects which involve Section 4(f) parklands, citizens should be particularly aware of the strong substantive requirements of this statute. If a locality, bent on carrying out a highway project, refuses to make a determination that the park or other protected land is significant, attempts should be made to find out whether any state or federal agency, which might issue a determination of significance, has any jurisdiction over the land.

MASS TRANSIT

Mass transit is of concern to environmentalists primarily as an alternative to transportation systems based on the private automobile. Transit lines and stations do affect patterns of land use, no doubt sometimes adversely, but the environmental impacts of transit facilities are tremendously less negative than those of highways and millions of private cars. Mass transit consumes far less energy as a mover of people, it creates much less air pollution in the process, and it works to preserve existing developed areas, serving as a counterforce to the spread of urban sprawl which is dependent on the automobile.

This section will focus on the programs of federal assistance which have been established to encourage and support public transportation.

The Urban Mass Transportation Administration (UMTA)

UMTA, an agency of DOT, is the federal agency that has prime responsibility for mass transit. It was created by the Urban Mass

Transportation Act of 1964,[64] which was the first federal legislation in this field. The act was passed when it had become apparent that the private transit industry was declining and that government support was essential for the development of efficient and coordinated mass transportation systems. It established a program of federal grants and loans with an annual budget of $75 million (compared to the *multibillion* dollar annual federal budget for highways) which initially was directed primarily toward the preservation of urban transit in selected cities through the conversion of failing private transit companies to public ownership. Today UMTA's annual capital assistance budget is nearly $2 billion and is devoted primarily to the rehabilitation and expansion of existing transit properties and to the construction of new transit systems. Capital grants are made at the level of 80 percent federal funding to 20 percent local matching. Multiyear funding commitments have already been made to assist Atlanta, Baltimore, and Philadelphia in the financing of their rapid transit systems.

Faced with both inflation and greatly increased demand for federal assistance for public transportation projects, UMTA does not have the funds needed to meet even existing mass transit needs. To clarify what factors will be weighed in its decisions regarding funds which have not yet been committed, UMTA published a proposed policy on August 1, 1975.[65] This policy indicated that as a condition of eligibility for federal assistance for any major mass transportation investment, applicants must carry out an analysis of transportation alternatives which explores how different modes of transit could be integrated in the metropolitan area and how incremental development could be carried out. In grant proposals UMTA wants to see not the use of a single technology over an entire metropolitan area, but "a mix of transit options—heavy or light rail, people movers, buses and paratransit—with the choice of service being dictated by the demands existing in a particular corridor or part of the urban area."[66] Further, it is looking for plans which propose transit development in incremental steps which are capable of efficient operation in themselves. Other factors which are very important to UMTA are cost-effectiveness, improved management of existing transportation systems, and the provision of full opportunity for timely involvement of the public in the alternative analysis process.

More efficient use and better management of existing transportation facilities were also central points in the joint regulations on urban transportation planning, discussed above, which were promulgated on September 17, 1975, by UMTA and FHWA.[67]

UMTA Grant Programs

1. Section 3 Grants

Section 3 of the Urban Mass Transportation Act of 1964, as amended, authorizes grants and loans to states and local public bodies and agencies for capital expenditures for mass transportation services.[68] The development of projects for these grants must be based on the certified 3–C planning process, discussed above. Moreover, each applicant proposing a project which "will substantially affect a community or its mass transportation service" must certify to UMTA that it has afforded adequate opportunity for public hearings; has considered the economic, social, and environmental impacts of the project; and has found the project to be consistent with official plans for the comprehensive development of the urban area. Each such project application must also include an environmental impact statement.[69]

2. Section 5 Grants

The National Mass Transportation Assistance Act of 1974 established a new program of grants which are to be allocated on a formula basis for capital outlays or operating expenses in urbanized areas with populations of fifty thousand or more.[70] Federal funds for capital projects under this section may cover up to 80 percent of costs, while those for operating expenses cannot exceed 50 percent of costs.

For urbanized areas with a population of 200,000 or more the governor of the state, responsible local officials, and publicly owned operators of mass transportation services must designate a recipient to receive and dispense the funds apportioned via the formula grants. Funds for urbanized areas with a population of less than 200,000 are made available to the governor of the state for expenditure in these areas.

The governor or designated recipient must submit to UMTA for approval a program of projects for the utilization of the funds authorized. This program of projects must be based on the 3–C planning process. Before approving any project UMTA must assure that possible adverse economic, social, and environmental effects of the project have been fully considered and that efforts have been made to eliminate such adverse impacts. The governor or designated recipient must certify that it has conducted public hearings (or has afforded to the opportunity for such hearings) at which economic, social, and environmental impacts were considered.

3. Other Programs

UMTA also has funds available for certain other purposes. For example, it is authorized to undertake or make grants for research and development (R & D) projects in all phases of urban mass transportation, including the development, testing, and demonstration of new facilities, equipment, techniques, and methods. In response to past criticisms that this program was guided more by a desire for technological virtuosity than by the need to improve existing technology, UMTA officials have stated a firm commitment to making certain that the R & D program addresses real public needs.[71]

Along with FHWA, UMTA is responsible for administering the rural highway transportation demonstration program. The purpose of this program is to carry out demonstration projects that encourage the development, improvement, and use of public mass transportation systems in which vehicles operating on highways transport passengers within rural and small urban areas and between such areas and cities. Project selection criteria and other aspects of the program are discussed in regulations promulgated in April 1975.[72]

It should be noted that UMTA is required by statute to make up to $500 million of the money available to finance activities under the Urban Mass Transportation Act, except under Section 5, available exclusively for assistance in areas with a population of less than fifty thousand.[73] Section 5, as has been indicated, applies exclusively to urbanized areas larger than this. Since it alone authorizes the use of UMTA funds for operating expenses, small areas of less than fifty thousand people cannot get money from UMTA for operating costs.

UMTA is also required by statute to make special efforts to encourage planning and design of mass transportation facilities to meet the needs of the elderly and the handicapped, and is authorized to make grants and loans to this end.[74]

Public Transportation Projects Under the Federal-Aid Highway Act

The Federal-Aid Highway Act of 1973[75] authorized for the first time the use of monies from the Highway Trust Fund for nonhighway public mass transit projects. The following transfers of funds from traditional road projects to transit needs are now authorized under 23 U.S.C. § 142:

1. The construction of exclusive or preferential bus lanes, highway traffic control devices, and parking facilities to serve bus and other public mass transportation passengers can be approved as highway projects on any of the four federal-aid highway systems. (Fringe and corridor parking facilities for urbanized areas with a population of over fifty thousand are also authorized for approval as projects on the federal-aid urban system by 23 U.S.C. § 137.)

2. Sums from the Highway Trust Fund apportioned for the urban system can be used for the following nonhighway projects:

a. Since fiscal year 1975, the purchase of buses can be approved as a project on the federal-aid urban system.

b. Since fiscal year 1976, the construction, reconstruction, and improvement of fixed rail facilities, including the purchase of rolling stock for fixed rail, can be approved as a project on the federal-aid urban system.

(Under special provisions for fiscal years 1974 and 1975, such nonhighway public mass transit projects could be approved for support from general funds in lieu of highway projects in urbanized areas with a population of over fifty thousand.)

3. Funds apportioned for the interstate system can be used to finance the federal share of projects for exclusive or preferential bus, truck, and emergency vehicle routes or lanes.

4. The states can be authorized to make highway rights-of-way available without charge to publicly owned mass transit authorities for rail or nonhighway public mass transit facilities.

Unfortunately, these opportunities to transfer funds from traditional highway projects to public transportation projects have been sadly underused. The record for transfers within the federal-aid urban system has been particularly disappointing. For example, out of a total availability of $480 million in fiscal year 1974 and $800 million in fiscal year 1975, the transfers approved amounted to only $34.6 million and $15.7 million, respectively.[76]

Also, FHWA and UMTA have not been able to agree on final regulations to implement the provisions of Section 142, though proposed rules were published in the *Federal Register* in September 1974.[77] The transfers which have been made have been approved under provisionary guidelines.

Another section of the Federal-Aid Highway Act authorizes what is called "interstate substitution," through June 30, 1981.[78] Under this mechanism, urbanized areas with a population of over fifty thousand can substitute a transit project involving the construction of fixed rail facilities or the purchase of rolling stock for any mode of public transportation for an interstate route or portion thereof which has already been approved. To achieve this, the state governor and the local governments concerned must request the Secretary of Transportation to withdraw his approval of the interstate segment. He, in turn, must find that the segment is not essential to the completion of a unified and connected interstate system or will not be essential if a transit substitution is made, and must receive assurances that the state does not intend to construct a toll road instead. If the interstate approval is withdrawn, then state and local officials may submit a public mass transit project for approval. If approved, this project is entitled to federal support from the general funds in an amount equal to that which would have been paid for the interstate segment. (A 1975 amendment allows the Secretary of Transportation to adjust the interstate cost estimate to reflect changes in construction costs.) The substitution funding is made at the level of an 80 percent federal share, in keeping with UMTA's programs rather than with the 90 percent share of the interstate system. Thus although the same amount of federal money is available, more state and local matching funds are required for substituted mass transit projects. This difference has been a prime reason why the substitution provision also has not been widely used.

Citizen Action

In general, citizens who are concerned about the unhealthy air in our cities and the ills of urban sprawl should support the development of mass transit as a mover of people within metropolitan areas. Pressure should constantly be exerted at local, state, and federal levels to provide adequate funds for this essential mode of transportation.

Even where funds are not available for the construction of new public transportation systems, it should be possible to improve the effectiveness of existing facilities through innovations such as the establishment of exclusive or preferential bus lanes and the adoption of disincentives like tolls and parking restrictions to discourage automobile use. The TSM element which is required by FHWA/UMTA regulations to play an important role in urban transportation planning is designed to promote just such actions. Citizens should, therefore, make every effort to assure that the federal requirements are being met in good faith by their MPO and state highway department and that needed innovations are being realistically planned.

Citizens should also push for the use of interstate substitution wherever it is desirable to replace a planned interstate segment that has not yet been constructed with a public transportation project. Most of the interstate system is now complete, but the mileage which remains includes some of the most controversial portions, which are largely located in metropolitan areas. If they do not already know what interstate segments remain unfinished in their area, citizens should find this out from their MPO and should carefully evaluate the possibility of replacing these segments with public transportation projects.

Also, citizens should fully understand the provisions established by Section 142 of the Federal-Aid Highway Act for transfers of highway funds from all four federal-aid highway systems to meet public mass transit needs. Public insistence on the use of funds for mass transit rather than roads can have a decisive influence on metropolitan and state highway officials responsible for transportation plans and programs.

RAILROADS

Like mass transit, railroads provide transportation services which are an alternative to motor vehicle operation. Moreover, in addition to moving people with less energy consumption and less air pollution, railroads also offer an alternative means of transporting freight that otherwise would be shipped by truck or airplane.

Unfortunately, by the early 1970s rail service in the United States was for the most part in a very sad state. In the Northeast, for example, most of the major carriers had gone bankrupt, the victims of poor management, labor problems, and an overwhelming government preoccupation with highway construction. Across the entire country, the highway obsession prevailed and light density branch lines and passenger service were all too frequently unprofitable problems. In latter-day attempts to save our railroad system, Congress has passed several significant railroad acts, which are discussed below.

The most critical and immediate environmental issue pertaining to railroads is the very real threat that service on many light density lines will be discontinued and the rail properties involved abandoned. When lines are abandoned, the rail rights-of-way are sold and tracks are dismantled—and thus the rail option with its environmental advantages is effectively lost. Congress itself has assessed this problem very realistically:

(1) The Nation is facing an energy shortage of acute proportions in the next decade.

(2) Railroads are one of the most energy-efficient modes of transportation for the movement of passengers and freight and cause the least amount of pollution.

(3) Abandonment, termination, or substantial reduction of rail service in any locality will adversely affect the Nation's long-term and immediate goals with respect to energy conservation and environmental protection.

(4) Under certain circumstances the cost to the taxpayers of rail service continuation subsidies would be less than the cost of abandonment of rail service in terms of lost jobs, energy shortages, and degradation of the environment.[79]

Whether Congress's actions, however, have been strong enough to prevent widespread abandonments is another question. The following discussion reviews the federal actions which have been taken in the attempt to strengthen the rail industry.

AMTRAK

In 1970 the National Railroad Passenger Corporation, known as AMTRAK, was created by the Rail Passenger Service Act.[80] The prime purpose of this act was to establish modern and efficient intercity rail passenger service through a new "for profit" corporation boosted by federal support. In the establishment of the original AMTRAK system, railroads were offered contracts under which they would be relieved of their entire responsibility to provide rail passenger service. AMTRAK itself is authorized to operate or contract for the operation of intercity rail passenger trains, as well as to contract with railroads or regional transportation authorities for the use of tracks and other facilities and for the provision of services. Congress also intended AMTRAK to develop and employ innovative marketing and operating concepts, and to propose new experimental routes to be added to the AMTRAK system.

Subsequent legislation has expanded the responsibilities of AM-

TRAK and provided continuing federal support, in recognition of the difficult financial problems which the corporation faces.[81] Important provisions of this legislation have authorized the use of federal funds for operating expenses and for critically needed upgrading of tracks and roadbeds along the Washington, D.C./New York/Boston corridor that have fallen into severe disrepair as a result of the bankruptcy of railroads in this area.

Rail Reorganization in the Northeast and Midwest

In response to the bankruptcy of principal railroad companies serving the Northeast and adjoining midwestern states, Congress passed the Regional Rail Reorganization Act of 1973.[82] The congressional findings which prompted this legislation included determinations that essential rail service of both regional and national significance was threatened with cessation or severe curtailment; that rehabilitation and modernization of rail properties were necessary; that rail service and rail transportation offer economic and environmental advantages with respect to land use, air pollution, noise levels, energy efficiency and conservation, resource allocation, safety, and cost per ton-mile of movement to such an extent that the preservation and maintenance of adequate and efficient rail service is in the national interest; and that these needs could not be met without substantial action by the federal government.[83] Major goals of the act were to provide for (1) "the reorganization of railroads in this region into an economically viable system capable of providing adequate and efficient rail service to the region," and (2) "assistance to States and local and regional transportation authorities for continuation of local rail services threatened with cessation. . . ."[84]

The act established the United States Railway Association (USRA), a nonprofit government corporation empowered to develop and implement a preliminary and final system plan for regional rail reorganization. The final system plan was required to designate which of the rail properties of the bankrupt railroads were to be

1. Transferred to the Consolidated Rail Corporation (ConRail), a for-profit corporation whose establishment was dictated by the act.

2. Offered for sale to a profitable railroad operating in the region.

3. Purchased, leased, or otherwise acquired from ConRail by AMTRAK.

4. Available for purchase or lease from ConRail by a state or a

local or regional transportation authority to meet the needs of commuter and intercity rail passenger service.

5. Suitable for use for other public purposes, including highways, other forms of transportation, conservation, energy transmission, education or health care facilities, or recreation.

Subject to certain limitations, rail service which is not included in the new regional system either through transferal to ConRail or sale to a profitable railroad, may be discontinued and rail properties may be abandoned. The limitations imposed by the act specify that such discontinuance and abandonment are not permitted where a shipper, a state, the United States, a local or regional transportation authority, or any responsible person offers to provide an acceptable rail service continuation subsidy or to purchase the rail properties for operation of rail service. Further, all discontinuance and abandonment must take place within two years after the effective date of the final system plan or after the final payment of any rail service continuation subsidy, whichever is later.

After ConRail has been in operation for two years, the Interstate Commerce Commission (ICC) may authorize it to abandon any rail properties on which it determines that service "is not required by the public convenience and necessity."[85] The ICC may also, at any time after the effective date of the final system plan, authorize the abandonment of rail properties which are not being operated by anyone.

The act established a program of federal financial assistance to support continuation of local rail services, as well as acquisition and modernization of rail properties. Under this program, states which met the eligibility criteria set out in the statute were entitled to federal assistance allocated on a formula basis for a maximum of two years. The federal contribution was to be available at the level of a 70 percent federal share to 30 percent state matching. In addition, the Secretary of Transportation was authorized to provide discretionary financial assistance to a state or a local or regional transportation authority in the region for the purpose of continuing local rail services. In 1974, moreover, an amendment to the act made rail freight services which met specified criteria also eligible for federal subsidies under this program.[86] As will be discussed below, federal financial assistance for rail service continuation was expanded by a new railroad act passed in February 1976.

The preliminary system plan required by the 1973 act was released by USRA in April 1975.[87] Subsequently, a series of public hearings on its provisions were conducted throughout the region by the Rail Services Planning Office, an agency created within the ICC by the act. The final system plan was delivered to Congress on July 26, 1975. Since Congress took no action to disapprove the final plan during a specified time period after its transmittal, the plan became effective in early November 1975. The date set for conveyance of rail properties to ConRail or profitable railroads was April 1, 1976.

The final system plan calls for the elimination from the regional rail system of nearly seven thousand miles of light density rail line —which is approximately 25 percent of all light density line in the region.[88] The lines slated for elimination are those which are not to be transferred to ConRail or purchased by profitable railroads, and thus will be saved only if rail service continuation subsidies are forthcoming from the state, a shipper, a public transportation authority, or other responsible person.

In determining to eliminate these light density lines from the regional rail system, the USRA focused its attention almost entirely on the goal of "profitability"—which was, in fact, only one of eight statutory goals for the final system plan set out in the act. In addition to creating a profitable or "financially self-sustaining" rail service system, the final system plan was also supposed to effectuate the following goals:

1. The establishment and maintenance of a rail service system adequate to meet the rail transportation needs and service requirements of the region;

2. The establishment of improved high-speed passenger service;

3. The preservation, to the extent consistent with other goals, of existing patterns of service and the utilization of those modes of transportation in the region which require the smallest amount of scarce energy resources and which can most efficiently transport energy resources;

4. The retention and promotion of competition in the provision of rail and other transportation services in the region;

5. The attainment and maintenance of any environmental standards, particularly the applicable national ambient air quality standards and plans established under the Clean Air Act of 1970,[89] taking into consideration the environmental impact of alternative choices of action;

6. The movement of passengers and freight in rail transportation

in the region in the most efficient manner consistent with safe operation, including the requirements of commuter and intercity rail passenger service; and

7. The minimization of job losses and associated increases in unemployment and community benefit costs in areas in the region presently served by rail service.[90]

Rather than considering these seven goals in the development of the final system plan, USRA took the position that they would be furthered by the subsidy program established by the act. In addition to this untenable side step, USRA's decision making on light density lines was characterized by serious shortcomings. The ICC, in its evaluation of the final system plan, stated that:

Failure to ferret out the facts concerning individual lines and methodological assumptions which we consider of questionable validity cast doubt on a number of the close line retention decisions.[91]

Finally, there is considerable question as to whether the abandonment of branch lines will indeed make the regional rail system more profitable, as USRA claims. The loss of these feeder lines at various points throughout the system may well result in a less integrated, less efficient, and less profitable system.

In declining to disapprove the final system plan, Congress acquiesced in USRA's decisions. This fact, along with the restrictions on judicial review established by the act,[92] limits the range of legal actions which can be taken to contest USRA's decisions. Further, no challenge to the final system plan has been possible on NEPA grounds, since the 1973 railroad act specifically exempted from NEPA any action taken under its authority before the effective date of the final system plan.

Some light was shed on this difficult situation by the passage in February 1976 of the lengthy and complex Railroad Revitalization and Regulatory Reform Act of 1976,[93] which included amendments to the Regional Rail Reorganization Act of 1973. Among the most important of these were the following:

1. Provisions were made for the inclusion of additional rail lines in the regional rail system via modification of the final system plan during a limited period of time.

2. Procedures were established for continuing reorganization

through transactions supplemental to the final system plan. These transactions may include transfer to the regional rail system of rail properties which were not so designated under the final system plan. The USRA must publish notice of every proposal for a supplemental transaction in the *Federal Register* and must afford all interested persons an opportunity to comment on the proposal.

3. The federal financial assistance program was expanded. First, the federal share in the existing two-year subsidy program was raised from 70 percent to 100 percent for the first year and 90 percent for the second year. After this two-year period, moreover, additional support will be available under a new nationwide rail freight assistance program, discussed further below, at the level of an 80 percent federal share for the third year and a 70 percent federal share for the fourth and fifth year. In addition, a new railroad trust fund, also discussed below, was established by the act to provide federal financial assistance to railroads across the country for facilities maintenance, rehabilitation, improvement, and acquisition projects and other financial needs approved by the Secretary of Transportation.

4. A new program of loans was established for the transitional period in which rail properties are conveyed from the bankrupt railroads to ConRail, AMTRAK, or profitable railroads. These loans are intended to foster orderly and efficient implementation of the final system plan and to prevent disruptions in ordinary business relationships.

5. ConRail and any affected profitable railroad are now required to provide rail passenger service, for a period of 180 days following conveyance of rail properties from a bankrupt railroad, on any properties where such service was being provided immediately prior to this conveyance—regardless of whether this service was specified by the final system plan. Provisions are made for 100 percent federal reimbursement of losses incurred during this period, as well as for 100 percent federal support for the costs of providing an additional 180 days service, for 90 percent support of still another year's service, and, finally, if the applicant assures the Secretary of Transportation that passenger service will be continued after the termination of federal assistance, for 50 percent federal support of a final 180 day period of service.

In summary, the new 1976 railroad act added new elements of flexibility and complexity to the rail reorganization process in the Northeast/Midwest region and made more federal assistance over a longer period of time available to aid this process. Nevertheless, federal assistance for railroads still trails far behind the multiple billions spent on highways and abandonment of light density lines is still a principal federal policy. Further, this situation is exacerbated by the fact that even though the federal assistance program has been expanded, the state transportation agencies responsible for administering assistance granted to the states generally have long been fierce advocates of highway construction and thus are not committed to rail rehabilitation. Hopefully, however, some of the new measures set out in the 1976 act will help forestall the widespread rail abandonments presaged by the USRA's final system plan.

Nationwide Federal Assistance and Study

The Railroad Revitalization and Regulatory Reform Act of 1976 dealt with railroad problems not only in the Northeast/Midwest region, but also in the country at large. Among the many provisions which it is not possible to examine here are changes in railroad rates and other financial matters, reform of the ICC, and encouragement of mergers and consolidations. One action which deserves special note in a citizens' handbook is the establishment of a new, independent Office of Rail Public Counsel, affiliated with the ICC. This office is charged with the responsibility of constructively representing the public interest in safe, efficient, reliable, and economical rail transportation services. It may petition the ICC for the initiation of proceedings on any matter within the commission's jurisdiction which involves railroad carriers subject to the act, and it may also seek judicial review of ICC actions. Further, the Office of Rail Public Counsel is required by statute to solicit, study, evaluate, and present in any ICC proceeding, the views of those communities and users of rail services affected by the proceeding whenever the director of the office determines "for whatever reason (such as size or location), that such community or user of rail service might not otherwise be adequately represented before the Commission in the course of such proceedings. . . ."[94]

As pointed out in the preceding section, the 1976 act established a new railroad trust fund, which is called the Railroad Rehabilitation and Improvement Fund. The monies in this fund are to be used to provide financial assistance to railroads for facilities maintenance, rehabilitation, improvement, and acquisition projects, as well as for other financial needs approved by the Secretary of Transportation.

To aid decision making regarding this federal support, the act requires the development through cooperative efforts of railroads (excluding railroads subject to reorganization pursuant to the Regional Rail Reorganization Act of 1973), the Secretary of Transportation, and the Rail Services Planning Office of (1) standards for classifying all main and branch lines according to the degree that they are essential to the rail transportation system, and (2) actual classifications of main and branch lines. Public hearings on these questions must be conducted by the Rail Services Planning Office before final determinations are made. Applications made by railroads to the Secretary of Transportation for rehabilitation and improvement financing must then include the classification of each main and branch line included in the project.

Also referred to above was the new federal financial support available to all fifty states, on a formula basis, for rail freight assistance programs. These programs must be designed to cover the costs of (1) rail service continuation payments; (2) purchasing rail properties to maintain existing or provide for future services; (3) rehabilitation and improvements; and (4) reducing the costs of lost rail service in a manner less expensive than continuing rail service. States must meet eligibility requirements set out in the statute in order to obtain this assistance, which is available at a federal share of 100 percent for the first year, 90 percent for the second, 80 percent for the third, and 70 percent for the fourth and fifth years. During the first two years this assistance is not available to states eligible for rail service continuation assistance under the Regional Rail Reorganization Act of 1973.

The 1976 act also makes the Secretary of Transportation, in cooperation with others, responsible for a number of special studies to be submitted to Congress. Among these are an analysis of the capital needs of certain railroads; a report on the conversion of railroad rights-of-way; a comprehensive study of the American railway system; a comprehensive study of federal aid to railroads and other modes of transportation, including the question of whether railroads have been at a disadvantage in this process; and a study of conglomerates and other corporate structures found within the rail transportation industry.

Finally, the act also provides for the establishment of a "rail bank," through which rail trackage and other rail properties can be preserved in those parts of the country where fossil fuels or agricultural production is located.

Citizen Action

The fight to save railroad services in the United States is an uphill battle. The billions of dollars which have been spent on highway construction have placed so much power behind highway interests, both inside and outside government, that efforts to win preservation and rehabilitation of railroads are carried out against very heavy odds. Thus there is a critical need for concerted and informed citizen action to take advantage of existing means of strengthening railroads and to push for more effective programs.

Citizens who want to join in the movement to preserve and upgrade railroad services should

1. Contact existing organizations which are working to prevent rail abandonments and to achieve improved rail services. Two important such organizations, both of which publish newsletters or public alerts, are

> National Association of Railroad Passengers
> 417 New Jersey Avenue, S.E.
> Washington, D.C. 20003
>
> North East Transportation Coalition
> Millerton, New York 12546

2. Write to the Office of Rail Public Counsel, requesting to be put on a mailing list for information regarding rail problems and the office's activities. The following is this agency's address:

> Office of Rail Public Counsel
> Rail Services Planning Office
> 1900 L Street, N.W.
> Washington, D.C. 20036

3. Contact the public information office of the U.S. Department of Transportation, Washington, D.C. 20590, and that of one's own state department of transportation requesting to be sent news releases and other materials concerning railroads.

4. Follow the activities of the congressional committees which

deal with railroad problems and legislation. These committees and their chairmen are as follows:

Senate Committee on Commerce
  Chairman: Warren G. Magnuson, Washington
  Subcommittee on Surface Transportation
  Chairman: Vance Hartke, Indiana
House Committee on Interstate and Foreign Commerce
  Chairman: Harley O. Staggers, West Virginia
  Subcommittee on Transportation and Commerce
  Chairman: Fred B. Rooney, Pennsylvania

Citizens should find out if their own representatives or senators serve on these committees, and if so, should write letters to these legislators expressing support for preservation of the nation's railroads.

5. Find out what state legislative committee or committees are responsible for railroad matters and what the state plans to do to assure continuation of service on light density lines and to prevent rail abandonments. It is also possible that someone on the governor's staff has special responsibility for railroad questions. Efforts should be made to see that the state meets all the federal criteria for financial assistance for rail service continuation subsidies, has appropriated the needed matching funds, and is moving ahead to obtain its full share of available federal support. State transportation departments which are dominated by highway officials may be very reluctant to develop an effective state railroad program and strong citizen pressure insisting that they do so is absolutely essential.

AIRPORTS

Airports create many serious environmental problems. Of these, the noise with which ascending and descending aircraft bombard communities is perhaps the most severe. In addition, airports attract large numbers of automobiles and trucks, with their concomitant air pollution, while the airplanes themselves also emit carbon monoxide, hydrocarbons, nitrogen dioxide, and smoke. Vast tracts of land, moreover, are needed to accommodate the operations of an airport. Since in developed areas frequently the only types of vacant land which lie within a convenient distance of the central business district are parks, wetlands, and other kinds of valuable open space, pressure to use such lands for airports or airport extensions has often been exerted. Once an airport is constructed, its paved surfaces give rise to storm water runoff that is often laden with oil and other pollutants. In addition to these direct effects, airports also have critical secondary impacts, since local governments and chambers of commerce often use them as means of attracting commercial and industrial development. Finally, growth in the air transportation industry also has a great impact on energy problems, since airplanes have a very high rate of fuel consumption.

Because of the adverse environmental effects involved, many communities have fought plans for new airports or expansions of existing ones. In one of the most widely publicized cases, fierce citizen opposition to the location of a huge jetport some fifty miles from Miami just north of the Everglades National Park led to the abandonment of that project. In fact, the difficulty of gaining approval for large new airports has led the Federal Aviation Administration (FAA), the DOT agency responsible for administering federal assistance for airport planning and development, to turn its attention more toward new small airports and improvements at existing airports, whereas it had earlier envisioned the construction of many large new metropolitan airports. In recent years the only new major metropolitan airports which have been built are Dulles Airport outside of Washington, D.C., and the Dallas-Fort Worth Airport. Both of these facilities are located at considerable distances from central business districts and both are very large, reflecting the purchase of much land to serve as noise buffer zones. In fact, the huge Dallas-Fort Worth Airport occupies over seventeen thousand acres and is larger than the whole of Manhattan Island.

Increasing use and expansion of existing airports has also met strenuous opposition. Legal actions against the city of Los Angeles led to a court ruling that the city was liable to property owners in the neighborhood of the airport for measurable reductions in property values resulting from the noise caused by increasing aircraft traffic.[95] The city has now, at great expense, purchased or moved homes on surrounding land to enlarge its noise buffer zone. The city of Romulus, a suburb of Detroit, obtained an injunction halting federal participation in the construction of a new runway on the grounds that the EIS prepared on the project was inadequate.[96]

In an attempt to clarify the context in which such legal battles have taken place, this section first explains the essential statutory framework of federal assistance for airports and then reviews the FAA's policies and procedures for environmental review.

The Airport and Airway Development Act of 1970

The federal government has assisted the construction of publicly owned airports since 1946, but this role was greatly expanded by the Airport and Airway Development Act of 1970.[97] The passage of this act was prompted by the enormous growth in air traffic during the 1960s and Congress's perception that the national network of airports and airways was inadequate to meet current and projected needs.

The act made federal funds available for both airport planning and development. It also required the Secretary of Transportation to prepare, and revise as necessary, a National Airport System Plan for the development of public airports for at least a ten-year period.[98] After the completion of this plan (accomplished in 1972), no application for development assistance could propose projects which were not included in the current revision of the plan. The act also established an Airport and Airway Trust Fund, to which are appropriated funds equivalent to taxes paid on aviation fuel, aircraft tires and tubes, air transportation, and the use of civil aircraft.

Federal grants for airport planning may not exceed two-thirds of the costs involved, while in the case of development grants, large airports can receive up to 50 percent federal funding and small airports, up to 75 percent.

Certain specific statutory requirements are set out for development grants.[99] No airport development project involving the location of an airport, a major runway extension, or runway location may be approved unless

1. The public agency sponsoring the project certifies that an opportunity has been afforded for public hearings to consider the economic, social, and environmental effects of the airport location and its consistency with the goals and objectives of whatever urban planning has been carried out by the community.

2. The governor or the state certifies that there is reasonable assurance that the project will be located, designed, constructed, and operated so as to comply with applicable air and water quality standards. Approval of project applications must be conditioned on compliance during construction and operation with applicable air and water quality standards.

The act specifically declares that it is "national policy that airport development projects authorized pursuant to this [statute] shall provide for the protection and enhancement of the natural resources and the quality of environment of the Nation."[100] In implementing this policy, the Secretary of Transportation must consult with the Secretary of the Interior and the Administrator of EPA regarding the effect any project involving airport location, a major runway extension, or runway location may have on natural resources including, but not limited to, fish and wildlife, natural, scenic, and recreation assets, water and air quality, and other factors affecting the environment. No such project found to have adverse effect may be authorized unless the Secretary of Transportation renders a finding, in writing, following a full and complete review which is a matter of public record, that "no feasible and prudent alternative exists and that all possible steps have been taken to minimize such adverse effects."[101]

A clear similarity exists between this language and that of Section 4(f) of the Department of Transportation Act of 1966, which has been discussed above under highways. However, Section 4(f), which also applies to airport grants, pertains specifically to the protection of park and recreation lands, wildlife and waterfowl refuges, and historic sites, while the airport act is broader in scope, requiring special consideration of all natural resources and the total quality of the environment.

All proposed airport development must be in accordance with federal standards, including those for site location, airport layout, grading, drainage, seeding, paving, lighting, and safety of approaches. A project may be approved only if the FAA is satisfied that the project is reasonably consistent with existing plans of planning agencies for the development of the area; that sufficient nonfederal monies are available; and that the project will be completed without undue delay. No airport development project may be approved unless a public agency or the federal government holds good title to the site of the landing area or gives satisfactory assurances that good title will be acquired. Before approval, the FAA must also receive satisfactory written assurances that:

> appropriate action, including the adoption of zoning laws, has been or will be taken, to the extent reasonable, to restrict the use of land adjacent to or in the immediate vicinity of the airport to activities and

purposes compatible with normal airport operations, including landing and takeoff of aircraft . . .[102]

Finally, no airport development project may be approved unless the FAA is satisfied that fair consideration has been given to the interests of communities in or near which the project may be located.

FAA Policies and Procedures for Environmental Review

As has been pointed out, the most severe immediate environmental impact of airports is noise. In 1968 growing public complaints about the noise caused by jets led Congress to authorize the FAA to regulate aircraft noise.[103] In 1969 the FAA promulgated a regulation which prescribed noise standards for type certification of subsonic transport category airplanes and for type certification of all subsonic turbojet powered planes.[104] Under this regulation significantly quieter aircraft such as the Boeing 747, the McDonnell Douglas DC–10, and the Lockheed L–1011 Tristar have been developed and certificated. In 1973 the FAA required all newly produced large turbojet planes to meet its aircraft noise criteria, regardless of when they were certificated. Retrofitting of airplanes certificated and produced prior to the establishment of noise standards is still under study and has not yet been required.

EPA was brought into the aircraft noise field by the Noise Control Act of 1972.[105] Under this act EPA was required, among other things, to undertake a special study of aircraft noise, including evaluation of the FAA regulations. On the basis of this study, it was to submit to the FAA proposed regulations for control and abatement necessary to protect the public health and welfare. The FAA was then to consider these proposed regulations and publish them in the *Federal Register* in a notice of proposed rule making. After this publication, the FAA was to hold public hearings and then either (1) adopt the regulations submitted by EPA or modifications thereof or (2) publish a notice in the *Federal Register* that it was not going to prescribe any regulations in response to EPA's submission, supported by a detailed explanation of its reasons for not doing so.

EPA did not deliver these proposed regulations to the FAA in one submission, but has submitted them in sections. Throughout 1975 the FAA fulfilled its statutory responsibility to publish the proposals in the *Federal Register,* but prospects for early adoption are dim. The Secretary of Transportation's decision in February

1976 to permit the supersonic Concorde to land at Kennedy and Dulles airports, despite EPA's strong objections based largely on noise considerations, was surely an ill omen in this field.

On July 9, 1975, the FAA announced an extended public comment period on the question of what type of airport noise policy it should adopt.[106] In this notice, the FAA identified possible airport use restrictions which might be imposed, set out four potential policy options, and raised specific questions about the alternative effects of the four proposals. These policy options were as follows:

1. Airport proprietors' actions unconstrained by the FAA (so long as restrictions do not interfere with clear federal responsibilities for aircraft operating procedures and the management and control of navigable airspace[107]).

2. Airport proprietors completely constrained by the FAA with a correlated development of a federal airport noise abatement plan.

3. Airport proprietors to establish noise abatement plans.

4. Continue the present policy (which emphasizes efforts to reduce aircraft noise at the source, as well as the development of noise abatement operating procedures).

Public hearings were held across the country on these policy options and the FAA accepted written comments until January 1, 1976. Analysis of these comments and selection of a course of action are now underway.

The measurement of noise impact is a very difficult task and a number of different techniques are presently used. For example, the FAA has developed and pushed for the use of the Aircraft Sound Description System (ASDS), which measures the number of minutes per day particular acres of land are exposed to aircraft noise levels of eighty-five decibels (a very high level of noise) or above. EPA, on the other hand, has favored composite noise level measurements, such as Composite Noise Rating (CNR) and Noise Exposure Forecast (NEF), which provide measurements of aggregate aircraft noise exposures in which all noise levels are taken into account and discriminations are made between daytime and nighttime noise levels, since nighttime noise is more disturbing. In *City of Romulus* v. *County of Wayne,*[108] the plaintiffs objected both to the FAA's excessive reliance on ASDS in the EIS prepared on a new runway project and to the agency's failure to explain what the noise measurements it presented meant in terms of an acceptable human environment.

The plaintiffs prevailed in the case, and federal participation in the project was enjoined pending the preparation of an adequate EIS.

The FAA's procedures for the preparation of EISs on airport projects were published in a notice of proposed rule making on August 20, 1975.[109] Comments were accepted until November 3, 1975, and final regulations are expected in the second half of 1976. Until that time, the proposed rules provide interim guidance.

With respect to noise, the proposed regulations state that "[u]ntil a single agreed upon Federal system is developed for compatible land-use designation, both the FAA's ASDS method and the CNR method (or other methods such as the NEF) shall be used to describe noise exposure conditions."[110]

Generally, the procedures for environmental review set out in the FAA's proposed regulations provide an effective framework for compliance with the letter and spirit of NEPA. The most serious problem in the environmental review of airports is that FAA generally prepares EISs *after* land for a new airport or expansion has been acquired by the airport sponsor. Clearly, once land has been acquired, some of the most important alternatives which NEPA requires to be considered—including the alternative of no construction—are effectively foreclosed.

Several court decisions have lent support to the approach of allowing sponsors who will later seek federal funds to proceed with a project without being subject to federal requirements. In *New Windsor* v. *Ronan,* the court rejected the plaintiff's argument that airport development, without federal money, could not proceed in the absence of federal authorization.[111] The court took this action even though it found that there was no serious doubt that the state desired and would later seek federal funds for the project. In *Boston* v. *Volpe* the FAA had made a tentative allocation of funds for a taxiway construction project, but the court held that this was not a "federal action" under NEPA and refused to enjoin the project pending the preparation of an adequate EIS.[112]

In a more recent case, however, a federal district court rejected the practice of local acquisition of land and subsequent federal reimbursement without an EIS.[113] In this case, which concerned the DuPage County Airport in Illinois, the court ordered the sponsor to deposit all federal funds received with the court until the county and the FAA had "caused a positive environmental impact statement to be prepared concerning the effect future airport development by the

County of DuPage and reimbursement therefor by the Federal Aviation Administration may have upon the environment. . . ."

The proposed FAA regulations suggest, at one point, that federal approval and environmental assessment must precede the decision regarding where a new airport is to be located:

> Because the location of a new airport profoundly affects the areas surrounding it, Federal approval of a proposed location is always preceded by an environmental assessment.[114]

Several paragraphs later, however, the regulations state that public sponsors may have the authority to acquire land adjacent to existing airports or for new airports, without prior approval by the FAA.[115] The regulations go on to warn that such prior acquisition could prejudice or preclude a favorable decision by the FAA on proposed changes in airport layout which would use the land or on requests for reimbursement for the property. Specifically, they state that:

> A sponsor who has acquired land without prior approval by the FAA must demonstrate to the satisfaction of the FAA that his action was consistent with the policies expressed in this order and has not precluded full and objective consideration of alternatives.[116]

The proposed regulations indicate that the environmental impact assessment report, which the FAA uses in its preparation of the EIS, is usually one of the elements of the airport master plan.[117] Another element of this master plan is a new or revised airport layout plan, which must be approved by the FAA. Although such approval does not commit the FAA to provide financial assistance to implement the proposed layout plan, it does constitute a "federal action" under NEPA. Thus airport layout plans may be unconditionally approved only if all FAA environmental requirements have been met. If environmental processing has not been completed on any proposed airport development shown on the plan, only a conditional approval may be granted. This provision has met with opposition among airport sponsors.

Citizen Action

It is essential that citizens who are concerned about the problems associated with airports become involved in the planning for specific facilities as early as possible. An excellent way of finding out what expansions of existing airports or new airports may be in the offing in one's area is to consult the most recent version of the National Airport System Plan (NASP). As has been discussed, the preparation of this plan was required by the Airport and Airway Development Act of 1970, and the FAA published the original twelve-volume edition in 1972.

In effect, the plan sets out airport development which the FAA considers desirable. Thus inclusion in NASP is no assurance that a project will be carried out, but is simply an indication that it might be. As has been pointed out, no airport development project may be proposed for federal assistance unless it is included in the current version of NASP. Nonetheless, despite its "wish list" character, NASP is an important introduction to the thinking of FAA and local airport planners. It is particularly important for citizens to scrutinize very carefully the projections of future air traffic it sets forth. Such projections, which serve as rationales for proposed development, have in the past frequently proved to be far too high.

NASP is updated on a quarterly basis, incorporating the results of various planning studies as well as indicating the completion of particular developments. The updated versions of the plan are not published, but are distributed as computer printouts to the various FAA field offices across the country. Since these documents are public information, they may be consulted by citizens in accordance with the FAA's procedures for making government materials available to the public for inspection and copying. Citizens who wish to review the most recent NASP printouts for their area should contact the FAA division or district office within whose jurisdiction they fall. A list of these regional field offices and their jurisdictions can be obtained from

> Airports Service
> Federal Aviation Administration
> U.S. Department of Transportation
> Washington, D.C. 20591

When a new airport or an important expansion is proposed for an area, citizens should push for the development of an airport master plan with a responsible land use element. They should also work to see that the local government carefully studies the relationship of the proposed airport development to adjacent land uses and, to the greatest degree possible, zones high noise areas for industrial rather than residential uses.

NOTES

1. In 1974 the Council on Environmental Quality, in association with the U.S. Department of Housing and Urban Development and the U.S. Environmental Protection Agency, published a study entitled *The Costs of Sprawl*, which documented many of the costs of scattered, low-density suburban development and estimated how these costs vary among different patterns of land use. Real Estate Research Corporation, *The Costs of Sprawl: Environmental and Economic Costs of Alternative Residential Development Patterns at the Urban Fringe* (Washington, D.C.: U.S. Government Printing Office, 1974).

2. Council on Environmental Quality, *Environmental Quality: The Fifth Annual Report of the Council on Environmental Quality* (1974), p. 39.

3. See Note 8 of Chapter 5 for a discussion of the very significant role which storm water runoff from city streets plays in water pollution.

4. Council on Environmental Quality, *Environmental Quality: The Second Annual Report of the Council on Environmental Quality* (1971), p. 212.

5. U.S. Environmental Protection Agency, *Report to the President and Congress on Noise*, S. Doc. No. 92–63, 92d Congress, 2d Sess. (February 1972).

6. Natural Resources Defense Council, *Transportation Controls for Clean Air* (January 1973).

7. *The World Almanac and Book of Facts, 1976*, published for *The Philadelphia Inquirer* (New York: Newspaper Enterprise Association, Inc., 1975), p. 962.

8. National Wildlife Federation v. Brinegar, Civil No. 1269–73 (D.D.C., August 22, 1975). See 40 *Federal Register* 53759 (November 19, 1975).

9. 23 U.S.C. § 103 (f); 23 C.F.R. Part 470.

10. PPM 21–1(5) (February 2, 1962), 2 ELR 46513, *amending* PPM 21–1 par. 8a (April 15, 1958), 2 ELR 46507. See Ronald C. Peterson and Robert M. Kennan, Jr., *The Federal-Aid Highway Program: Administrative Procedures and Judicial Interpretation*, 2 ELR 50001, 50005 and 50007 (1972).

11. 23 C.F.R. § 795.2 (e).

12. 23 U.S.C. § 106 (a); 23 C.F.R. Part 630.

13. 23 U.S.C. §§ 109 (h) and 128; 23 C.F.R. Part 790.

14. 23 C.F.R. § 1.12.

15. 23 C.F.R. §§ 635.107 (a) and 635.111 (a).

16. This process was carefully analyzed in 1972 in Peterson and Kennan, *The Federal-Aid Highway Program*, 2 ELR 50001.

17. 23 U.S.C. § 118 (b).

18. As has been pointed out, Section 106 (a) states that PS&E approval contractually obligates the federal government to pay the federal share of a project. However, FHWA has considered certain authorizations to proceed with work to constitute contractual obligation of federal funds. See Peterson and Kennan, *The Federal-Aid Highway Program*, 2 ELR 50010.

19. This problem and related litigation are analyzed in John W. Vardaman, Jr., "Federal Environmental Statutes and Transportation," *Federal Environmental Law* (St. Paul: West Publishing Co., 1974), as well as in Peterson and Kennan, *The Federal-Aid Highway Program*, 2 ELR 50011.

20. 23 C.F.R. §790.3 (d).

21. 23 C.F.R. § 790.9 (e).

22. See Chapter 3 for further discussion of this problem.

23. 23 C.F.R. § 771.5(f).

24. 23 U.S.C. § 117. Revised interim regulations implementing this statute were published by FHWA at 40 *Federal Register* 6914 (February 13, 1976); 23 C.F.R. Part 640 (interim).

25. 40 *Federal Register* 6914 (February 13, 1976).

26. 42 U.S.C. § 4332 (2) (C).

27. 39 *Federal Register* 41804 (December 2, 1974); 23 C.F.R. Part 771.

28. *Ibid.*, § 771.5 (a). A "highway section" is defined as a highway development proposal between logical termini (population centers, major traffic generators, major crossroads, etc.) as normally included in a location study or multiyear highway improvement program.

29. 23 C.F.R. § 771.5 (b).

30. See Notes 20 and 21 of Chapter 3.

31. Public Law No. 94–83, 89 Stat. 424 (August 9, 1975); 42 U.S.C. § 4332 (2) (D).

32. 23 C.F.R. § 771.9 (d).

33. 23 C.F.R. § 771.10 (e) (3).

34. 49 U.S.C. § 1653 (f). Virtually identical language is repeated in 23 U.S.C. § 138.

35. *Ibid.*

36. E.g., Named Individual Members of San Antonio Conservation Society v. Texas Highway Department, 446 F.2d 1013, 2 ERC 1871 (5th Cir. 1971); Arlington Coalition on Transportation v. Volpe, 458 F.2d 1323, 3 ERC 1995 (4th Cir. 1972).

37. Citizens to Preserve Overton Park, Inc. v. Volpe, 401 U.S. 402, 411, 2 ERC 1250, 1254 (1971). This rule was applied in a recent decision by the U.S. Court of Appeals for the Fourth Circuit. Coalition for Responsible Regional Development v. Brinegar, 518 F.2d 522, 8 ERC 1425 (4th Cir. 1976).

38. *Ibid.*

39. 401 U.S. at 412–413.

40. 39 *Federal Register* 41813 (December 2, 1974); 23 C.F.R. § 771.19.

41. PPM 20–8, 2 ELR 46505. The amended version of this policy and procedure memorandum is now found at 23 C.F.R. Part 790.

42. 39 *Federal Register* 41819 (December 2, 1974); 23 C.F.R. Part 795.

43. In D.C. Federation of Civic Associations v. Volpe the court held that an earlier hearing did not adequately deal with the design details of the proposed Three Sisters Bridge across the Potomac, since the final design varied from the plans discussed at the hearing in such items as the angle at which the bridge would cross the river, the placing of approach ramps, and the number of spans in the bridge. 316 F. Supp. 754, 1 ERC 1484 (D.D.C. 1970).

44. 23 C.F.R. § 790.1 (b).

45. 39 *Federal Register* 41804 (December 2, 1974).

46. 23 C.F.R. § 795.10 (b) (7) (i).

47. 23. U.S.C. § 134 (a).

48. 23 C.F.R. § 450.122.

49. 40 *Federal Register* 42976 (September 17, 1975); 23 C.F.R. Part 450.

50. The regulations encourage but do not require the designation of the A–95 areawide clearinghouse agency, discussed in Chapter 13, as the MPO for a region.

51. Richard A. Bouchard, "Environmental Factors in Urban Transportation Planning," *1970 Proceedings, American Association of State Highway Officials*, pp. 281–282, as quoted in Vardaman, "Transportation," *Federal Environmental Law*, p. 1342.

52. 23 C.F.R. § 450.120 (a) (3).

53. 42 U.S.C. § 1857 *et seq.*

54. 42 U.S.C. § 1857c–5 (a) (2) (B).

55. Natural Resources Defense Council v. Environmental Protection Agency, 475 F.2d 968, 4 ERC 1945 (D.C. Cir. 1973).

56. Friends of the Earth v. Wilson, 389 F. Supp. 1394, 7 ERC 1939 (S.D.N.Y. 1974).

57. These notices of violation are filed in the Region 2 enforcement docket as Index Nos. 50216 and 50217.

58. Friends of the Earth v. Carey, 401 F. Supp. 1386, 8 ERC 1585 (S.D.N.Y. 1975), _____F.2d _____, 8 ERC 1933 (2d Cir. 1976).

59. 8 ERC at 1937–1938.

60. Commonwealth of Pennsylvania v. Environmental Protection Agency, 500 F.2d 246, 6 ERC 1769 (3d Cir. 1974).

61. Brown v. Environmental Protection Agency, 521 F.2d 827, 8 ERC 1053 (9th Cir. 1975).

62. District of Columbia v. Train, 521 F.2d 971, 8 ERC 1289 (D.C. Cir. 1975).

63. 39 *Federal Register* 44441 (December 24, 1974); 23 C.F.R. Part 770. In April 1975 FHWA and EPA issued further more detailed, but nonregulatory guidelines explaining the actual procedures which should be involved in making the required 109 (j) consistency determinations. U.S. Department of Transportation, Federal Highway Administration, *Guidelines for Analysis of Consistency Between Transportation and Air Quality Plans and Programs* (Washington, D.C.: April 1975).

64. 49 U.S.C. § 1601 *et seq.*

65. 40 *Federal Register* 32546 (August 1, 1975).

66. Robert E. Patricelli, Administrator of UMTA, speech before the first APTA annual conference, New Orleans, September 30, 1975, as reprinted in DOT, *News* (no date), p. 3.

67. 40 *Federal Register* 42976 (September 17, 1975); 23 C.F.R. Part 450.

68. 49 U.S.C. § 1602.

69. § 14; 49 U.S.C. § 1610.

70. Public Law No. 93–503, 88 Stat. 1565 (November 26, 1974), amending 49 U.S.C. § 1604.

71. C. Kenneth Orski, Associate Administrator for Policy and Program Development of UMTA, speech before the fifty-fifth annual meeting of the Transportation Research Board, Washington, D.C., January 21, 1976, as reprinted in DOT, *News* (no date), p. 12.

72. 40 *Federal Register* 16301; 23 C.F.R. Part 820 (April 11, 1975).

73. § 4 (c); 49 U.S.C. § 1603 (c).

74. § 16; 49 U.S.C. § 1612.

75. Public Law No. 93–87, 87 Stat. 250 (August 13, 1973).

76. Patricelli, speech, September 30, 1975, as reprinted in DOT, *News* (no date), p. 9.

77. 39 *Federal Register* 32298 (September 5, 1974); 23 C.F.R. Part 810 (proposed). An internal DOT document entitled "Preliminary Guidance on Advancing Public Transportation Projects Now Applicable under Provisions of the Federal-Aid Highway Act of 1973" (November 15, 1973) was also published at 40 *Federal Register* 53958 (November 19, 1975), as part of materials published by DOT under court order. See Note 8 above.

78. 23 U.S.C. § 103 (e) (4); 23 C.F.R. § 476.300 *et seq.*

79. 45 U.S.C. § 761.

80. 45 U.S.C. § 501 *et seq.*

81. Public Law No. 92–316 (June 22, 1972); Public Law No. 93–146 (November 3, 1973); Public Law No. 93–496 (October 28, 1974); Public Law No. 94–25 (May 26, 1975); and Public Law No. 94–210 (February 5, 1976).

82. Public Law No. 93–236, 87 Stat. 986 (January 2, 1974), 45 U.S. § 701 *et seq.*

83. 45 U.S.C. § 701 (a).

84. 45 U.S.C. § 701 (b) (2) and (5).

85. 45 U.S.C. § 744 (e).

86. Public Law No. 93–488, § 1 (d), 88 Stat. 1464 (October 26, 1974); 45 U.S.C. § 762 (c) (2).

87. 40 *Federal Register* 16377 (April 11, 1975).

88. The plan stated that 5,757 miles of "active roadway" and 1,158 miles of out-of-service trackage, or a total of 6,915 miles of rail line, were excluded from the regional rail system. U.S. Railway Association, *Final System Plan,* II:3.

89. 42 U.S.C. § 1857 *et seq.* See Chapter 4 and the section on transportation control plans above in this chapter.

90. 45 U.S.C. § 716 (a).

91. Interstate Commerce Commission, *Evaluation of the U.S. Railway Association's Final System Plan,* report of the Interstate Commerce Commission to the United States Congress (Washington, D.C.: August 25, 1975), p. 47.

92. See 45 U.S.C. § 719.

93. Public Law No. 94–210, 90 Stat. 31 (February 5, 1976).

94. *Ibid.,* § 304 (a), amending 49 U.S.C. § 27.

95. Aaron v. City of Los Angeles, 40 Cal. App.3d 471, 7 ERC 1657, *cert. denied,* 419 U.S. 1122, 7 ERC 1657 (1975).

96. City of Romulus v. County of Wayne, 392 F. Supp. 578, 7 ERC 1866 (E.D. Mich. 1975).

97. 49 U.S.C. § 1701 *et seq.*

98. The authority for the preparation of this plan was delegated by the Secretary of Transportation to the FAA. The first edition was published in 1972. U.S. Department of Transportation, Federal Aviation Administration, *1972 National Airport System Plan* (Washington, D.C.: U.S. Government Printing Office, 1972), 12 volumes.

99. 49 U.S.C. §§ 1716 and 1718.

100. 49 U.S.C. § 1716 (c) (4).

101. *Ibid.*

102. 49 U.S.C. § 1718 (4).

103. 49 U.S.C. § 1431.

104. 14 C.F.R. Part 36.

105. Public Law No. 92–574, § 7 (b), 86 Stat. 1239 (October 27, 1972), amending 49 U.S.C. § 1431.

106. 40 *Federal Register* 28844 (July 9, 1975).

107. In City of Burbank v. Lockheed Air Terminal the U.S. Supreme Court invalidated a municipal ordinance which prohibited jet landings and takeoffs from the Hollywood-Burbank Airport between 11 p.m. and 7 a.m. The Court held that such control over flight operations is preempted by federal law. 411 U.S. 624, 5 ERC 1321 (1973).

108. 392 F. Supp. 578, 7 ERC 1866 (E.D. Mich. 1975).

109. 40 *Federal Register* 36516 (August 20, 1975). This notice included both proposed amendments to 14 C.F.R. Part 152 and an internal directive, FAA Order 5050.2A, "Instructions for Processing Airport Development Actions Affecting the Environment," which is incorporated by reference in 14 C.F.R. § 152.23 (proposed).

110. 40 *Federal Register* 36521 (August 20, 1975), paragraph 44.

111. New Windsor v. Ronan, 329 F. Supp. 1286, 3 ERC 1023 (S.D.N.Y. 1971).

112. Boston v. Volpe, 464 F.2d 254, 4 ERC 1337 (1st Cir. 1972).

113. Board of Education of Community Unit School District 303, Kane and DuPage Counties, Illinois v. Brinegar, Civil No. 72–C–3126 (N.D. Ill., January 11, 1974).

114. 40 *Federal Register* 36520 (August 20, 1975), paragraph 34.

115. *Ibid.,* paragraph 38.

116. 40 *Federal Register* 36520 (August 20, 1975), paragraph 38.

117. In 1971 the FAA published a readable booklet explaining the components of the airport master plan which is for sale from the Superintendent of Documents. U.S. Department of Transportation, Federal Aviation Administration, *Airport Master Plans* (Washington, D.C.: U.S. Government Printing Office, 1971). AC 150/5070–6.

CHAPTER 11

The Public Lands of the United States

A PPROXIMATELY ONE-THIRD of the land in the United States is owned by the federal government and managed by federal agencies. Most of these public lands are located in the eleven western states and in Alaska, where the federal government still owns vast acreages, but there are also important holdings in the eastern states as well.

In a book such as this, it is not possible to set out in detail the complex myriad of statutes, agency regulations, and policies which govern the management and use of these lands.[1] What can be presented, however, is an account which clarifies the following:

1. What kinds of public lands there are.
2. What agencies are responsible for their management.
3. What important private uses are made of the public lands and what the environmental impacts of these uses are.
4. How citizens can seek to assure that the public lands are managed and used for the maximum benefit of the general public.

The Public Lands

The public lands of the United States are remarkably diverse in character. They range from the northern tip of Alaska to the southern end of Florida, encompassing all types of climates, terrains, and vegetation. The highest point in North America, Mount McKinley, lies on public land, and so does the lowest point in the United States, Death Valley. Mountains, valleys, tundra, river deltas, swamps, and seashores are all represented in the vast federal holdings, as are a broad range of actual or potential resources, including timber, minerals, forage, watersheds, sites for the expansion of towns and cities, and settings for recreation and associated activities.

During the nineteenth century a basic policy of the United States government was to encourage westward expansion and settlement through the disposal of public lands. Homestead grants made land available to settlers, land grants to the new states encouraged education and other supportive uses, and grants such as those for railroad construction stimulated the construction of public facilities. Beginning with the establishment of Yellowstone Park in 1872, however, the federal government began to reserve certain portions of its land for special purposes and permanent federal ownership.[2] During the ensuing years, millions of acres of federal lands were withdrawn from entry under the disposal laws, often to protect natural resources from private exploitation, as well as to serve emerging national needs. In addition, the federal government began to purchase or repurchase selected tracts of land for particular purposes.

Today the public lands include both (1) the so-called "public domain" lands which have never left federal ownership since they were ceded to the federal government by the original states or were acquired from other countries; and (2) lands which have been acquired by the federal government for specific purposes. The public domain includes (1) those lands which have been reserved or set aside for particular purposes, such as national forests, national parks, wildlife refuges, wilderness areas, and defense installations; (2) those lands which have not been so reserved; and (3) those lands which have been withdrawn from entry, but have not yet been classified for particular purposes.

In 1964, when it established the Public Land Law Review Commission, Congress stated that:

> it is hereby declared to be the policy of Congress that the public lands of the United States shall be (a) retained and managed or (b) disposed of, all in a manner to provide the maximum benefit for the general public.[3]

As one commentator has observed, "[b]y that declaration Congress made it clear that it was ending the long-standing statutory preference for disposal of the federal lands as a dominant policy, and was adopting a general goal—maximum benefit for the general public—which could be implemented by either disposal or retention. Thus those two alternatives were finally and properly viewed as means towards larger objectives, not as ends in themselves."[4]

The Public Land Law Review Commission itself, in its recommendations which were released in 1970, urged that future disposal of public lands be made only when such action would provide the maximum benefit for the general public. Regarding the lands retained in federal ownership, the commission stressed that their "values must be preserved so that they may be used and enjoyed by all Americans."[5]

Managing Agencies

The following four agencies manage most of the public lands of the United States:

1. The Forest Service of the U.S. Department of Agriculture.
2. The Bureau of Land Management (BLM) of the U.S. Department of the Interior.
3. The Fish and Wildlife Service of the U.S. Department of the Interior.
4. The National Park Service of the U.S. Department of the Interior.

In addition, sizeable acreages are also administered by the various military departments, the Energy Research and Development Administration, and the Bureau of Reclamation of the U.S. Department of the Interior.

1. The Forest Service

The Forest Service is responsible for the national forests, which comprise about one-fourth of all public lands or around 187 million acres. The vast bulk of these national forests (over 160 million acres) is located in the western states, including Alaska. In all, there are 155 different national forests in forty states.

The Forest Service manages the national forests under two principal acts, the Organic Act of 1897,[6] which was the first comprehensive act governing the management of the national forests, and the Multiple Use-Sustained Yield Act of 1960.[7] Under the Organic Act national forests were to be established to provide favorable conditions of water flow and to furnish a continuous supply of timber for the use of American citizens. These purposes were enlarged by the Multiple Use-Sustained Yield Act to include outdoor recreation, range, timber, watershed, and fish and wildlife purposes. Renewable resources are to be managed on a sustained yield basis, which means "the achievement and maintenance in perpetuity of a high-level annual or regular periodic output of the various renewable resources of the national forests without impairment of the productivity of the land." In making its management decisions, the Forest Service must give due consideration to the relative values of the various resources in particular areas. Finally, the main goal of the multiple-use law is to produce "management of all the various renewable surface resources of the national forests so that they are utilized in the combination that will best meet the needs of the American people. . . ."[8]

Various clauses of the Organic Act have been interpreted as restraints on the Forest Service. As is discussed below, the requirements that all trees to be cut must be individually marked and that only dead, matured, or large trees may be cut have been held by the courts to prohibit the presently widespread practice of clear-cutting in the national forests.[9]

Under the terms of the Multiple Use-Sustained Yield Act, the Forest Service draws up multiple use plans for the national forests on a forest-by-forest basis. These plans then govern management decisions on matters such as the sale of timber, methods of timber harvest, and watershed protection. There has been considerable debate, however, regarding whether these decisions have in fact served the broad purposes of the act and some have argued that the terms of the act itself are so discretionary that they impose virtually no congressional standards on the Forest Service.[10]

The Forest and Rangeland Renewable Resources Planning Act of 1974[11] requires the Forest Service to carry out *long-term* planning for the national forests in accordance with principles set forth in the Multiple-Use Sustained Yield Act and the National Environmental Policy Act (NEPA).[12] Under the new 1974 act, the Forest Service must prepare a renewable resource program first for the four-year period from 1976 through 1980 and subsequently for each decade. These programs must include an inventory of specific needs and opportunities for public and private program investments in the national forests, along with an analysis of anticipated costs and benefits, priorities, and personnel requirements.

2. The Bureau of Land Management (BLM)

The BLM is responsible for the administration of some 470 million acres or over 60 percent of all federal lands. Most of this acreage is comprised of public domain lands which have not been reserved for particular uses. Almost two-thirds of the BLM lands are in Alaska, and the remainder are almost entirely in the eleven western states. Essentially, these are lands which are not suitable for agriculture and have not been included in the national forests or national parks systems.

The BLM also plays the lead role, along with the Geological Survey of the Department of the Interior, in the supervision of the resource development of the submerged lands of the Outer Continental Shelf.[13] The accelerated program of offshore oil leasing which has followed in the wake of the energy crisis has greatly increased the significance of this responsibility.

There is no comprehensive, organic act regulating the vast holdings of the federal government which fall within the jurisdiction of the BLM. Bills which would provide such an act for the BLM have been considered by Congress, but have not been passed. Many of the old laws governing private use or disposal of public domain lands (the Homestead Laws, for example) are still on the statute books, but only a limited number have relevance and importance today. Among these are the Mineral Leasing Act of 1920,[14] an antiquated law which governs the leasing of mineral rights for coal, oil, gas, and oil shale, and the Taylor Grazing Act of 1934,[15] which established a permit and fee system for livestock grazing on public domain lands.

In 1964 Congress passed the Classification and Multiple-Use Act,[16] which charged the BLM with the responsibility of classifying the public domain lands for disposal and management purposes. Under this now expired act, the BLM was given the authority to manage its lands on a multiple use-sustained yield basis similar to that authorized for the Forest Service. However, the BLM's list of specified management purposes included not only the five set out for the Forest Service (namely, outdoor recreation, range, timber, watershed, and fish and wildlife), but also industrial development, mineral production, occupancy, and wilderness preservation.

3. The Fish and Wildlife Service

This agency administers the National Wildlife Refuge System, which includes over 340 national wildlife refuges and game ranges, comprising over 30 million acres, and about a hundred small fish hatcheries. By statute, the components of this system are those areas under the jurisdiction of the Department of the Interior which are administered "as wildlife refuges, areas for the protection and conservation of fish and wildlife that are threatened with extinction, wildlife ranges, game ranges, wildlife management areas, or waterfowl production areas."[17]

4. The National Park Service

This agency administers the National Park System, which includes over 23 million acres of land. The National Park Service Act of 1916 established that all national parks are to be managed:

> to conserve the scenery and the natural and historic objects and the wildlife therein and to provide for the enjoyment of the same in such manner and by such means as will leave them unimpaired for the enjoyment of future generations.[18]

The individual components of the system are governed by particular statutes which generally aim to maintain the land in its natural state, but differ in the details of management.

The individual components include not only the national parks, but other types of areas as well. For administrative purposes, the National Park Service has grouped its lands into the following three categories: natural areas, historical areas, and recreation areas. The natural areas include the national parks and national monuments of scientific significance. The historical areas include those lands which have historical or archaeological significance. The recreation areas include those areas which were established primarily for recreational purposes, notably national recreation areas, seashores, lakeshores, scenic parkways, and wild and scenic rivers.

Private Uses of Public Lands

Although much of the prime land once owned by the federal government was transferred into private ownership during the nineteenth and early twentieth centuries, the public lands are today still rich with multiple resources. Generally, authorization and procedures exist for private use, development, lease, or purchase of these resources. The most prevalent such uses involving the following resources will be reviewed here: timber, mineral, grazing, water, and recreation resources. Various occupancy uses will also be briefly examined. Finally, attention will be turned toward the wilderness resources represented in the National Wilderness Preservation System, through which a heritage of lands substantially untouched by man is to be preserved for future generations.

1. Timber Resources

As a result of the reservation of vast acreages of timberland around the turn of the century, the federal government now plays a very important role in timber production in this country. It owns approximately 20 percent of the nation's commercial forest land, almost 40 percent of its supply of merchantable timber, and over 60 percent of its softwood sawtimber. About 100 million acres of public lands are classed as commercial forest lands, which are lands suitable for logging and the production of raw materials for the timber industry. Most of these lands lie within the national forests and are managed by the Forest Service.[19]

Rights for private parties to cut timber on federal lands are periodically put up for sale to applicants who meet specified criteria, and are awarded to the highest bidder. In the timber sales contracts which are then drawn up, the Forest Service has the right to stipulate methods of operation and safeguards which must be taken to prevent or minimize adverse effects on lands and waters.

In recent years, the amount of timber cut in the national forests has been increasing considerably, and now accounts for nearly one-third of the nation's total production. In the timber management plans which it develops on a forest-by-forest basis, the Forest Service determines "allowable cuts," which establish the amount of timber which may be cut from specified areas over a given period of time. These determinations are supposed to be designed to assure a sustained yield of timber from the area involved.

There is evidence, however, that this is not always the case. Two reports published by the Forest Service during the last five years have concluded that the maximum allowable timber harvest levels in selected national forests have been overestimated by as much as 30 percent.[20] In the past, actual cutting has usually fallen below the allowable cuts established, but more recent developments reveal strong pressures to increase tremendously the amount of timber taken from the national forests. For example, in response to rising timber prices the Nixon Administration decided to increase national forest timber sales by at least one billion board feet in fiscal 1974. Concerned by the serious environmental implications of this decision, the Natural Resources Defense Council (NRDC) initiated legal action to require the Forest Service to prepare an environmental impact statement under the National Environmental Policy Act (NEPA)[21] before proceeding with this sales drive, which was known as "Supersell" within the Forest Service.[22] In February 1974 the District Court for the District of Columbia upheld NRDC's position that such an impact statement was required. The Forest Service neither appealed the decision nor prepared an environmental impact statement, and the Supersell program was dropped.

A number of serious environmental effects are associated with timber cutting. Logging and the construction of necessary roads and facilities cause increased soil erosion, landslide potential, and water pollution, and can seriously affect the recreational, wildlife, and aesthetic values of a forest. For example, fish habitats are damaged both when streams are clogged with soil and logging debris and when water temperatures rise as a result of the removal of protective shade trees. Wildlife habitats may be damaged or destroyed by the removal both of food supply and of protective cover. These adverse impacts are greatly increased by such practices as clear-cutting and low-cost logging road construction.

As has been pointed out above, the Forest Service is charged by the Multiple Use-Sustained Yield Act of 1960 to administer the national forests for outdoor recreation, range, timber, watershed, and fish and wildlife purposes. In practice, however, there has been great pressure both from outside and within the agency to treat timber cutting as the dominant use of the national forests. Recently, a study team of the National Academy of Sciences concluded that:

> the [national] forests are managed for multiple use but we find in current practice that the extraction of saw timber gets the overwhelming attention from the Forest Service. There is much concern that irreversible harm to the environment may be caused by unwise forest management, for example by unwarranted clear-cutting.[23]

Clear-cutting has long been at the center of controversies over national forest management. The most widely used method of harvesting timber at the present time, it involves the cutting of all trees, regardless of age or condition, in an entire block of forest land. Even some of its severest critics acknowledge clear-cutting as an acceptable method of harvesting under the right conditions and within limits, but there has been much debate on how large the cuts should be and on what kinds of terrain or soil they should be allowed. The gigantic two hundred to one thousand acre clear-cuts which extend for mile after mile in the Bitterroot National Forest in Montana have caused substantial environmental and aesthetic damage. Even an in-house study team sent by the Forest Service to the Bitterroot criticized this clear-cutting as an example of poor forestry, concluding that "there is an implicit attitude [in] the Bitterroot National Forest that resource production goals come first and land management considerations take second place."[24]

In May 1973 the West Virginia Division of the Izaak Walton League, joined by the Sierra Club, the West Virginia Highlands Conservancy, the Natural Resources Defense Council, and one individual, filed a suit challenging extensive clear-cutting and other harvesting practices used in the Monongahela National Forest in West Virginia.[25] The plaintiffs argued that these practices violated provisions of the Organic Act of 1897, the first comprehensive act governing the management of the national forests. The federal district court agreed with this position, accepting the arguments of the plaintiffs that the plain language of this act requires that in all Forest Service timber sales: (1) all the trees to be cut must be individually marked; (2) only dead, matured, or large trees may be cut; and (3) all timber cut must be removed. The court found that in the seventy-seven years since the passage of the Organic Act there has been a "gravitation" away from its congressional mandates, but held that if clear-cutting does in fact represent a silviculturally sound method of harvesting, then such evidence should be presented to Congress. The unilateral adoption of these techniques by the Forest Service was found to be in violation of the intent of Congress expressed in the Organic Act.

In August 1975 the U.S. Court of Appeals for the Fourth Circuit affirmed the district court's decision. The Forest Service has decided not to appeal to the Supreme Court, but it is expected that advocates of clear-cutting both within the Forest Service and from the timber industry will urge Congress to pass new legislation amending the Organic Act. This means that during the next few years Congress will probably be reviewing the management of the national forests, thereby providing an opportunity for a national debate on Forest Service practices.

Two important legal suits have challenged Forest Service management practices in *de facto* wilderness areas. The first of these, *Sierra Club* v. *Butz,*[26] attacked the review process used by the Forest Service in determining which of approximately 55 million acres of roadless areas within the national forests should be studied for possible designation as "wilderness areas" under the Wilderness Act of 1964,[27] which is discussed below. Once designated for such study, areas are protected from actions, such as logging, which would disqualify them for wilderness designation. Shortly after the suit was filed, the district court enjoined the Forest Service from taking any steps to develop the land in question until the case had been decided. In November 1972, just before the trial, the Forest Service capitulated in major part and agreed to prepare environmental impact statements on all contracts to develop roadless areas entered into after July 1, 1972. The preparation of impact statements on the several dozen roadless areas covered by contracts entered into before that date was left to further litigation.

In March 1973 *Wyoming Outdoor Coordinating Council* v. *Butz*[28] challenged two pre-July 1, 1972, timber contracts for *de facto* wilderness areas in the Teton National Forest. The plaintiffs sought to halt these contracts, pending the preparation by the Forest Service of an environmental impact statement. The district court upheld the Forest Service, but the U.S. Court of Appeals for the Tenth Circuit reversed this decision, emphasizing "an overriding public interest in preservation of the undeveloped character of the area" and observing that the clear-cutting planned "obviously will have a significant effect on the environment for many years."[29]

It is clear that the environmental impact statement process has been a vital means of ensuring public scrutiny of the management of the national forests by the Forest Service. Another suit brought in the effort to obtain full consideration of environmental values by the Forest Service sought an order requiring the agency to prepare environmental impact statements on its annual programs.[30] This suit was settled after Congress passed the Forest and Range Renewable Resources Act of 1974, which requires the Forest Service to develop long-range programs for managing the national forests.[31] The first of these programs must cover the period from 1976 to 1980, whereas subsequent programs will be for ten-year periods. When the Forest Service agreed to prepare environmental impact statements as part of this planning process, the lawsuit seeking preparation of impact statements on annual programs was dropped.

2. Mineral Resources

The public lands, including the Outer Continental Shelf (OCS), furnish a large proportion of the minerals produced in the United States. Reflecting the national drive for energy self-sufficiency, moreover, increased attention to the fuel resources of the public lands can be expected in the future. The accelerated program now underway to increase the exploration and exploitation of the oil and gas resources of the OCS and the completion of oil-drilling and transport facilities in Alaska will dramatically increase the output of oil from federal lands. Extraction of oil from oil shale, which is currently being explored on an experimental basis, can be expected to be pursued on a much larger scale if it is found to be economically feasible and environmentally responsible. Finally, the pressures of both the energy crisis and air pollution control have stimulated increased interest in the mining of the low-sulphur coal found in the Northern Plain states of Wyoming, Montana, and the western Dakotas.

Development of mineral resources found on the public lands is basically governed by three acts: (1) the Mining Act of 1872,[32] which generally covers hard rock or metallic minerals such as gold and silver; (2) the Mineral Leasing Act of 1920,[33] which covers coal, oil, gas, and oil shale; and (3) the Outer Continental Shelf Lands Act of 1953.[34]

The Mining Act of 1872, which was passed to encourage mineral exploration, discovery, and development, sets out statutory criteria for the acquisition of a patent or title to mineral-bearing lands and leaves little if any room for discretion or regulation by federal agencies. Basically, the act provides that a person who has discovered valuable minerals on federal land and who meets certain location and work requirements can acquire the land required to develop these minerals for a nominal fee. Thus no environmental limits are placed on where such mining activities can occur and no restrictions can be placed on the methods of operation, since the land becomes privately owned. Also, no provision is made for any federal determination that the land should remain in federal ownership to serve other public purposes.

Some agency actions have been taken, however, that affect mining activities carried out under this law. The Forest Service has now issued regulations which provide that although the agency cannot deny prospectors access to lands which it manages, it can regulate and control their prospecting.[35] Also, increasingly stringent criteria have been used in determining whether or not mineral claims are "valuable," as is required by the statute.[36]

Under the Mineral Leasing Act of 1920, the federal government retains title to land and/or mineral rights (the federal government always retains title to the mineral rights, but some lands involved are privately owned), but grants leases for the exploration and development of oil, gas, coal, and other specified minerals. The lands bearing these minerals are generally those managed by the BLM, which is responsible for administering the leasing program. Generally, the BLM has complete discretion regarding whether or not to grant particular leases, but when the lands involved are managed by another federal agency, the BLM usually obtains the advice and approval of this agency.

Both prospecting permits and leases may be issued under the act. If it is known that minerals are present in commercial quantities, leases must be made on a competitive bid basis. Prospecting permits are available for other areas. If a prospector discovers a deposit, he may acquire a lease on a non-competitive, preference basis. The degree to which environmental protection must be taken into account by the BLM in the leasing process is the subject of pending litigation.[37]

The Outer Continental Shelf Lands Act of 1953 governs mineral leases for the exploration and development of deposits of oil, gas, and other minerals in the OCS. The BLM is responsible for the administration of this leasing program, and for the preparation of environmental impact statements both for the program as a whole and for the leasing planned in particular geographical areas. The Geological Survey, another agency within the Department of the Interior, is responsible for pre-lease resource evaluation and for supervision of leases once they are made.

Mineral and fossil fuel extraction involve many environmental impacts. Two types of operations which perhaps cause the most serious problems are strip mining and offshore oil drilling. Strip mining has long been a focus of national consciousness, as repeated efforts have been made to pass national strip-mining legislation. Two bills passed by Congress in 1974 and 1975 were both killed by presidential vetoes, and an attempt in June 1975 to override the second veto failed by only three votes. The virtual devastation caused by this technique of surface mining has been widely documented. Adverse effects include severe disturbances of land contours and groundwater aquifers, destruction of vegetation cover, erosion and landslides, safety hazards, and severe aesthetic blight. Because of soil characteristics, climate, or other factors, moreover, revegetation or reclamation may not be possible, even if attempted. Finally, the sociological implications of strip mining are extremely adverse, involving as they do the disruption of rural environments in areas where the local populace is generally very poor and unable to prevent mining or force reclamation. In addition, strip mining also brings rapid and uncontrolled urbanization and industrialization with concomitant social dislocations into rural areas.

The environmental impacts of offshore oil drilling are another very serious problem facing the country. With the goal of greatly increased domestic oil production, substantially increased exploitation of OCS oil is projected, though not at the accelerated rate originally visualized by the Nixon Administration. In addition to the effects which the actual drilling will have on oceanic ecological systems, there will be greatly increased pressures on ecologically fragile and already overburdened coastal areas, which will have to accommodate supporting and associated industries, harbors, distribution facilities, and related residential and commercial development. The concern which these problems has evoked and the need for adequate funds to address them have been discussed in Chapter 6, which deals with coastal zone management.

In July 1975 the BLM made available to the Council on Environmental Quality and the public its final environmental impact statement (EIS) on the "Proposed Increase in Oil and Gas Leasing on the Outer Continental Shelf."[38] As is documented in this overall, programmatic EIS, such an acceleration would involve the opening of so-called "frontier areas," which have little or no history of OCS leasing. These include the Atlantic coast, the "lower 48" Pacific coast, and the coast of Alaska.[39] Leasing would also continue in the Gulf of Mexico, where practically all past offshore drilling has taken place.

In June 1975 the BLM released a proposed schedule for OCS leasing through 1978.[40] This schedule encompasses a total of twenty-four lease sales—six for the Gulf of Mexico, three for the Pacific coast, nine for Alaska, and six for the Atlantic coast. Six of these sales are planned for each year from 1975 through 1978. The goal originally set forth by President Nixon in January 1974 of leasing 10 million OCS acres in 1975—triple the acreage then planned to be leased—was rejected as "unattainable" and specific acreage figures are no longer used as planning targets.[41] The Geological Survey has also now sharply reduced its estimates of the recoverable oil and gas resources of the Atlantic coast.[42]

Prior to each of the twenty-four proposed lease sales, the BLM must prepare a site-specific EIS for that particular sale. The following is the basic sequence of actions that the BLM has announced in the *Federal Register* it will carry out before each sale:[43]

1. Issuance of a request for reports from interested federal agencies.
2. Preparation of environmental baseline studies.
3. Call for nominations of tracts and comments from industry and all other interested groups and individuals.
4. Acceptance of nominations and comments.
5. Tentative selection of tracts for further environmental analysis.
6. Preparation of a site-specific draft EIS.
7. Holding of a public hearing.
8. Preparation of a final EIS.
9. Preparation of a "Program Decision Option Document" for use by the Secretary of the Interior in deciding whether or not to hold the sale.
10. Presale evaluation of tracts.
11. Publication of a notice of sale in the *Federal Register.*

When the BLM issues a call for nominations, which is a formal request to industry and the public for recommendations regarding which particular tracts should be leased, it also specifically requests (1) identification of areas which "because of conflicting and environmental concerns" either should not be leased or should be leased only under special conditions; and (2) particular environmental and scientific information "which might bear upon potential leasing and development of particular tracts."[44] This information is requested from government, industry, universities, research institutes, environmental organizations, and members of the general public. The final decision regarding whether a lease sale will be made and, if so, which particular tracts will be put up for competitive bidding, can be made only after full compliance with all agency procedures and EIS requirements under NEPA.

The BLM estimates that the time interval between a call for nominations of tracts in a particular area and the actual decision on whether or not to hold the sale will generally be about twelve to eighteen months. During the four-year period from 1975 through 1978, the leasing process will be initiated on a staggered basis in the twenty-four different sales areas.

There are three major opportunities for citizen participation in the OCS leasing procedures for a particular sale area. First, citizens may submit information to the BLM when it issues the call for nominations of tracts and comments for that area. Second, they may submit comments on the draft site-specific EIS which is prepared. And third, they may appear at the public hearing held on the draft EIS. Public comments may also be submitted on the final EIS, but this statement is released at a very late stage of the planning process.

Among the major issues raised by the accelerated OCS leasing program are the following:

1. Jurisdictional conflicts between the coastal states and the federal government regarding ownership of offshore oil and gas have gone all the way to the U.S. Supreme Court. In March 1975, in *United States* v. *Maine*,[45] the Court ruled that the federal government has sovereign rights over the resources of the Atlantic OCS. In *United States* v. *Alaska*,[46] handed down in June 1975, the Court held that the United States rather than the state of Alaska has paramount rights to the subsurface lands beneath lower Cook Inlet.

2. In general, the states and some local governments have raised objections to the federal OCS leasing program on grounds such as insufficient state and local involvement in OCS decision making, inadequate federal assessment of environmental factors, and insufficient financial and safety assurances. As has been pointed out, the development of state and local planning for the broad range of anticipated impacts and the provision of the funds needed for such planning are critical problems.

3. There has been considerable discussion on the question of whether the exploratory phase of oil drilling should be separated from the development phase. Some argue that the federal government, rather than oil companies, should be responsible for exploratory drilling. Others support industry exploration, but contend that once exploration is completed, an environmental assessment should be required before actual development can begin.

3. Grazing Resources

Over one-third of the public lands are used by ranchers for grazing cattle and sheep under permit and fee systems which are primarily administered by the BLM and the Forest Service. This means that more public lands are used for grazing than for any other economic activity. The federal rangelands provide about 3 percent of the total forage consumed by American livestock, but they provide 12 percent of forage consumption in the western states. In 1971 the BLM and the Forest Service authorized about 11.5 million head of livestock owned by 35,720 operators to consume 33 million "animal unit months" of vegetation. (An animal unit month is the amount of forage required to sustain one mature cow or five sheep for one month.) The average length of time spent on public lands by the animals involved was 6.7 months for cattle and 5.5 months for sheep. Many operators run livestock on both Forest Service and BLM lands, using the latter—which are generally at lower elevations—in the spring and the former during the summer.

The permit system for grazing in the national forests was authorized by the Organic Act of 1897 and that for grazing on the unreserved lands of the public domain administered by the BLM was established by the Taylor Grazing Act of 1934. Under both of these programs preference in the issuance of permits has been given to landowners engaged in ranch operations which were using the public lands at the time the legislation was passed. Preference for renewals is granted to those holding the original permits or their successors.

The BLM and the Forest Service may grant grazing permits for a maximum term of ten years, but in practice usually grant them for much shorter periods. For example, virtually all BLM grazing permits must be renewed annually. Renewal is generally automatic unless there is another federal use for the land or the terms of the permit have been violated. Agency-established fees are charged for this forage, but at rates far below what the operators would have to pay for privately owned forage. Even adjusting for services rendered by private owners, the federal fees are still less than half of the going private rate. Federal grazing fees are now increasing, however, as both the BLM and the Forest Service are more or less committed to raising fees until they equal the 1966 fair market value. The opposition of ranchers to increases in grazing fees has always been strenuous.

The environmental damage which has occurred on public lands

as a result of poor range management has never been as well known to the public as the degradation caused by clear-cutting and strip mining. Nonetheless, improper and short-sighted grazing policies have led to severe ecological problems over vast areas of land. They have led to fundamental and often irreversible changes in plant ecology, greatly increased erosion, dwindling fish and wildlife populations, and a marked deterioration in water quality.

The principal cause of such adverse impacts is overgrazing. For many decades excessive livestock grazing has been allowed on public lands which are ecologically fragile. Such lands receive little precipitation and have steep slopes and/or fragile soil conditions. In addition, grazing has often been allowed both too early in the spring and too late in the fall. In the common sequence of events, forage vegetation which has been too closely cropped and heavily trampled by livestock becomes severely stunted or dies out altogether; then the forage plants which were effective as soil retainers are replaced by species which are ineffective and, in some cases, also noxious; finally rainfall causes extensive erosion and stream siltation, and the land deteriorates to a desert-like state in which such plants as sagebrush predominate. A recent BLM study has shown that 83 percent of its grazing lands are in fair to bad condition, while only 15 percent are in good condition, and 2 percent are in excellent condition.[47] In addition to overgrazing, other management policies which have adverse environmental effects include extensive use of herbicides and mechanical land treatments which destroy existing vegetation, replacing it with forage intended for livestock. The construction of fences also interferes with the migration routes of big game animals.

The total impact of short-sighted grazing policies leads to a very bleak picture of badly deteriorated rangeland where original grasses have been largely destroyed and erosion prevails; of grazing wildlife competing with domestic livestock for a dwindling supply of forage; of deteriorating habitat conditions for all forms of wildlife; and of streams filled with sediment.

Among the actions which have been taken to try to bring about ecologically more responsible management of the range resources of the public lands has been a successful suit to require the BLM to prepare site-specific environmental impact statements in connection with all grazing activities.[48] Through efforts such as these, it may be possible to force the BLM to fulfill its statutory obligation in grazing districts "to preserve the land and its resources from destruction or unnecessary injury"[49]—a mandate which has to date been badly overshadowed by other objectives.

4. Water Resources

Federal lands are the source of most of the water in the eleven western states, supplying around 60 percent of the natural runoff in that part of the country. Most of these water supply lands are administered by the Forest Service (88 percent) or the National Park Service (8 percent). The vast federal holdings administered by the BLM do not contribute much to the water yield of the public lands, but by virtue of their location, do affect water quality.

The economic importance of the water supply from public lands is substantial. Over $12 billion in public and private funds have been invested in water storage facilities, and additional billions have been used to provide irrigation for millions of acres of land. Most of the urban areas in the West and about 96 percent of the population are dependent to some degree on water from the public lands. Almost the entire hydroelectric industry is dependent on water which originally comes from federal lands.

The two federal agencies which have primary responsibility for the development of water resources are (1) the Army Corps of Engineers, an agency of the U.S. Department of the Army, which carries out projects throughout the country, and (2) the Bureau of Reclamation of the U.S. Department of the Interior, whose operations are restricted to the eleven western states and Hawaii, North and South Dakota, Oklahoma, Texas, Nebraska, and Kansas.

Both the Bureau of Reclamation and the Corps of Engineers plan and construct projects (typically involving dams, reservoirs, canals, and aqueducts) which provide, at a fee, water for irrigation, municipal and industrial use, and electrical power. The projects are also intended to provide flood control, as well as other incidental benefits. Some of these projects are enormous. The Bureau of Reclamation's Central Utah Project is a giant $1.5 billion complex of dams, canals, and aqueducts, and the Central Arizona Project is even larger. By 1972 bureau projects were furnishing irrigation water to almost nine million acres of land, municipal and industrial water to a population of over 14.5 million people, and electrical generating capacity of 7.6 million kilowatts.

Projects may be proposed for privately owned as well as public lands. However, once a project is decided upon, the private lands required for its construction are acquired or condemned, if necessary, and are subsequently managed by the federal agency involved.

The development of water resources through the construction of public works can have a wide range of adverse environmental effects. The exchange of free-flowing streams for relatively stagnant reservoirs in a large fraction of the significant river systems of the western states has led to serious disruptions or destruction of ecological systems. Further, areas of archaeological, historical, scenic, biological, and/or geological importance, as well as significant wildlife habitats, have been permanently lost as a result of water projects. Natural limitations to urban growth have been removed, and land has been transferred from low intensity human use to heavy cultivation. Buildup of salts in the soil and in groundwater supplies has occurred, as has drainage of salts and fertilizer-laden water into natural watercourses. Unfortunately, many of these effects are essentially irreversible.

5. Recreation Resources

The public lands possess many different recreation resources and are used for a wide variety of recreational purposes. Traditionally, fees have not been charged for recreational use of the public lands, in keeping with the general belief that all citizens have the right to enjoy these resources without charge. As increased usage by the public has snowballed, however, support for user fees and protective regulations has grown.

Yosemite National Park is the classic example of the kind of pressures which are being placed on the national parks. Annual visits to this park rose from 640,000 in 1946 to 2.3 million in 1969. On Memorial Day weekend in 1969, some 70,000 people and their vehicles entered the seven square miles of the park's valley floor. This kind of excessive overcrowding leads to any number of environmental ills, air pollution being not the least, and precludes the recreational experience sought. Overuse has also been a serious problem in some areas of the National Wilderness Preservation System, discussed below, where littering, other careless actions, and concentrated use have compromised the undisturbed character and fragile ecology of the land. As a result of such pressures, in the summer of 1973 the National Park Service instituted an experimental reservation system for certain uses of the national parks, and permits are now required for overnight stays in some wilderness areas.

The need for greater regulation of particular recreational uses on the public lands has also been recognized. For example, on February

8, 1972, an Executive Order was issued by the President regarding the use of off-road vehicles (ORVs) on the public lands.[50] The use of such vehicles, which include motorcycles, minibikes, trail bikes, snowmobiles, dune-buggies, and all-terrain vehicles, has caused serious environmental damage to the public lands in a number of areas.[51] Among the destructive effects caused have been damage to soil, destruction of vegetation, erosion, water pollution, air and noise pollution, disruption of wildlife habitats, and littering, as well as facilitation of illegal logging and vandalism. In the Mojave Desert ORV users have removed pre-Columbian artifacts and have defaced primitive cliff dwellers' paintings.

The Executive Order acknowledged the seriousness of the problems created by ORV use on the public lands and directed the Secretaries of the Interior, Defense, and Agriculture and the Directors of TVA within six months to issue regulations "to provide for administrative designation of the specific areas and trails on public lands on which the use of off-road vehicles may be permitted, and areas in which the use of off-road vehicles may not be permitted, and set a date by which such designation of all public lands shall be completed." The order further required that these designations be made in accordance with specified criteria.

In April 1974, more than a year and a half after the six month deadline had expired, the BLM promulgated regulations on ORV use on the public lands under its jurisdiction.[52] These regulations, which set forth a blanket designation of all BLM lands as "open" to ORV use unless otherwise restricted, were challenged in a lawsuit by the National Wildlife Federation.[53] The court found that the regulations failed to comply with numerous requirements of the Executive Order and with NEPA, and ordered the BLM to issue new regulations.

6. Occupancy Uses

Occupancy uses involve the use of public lands for the location or siting of various kinds of structures or facilities, in contrast to utilization or development of particular resources. Among the most common of such occupancy uses are rights-of-way for transportation, utility, and commercial facilities; residential uses, including second homes; commercial and industrial sites; and public service facilities.

The federal laws and regulations governing occupancy uses are extremely varied, complicated, and often inconsistent. Initially, such uses were authorized on the public lands on a case-by-case basis.

Later, when general legislation was passed, it usually was narrow in scope, included few statutory standards, and left much to agency discretion. Congress, moreover, has made little effort to coordinate different statutes. For example, it may be possible under one law to obtain fee title to land for a particular purpose, while under another law only a revocable permit may be obtained for the same purpose. With regard to federal right-of-way laws, the U.S. Court of Appeals for the D.C. Circuit has observed:

> As a cursory glance at those sections of the United States Code which deal with the public lands will indicate, these laws are hardly a model of neat organization and uniform planning. . . . This is an area of the law where it truly can be said that most statutes are *sui generis*.[54]

Nonetheless, many serious environmental problems are associated with various occupancy uses and a number of very important environmental lawsuits have been based on the provisions of statutes governing particular uses. For example, the Trans-Alaska pipeline case,[55] which delayed construction of the oil pipeline from the North Slope until specific congressional authorization was passed, was won by environmentalists on the basis of a showing that the proposed rights-of-way for the pipeline violated the Mineral Leasing Act of 1920. The congressional action which gave the project a go-ahead exempted the pipeline from the restrictions of this act.

7. Wilderness Preservation

Certain areas of the public lands are set aside for wilderness preservation in which there is to be no substantial human use of the land or its resources. Such action was mandated by the Wilderness Act of 1964,[56] which established the National Wilderness Preservation System "to secure for the American people of present and future generations the benefits of an enduring resource of wilderness." The act requires that the wilderness areas of the system be "administered for the use and enjoyment of the American people in such manner as will leave them unimpaired for future use and enjoyment as wilderness."[57]

Wilderness areas are defined by the act in the following manner:

> A wilderness, in contrast with those areas where man and his own works dominate the landscape, is hereby recognized as an area where the earth and its community of life are untrammeled by man, where man himself is a visitor who does not remain. An area of wilderness is

further defined to mean in this chapter an area of undeveloped federal land retaining its primeval character and influence, without permanent improvements or human habitation, which is protected and managed so as to preserve its natural conditions and which (1) generally appears to have been affected primarily by the forces of nature, with the imprint of man's work substantially unnoticeable; (2) has outstanding opportunities for solitude or a primitive and unconfined type of recreation; (3) has at least five thousand acres of land or is of sufficient size as to make practicable its preservation and use in an unimpaired condition; and (4) may also contain ecological, geological, or other features of scientific, educational, scenic, or historical value.[58]

The act designated fifty-four national forest areas containing some 9.1 million acres as the original components of the National Wilderness Preservation System. It also charged the Secretary of Agriculture and the Secretary of the Interior to review several million acres of additional land in the national forests, the national park system, and national wildlife refuges for possible inclusion in the system. On its own initiative, moreover, the Forest Service began a review of some fifty-six million roadless acres of national forest land to determine their suitability for potential uses, including wilderness designation. Legal suits challenging the way in which the Forest Service has carried out this review of *de facto* wilderness areas have been discussed above.

In carrying out its responsibilities under the Wilderness Act, the Forest Service initially took a hard line on the definition of wilderness and held that to qualify for inclusion in the system, an area had to be virgin and must never have been logged. Also, areas in which there were roads (though possibly not jeep trails) were virtually excluded from consideration. These inclusion criteria became a particularly important issue in the East, where practically all areas have at some time been logged, though in many cases this was done over a hundred years ago. Conservationists maintained that there were many areas in the East which, although not pristine, either had already reverted to a wilderness state or could do so, if they were protected.

Congress responded to this situation by passing the so-called Eastern Wilderness Act, signed by the President on January 3, 1975.[59] This new act, which applies to national forest areas east of the 100th meridian, immediately added sixteen areas comprising some 207,000 acres in thirteen eastern states to the National Wilderness Preservation System. Further, it designated an additional seventeen areas comprising 125,000 acres as wilderness study areas which must be reviewed for possible inclusion in the system and must receive interim protection during the maximum five-year study period. The act also specifically left open to Congress the right to designate other national forest areas in the East as study areas.

Citizen Action

All of the federal agencies which are involved in public land management must prepare environmental impact statements under the National Environmental Policy Act for at least some of their activities. The following are among the agency actions for which such impact statements can be expected:

1. Forest Service: management plans for individual forests and long-term management plans; proposals to establish wilderness areas; special programs such as pesticide and herbicide applications; and some mining activities within the national forests.

2. National Park Service: management plans for national parks, including commercial uses within the parks; and wilderness area proposals.

3. Bureau of Land Management: overall management programs; certain management actions such as grazing, pesticide and herbicide use, and vegetation manipulation; and mining activities, including offshore oil leasing.

4. Bureau of Reclamation and Corps of Engineers: major water resource projects, including dams and channelization.

Some agencies, such as the Bureau of Reclamation and the Corps of Engineers, have a backlog of projects which predate NEPA at least in congressional authorization. Nonetheless, many successful suits have been brought to require environmental impact statements for such projects.[60]

As has been discussed in Chapter 3, all draft and final impact statements must be made available for public review and comment. Notice of this availability is given in the *Federal Register* and in local newspapers in the area of a proposed project. Citizens should take care to read draft impact statements and proposals very carefully and to prepare thoughtful criticisms.

Agency planning procedures offer another means through which citizens can influence public land policies and decisions. Both the Forest Service and the BLM have established planning procedures for the management of the national forests and grazing districts. In both cases, the procedures set up are designed to allow for public participation.

Further, the federal Water Resources Council has issued "Standards for Planning Water and Related Land Resources," which include provisions for public participation.[61] These standards apply to

> *Federal and federally assisted programs and projects.* These standards apply to the planning and evaluation of the effects of the following water and land programs, projects, and activities carried out directly by the Federal Government and by State or other entities with Federal financial or technical assistance:
>
> (a) Corps of Engineers civil functions;
>
> (b) Bureau of Reclamation projects;
>
> (c) Federally constructed watershed and water and land programs;
>
> (d) National parks and recreation areas;
>
> (e) Wild, scenic, recreational rivers and wilderness areas;
>
> (f) Wetland and estuary projects and coastal zones;
>
> (g) Federal waterfowl refuges;
>
> (h) Tennessee Valley Authority;
>
> (i) Federal assistance to State and local government sponsored watershed and water and land resources programs (Watershed Protection and Flood Prevention Projects and Resource Conservation and Development Projects).[62]

The standards established are intended to augment NEPA, and apply to all levels of planning, including framework studies, regional plans, and implementation studies. All federal agencies affected must revise their regulations to conform to the standards. The following are the provisions for public participation which must be made in agency planning:

> Direct input from the public involved at the local and regional level is important and will be accomplished by:
>
> a. Soliciting public opinion early in the planning process;
>
> b. Encouraging periodic expression of the public's views orally, and recording their opinions, and considering them;
>
> c. Holding public meetings early in the course of planning to advise the public of the nature and scope of the study, opening lines of commu-

nication, listening to the needs and views of the public and identifying interested individuals and agencies;

d. Making available all plans, reports, data analyses, interpretations, and other information for public inspection.

Efforts to secure public participation should be pursued vigorously through appropriate means of public hearings, public meetings, information programs, citizen committees, etc.

Definition and specification of the components of the environmental quality objective will require direct consultation with groups identified with environmental concerns as well as with those groups within a planning setting whose actions have significant impacts on the environment.[63]

A number of national and regional environmental organizations have been particularly concerned about the management policies and practices adopted by federal agencies for the public lands, which, as has been noted, comprise one-third of the nation's land. Individuals and groups who want to work for environmentally responsible federal decisions and actions concerning the public lands may want to join efforts already being made by such organizations. Although it is not possible here to list every national and regional organization which has been involved with public land issues, the following are organizations whose work has been particularly important: Environmental Defense Fund (EDF), Environmental Policy Center, Friends of the Earth, The Institute of Ecology, The Izaak Walton League of America, National Audubon Society, National Parks and Conservation Association, The National Wildlife Federation, Natural Resources Defense Council (NRDC), Northern Plains Resources Council, Oregon Environmental Council, Powder River Basin Resources Council, Rocky Mountain Center on Environment (ROMCOE), Sierra Club, Wilderness Society, Wyoming Environmental Institute, and Wyoming Outdoor Coordinating Council.

NOTES

1. In 1964 Congress appointed a Public Land Law Review Commission, which prepared the following three volumes as part of its research program: *One Third of the Nation's Land: A Report to the President and to the Congress by the Public Land Law Review Commission* (Washington, D.C.: U.S. Government Printing Office, 1970); *Digest of Public Land Laws* (Washington, D.C.: U.S. Government Printing Office, 1968); and Paul Wallace Gates and Robert W. Swensen, *History of Public*

Land Law Development (Washington, D.C.: U.S. Government Printing Office, 1968).

2. In 1864 Congress had granted Yosemite Valley and the Mariposa Grove to the state of California solely for use as a public park. Yosemite did not become a national park until 1890, but the 1864 grant is often regarded as the beginning of the public park system.

3. 43 U.S.C. § 1391.

4. Jerome C. Muys, "The Federal Lands," *Federal Environmental Law* (St. Paul, Minn.: West Publishing Co., 1974), p. 497.

5. Public Land Law Review Commission, *Report,* p. 1.

6. 16 U.S.C. § 475.

7. 16 U.S.C. §§ 528–531.

8. 16 U.S.C. § 531.

9. West Virginia Division of the Izaak Walton League v. Butz, 367 F. Supp. 422, 6 ERC 1016 (N.D.W.Va. 1973), 522 F.2d 945, 8 ERC 1076 (4th Cir. 1975).

10. Sierra Club v. Morton, 405 U.S. 727, 748, 3 ERC 2039 (1972) (Douglas dissenting); Reich, "The Public and the Nation's Forests," 50 *Cal. L. Rev.* 387 (1962).

11. 16 U.S.C. § 1601 *et seq.*

12. 42 U.S.C. § 4321 *et seq.* See Chapter 3 for a full discussion of NEPA.

13. This role was assigned to the BLM by the Outer Continental Shelf Lands Act of 1953. 43 U.S.C. §§ 1331–1343.

14. 30 U.S.C. § 181 *et seq.*

15. 43 U.S.C. § 315 *et seq.*

16. 43 U.S.C. §§ 1411–1418.

17. 16 U.S.C. § 668dd (a).

18. 16 U.S.C. § 1.

19. In the western states the BLM manages twenty-three million acres of commercial timberlands. These lands represent 4.5 percent of the total forest area in the United States and 2 percent of the nation's wood supply.

20. U.S. Department of Agriculture, Forest Service, *Stratification of Forest Lands for Timber Management Planning on Western National Forests* (Washington, D.C.: U.S. Government Printing Office, 1971); U.S. Department of Agriculture, Forest Service, *Forest Regulation Study* (Washington, D.C.: U.S. Government Printing Office, 1973).

21. 42 U.S.C. § 4321 *et seq.* See Chapter 3.

22. Natural Resources Defense Council v. Butz, 6 ERC 1895 (D.D.C., February 25, 1974).

23. National Academy of Sciences, Environmental Studies Board, "Gates Report" (1972). For a critical analysis of the Forest Service's management of the national forests, see Daniel R. Barney, *The Last Stand,* Ralph Nader's Study Group Report on the National Forests (New York: Grossman Publishers, 1974).

24. U.S. Department of Agriculture, Forest Service, *Management Practices on the Bitterroot National Forest: A Task Force Appraisal* (1970), p. 9.

25. West Virginia Division of the Izaak Walton League v. Butz, 367 F. Supp. 422, 6 ERC 1016 (N.D.W.Va. 1973), 522 F.2d 945, 8 ERC 1076 (4th Cir. 1975).

26. 349 F. Supp. 934, 4 ERC 1673 (N.D.Cal. 1972).

27. 16 U.S.C. §§ 1131–1136.

28. 484 F.2d 1244, 5 ERC 1844 (10th Cir. 1973).

29. 484 F.2d at 1250.

30. Natural Resources Defense Council v. Butz, Civil No. 74–585 (D.D.C. 1974).

31. 16 U.S.C. § 1601 *et seq.*

32. 30 U.S.C. § 21 *et seq.*

33. 30 U.S.C. § 181 *et seq.*

34. 43 U.S.C. §§ 1331–1343.

35. 39 *Federal Register* 31317 (August 28, 1974); 36 C.F.R. Part 252.

36. Muys, "The Federal Lands," p. 525.

37. Natural Resources Defense Council v. Berklund, Civil No. 75–0313 (D.D.C. 1975).

38. U.S. Department of the Interior, *Final Environmental Impact Statement, Proposed Increase in Oil and Gas Leasing on the Outer Continental Shelf* (July 1975), 3 vols. (Hereafter, Final EIS).

39. The Atlantic and Alaskan OCS areas have no drilling history. In Alaska there has been oil development under state jurisdiction in the coastal water areas of Cook Inlet, but there has never been any oil drilling in the coastal waters of the Atlantic states. Some drilling has taken place in both the coastal and OCS waters off the coast of Southern California, but federal leasing was suspended after the Santa Barbara oil spill in 1969 and only limited drilling occurred on existing leases.

40. See 40 *Federal Register* 25833 (June 19, 1975).

41. Final EIS, 1: 1 and 13.

42. U.S. Department of the Interior, Geological Survey, *Geological Estimates of Undiscovered Recoverable Oil and Gas Resources in the United States,* Geological Survey Circular 725 (1975).

43. 40 *Federal Register* 25833 (June 19, 1975).

44. See, e.g., 40 *Federal Register* 13322 (March 26, 1975).

45. 420 U.S. 515, 7 ERC 1753 (1975).

46. 422 U.S. 184 (1975).

47. U.S. Department of the Interior, Bureau of Land Management, *Range Condition Report,* prepared for the U.S. Senate Committee on Appropriations (January 1975), p. II–12.

48. Natural Resources Defense Council v. Morton, 388 F. Supp. 829, 7 ERC 1298 (D.D.C. 1974).

49. 43 U.S.C. § 315 (a).

50. Executive Order 11644, 37 *Federal Register* 2877 (February 9, 1972); 3 C.F.R. E.O. 11644.

51. See 4 ELR 10180.

52. 39 *Federal Register* 13613 (April 15, 1974); 43 C.F.R. Part 6290.

53. National Wildlife Federation v. Morton, 393 F. Supp. 1286, 7 ERC 2128 (D.D.C. 1975).

54. Wilderness Society v. Morton, 479 F.2d 842, 881, 4 ERC 1977, 2002 (D.C. Cir. 1973).

55. *Ibid.*

56. 16 U.S.C. §§ 1131–1136.

57. 16 U.S.C. § 1131 (a).

58. 16 U.S.C. § 1131 (c).

59. Public Law 93–622, 88 Stat. 2096.

60. See, e.g., Environmental Defense Fund v. Corps of Engineers, 325 F. Supp. 728 (E.D.Ark. 1971), *aff'd,* 470 F.2d 289 (8th Cir. 1972); Environmental Defense Fund v. Corps of Engineers, 324 F. Supp. 878 (D.D.C. 1971); see also, Natural Resources Defense Council v. Grant, 341 F. Supp. 356 (E.D.N.C. 1972).

61. 38 *Federal Register* 24778 (September 10, 1973).

62. *Ibid.* at 24790.

63. *Ibid.* at 24827.

CHAPTER 12

State Land Use Controls

E ACH STATE IN the union has the power to enact legislation to protect the health, safety, morals, and general welfare of its citizens. At least to some extent, however, every state has delegated to its local and county governments the authority to exercise this "police power of the state" to enact land use regulations. In fact, traditionally, land use control has been strictly a local matter, since for many years the states were reluctant either to involve themselves in land use matters or to interfere with the actions of local governments.

These circumstances have changed dramatically in a number of states, as state governments have reevaluated their responsibilities regarding land use problems and have passed legislation establishing comprehensive statewide land use programs or acts addressing particular issues. Table 9 summarizes some aspects of state legislative activity related to land use, as of April 1975.

It is not possible here to review all of the actions which have been taken in the fifty states or to explain the countless organizational variations which bear on state land use planning and decision making. The literature on this subject is already vast, and continues to grow apace.[1] This chapter will, therefore, focus first on generic types of state legislation and programs which have been adopted, providing as many specific examples as space permits, and second on statewide land use programs which have been adopted by six states.

GENERIC TYPES OF STATE LEGISLATION AND PROGRAMS AFFECTING LAND USE

In most states many state agencies have responsibilities which involve or affect land use. For example, in California at a minimum the following seventeen state agencies or institutions have land use planning or regulatory responsibilities: the Office of Planning and Research, the Council on Intergovernmental Relations, the Department of Transportation, the Department of Housing and Community Development, the State Public Works Board, the Air Resources Board, the State Water Resources Control Board, the State Coastal Zone Conservation Commission, the State Energy Resources Conservation and Development Commission, the Department of Fish and Game, the Department of Parks and Recreation, the Department of Water Resources, the Department of Navigation and Ocean Development, the Solid Waste Management Board, the University of California, the State Lands Commission, and the Public Utilities Commission.[2]

This typical pattern results from the fact that what happens to land has such a significant impact on so many other concerns, as well as from the past reluctance of states to contend with land problems in an outright and unified fashion. Moreover, even where states have adopted statewide land use programs of planning and/or regulation under the administration of a land use commission or agency, older land-related responsibilities usually still rest in the hands of other agencies, and coordination among the different fields is still essential.

This section sets out for citizens the most important kinds of legislation and programs affecting land use that may have been adopted in their state. A given state may have adopted only a few or nearly all of the different types of laws described and, of course, in each case modifications relating to particular circumstances in that state have probably been incorporated. The essential questions which citizens concerned with land use problems need to answer are

· Which of these laws with bearing on land use decision making have been enacted by the state?
· Which agencies, boards, commissions, offices, departments, divisions, committees, or other bodies have been given the responsibility of implementing and enforcing these laws?

Table 9
Status of State Activity Related to Land Use Management, April 1975

	Enabling Legislation				
State	Municipalities	Counties	Regional Agency Advisory Only	Regional Agency Review Authority	Procedures for Coordination of Functional Programs
Alabama	Yes	Yes	Yes	No	No
Alaska	Yes	Yes	N/A	N/A	Yes
Arizona	Yes	Yes	Yes	No	Yes
Arkansas	Yes	Yes	Yes	No	No
California	Yes	Yes	Yes	Yes	Yes
Colorado	Yes	Yes	No	Yes	No
Connecticut	Yes	N/A	Yes	No	Yes
Delaware	Yes	No	Yes	No	Yes
Florida	Yes	Yes	No	Yes	Yes
Georgia	Yes	Yes	Yes	No	Yes
Hawaii	No	Yes	N/A	N/A	Yes
Idaho	Yes	Yes	Yes	No	No
Illinois	Yes	Yes	Yes	No	No
Indiana	Yes	Yes	Yes	No	Yes
Iowa	Yes	Yes	Yes	No	No
Kansas	Yes	Yes	Yes	No	No
Kentucky	Yes	Yes	Yes	No	No
Louisiana	Yes	Yes	Yes	No	No
Maine	Yes	Yes	Yes	No	Yes
Maryland	Yes	Yes	Yes	No	Yes
Massachusetts	Yes	Yes	Yes[3]	No	No
Michigan	Yes	Yes	Yes	No	No
Minnesota	Yes	Yes	Yes[4]	No	No
Mississippi	Yes	Yes	Yes	No	No
Missouri	Yes	Yes	Yes	No	No
Montana	Yes	Yes	Yes	No	No
Nebraska	Yes	Yes	Yes	No	No
Nevada	Yes	Yes	Yes	No	Yes
New Hampshire	Yes	Yes	Yes	No	No
New Jersey	Yes	No	Yes	No	No
New Mexico	Yes	Yes	Yes	No	Yes
New York	Yes	Yes	Yes	Yes	Yes
North Carolina	Yes	Yes	Yes	No	No
North Dakota	Yes	Yes	Yes	No	No
Ohio	Yes	Yes	Yes	No	No
Oklahoma	Yes	No	Yes	No	No
Oregon	Yes	Yes	Yes	No	No
Pennsylvania	Yes	Yes	Yes	No	No
Rhode Island	Yes	N/A	No	No	Yes
South Carolina	Yes	Yes	Yes	No	No
South Dakota	Yes	Yes	Yes	No	No
Tennessee	Yes	Yes	Yes	No	Yes
Texas	Yes	No	Yes	No	Yes
Utah	Yes	Yes	Yes	No	Yes
Vermont	Yes	N/A	Yes	No	Yes
Virginia	Yes	Yes	Yes	No	No
Washington	Yes	Yes	Yes	No	No
West Virginia	Yes	No	Yes	No	Yes
Wisconsin	Yes	No	Yes	No	Yes
Wyoming	Yes	Yes	No	Yes	Yes

[1]Coastal Zone Management
No state has an approved Coastal Zone Management Program at present

[2]State Land Use Program Code:
1. No activity at state level.
2. Study (executive or legislative) or state legislative consideration in progress.
3. State land use program legislation enacted.
    Authorization for:
        (a) inventorying existing land resources, data and information collection
        (b) policy study or promulgation by agency or commission
        (c) identification of land areas or uses of more than local concern
        (d) regulation or management of land areas and uses identified
        (e) direct state implementation or state review of local government implementation

[3]Massachusetts
Areawide Council for Martha's Vineyard has authority to administer controls

Table 9
Status of State Activity Related to
Land Use Management, April 1975

Functional Programs

Land Use-Value Tax Assessment Law	Surface Mining	Floodplain Regulations	Power Plant Siting	Wetlands Management	Critical Areas	Coastal Zone Mgmt. Program Participation[1]	State Land Use Program (see Code)[2]
No	Yes	No	Yes	No	No	Yes	1
Yes	Yes	No	Yes	No	No	Yes	2
No	No	Yes	Yes	No	No	N/A	2
Yes	Yes	Yes	Yes	No	No	N/A	2
Yes	Yes	Yes	Yes	No	No	Yes	2
Yes	Yes	Yes	Yes	No	Yes	N/A	3a-c
Yes	No	Yes	Yes	Yes	No	Yes	2
Yes	No	No	No	Yes	No	Yes	2
Yes	No	No	Yes	No	Yes	Yes	3a-e
No	Yes	No	No	Yes	No	Yes	2
Yes	No	Yes	No	No	No	N/A	3a-e
No	Yes	No	No	No	No	Yes	2
Yes	Yes	No	No	No	No	No	2
Yes	Yes	Yes	No	No	No	N/A	2
Yes	No	Yes	No	No	No	N/A	2
No	Yes	No	No	No	No	N/A	2
Yes	Yes	No	Yes	No	No	N/A	2
Yes	No	No	No	Yes	No	Yes	2
Yes	Yes	Yes	Yes	Yes	Yes	Yes	2
Yes	Yes	Yes	Yes	Yes	Yes	Yes	3a-c
Yes	No	No	Yes	Yes	No	Yes	2
Yes	Yes	Yes	No	No	No	Yes	2
Yes	No	No	Yes	Yes	Yes	Yes	2
No	No	No	No	No	No	Yes	2
No	No	No	Yes	Yes	No	N/A	2
Yes	Yes	Yes	Yes	No	No	N/A	2
Yes	No	Yes	Yes	No	No	N/A	2
Yes[5]	No	No	Yes	No	Yes	N/A	3a-c
Yes	No	No	Yes	Yes	No	Yes	2
Yes	No	Yes	No	Yes	No	Yes	2
Yes	Yes	No	Yes	No	No	N/A	2
Yes	Yes	No	Yes	Yes	No	Yes	2
No	Yes	Yes	No	Yes	Yes	Yes	3a-c
Yes	Yes	No	No	No	No	N/A	2
Yes	Yes	No	Yes	No	No	Yes	2
No	Yes	Yes	No	No	No	N/A	2
Yes	Yes	No	Yes	No	Yes	Yes	3a-c
No	Yes	No	No	No	No	Yes	2
Yes	No	No	Yes[6]	Yes	No	Yes	2
No	Yes	No	No	No	No	Yes	2
Yes	Yes	No	No	No	No	N/A	2
No	Yes	No	Yes[7]	No	No	N/A	2
Yes	No	No	No	Yes	No	Yes	2
Yes	No	No	No	No	Yes	N/A	2
Yes	No	Yes	Yes	Yes	No	N/A	3a-e
Yes	Yes	No	No	Yes	No	Yes	2
Yes	Yes	Yes	Yes	Yes	No	Yes	2
No	Yes	Yes	No	No	Yes	N/A	2
Yes	Yes	Yes	Yes	No	No	Yes	2
Yes	Yes	No	Yes	No	No	N/A	3a-d

[4]Minnesota
Twin Cities Metropolitan Council has regulatory authority

[5]Nevada
Must be ratified in a referendum to take effect

[6]Rhode Island
Within the coastal zone a development permit is required from the Coastal Council

[7]Tennessee
Power plant siting is conducted by TVA only

Source: U.S. Department of Interior
        Office of Land Use and Water Planning

· What procedures must these bodies follow?
· Are permits, licenses, or approvals required by the law?
· If so, to what types and dimensions of development projects do they apply?
· What provisions are made for citizen participation in the implementation and enforcement of the law? For public hearings or meetings? For public notice of permit applications filed?

With such information in hand, citizens will be able to determine the relevance of state laws to particular land use problems and to evaluate the degree to which the state government is responsibly addressing the land use problems of the state.

Protection of Wetlands and Shorelands

During the 1960s states began to pass special legislation to protect wetlands, one of our most critical natural resources. As has been discussed in the first chapter of this book, wetlands play a uniquely important role in nurturing plant and animal organisms at the bottom of the food chain; they are vital to fish and shellfish, which feed on this biota and spawn in the wetlands' protective reaches; they are essential to water systems, absorbing and holding excess water and recharging groundwater aquifers; they provide natural protection against floods and storm tides; they are natural oxidation basins in which runoff is converted into useful nutrients; they reduce sedimentation in rivers; and they serve as habitats for countless species of birds and wildlife.

In recognition of the great ecological significance of once scorned marshes and swamps, many states have now taken action to stop their widespread destruction. Massachusetts's law governing tidal wetlands includes not only a permit system for development in these wetlands, but also provisions for protective orders which are filed with the title to the land and become binding restrictions on its use. In that state, moreover, local conservation commissions, which are discussed in Chapter 14, have been given regulatory authority over wetlands by the state.

A popular mechanism adopted by states to protect wetlands is the requirement of a permit for specified types of development and activities, notably dredging and filling. For example, in New York the activities subject to regulation in tidal wetlands include:

any form of draining, dredging, excavation, and removal either directly or indirectly, of soil, mud, sand, shells, gravel or other aggregate from any tidal wetland;

any form of dumping, filling, or depositing, either directly or indirectly, of any soil, stones, sand, gravel, mud, rubbish, or fill of any kind;

the erection of any structures or roads, the driving of any pilings or placing of any other obstructions, whether or not changing the ebb and flow of the tide; and

any other activity within or immediately adjacent to inventoried wetlands which may substantially impair or alter the natural condition of the tidal wetland area.[3]

The typical pattern under a state permit program is for the state to inventory and map its wetlands, a process which is considerably less difficult for tidal wetlands than for freshwater wetlands which are scattered across the state. Once the inventory and maps are complete, then the boundaries of the permit program must be established. Public hearings are almost always required during this process. Once boundaries are determined, then permit regulations go into effect or, in some cases, further land use restrictions are developed and adopted. A very important element of this process is the establishment by the state of interim controls over development to cover the period of time necessary to prepare the inventory and maps, to establish boundaries, and to adopt regulations.

A number of states have passed shoreland management acts, which include many wetlands within their scope. These acts frequently require local and/or county governments to adopt shoreland management ordinances and often authorize the state to establish setback and other requirements which must be included in these ordinances. Also common, as is the case in Maine, whose shoreland law is discussed in the next section, the state often retains approval authority over local actions and the right to adopt regulations when localities fail to act within a specified time.

The apprehension felt in many areas that wetlands and shorelands protection statutes and regulations could not withstand constitutional challenges on the "takings" issue has been substantially eased by many recent court decisions upholding such laws and regulations. As has been discussed in Chapter 2, a landmark decision by the Supreme Court of Wisconsin in 1972 held that:

An owner of land has no absolute and unlimited right to change the essential natural character of his land so as to use it for a purpose for which it was unsuited in its natural state and which injures the rights of others. . . . The changing of wetlands and swamps to the damage of the general public by upsetting the natural environment and the natural relationship is not a reasonable use of that land which is protected from police power regulation. . . . [N]othing this court has said or held in prior cases indicate [sic] that destroying the natural character of a swamp or a wetland so as to make that location available for human habitation is a reasonable use of that land when the new use, although of a more economical value to the owner, causes a harm to the general public.[4]

Although variations in court decisions continue to exist in this area, the most predominant trend in recent decisions on wetlands cases reflects the judgments of the Wisconsin court.

With the advent of the federal Coastal Zone Management program, discussed below and in Chapter 6, wetlands and shorelands programs are being integrated into the coastal zone management programs that are being developed.

Coastal Zone Management

All thirty of the states eligible to participate in the federal assistance program established by the Coastal Zone Management Act of 1972[5] have now received federal grants to develop water and land use management programs for their coastal zones. Several states, beginning with the state of Washington, have successfully completed the planning stages and are now receiving federal funds to assist implementation of their programs.

The specific requirements, goals, and problems of this cooperative federal-state program, which applies to states bordering on the Great Lakes as well as to coastal states, are discussed in Chapter 6. It is important to note, however, that the opportunity to receive federal funds to help the state address development problems in its coastal areas has focused attention on state land use planning in many states where the state government had been making little effort to deal with its land use problems.

Several states have passed strong coastal zone acts of their own. The Delaware Coastal Zone Act,[6] enacted in 1971, prohibits any further development (1) which is for heavy industrial purposes, or (2) which involves offshore gas, liquid, or solid bulk product transfers. Other manufacturing uses are regulated through a state permit system. A public hearing must be held on each permit application and local government approval must be given before any permit may be approved by the state. Statutory guidelines govern the consideration of applications by the State Planning Office, which is the administering agency. The stimulus for the passage of this stringent act was the threat of additional heavy industrialization related to petroleum products on the short Delaware coastline, which by 1971 was already the receiving point for 70 percent of the oil imported into the eastern United States.

The California Coastal Zone Conservation Act of 1972[7] and the events leading up to its adoption have been reviewed in Chapter 6. Essentially, this act provides (1) for the preparation of a state coastal plan by the state Coastal Zone Conservation Commission and six regional commissions and (2) for the interim regulation of development by these commissions in a designated coastal zone which extends three miles seaward and 1,000 yards landward.

Floodplain Controls

The very important land use aspects of the National Flood Insurance Program are discussed in Chapter 7. As is explained there, local governments with flood-prone areas must adopt land use restrictions meeting criteria established by the Federal Insurance Administration to avoid stringent federal sanctions. Many states are working with the federal and local governments in the implementation of this program, as well as administering their own state floodplain programs. Under state administrative action or legislation, a number of states are providing technical assistance, such as development of model floodplain regulations, to local governments. In Minnesota the Department of Natural Resources has established statewide floodplain standards which specify requirements for local zoning and subdivision ordinances. In New York, if a local government fails to qualify for the National Flood Insurance Program or has its eligibility revoked, the Department of Environmental Conservation is authorized to promulgate and administer floodplain regulations in that community.

Wild and Scenic Rivers

More than half of the states have established their own wild and scenic river systems patterned after the National Wild and Scenic

River System described in Chapter 8. These state programs provide protection for wild, scenic, and recreational rivers which are not included in the federal system.

Generally, the state programs establish criteria on the basis of which the state legislature or governor may designate rivers to be part of the state system and specify the kinds of protection which will or may be accorded rivers in the system. River studies, often involving citizen participation, are carried out to determine whether particular rivers meet these criteria. Public hearings are usually held to review a river's eligibility for inclusion in the state system. It is extremely important for citizens to make a strong showing at these hearings and, if necessary, help convince the public of the need to protect the rivers in question from uncontrolled development. Often rivers proposed by the state are already receiving some type of governmental protection as a result of their location in state, federal, or local parks. Thus winning protection for completely unrestricted rivers will usually require even more energetic citizen efforts.

Once a river is designated by the legislature or governor, a management plan must be developed for the river segment involved. These plans generally combine provisions for local land use controls and outright purchase of land along the river by the state or local government. Often a citizens' advisory committee is set up to assist the agency responsible for developing the management plan. Public hearings and meetings are also an important part of this process.

Critical Areas Programs

Many states have enacted special legislation to protect certain areas of the state. Examples of this type of action are the many wetlands, shorelands, and floodplain statutes which have been enacted; the coastal zone laws passed by California and Delaware; state wild and scenic rivers systems; Vermont's permit requirement for all lands over 2,500 feet; and the establishment by New York of the Adirondack Park Agency and by California of the San Francisco Bay Conservation and Development Commission, both of which are discussed in Chapter 13.

In addition to these actions, however, some states have established a more general mechanism for designation and regulation of "critical areas," which may include a number of different types of areas of particular state concern. Two major categories of critical areas for which it is argued protection is needed are (1) areas that are ecologically fragile, and (2) areas that may be subject to heavy development pressures. Florida's well-developed critical areas program is explained in the next section, and mention is made of actions relating to critical areas that have been taken by Maine, Wyoming, and Oregon. Minnesota has also enacted a strong program similar to Florida's, in which provision is made for administrative designation of critical areas and local adoption of land use regulations, subject to state review and enforcement. Nevada has adopted a program in which the director of the Department of Conservation and Natural Resources, with the concurrence of the governor, designates areas of critical environmental concern, and the state land use planning agency adopts standards and land use plans for these areas. Other states, such as Colorado and Maryland, are developing programs based on local initiatives.

Agricultural Use Tax Assessment

The loss of agricultural land to urban sprawl has been exacerbated by property tax assessment practices which assess farmland in terms not of its agricultural use, but of its development potential. This has caused property taxes to soar, greatly increasing pressures on farmers to sell out to developers.

To counteract this trend, many states have enacted laws authorizing use-value assessment of lands which farmers agree to keep in agricultural production. Generally, the farmer must sign a contract or agreement with the local or county government that he will continue to farm the land for a specified period of time, such as five to ten years. If he fails to do so, he must pay a rollback tax penalty. In New York farmers may join together to form agricultural districts which are established under procedures administered by the counties and the state Department of Environmental Conservation. Once such districts are set up, not only do special tax provisions apply within their boundaries, but also measures to protect and encourage agricultural uses. Some states authorize use-value assessments for forestland and other types of open space, as well as for farmland.

Management of State Lands

State parks and recreation departments, divisions, offices, or commissions play an important role in acquiring and managing state open space and recreational lands. Departments of natural resources, departments of conservation, and other agencies may also be responsible for parklands and recreational programs, as well as for the management, classification, and protection of state resource lands, such as state forests.

The prime focus of this book is on the regulation of private land use, but effective management of public lands and control of private uses of public land are very significant land use concerns. In Chapter 11 these topics have been reviewed with regard to the vast federal holdings which constitute one third of the nation's land. They are equally important on the state level, though the variations in organizational framework and statutory mandates make it impossible to provide detailed treatment here.

Boards of Land Commissioners

Many of the western states still own large acreages of land ceded to the state during the last century for public schools or other public purposes. A number of these states have boards of land commissioners, generally established by the state constitution, which are responsible for the sale, lease, or use of resources on these lands. The proceeds from the sale or lease of the lands, as well as from resource uses such as the sale of timber, generally go to a public school income fund.

Procedures and standards governing the actions of the boards of land commissioners are generally set out in the state constitution, but may also be supplemented by statutory provisions. Of particular significance are requirements establishing that if the state lands are sold, they must be sold at public auction for not less than their duly appraised value. Litigation on this point has arisen where boards of commissioners have sought to sell lands to particular developers at discount prices.

Some states have identified state public school lands which have particular environmental value. In Colorado, for example, the Department of Natural Resources has identified lands under the jurisdiction of the board of land commissioners which are environmentally or economically unique, and the board has held public hearings on these determinations.

Fish and Wildlife Protection

Most states have established a fish and wildlife agency which is primarily responsible for assuring that the state's fish and wildlife populations are maintained and their habitats protected. To carry out these objectives, such agencies are generally empowered to acquire and manage land for fish hatcheries and wildlife preserves; to undertake stream improvement projects; to issue fishing and hunting licenses, as well as to establish and enforce fishing and hunting regulations; and to evaluate proposed stream disruptions for compatibility with fishery resources.

Protection of Water Resources

The state action required in the implementation of the Federal Water Pollution Control Act Amendments of 1972[8] is discussed in Chapter 5. As noted there, the National Pollutant Discharge Elimination System (NPDES), the permit program for discharges of pollutants, may be administered either by the U.S. Environmental Protection Agency (EPA) or by the state. This division stems from the act's provision that the states may seek authorization from EPA to administer the NPDES program in its behalf. If a state has obtained such authorization from EPA, then it rather than the federal agency is responsible (1) for the issuance of permits, in accordance with federal standards, to industrial and municipal dischargers of water pollutants into surface waters; (2) for the enforcement of permit conditions; and (3) for the imposition of heavy fines on violators of the act or of permit conditions. If a state has not received such authorization, then EPA is responsible for administering the NPDES program in the state. The NPDES program may replace some of a state's earlier requirements regarding sewage effluent, but it is likely that the state will have other sewage control requirements which affect development. For example, approval of septic tanks by health department or other state officials may be required.

State laws on water pollution may be more stringent and extensive than the federal program. For example, the New York discharge permit law applies to discharges into the groundwaters of the state as well as to those into surface waters.

Under federal law, the states have established water quality standards for their surface waters, which must be revised and approved by EPA at least every three years. In addition, each state is now required to develop and implement an antidegradation policy for waters whose quality is better than that required by standards. EPA's regulations governing these responsibilities are discussed in Chapter 5.

As has also been explained in Chapter 5, the states are responsible for the implementation within their borders of Section 208 of the Federal Water Pollution Control Act Amendments. This important statute requires the development of water quality management plans which apply to both point and nonpoint sources of pollution and which include provisions for establishing regulatory mechanisms. The state must (1) oversee the work done by designated areawide 208 planning agencies, and (2) carry out 208 planning for all areas which have not been designated. The 208 plans that are developed will be extremely important, since they will provide the framework within which many other aspects of the water act will be implemented.

The states have also established standards for drinking water, exercised control over their water supply, and set up permit programs for stream disruptions and diversions. Drinking water standards are frequently enforced through required approvals from health department officials. In many states lots in subdivisions of certain sizes cannot be sold unless health department officials have approved plans for an adequate and safe drinking water supply.

Control over the supply and distribution of water in the state is usually an important state function, especially in the arid western states. State water supply permits are frequently required for both municipalities and large-scale subdivisions, and in some particular areas a permit must be obtained to drill an individual well. Water rights are a much more complicated issue and determinant of land use in the West, where they are generally separable from the land, like mineral rights, and may be subject to adjudication by state authorities.

Most states also require permits for certain types of stream disruptions and diversions. Interstate diversions of rivers are sometimes the subject of interstate compacts. Generally, any significant damming or diversion of a river or stream will require a state permit, as may dredging or filling operations.

Soil Conservation Commissions or Boards

Many states have soil conservation commissions or boards which coordinate the work of the soil conservation districts in the state. These districts were established in connection with the program of the Soil Conservation Service of the U.S. Department of Agriculture, which provides resource data and technical assistance regarding soil and water conservation in rural and urbanizing areas. The state boards generally administer various soil erosion, flood control, and watershed projects.

Air Pollution

The responsibility of each state to develop an implementation plan under the Clean Air Act of 1970[9] has been discussed in Chapter 4. As pointed out there, the portions of these plans which pertain most immediately to land use are those dealing with the location of new stationary sources of air pollution, indirect source review, air quality maintenance plans, and prevention of significant deterioration in clean air areas. The transportation control plans of state implementation plans have been discussed in Chapter 10.

It is essential for citizens to find out how these air pollution control programs are being carried out by their state and to participate as actively as possible in the drive to achieve and maintain the national ambient air quality standards.

Some states have established air pollution control programs which go beyond federal requirements. Also, while implementation of requirements for indirect source review has been delayed at the federal level, some states are already operating their own indirect source review programs which require permits for the construction of facilities, such as shopping centers and sports stadiums, which attract large numbers of automobiles.

Solid Waste Management

Many states are involved in the development of solid waste plans, the establishment of state standards with which local governments and counties must comply, and/or the administration of a state permit program.

Federal assistance for state solid waste planning is available at a level of 75 percent under the Solid Waste Disposal Act,[10] which is administered by the U.S. Environmental Protection Agency. This law provides technical and financial assistance to the states for the planning and development of solid waste management programs, including resource recovery and the management of hazardous wastes. It does not establish federal solid waste standards, but does require that the plans developed incorporate federal air and water quality standards. The state plan must contain forecasts for a short-term horizon of five years and a long-term horizon of twenty years.

It must be integrated with existing comprehensive state and local plans and must contain a framework for local government planning, as well as recommendations for legislative action.

Many states have established solid waste standards which local governments must meet, some require local solid waste planning, and some operate permit programs. For example, in Arkansas the Solid Waste Division of the Department of Pollution Control and Ecology sets standards, enforces regulations, and issues permits to cities and counties, which are required to develop solid waste management systems. No such system may be constructed or modified without the approval of the division. In California solid waste plans meeting minimum state requirements must be prepared by each county, in cooperation with local jurisdictions, or by a regional planning agency authorized by the county and a majority of the cities within the county.

States have also taken other steps to abate solid waste problems. For example, Oregon has banned nonreturnable beer and soft drink containers and Pennsylvania has established a $20 million revolving fund to provide loans to municipalities and agencies of up to 50 percent of the costs of developing solid waste/resource recovery systems.

Noise Pollution

More and more states are establishing programs to control noise pollution. Noise abatement laws have traditionally included provisions for reducing noise at the source—such as requirements for mufflers on automobiles, motorcycles, boats, and now snowmobiles —but increasing attention is being paid to the use of zoning to limit the impact of noise, particularly in high noise areas such as lands adjacent to highways or airports. In Minnesota, for example, the state has passed enabling legislation specifically authorizing municipalities and counties to adopt airport zoning controls. To give teeth to this legislation, the state requires that no airport in the state system may receive financial assistance unless an airport zoning ordinance has been adopted or there is the intent to zone.

State Comprehensive Planning

As is discussed in the next section, some states have adopted mandatory programs of statewide land use planning, either by a state agency or through a cooperative state and local planning process. In Oregon counties and cities are required to bring their comprehensive plans into conformity with the state planning goals which have been developed and to implement these goals through the adoption of local ordinances and programs.

Whether or not a state is specifically working on the development of a state land use plan or statewide land use planning goals, usually some state agency serves as the lead agency for comprehensive planning in the state. Usually this agency receives some funding under the HUD "701" program, which is explained in both Chapter 13 and Chapter 14, and is responsible for channeling 701 comprehensive planning funds to localities in the state that are not eligible to apply directly to HUD or which opt to apply through the state. The state comprehensive planning agency may also use some of its own HUD money to provide technical assistance to localities.

Many other state agencies are also likely to have planning divisions which are concerned with land use problems, and it is not uncommon for conflicts to develop among the personnel of different agencies with overlapping concerns. For example, coastal zone management planning in New York was initially hampered by disagreement regarding which state agency should have prime responsibility for developing the program. In environmental matters, such differences often develop between comprehensive planning agencies and more functional agencies which have expertise and regulatory responsibilities in particular areas.

The questions of how state land use planning ought to be conducted, how it ought to be coordinated with comprehensive state planning and with planning in other areas, and how implementation of land use plans can best be achieved are very complex and very difficult. The most valuable information on these issues should come from the experiences of states which are developing statewide land use programs.

The State A–95 Clearinghouse

The A–95 project review system established by the federal Office of Management and Budget (OMB) under the Intergovernmental Cooperation Act of 1968[11] is explained in Chapter 13. Essentially, this system provides the opportunity for state and areawide "clearinghouse" agencies to review applications for federal assistance to development projects. Applicants who intend to propose such projects to federal agencies must send preliminary summaries to the clearinghouses for consideration. If the clearinghouses find that the project would conflict with existing comprehensive plans and goals, they may schedule conferences with the developer to try to resolve the problems involved and may prepare comments on the project which must be submitted to the federal funding agency along with the completed application.

The basic intent of this program is to identify at a very early stage conflicts between federally assisted projects and the plans and activities of states, regions, and localities. It seeks to establish lines of communication between the different levels of government and to foster coordinated plans and actions.

OMB does not specify how the states must organize or operate their A–95 clearinghouses. It does require, however, that notice of all applications be sent to the state clearinghouse, which usually is the state comprehensive planning agency funded under the HUD 701 program to conduct comprehensive planning. Review of a given application may be carried out by the state clearinghouse or by an areawide clearinghouse or by both, depending on the nature of the project.

Transportation Programs

Every state has a state highway department or agency which is responsible for the construction of state roads and for state participation in the federal-aid highway program. The latter has been discussed at some length in Chapter 10, as well as in Chapter 3. The ways in which the states carry out their state road-building programs vary considerably from state to state. Citizens who are concerned about the land use implications of road construction need to find out whether their state has established environmental standards for the planning and construction of roads, whether the secondary effects of roads on growth and development are taken into consideration, and what provisions have been made for public notices, public hearings, and public information meetings.

Many states have now established departments of transportation, with responsibilities for other modes of transportation as well as highways. This indicates a broader and more interdisciplinary approach to transportation problems, but highway officials are still likely to hold the most power in the department. It is very important for citizens to find out how transportation planning is carried out in their state and to gain access to the planning of major programs and projects at the earliest stages possible.

State NEPAs

As has been discussed in Chapter 3, a number of states have adopted programs of environmental impact review based on the National Environmental Policy Act (NEPA).[12] Particular variations in these state laws are summarized in that discussion. Once it is determined whether or not one's state has such a law, the most important points to clarify are

• For what kinds of activities must environmental impact statements (EISs) be prepared?
• Who must prepare the EISs? State agencies only? Local governments? Private individuals proposing projects?
• What procedures are set out for submission and review of EISs?
• What provisions are there for citizen comments and public hearings?
• How many of the above matters are set out in statutory requirements and how many are left to the discretion of the state agency administering the program?

Whenever citizens in a state which has a state NEPA law are involved in a land use dispute concerning a proposed project, they should determine whether or not this project falls under the state or federal EIS requirements. If it is possible that it does, every effort should be made to win this important type of environmental review. Since most state agencies responsible for the implementation of state NEPAs have limited staff resources, the degree of public controversy surrounding a particular project may be a prime determinant in establishing whether or not an EIS is actually required. In Minnesota, if 500 citizens sign a petition requesting an EIS on a particular project, one must be prepared.

Land Subdivision Registration Requirements

Some states have enacted laws to protect purchasers of subdivided lands. Often these laws are similar to the federal Interstate Land Sales Full Disclosure Act,[13] which is explained in Chapter 9. They require subdividers of land which fall within the scope of the law to prepare disclosure statements which must be filed with the state and presented to purchasers prior to a sale. These disclosure statements generally must include information on such matters as the physical characteristics of the subdivision, the services to be provided by the developer, distances to schools and shopping areas, the business background of the principals of the development company, the company's affiliations and financial status, the presence of any natural hazards, and the methods of water supply and sewage disposal to be employed.

As has been discussed in Chapter 9, federal disclosure requirements, which are administered by the Office of Interstate Land Sales Registration (OILSR), are more stringent than those of almost all the states. While at one time OILSR accepted filings made under state laws in California, Florida, Hawaii, and New York as meeting federal requirements, this practice was terminated after the federal law and regulations were substantially strengthened in 1973 and 1974. Only California has been reinstated for such treatment, following improvements in the California requirements.

State subdivision laws may, however, apply to subdivisions which are not covered by the Interstate Land Sales Full Disclosure Act. For example, the federal law does not apply to subdivisions of less than fifty lots, and developers may seek an exemption for subdivisions which are sold "entirely or almost entirely" *intrastate.* Thus a state law may impose requirements which must be met by developments that are exempt from federal filings.

The subdivided lands law of Minnesota is intended to provide consumer protection not simply through disclosure requirements, but also through affirmative action by state agencies to determine that subdivisions covered by the law comply with environmental standards. The law requires that subdivided lands, unless exempted, must be registered and must meet local, state, and federal environmental standards before lots may be advertised or sold. The environmental standards may include, but are not limited to, water and air quality; shoreland, floodplain, and wild and scenic river protection; and drainage requirements. The state Environmental Quality Commission is responsible for promulgating state environmental standards and the state Department of Natural Resources is responsible for determining compliance. Although the effect of this law is considerably weakened by the breadth of its exemptions and by inadequate implementation, the concept of requiring compliance with environmental standards before subdivision lots may be sold is extremely important. It is, in fact, probably a more effective means of protecting consumers than the requirement that they be given a lengthy and complex document to read and analyze.

Power Plant Siting

Many states have laws requiring that a permit, a certificate of environmental compatibility, and/or a statement of public need be issued for the location and construction of power plants. Often these laws preempt other state and local controls, establishing that no other permits, approvals, or hearings may be required. However, the responsible state agency must generally consult with other agencies and hold a public hearing before issuing a permit. The criteria which must be met before permits may be granted are set out in state statutes and agency regulations. In some cases, a large application fee provides revenue for the state to assess the impact of the proposed utility construction. Inventories of potential power plant sites are being prepared in certain states.

State power plant siting laws operate in conjunction with the following federal requirements:

1. All nuclear power plants must be licensed by the Nuclear Regulatory Commission, a successor agency to the Atomic Energy Commission.

2. All plants involving encroachment on a navigable stream must obtain a permit from the U.S. Army Corps of Engineers.

3. Any power plants or transmission lines "across, along, from, or in any of the streams or other bodies of water over which Congress has jurisdiction . . . or upon any part of the public lands and reservations of the United States" must be licensed by the Federal Power Commission.[14]

Any federal involvement in a project, including licensing as well as financial assistance, which constitutes "a major federal action significantly affecting the quality of the human environment" will require the preparation of an environmental impact statement under the National Environmental Policy Act. This critical federal legislation and its requirements are reviewed in Chapter 3.

Power plants must also meet the requirements of the air and water pollution abatement programs developed under the Clean Air

Act of 1970 and the Federal Water Pollution Control Act Amendments of 1972, which are the subjects of Chapters 4 and 5, respectively. Specifically, the U.S. Environmental Protection Agency has established new source standards of performance for fossil fuel electric generating plants that must be incorporated in state programs designed to prohibit the construction of new stationary sources which would cause or exacerbate an air quality standard violation. Power plant siting must also be guided by the regulations developed by EPA and the states to prevent significant deterioration of clean air areas.

Under the National Pollutant Discharge Elimination System of the water act, all power plants must obtain a permit from EPA or the state, if it has been authorized to act in EPA's behalf, for any discharge of pollutants, including thermal water, into surface waters. These permits, except those for new sources, are exempt from the provisions of NEPA.

State power plant siting laws sometimes apply only to certain kinds of power plants. For example, the New York State law applies only to electric steam generating plants with the capacity of producing fifty thousand kilowatts of power. This includes both fossil fuel and nuclear power plants, but excludes pumped storage plants and hydroelectric facilities. Vermont has just passed a law which requires approval by the state legislature before any new nuclear power plant may be built in the state.

The location of transmission facilities such as electric power lines and natural gas supply lines may also be regulated under the state power facilities siting law. Here again, only certain types and dimensions of lines may be covered by the law.

Passage or strengthening of power plant or energy facilities siting laws has significantly increased during the past few years in the western plains or mountain states such as Montana, North Dakota, and Wyoming, where plans are being made for the accelerated development of energy resources through strip mining of coal and oil shale operations. Wyoming's new law applies to other types of industrial plant sitings as well as to utilities. Montana prohibits the transfer of agricultural water rights to any other uses and requires applicants for a permit to demonstrate that they will not adversely affect existing water users. The use of scarce water resources in mining and processing operations and the impact on sparsely populated rural areas of the rapid growth generated by such development are major concerns in these states.

Strip Mining

Since Congress failed to override President Ford's vetoes of federal strip-mining legislation in both 1974 and 1975, the strip-mining acts passed by the individual states have taken on new importance. More than half the states have passed such legislation, which varies in strength and effectiveness.

A common mechanism for the implementation of state strip-mining and reclamation laws is the requirement that anyone seeking to carry out mining activities must obtain a permit and must agree to reclaim the land mined through restoration of topsoil, planting or alternate procedures to prevent erosion, and contouring or terracing. Performance bonds may be required to assure that the reclamation is completed. Some states, such as Minnesota, are making efforts to identify those lands which cannot be reclaimed with existing techniques.

Most state strip-mining acts do not contain provisions for reclamation of lands which have been strip mined in the past. The federal legislation passed by Congress but killed by the President would have generated revenue for the reclamation of lands previously stripped and abandoned through the imposition of a per-ton user's tax on coal.

Oil and Gas Commissions

Some states have an oil and gas commission from which a permit must be obtained before a well can be drilled for oil or gas. These commissions are usually empowered to inspect drilling operations and are responsible for preventing water pollution by such operations.

SIX STATEWIDE LAND USE PROGRAMS

This section describes the programs which have been developed by six states to deal with their land use problems on a statewide basis. There is considerable variation among these different programs. Hawaii is unique in possessing a system of statewide zoning. In Vermont, Maine, and Oregon, state agencies have direct permit-granting authority over specified types of development or activities. In Vermont, however, these permits are issued through a system of district commissions, while Maine and Oregon have no regional mechanism for the granting of permits. The laws of Vermont and Maine apply to industrial, commercial, and residential development, but Oregon's state permits apply to designated activities of statewide significance, such as the planning and siting of public facilities. Maine has no provisions for the development of a state land use plan; Vermont has failed to adopt the land use plan envisioned by its land use law; and Oregon has developed statewide land use planning goals which must be incorporated in the required comprehensive plans of its counties and cities and then implemented through local regulations and programs.

Florida's unique program, which is based on the Model Land Development Code of the American Law Institute, has a two-pronged attack in which the efforts of state, local, and regional bodies are coordinated: (1) state-designated areas of critical state concern are to be administered by local governments under regulations which they have adopted pursuant to state guidelines; and (2) developments of regional impact, as defined by the state, must be reviewed by the regional planning agency and approved by the local government. If local governments fail to adopt and obtain state approval of regulations for a critical area, the state may adopt such regulations. The decisions of local governments on developments of regional impact may be appealed to the governor and his cabinet by the regional planning agency, the State Division of Planning, and the developer.

Wyoming is a newcomer to the ranks of states which are addressing their land use problems on a statewide basis, but has only established a statewide planning program, without provisions for implementation of this planning through the adoption of regulations. The program is based on a coordinated planning effort by the state, counties, and local governments, and the state is making funds available to counties and localities for the mandatory land use planning.

Hawaii

Hawaii has the oldest and strongest state land use program in the nation, having adopted statewide zoning in 1961.[15] The prime motivation for this action was the desire to protect agricultural land, upon which the state's economy was based, from the effects of the booming growth that had begun in Hawaii in the mid-1950s and was accelerated by the approval of statehood in 1959. The islands' long tradition of centralized government encouraged the development of a statewide system to deal with the problems faced, though county governments play a critical role in the program which has been developed.

The land use program operates under the direction of the state Land Use Commission, which is composed of nine private citizens, the chairman of the state Board of Land and Natural Resources, and the director of the Department of Planning and Economic Development. As mandated by the Land Use Law, the commission has divided the entire state into the following four types of districts:

1. Urban districts. These include all existing urban land plus a reserve of land to accommodate urban growth for ten years. Within these districts county zoning regulations control land uses. The reclassification of land from other types of districts to urban districts is, however, the responsibility of the Land Use Commission.

2. Rural districts. These include small farms and low density (by Hawaiian standards) residential development on lots of at least one-half acre. No districts of this type have been created on the island of Oahu, nor is the classification heavily used on the other islands. Land use in rural districts is governed by regulations adopted by the Land Use Commission, but administered by the counties, which may establish more restrictive regulations than those provided by the commission. Special permits for other uses may be granted by county planning commissions, if approved by the Land Use Commission.

3. Agricultural districts. These include lands suitable for intensive cultivation, as well as some lava flows which are unsuitable for agricultural use, but were not set aside for conservation purposes. The minimum lot size is one acre. As in rural districts, land use is governed by regulations of the Land Use Commission which are administered by the counties, and special use permits may be issued if approved by both the county planning commission and the Land Use Commission. Uses permitted include cultivation of crops, raising livestock, grazing, farm buildings, sugar mills and other activities typically associated with Hawaiian agriculture, utility lines, and some open air recreation.

4. Conservation districts. These originally included only the state-owned Forest and Water Reserves Zones which had been established for conservation purposes in 1957. These zones included not only lands needed for the protection of natural resources, but also areas subject to natural hazards such as flooding, erosion, landslides, and volcanic activity. Under its power to reclassify land, the commis-

sion has now added to the conservation districts a considerable amount of private land, much of which is mountainous terrain with slopes of more than 20 percent. A 1970 law enabled the commission to add to these districts a shoreline band of forty feet extending along the entire Hawaiian coastline. Land use within the conservation districts is regulated solely by the state Board of Land and Natural Resources.

Under a new law passed in 1975, district reclassifications made by the Land Use Commission must be consistent with an Interim Statewide Land Use Guidance Policy, pending the preparation of a Land Use Guidance Policy, which will be a state land development plan to guide reclassifications. This plan is to be developed by the state Department of Planning and Economic Development. The interim policy now in effect seeks to prevent urban sprawl and to place tighter constraints on reclassifications of land to urban districts. The interim policy also encourages lower income housing developments.

Vermont

Vermont was the first mainland state to adopt a comprehensive statewide approach to its land use problems. This occurred in 1970 when the state legislature, backed by strong citizen support, passed Act 250, which immediately instituted a statewide program for the regulation of specified types of development and scheduled a three-stage planning program which was to culminate in a state land use plan.[16]

The primary stimulus for the passage of Act 250 was the heavy pressure for recreation and second home development which had emerged in this rural state once interstate highways completed in the 1960s opened up the area to the millions of city dwellers in the Northeast. In the late 1960s, moreover, most townships had not adopted any type of land use controls capable of controlling rapid development. This situation was exacerbated by the ecological fragility of much of the state and the strong desire of many of its residents to retain their rural life-styles. A particularly acute problem was posed by the plans of second home developers to rely on individual septic tanks in areas where terrain and soil conditions were not suitable—where there were steep slopes and where impermeable bedrock was covered with only a thin layer of topsoil.

In mid-1968 these problems were highlighted when the governor of the state made a much publicized visit to the site of a proposed twenty thousand acre second home subdivision to be built on property owned by a large paper company in an area where there were no existing local zoning or subdivision regulations and the soil was clearly inhospitable to septic tanks. In 1969 the governor appointed a study commission to hold public hearings and to issue a report and recommendations on environmental controls. Almost all of the recommendations of this commission were incorporated in Act 250.

The regulatory system established by Act 250 vests permit-granting authority in a state Environmental Board, which is assisted by eight District Commissions. All the members of these bodies are citizens appointed by the governor, except that the chairmanship of the Environmental Board has evolved into a full-time, salaried position. Permits are required for the following kinds of development projects:

1. Subdivisions of ten or more lots in parcels of ten acres or under;
2. Construction of ten or more dwelling units;
3. Commercial or industrial improvements on more than ten acres;
4. All commercial, industrial, or residential development above the elevation of 2,500 feet;
5. Any state or municipal construction on more than ten acres; and
6. Within municipalities which have not adopted permanent zoning and subdivision ordinances, commercial or industrial improvements on more than one acre.

Activities which are specifically excluded from the permitting process are (1) construction for farming, logging, or forestry purposes below 2,500 feet; and (2) electric generation or transmission facilities. The latter are regulated exclusively by the Public Service Board. The law also contained a "grandfather" clause, which exempted from its provisions existing developments, developments which had already received health department permits for sewage disposal and water supply, and highways upon which hearings had already been held.

The District Commissions are responsible for issuing permits, but other state and local bodies and officials are statutory parties to permit proceedings. When an application is filed, public notice must be given and copies of the application must be sent to the local selectmen, the local planning commission, the regional planning commission, the Environmental Board, the local state forester, and the Agency 250 Review Committee, which is an interagency review committee composed of members of various state agencies. The Protection Division of the Agency of Environmental Conservation also reviews each application and makes certain that all interested agencies have an opportunity to comment on it.

The District Commission then holds a public hearing on the application. Statutory provisions establish that the commission may grant the permit only if it finds that the proposed project:

1. Will not result in undue water or air pollution.

2. Has sufficient water available for its reasonably forseeable needs.

3. Will not cause an unreasonable burden on any existing water supply to be used.

4. Will not cause unreasonable soil erosion or reduction in the capacity of the land to hold water which may result in a dangerous or unhealthy condition.

5. Will not cause unreasonable congestion or unsafe conditions with respect to the use of highways, waterways, railways, airports, and other means of transportation, existing and proposed.

6. Will not cause an unreasonable burden on the ability of a municipality to provide educational services.

7. Will not place an unreasonable burden on the ability of local governments to provide municipal or governmental services

8. Will not have an undue adverse effect on the scenic or natural beauty of the area, aesthetics, historic sites, or rare and irreplaceable natural areas.

9. Is in conformance with the statewide plans to be developed under Act 250.

10. Is in conformance with any duly adopted local or regional plan or capital program.

A permit cannot be denied solely because it does not meet criterion 5, 6, or 7. With respect to criteria 1 through 4, and 9 and 10, the burden of proof lies with the developer, whereas opposing parties must prove their case regarding criteria 5 through 8.

Moreover, the District Commission may consider other criteria in evaluating permit applications, and it may attach conditions or requirements to any permit granted. Such conditions have proved to be an important mechanism for obliging developers to make needed improvements, such as changing the method of sewage disposal, reducing density, increasing setbacks from highways, and building culverts and retaining walls for erosion control.

A District Commission's decision on a permit application may be appealed to the state Environmental Board for *de novo* consideration or, under a later amendment, to the county court. Further appeals go directly to the Vermont Supreme Court.

The three-stage statewide planning process established by Act 250 called for the development and adoption of the following three plans:

1. An Interim Land Capability Plan
2. A Land Capability and Development Plan
3. A Land Use Plan

The first of these plans, which was adopted in 1972, was basically a statement of general state policies and a series of maps indicating areas of the state which had physical limitations for development and those which were particularly suitable for agricultural or forest use.

The second plan, the Land Capability and Development Plan, was approved by the state legislature in April 1973. It expanded and clarified the statutory criteria for judging permit applications and set out nineteen planning principles regarding such matters as natural resources, conservation of energy, economic development, and transportation.

The final plan, the Land Use Plan, which was to have established "the proper use of the lands of the state whether for forestry, recreation, agriculture, or urban purposes," has never made it through the Vermont legislature, failing in both 1974 and 1975. As originally prepared, the plan would have divided the state into five types of areas: urban, village, natural resource, conservation, and rural. Local governments were to be responsible for preparing land use plans for urban and village areas; but if they failed to act, the state would be authorized to act for them. This type of statewide zoning was rejected by the legislature, as was a weaker version of the plan submitted later.

The failure of this planning effort has a number of facets. For example, many problems developed in the preparation of the plan, notably conflicts between the State Planning Office, which was responsible for drafting the plan, and the Environmental Board, which was responsible for approving it before submission to the governor and the legislature. Moreover, the downturn of the national economy and the impact of the energy crisis on the tourist industry have affected the climate of opinion in the state, strengthening opposition to further restraints on development.

Thus Act 250 has produced in Vermont a state supervised regulatory program requiring permits for developments which are of specified dimensions or which are located above 2,500 feet. This program has, of course, not been without its problems, but it has undeniably raised the standards of development in the state and has provided protection for natural resources and ecosystems which would not have been forthcoming from piecemeal or nonexistent regulation by local governments. The planning side of the state land use program has, however, come to an unsuccessful standstill and it is not clear what future actions will be taken in this area.

Vermont was also the first state to establish a special capital gains tax on the profits from land sales.[17] Essentially, this graduated tax, which was authorized in 1973, imposes heavy penalties on sales of land that is held for less than six years. When a piece of land is sold, the amount of the capital gains tax is determined by how long the land has been owned by the seller and by the percentage of profit realized. A maximum tax of 60 percent is imposed on sales of land held for less than one year in which the profit realized is 200 percent or more. At this level of profit the tax decreases 10 percent each year for six years. Lower taxes are imposed on sales in which there is less profit. The primary reason for the passage of this law was the desire to discourage speculative sales of land.

Maine

Maine does not have a single comprehensive statewide land use law, but rather has several key programs which together compromise a significant statewide effort to deal with land use problems. Establishment of these programs was prompted primarily by the environmental awareness and action of Maine citizens during the early 1970s. They perceived first that development pressures were building to locate oil refineries and deepwater ports for supertankers along the scenic Maine coast, as well as to construct large second home subdivisions in the state. Second, they realized that the absence of local controls left the state extremely vulnerable to these pressures.

Efforts to spur adoption of land use controls, as well as other types of environmental legislation, were spearheaded by the Natural Resources Council of Maine, a statewide environmental citizens' group. Under the leadership of this organization, citizens conducted a very effective public campaign for the adoption of needed protective measures. In fact, when the site location act, discussed below, was passed by the state legislature, there was only one dissenting vote.

1. The Site Location of Development Act [18]

Enacted in 1970, in response to the prospect of increased industrial development, this law requires that a permit be obtained from the state Department of Natural Resources for any commercial, residential, or industrial development which:

a. Requires a license from the department under its air and water pollution control programs;

b. Occupies over twenty acres;

c. Contemplates drilling for or excavating natural resources; or

d. Occupies on a single parcel, a structure or structures in excess of a total floor area of sixty thousand square feet.

Development carried out by public agencies is not regulated.

The act requires that the department's decisions on permits must be governed by the following four criteria:

a. Financial capacity. The proposed development must have the financial capacity and technical ability to meet state air and water pollution control standards, and must have made adequate provision for solid waste disposal, the control of offensive odors, and the securing and maintenance of a sufficient and healthful water supply.

b. Traffic movement. The proposed development must have made adequate provision for loading, parking, and traffic movement from the development area onto public roads.

c. No adverse effect on the natural environment. The proposed development must have made adequate provisions for fitting itself harmoniously into the existing natural environment and must not adversely affect existing uses, scenic character, natural resources, or property values in the municipality.

d. Soil suitability. The proposed development must be built on soil types which are suitable to the nature of the undertaking.

Each permit granted is subject to certain standard conditions—such as, that approval is limited to the project as set forth in the application, that all other required licenses and approvals must be obtained, and that the applicant must provide all other information subsequently requested by the department. Specific conditions may be, and often are, attached to a particular permit. These frequently are imposed on the recommendation of other state agencies which are given the opportunity to review project applications.

2. The Maine Land Use Regulation Commission

Fifty-one percent of Maine's land lies within unorganized areas in which there are no local governments. These counties occupy the northern half of the state and are largely unpopulated. The Maine Land Use Regulation Commission was authorized in 1971 to develop land use controls for these unorganized areas.[19] It is responsible (a) for classifying the land into protection, management, development, and holding districts, and (b) for preparing, implementing, and enforcing land use guidance standards for each of the four types of districts. If an area decides to become incorporated, these controls and standards remain in effect until the new municipality adopts land use regulations that are at least as stringent.

In 1975 the commission submitted to the governor a plan in which 5 million acres would be classified for protection in their present wilderness state. The governor approved parts of this plan, but returned the entire document to the commission for revision and resubmission.

3. The Mandatory Shoreline Zoning and Subdivision Control Act[20]

This act was passed in 1971 when only 15 percent of Maine's organized municipalities had adopted zoning, and even the state capital had no zoning ordinance. It requires every municipality to adopt zoning and subdivision controls for all land that lies within 250 feet of any navigable pond, lake, river, or saltwater body (which includes any pond or lake of more than ten acres). The state is authorized to adopt ordinances for localities which fail to comply with the law. By the end of 1975 over two-thirds of the state's municipalities had adopted zoning ordinances which had been approved by the state. Localities not complying have had development moratoriums imposed upon them. In 1975 municipalities were also authorized to adopt special zoning and subdivision controls to avoid problems associated with floodplain development.

4. The State Register of Critical Areas Act[21]

Enacted in 1974, this act provided $30,000 for the initiation of a state inventory of critical natural areas and important scenic, scientific, and historic areas. Once an area is designated, localities must develop plans to protect it within six months.

5. Protection of Coastal Wetlands[22]

Since 1967 Maine has required that permits be obtained for alterations of coastal wetlands. The permits are issued by the Board of Environmental Protection, unless the municipality has been authorized by the board to carry out this responsibility. Such authorization is permitted only where the municipality has (a) established a planning board, (b) adopted a zoning ordinance approved by the board and the Land Use Regulation Commission, and (c) made provision by ordinance or regulation for prompt notice to the board and the public of the receipt of applications for permits.

Florida

Long the locale of intensive growth and development, Florida was jolted into a new perspective on its ecological limitations by a severe drought in 1971 which brought water rationing to three heavily populated counties in the southeastern part of the state. Scientific analysis of this experience identified its cause as the widespread destruction, through drainage, dredging, and filling, of the state's wetlands, which are necessary for recharging the groundwater aquifer.

The 1971 water shortage led the governor of the state to call a water resources conference, which resulted in the formation of a task force to study the issues of water and land management. This task force developed several pieces of environmental and planning legislation which were subsequently enacted by the legislature in 1972. Of these, the most important was the Environmental Land and Water Management Act of 1972.

1. The Environmental Land and Water Management Act of 1972[23]

This act was based on the Model Land Development Code of the American Law Institute (ALI), which both establishes the state's interest in development problems and provides for a partnership between the state and local governments in dealing with these problems.[24] Like the model code, the Florida law focuses the state's attention on areas of critical state concern and developments of regional impact, two features also stressed in proposed federal land use bills which have been inspired by the ALI model code.

Under the Florida law, an area of critical state concern may be:

a. An area containing or having a significant impact upon environmental, historical, natural, or archaeological resources of regional or statewide importance;

b. An area significantly affected by or having a significant effect upon an existing or proposed major public facility or other area of major public investment; or

c. A proposed area of major development potential, which may include a proposed site of a new community designated in the state land development plan.

The Division of State Planning, the lead agency for state land use planning, is responsible for recommending areas for designation as areas of critical state concern to the governor and his six cabinet members, all of whom are elected. Local governments, regional planning councils, or interested groups may nominate areas for recommendation to the Division of State Planning. These nominations are reviewed in a standardized manner for conformity with the legislative intent, critical nature, scope, and priority. Based on the priorities determined, areas which might be designated are studied as resources permit. The Division of State Planning holds public hearings to gather information on particular areas and works closely with local governments in defining the boundaries of those areas which are recommended.[25]

The governor and the cabinet may approve, modify, or reject the recommendations of the Division of State Planning. If an area is approved as an area of critical state concern, local governments have six months to prepare land development regulations for it, in accordance with state guidelines. If local regulations are not submitted to and approved by the state within this time period, the Division of State Planning must prepare regulations for the area and submit them to the governor and the cabinet for adoption. Local governments are responsible for administering the land use regulations in the critical areas. If they fail to enforce these controls adequately, the state may institute appropriate judicial proceedings.

Two significant weaknesses in Florida's critical areas program are (a) the absence of provisions for interim controls pending the adoption of permanent land use regulations, and (b) the limitation that no more than 5 percent of the state's total land area may be designated as critical areas. The latter problem was bypassed by the state legislature in 1973 when it passed a special act designating the Big Cypress Swamp as an area of critical state concern. In taking action to protect this vitally important groundwater recharge area just north of the Everglades National Park, the legislature exempted it from the 5 percent rule.

The Big Cypress Swamp was the first area established as an area of critical state concern, but other areas, notably the Florida Keys, have since been designated by the governor and the cabinet under the administrative procedures set out by the Environmental Land and Water Management Act.

The act also establishes means of dealing with "developments of regional impact" (DRIs). The law defines a DRI as "any development which, because of its character, magnitude, or location, would have a substantial effect upon the health, safety, or welfare of citizens of more than one county." Guidelines and standards for identifying particular types of DRIs have now been prepared by the Division of State Planning and approved by the governor, the cabinet, and the legislature. These DRIs include airports, attractions and recreation facilities, electrical generating facilities and transmission lines, hospitals, industrial plants and industrial parks, mining operations, office parks, petroleum storage facilities, port facilities, residential developments, schools, and shopping centers.

A developer wishing to construct a project covered by the DRI process must file an application form with the local government, the appropriate regional planning agency, and the Division of State Planning. This application must provide detailed information regarding how the project will affect the region in terms of such factors as water supply and water quality, air quality, noise levels, sedimentation, erosion, animal life, sewage disposal, solid waste management, power supply, schools, transportation, jobs, taxes, and housing.

The DRI process operates only in areas where local zoning or subdivision regulations are in effect. If a developer proposes a project in a local jurisdiction which does not have such controls, he must wait ninety days after submitting his proposal to allow time for the locality to enact them or for the state to designate the area as an area of critical state concern. If neither of these actions takes place, the developer may proceed without further review under the Environmental Land and Water Management Act, though he may still be subject to other state permit requirements such as those pertaining to water pollution and dredging and filling operations.

When a DRI is proposed in a locality that has zoning and subdivision regulations, the regional planning agency for the area has thirty days in which to prepare an advisory report for the local government on the regional impact of the proposed development. This regional review covers the impact of the project on five major areas: (a) environment and natural resources, (b) economy, (c) public facilities, (d) public transportation, and (e) housing.

The local government must consider the report of the regional planning agency in making its decision to approve the proposed DRI, to deny it, or to approve it with conditions. During this decision-making process, a public hearing must be held, public notice of which must be given four weeks in advance.

The local government's decision on a DRI application may be appealed to the governor and cabinet by the regional planning agency, the Division of State Planning, or the developer. Decisions of the governor and cabinet must be rendered within 120 days and are subject to judicial review.

This DRI process has greatly strengthened regional planning bodies in Florida. When the act was passed in 1972 only two weak regional planning councils and several loosely organized multijurisdictional bodies existed in the state. The Division of State Planning has now designated ten regional planning areas in the state and regional planning councils have been formed in almost all of these areas.

The Environmental Land and Water Management Act, along with the Comprehensive Planning Act of 1972,[26] which created the Division of State Planning, mandates this agency to prepare a state land development plan. It is expected that preparation of this plan will require several years, but that interim plans and policies will be issued to guide land management strategies across the state.[27]

2. Other Laws

Several other important new Florida laws have very important land use implications. The Land Conservation Act of 1972 authorized $200 million in bond funds for the state to acquire environmentally endangered lands and $40 million for the acquisition and improvement of recreational facilities.[28] The Florida Water Resources Act of 1972 governs water management throughout the state, utilizing the police power to enforce water budgeting.[29] The New Communities Act of 1975 extends broad new incentives to developers who wish to undertake the planning, financing, and construction of new communities.[30] The Local Government Comprehensive Planning Act of 1975 requires all counties and municipalities in the state to prepare and adopt a comprehensive plan by July 1, 1979.[31] If a city fails to prepare a plan, the county is authorized to conduct this planning and to bill the city for it. If counties do not develop comprehensive plans, the state may do so and bill the counties. Each plan must include as elements a future land use plan, a traffic circulation plan, a mass transit plan, and a public service and water use plan.

Oregon

Oregon's Land Use Law,[32] commonly known as Senate Bill 100, was passed in 1973, following in the wake of legislation on other land-related issues such as protection of public access to ocean beaches, protection of certain rivers, planning for coastal development, and required adoption and implementation of comprehensive plans by cities and counties. The year 1973 also saw enactment of an act requiring all cities and counties to adopt subdivision ordinances; an act establishing farm use zoning and tax deferrals; and laws to increase the effectiveness of city and county planning commissions.

Senate Bill 100 was enacted after extensive public debate on state land use legislation in which a slide presentation on land use planning toured the state and a weekly newsletter was sent out to a mailing list of some seven thousand people while the legislature was in session. The bill eventually adopted was a considerably compromised version of that originally prepared, but nonetheless established a framework for statewide land use action.

The act created a Land Conservation and Development Commission (LCDC) with seven members appointed by the governor and approved by the legislature. Staff services for the commission are provided by the Department of Land Conservation and Development. LCDC was charged by the act to adopt statewide planning goals and guidelines by January 1, 1975. Unless granted an extension by LCDC, all of the state's counties and cities, as well as special districts and state agencies, must have adopted comprehensive land use plans which conform to these statewide goals by January 1, 1976. Further, these comprehensive plans must be implemented through the enactment of zoning, subdivision control, and other ordinances. County governments are required by the act to coordinate the planning activities of all localities within their boundaries (except for cities of over 300,000 of which Portland is presently the only instance). Counties may also opt to form multicounty agencies to carry out this function. Special legislation passed in 1973 mandated the establishment of a regional planning district for the tri-county Portland metropolitan area.

LCDC has review and approval authority over the land use plans of all counties and local governments. If any county or city fails to adopt and implement a comprehensive plan which conforms to the statewide goals, LCDC is authorized, after public notice and hearing, to adopt or implement such plan or ordinances.

In developing the statewide land use goals and guidelines which became operative on January 1, 1975, LCDC conducted across the state fifty-six public workshops, eighteen public hearings, and a number of public meetings to consider drafts. Fourteen goals and guidelines were finally adopted on the following subjects: (1) citizen involvement; (2) land use planning; (3) agricultural lands; (4) forest lands; (5) open spaces, scenic and historic areas, and natural resources; (6) air, water, and land resources quality; (7) areas subject to natural disasters and hazards; (8) recreational needs; (9) economy of the state; (10) housing; (11) public facilities and services; (12) transportation; (13) energy conservation; and (14) urbanization.

The guidelines accompanying most of the goals are divided into two sections: planning and implementation. The planning guidelines relate primarily to the process of bringing plans into conformance with the goals, whereas the implementation guidelines address the problem of actually carrying out the goals. The planning guidelines for land use planning recommend that local plans include areawide planning goals, identification of critical areas, elements that address any special needs or desires of the people in the area, and schedules which reflect the anticipated future situation at appropriate intervals. The implementation measures recommended include ordinances controlling the use of and construction on land, such as zoning and subdivision ordinances, building codes, and sign ordinances; plans for public facilities which are more specific than those included in the comprehensive plan; capital improvement budgets; state and federal regulations affecting land use; and annexation, consolidations, mergers, and other reorganization measures.

LCDC holds that all of the goals and guidelines are of equal importance and that their order does not reflect priorities. Some indication of priorities has been given, however, in the following requirements which the commission established for cities and counties to which it granted planning extensions in January 1975:

1. Extensions are for one year only. Cities or counties requiring more time must submit revised extension requests at the end of 1976.

2. All urban areas must designate urban growth boundaries as soon as possible, and perhaps as a preliminary condition of receiving a planning extension.

3. All agricultural lands must be protected with exclusive farm use zoning as soon as possible this year.

In 1975 the Oregon state legislature included $4.4 million for planning grants to county and city governments in LCDC's overall 1975–1977 budget of $5.5 million. These grants will help pay the local costs of meeting the state goals.

As originally drafted, Senate Bill 100 would have given LCDC permit authority in areas of critical state concern, but this provision was deleted before the act was passed. The question of designation of critical areas was deferred for later legislative consideration, though LCDC was authorized to review and recommend such designations to the legislature.

The act did, however, authorize the commission to designate and require permits for *activities* of statewide significance. It established that these activities might include the following, if determined by LCDC to be of statewide significance by virtue of their nature or magnitude: the planning and siting of public transportation facilities, sewerage systems, water supply systems, solid waste disposal sites and facilities, and schools. Additional activities may also be recommended for designation by LCDC. Permits for designated activities must be issued on the basis of statewide planning goals and guidelines applicable to activities of statewide significance.

In practice, this permit system, which is a mechanism for state control of the public infrastructure necessary for development, is administered by the Department of Land Conservation and Development, though final authority rests in the commission. County and state agencies which are affected by the activities involved are required to review and comment upon permit applications.

Wyoming

In 1975 Wyoming passed a statewide planning law[33] which is primarily intended to help prepare the state for increased development of its energy resources and the growth this process is expected to generate. One of the least densely populated states in the nation, Wyoming is predominately rural, with an economy based on mining and ranching.

Within the next decade the state's mineral resources are expected to draw new mining operations and accompanying boomtown growth to some areas. In the northeastern portion of the state, the Powder River Basin contains the largest reserve of strippable coal in the nation. In addition, further oil, gas, and uranium mining is anticipated. No plans have yet been charted for mining the oil shale in a section of the Green River formation, but this must be considered a possibility.

In conjunction with this mining development, construction of new power plants is also presaged. Coal developers anticipate mine mouth plants with either liquidification or gasification processes. Another alternative which has been suggested is the construction of a coal slurry pipeline that would transport the coal to Arkansas for power development.

One of the most serious problems involved in this potential development is the demands which it would make on one of Wyoming's most scarce resources: water. The state has a limited water supply, and in the eastern section surface water rights are owned by ranchers. Obtaining water needed for new mining and mining-related industry will be very difficult, since all of the alternatives proposed to date (including the use of groundwater or further diversions from either the Yellowstone or the Green River) all involve considerable problems and controversy.

The alteration of grazing land by strip mining is another severe problem, particularly since it is questionable whether present techniques of reclamation will be effective on arid grasslands.

Equally difficult to deal with will be the rapid population growth that is expected to accompany mining development. In a dramatic foreshadowing of possible things to come, the small town of Rock Springs more than doubled in population—growing from 11,000 to 26,000—in the four years from 1970 to 1974, as a result of growth stimulated by a coal-fired power plant, a sodium carbonate mining operation, and soda ash refining plants. This uncontrolled and unplanned for growth led to housing shortages, overcrowded mobile home parks, overburdened sewers which necessitated a housing construction moratorium, and subsidence of land over abandoned coal mines.

Faced with such problems, the state initiated study of land use issues in 1973 with the formation of the Wyoming Conservation and Land Use Study Commission. This commission was charged to study past, present, and future land use controls in the state at all levels of government; to conduct public hearings throughout the state; to study the public education needed in state land use planning; and to make recommendations to the legislature regarding needed legislation and constitutional amendments for statewide land use policy and planning and needed consolidation and strengthening of land use controls.

The study commission reported back to the legislature in the fall of 1974, and in March 1975 the latter established a statewide land use planning program. It created a state Land Use Commission, composed of nine members selected by the governor from a list provided by an advisory council, which, in turn, is appointed by the governor from a list compiled by the county commissioners.

Within one year of its establishment, the Wyoming Land Use Commission must adopt state land use goals, policies, and guidelines, which will include definitions of different types of land uses. Once these are prepared, local governments must develop a local land use plan or opt to cooperate with the county in the development of a plan. Each county must develop a land use plan which incorporates the plans of its municipalities. These local and county land use plans must be consistent with the state land use goals, policies, and guidelines and are subject to review and approval by the Land Use Commission. The plans must be completed and approved within one year. Once the local and county plans are approved, the commission must develop a state land use plan, which must be completed by January 1, 1979. This plan is to be implemented by the counties.

The act included a two-year appropriation of $460,000 to aid local and county governments in the preparation of their land use plans. It also created a land use information service to make needed information and data available to local planning units. To carry out the policies and guidelines established by the commission, the act created an Office of Land Use Administration within the governor's office.

The act also contains a clause which allows the Land Use Commission to designate areas of "critical or more than local concern" and to establish development guidelines for these areas. Areas which may be designated are those "where uncontrolled or incompatible large scale development could result in damages to the environment, life or property, where the short or long term public interest is of more than local significance." Such areas include fragile or historic lands, natural hazard lands, renewable resource lands, and other areas determined by the commission to be of more than local concern.

CITIZEN ACTION

This chapter has provided generic information on state laws affecting land use, as a guide for determining what laws and programs exist in a particular state. It has discussed the statewide programs developed by six different states, to demonstrate the kinds of initiatives that are being taken to confront land use problems.

As was emphasized at the beginning of this chapter, citizens need to find out

· Which of the many possible types of laws and programs affecting land use have been adopted in their state.
· What agencies are responsible for implementing and enforcing these laws.
· What procedures and standards these agencies must follow.
· What permits, licenses, or approvals are or may be required of developers under state law.
· What requirements there are for public notice of applications for permits, public hearings, and public information meetings.

Often citizens will find that existing groups or organizations are already involved in land use questions and may have amassed much needed information and expertise. Such groups may include local environmental or citizens' organizations; local chapters of national organizations; in the Northeast, local conservation commissions; associations of backpackers, nature enthusiasts, hunters, or fishermen; and lobbying groups in the state capital.

Where possible, citizens should get to know the personnel of state agencies who are responsible for administering land-related programs, as well as regional federal officials who coordinate federal-state activities. They should also get on any mailing lists through which information on state land use programs is disseminated. When public meetings or hearings are held, citizens should make a strong showing and be well prepared to discuss the issues involved.

Once citizens know how state programs affecting land use operate, they will be able to apply this knowledge to particular land use problems. For example, if they know all the state laws applicable to subdivisions—including requirements for sewage disposal plans, water supply permits, disclosure filings, and perhaps for wetlands alteration permits, stream disruption permits, and environmental review —they may be able to achieve review of the development at the state level which was unobtainable from a growth-oriented local government.

A key determination which citizens working for more effective land use planning and regulation at the state level need to make is whether they should focus their attention on winning passage of new legislation or on achieving better implementation of existing legislation—or even possibly on defending existing legislation that is under attack. In states which have done virtually nothing, clearly efforts should be made to establish needed protective laws. In other states, however, it may be more important to concentrate on correcting inept or inadequate implementation of laws which, on the books, are reasonably strong. In either case, it is essential for citizens to evaluate very carefully the political factors which are at work. For example, they should find out where the governor and key state legislators stand on land use issues and what actions they and their staffs are taking.

The need for public education regarding state involvement in land use matters is very acute in many areas. The past failures of piecemeal or nonexistent local action to protect critical environmental values should be documented and the constructive role which the state can play emphasized.

NOTES

1. The first really significant study of state actions in the realm of land use control was Fred Bosselman and David Callies, *The Quiet Revolution in Land Use Control,* prepared for the Council on Environmental Quality (Washington, D.C.: U.S. Government Printing Office, 1971). It is for sale by the Superintendent of Documents, U.S. Government Printing Office, Washington, D.C. 20402. The most

recent compendium of actions taken by all fifty of the states is *Land Use Planning Reports: A Summary of State Land Use Controls* (Washington, D.C.: Plus Publications, January 1976). This report is available for $9.50 from Plus Publications, Inc., 2814 Pennsylvania Ave., N.W., Washington, D.C. 20007. A weekly newsletter entitled *Land Use Planning Reports,* also published by Plus Publications, reports on current land use control developments at the federal, state, and local level. Its subscription price is $90 per year. *Land Use Planning Abstracts* (New York: Environmental Information Center, 1975) is an extensive reference source, published annually, which includes information on all types of materials on land use.

It is not possible here to provide a full list of publications pertaining to state land use controls, but the following is a sampling of this literature: California Land-Use Task Force, *The California Land: Planning for People,* sponsored by the Planning and Conservation Foundation (Los Altos, California: William Kaufmann, Inc., 1975); Luther J. Carter, *The Florida Experience: Land and Water Policy in a Growth State* (Baltimore and London: published for Resources for the Future by the Johns Hopkins University Press, 1974); Raymond R. Christman, *State Land Use Programs: Issues and Options* (Pittsburgh: Pennsylvania Land Policy Project, 1975); Wendell Fletcher and William Duddleson, *A Comparative Anatomy of Eight State Land-Use Control Programs* (Washington, D.C.: The Conservation Foundation, 1974); Elizabeth Haskell and Victoria Price, *State Environmental Management: Case Studies of Nine States* (New York: Praeger, 1973); Hawaii State Land Use Commission, *Report to the People* (February 1975); Robert G. Healy, *Land Use and the States* (Baltimore and London: published for Resources for the Future by the Johns Hopkins University Press, 1976); Jon A. Kusler, *State Land Planning and Regulatory Functions; Proposals and Programs for the Several States and a Draft Bill for Wisconsin,* a working paper of the Institute for Environmental Studies (Madison: University of Wisconsin, 1972); Charles E. Little, *The New Oregon Trail* (Washington, D.C.: The Conservation Foundation, 1974); Phyllis Meyers, *Slow Start in Paradise* (Washington, D.C.: The Conservation Foundation, 1974); Phyllis Meyers, *So Goes Vermont* (Washington, D.C.: The Conservation Foundation, 1974); Phyllis Meyers, *Zoning Hawaii* (Washington, D.C.: The Conservation Foundation, 1976); Minnesota State Planning Agency, *Programs, Policies and Legal Authorities Affecting the Use of Land in Minnesota* (May 1975); Natural Resources Defense Council, *Land Use Controls in New York State,* ed. Elaine Moss (New York: The Dial Press/James Wade Books, 1975); *Oregon Land Use Legislation* (Salem, Oregon: Office of the Governor, 1973); Thomas M. Schmidt, *Laws Which Regulate Land Use in Pennsylvania* (Pittsburgh: Pennsylvania Land Use Project, 1975), Task Force on Natural Resources and Land Use Information and Technology, *Land: State Alternatives for Planning and Management* (Lexington, Ky.: The Council of State Governments, 1975); Task Force on Natural Resources and Land Use Information and Technology, *Organization, Management and Financing of State Land Use Programs* (Lexington, Ky.: The Council of State Governments, 1974); and Wyoming Conservation and Land Use Study Commission, *Statewide Land Use Planning Program for Wyoming* (October 1974).

2. California Land-Use Task Force, *The California Land: Planning for People,* sponsored by the Planning and Conservation Foundation (Los Altos, California: William Kaufmann, Inc., 1975), pp. 16–22.

3. N.Y. Environmental Conservation Law § 25–0401(2).

4. Just v. Marinette County, 201 N.W.2d 761, 768, 4 ERC 1841, 1844–1845 (Wis. 1972).

5. 16 U.S.C. § 1451 *et seq.*

6. 7 Del. Code, Chapter 70, § 7001 *et seq.*

7. Cal. Pub. Res. Code § 27000 *et seq.*

8. 33 U.S.C. § 1251 *et seq.*

9. 42 U.S.C. § 1857 *et seq.*

10. 42 U.S.C. § 3251 *et seq.*

11. 42 U.S.C. § 4201 *et seq.*

12. 42 U.S.C. § 4321 *et seq.*

13. 15 U.S.C. § 1701 *et seq.*

14. 16 U.S.C. § 797(e).

15. Haw. Rev. Stat. Chapter 205.

16. 10 Vt. Stat. Ann. § 6001 *et seq.*

17. Act 81 of the 1973 Vermont laws, amending 32 Vt. Stat. Ann. §§ 5951, 5960 (e), 5967–5968, 5973; adding 32 Vt. Stat. Ann. §§ 5976–5977 and 32 Vt. Stat. Ann. §§ 10001–10010.

18. 38 Me. Rev. Stat. Ann. § 481 *et seq.*

19. 12 Me. Rev. Stat. Ann. § 681 *et seq.*

20. 12 Me. Rev. Stat. Ann. § 4811 *et seq.*

21. 5 Me. Rev. Stat. Ann. § 3310 *et seq.*

22. 38 Me. Rev. Stat. Ann. §§ 471–478.

23. 14 Fla. Stat. Ann. § 380.012 *et seq.*

24. The American Law Institute, A Model Development Code, Proposed Official Draft, Article 7 (Philadelphia: The American Law Institute, 1975).

25. Task Force on Natural Resources and Land Use Information and Technology, *Organization, Management and Financing of State Land Use Programs* (Lexington, Ky.: The Council of State Governments, 1974), p. 48.

26. *Ibid.*

27. 1 Fla. Stat. Ann. § 23.011 *et seq.*

28. 12 Fla. Stat. Ann. § 259.01 *et seq.*

29. 14 Fla. Stat. Ann. § 373.013 *et seq.*

30. 8 Fla. Stat. Ann. § 163.601 *et seq.*

31. 8 Fla. Stat. Ann. § 163.601 *et seq.*

32. Ore. Rev. Stat. Chapter 197.

33. Wy. Stat. § 9–849 *et seq.*

CHAPTER 13

Regional Land Use Controls

A VERY SERIOUS dilemma exists in this country in that many land use and environmental problems are regional in nature, but in most cases we have not yet developed an effective regional means of dealing with them. Most political boundaries between units of local government are the result of historical chance or haphazard growth and thus do not bear a logical relation to the present distribution of population and pressures for development. Metropolitan areas throughout the country extend through many towns, cities, and counties, and frequently are located in more than one state. In addition, increased access to more distant rural areas, along with the increasing mobility and affluence of the American population, has brought once remote and isolated areas into the orbit of influence of regional and national centers. Consequently, regional and interdisciplinary management of problems is needed in such areas as transportation, air pollution, water supply and sewage disposal, solid waste, open space preservation, housing, employment, and racial discrimination.

If one looks at the relation of local units of government to major natural systems such as mountainous areas or the shores of large lakes, it is equally clear that a single unit of local government rarely has the power to regulate directly an entire ecosystem. Yet the integrity of an ecosystem is dependent upon coordinated control of conservation and development.

Historically, moreover, state governments have been reluctant to take to themselves the job of land use management, to interfere with the powers traditionally delegated to local units of government, or to foster the development of strong regional bodies which might be competitive with the state itself. As a result, regional planning commissions and voluntary associations of local governments have generally been authorized under state enabling acts which make the decision of whether to employ the regional approach one of local choice and also leave the financing of such efforts up to local discretion.[1] The greatest growth in the organization of regional planning commissions and councils of governments occurred during the 1960s as a result of two federal programs, the HUD "701" program and the A-95 review process, which established funds and responsibilities for such bodies. Both of these programs are discussed further below.

Regional, metropolitan, areawide, or joint planning commissions are usually composed of citizens appointed by the localities involved or by the state government. They generally have been empowered to serve advisory functions—to gather and distribute information relevant to land use and development, to provide support and advice to local planning boards or commissions, and to prepare a regional plan. The implementation of regional plans, on the other hand, has generally been left to the constituent local governments. Thus a regional plan usually has no binding force or effect and, in the final analysis, local rather than regional interests prevail. This has meant that while some regional planning commissions have developed real or apparent planning expertise, their work generally has not been an effective force in regulating the development of the country's landscape.

Councils, associations, or conferences of local governments (commonly known as councils of governments or COGs) are voluntary associations composed of elected officials of local member jurisdictions. They grew in popularity during the 1960s when the inability of regional planning commissions to implement their plans and their remoteness from actual policy and decision making began to be points of considerable controversy. The hope in establishing COGs with regional planning responsibilities was that in this way such planning would become a more integral part of the political process. However, although COGs have served as forums in which elected officials can air their common problems and concerns, COGs are also

voluntary confederations which have no authority to compel participation, attendance, or implementation of policy decisions. Consequently, they too are dependent on the goodwill of their constituent
local governments and reflect the interests of those governments.
Thus, like regional planning commissions, COGs usually have not
been able to hammer out solutions to difficult environmental and
land use problems.

Another important factor in American regionalism is the fragmentation of governmental authority into numerous special districts
and areawide agencies.[2] Special districts are limited purpose governmental units that are separate corporate entities designed to provide
a particular service or services. Regional or local in character, they
exist in great profusion and with irregular boundaries in all states
except Alaska. Not generally classed as special districts are the thousands of school districts across the country.

Examples of special districts are districts or authorities concerned with housing, sewers, water supply, soil conservation, drainage, flood control, parks and recreation, transit, highways, electric
power, gas supply, hospitals, cemeteries, and fire protection. Their
boundaries may encompass an area larger or smaller than a given
local government and in some cases even cross state lines. There is
considerable diversity among special districts in organization, number of jurisdictions served, type and number of services provided, size
of budget, and number of employees. Some special purpose units are
so closely related to cities, counties, or other general purpose governments that the U.S. Bureau of the Census classifies them as subordi-
nate agencies of these governments; many others are substantially
autonomous.

Special districts are created for a wide variety of reasons and have
been promoted by local, state, and the federal government. The chief
reason for their popularity is their capacity to provide unique structural solutions to pressing problems of a particular kind. They can
usually be created with only minor alterations to the existing system
of local government and they are frequently fiscally self-sufficient,
traditionally obtaining the bulk of their revenues from nontax
sources such as bond proceeds and user charges. Other arguments
for their use emphasize technical specialization, efficiency, and the
geographic flexibility which allows special districts to conform to the
service boundaries of a particular function.[3]

These technical and political advantages have led to a great
proliferation of special districts. During the past twenty years they

have, in fact, increased by more than 90 percent, far outpacing the growth of any other unit of local government.[4] This has resulted in great jurisdictional complexity and what has been called "a boundary mess." In recognition of the difficulties of communication and coordination caused by such a multiplicity of governmental units, action has been taken at all levels of government to curb the growth of special districts. Some local governments have consolidated certain districts; the federal government has taken steps to assure that general purpose governments rather than special districts are the prime recipients of federal grants; and a few states have established boundary commissions.

In addition to special districts, since the 1960s federal programs requiring an "areawide" approach have led to the creation of areawide districts or program areas for planning, grant administration, and implementation of federal standards. The more common of these program areas or agencies—a number of which have direct or indirect associations with land use—include air quality control regions, air quality maintenance areas, areawide water quality management or designated "208" agencies, river basin commissions, metropolitan transportation planning organizations, regional criminal justice planning boards, manpower area planning councils, areawide comprehensive health planning organizations, economic development districts, and resource conservation and development councils. The programs involving air quality control regions and maintenance areas, 208 planning, coastal zone management, and metropolitan transportation planning organizations have been discussed in some detail in Chapters 4, 5, 6, and 10, respectively.

In some of the federal programs which have an areawide approach, such as air quality control, the state is responsible for planning and action on a regional basis and may or may not designate areawide organizations to participate in this work. In a majority of cases, however, the federal government requires some type of regional organization, though there is variation regarding whether the comprehensive planning organization for the region, a specially created single purpose organization, or other types of organizations are preferred.

The prime federal motivation in structuring assistance programs in an areawide manner has been the desire to encourage efforts to find regional solutions to regional problems, a need accentuated by the failure of states and localities in most areas to develop effective mechanisms through which regional needs can be identified and addressed. Yet as various functional federal areawide programs have grown up, each with its own requirements for organization, geographical boundaries, planning, administration, and coordination with state and local governments, substate regionalism has become even more complex than ever.

In addition, it has become apparent that areawide problems are not only interrelated in a geographical sense, they are also interrelated in an interdisciplinary sense. That is, in a metropolitan area, not only must there be coordination in determining where sewage treatment plants and interceptor lines are located, there must also be coordination between sewage treatment decisions and air quality maintenance plans. Likewise, transportation planning must be consistent with air quality control planning, and coastal zone management plans must be coordinated with efforts to abate both air and water pollution. This needed coordination is, moreover, not a simple matter, since many technical issues and the expertise of many different kinds of specialists are involved. The hard truth which has to be faced is that not only must we learn to deal with regional aspects of particular problems, we must also learn to understand and cope with the interrelationships between different kinds of problems.

Increasingly, efforts have been made by the federal government to establish linkages and coordination between areawide programs supported by federal assistance. The statutory requirement that the construction of federal-aid highways be consistent with state implementation plans under the Clean Air Act has been described in Chapter 4. Further, interagency agreements have been signed to coordinate the HUD 701 land use requirements with those of the Coastal Zone Management program and the U.S. Environmental Protection Agency's Section 208 program. Similar agreements have also been made between the 208 program and the Coastal Zone Management program, and between the 208 program and the U.S. Army Corps of Engineers. In all of these programs, the ruling federal regulations emphasize that areawide planning programs must be coordinated with each other and with state, local, and regional comprehensive planning efforts.

The many layers of complexity which exist on the areawide or regional front, crowned by the voluntary nature of many regional organizations, have led some to believe that the answer lies in some form of regional government, while others (such as the prestigious American Law Institute) have concluded that the weaknesses of regional organizations are so critical that the state itself must take full responsibility for regional programs. It is not possible to analyze here the various ideas which have been put forward, though it is important to stress how far we are from any kind of consensus. As an analyst of the California coastal planning process has observed:

> In [one] view, linkages are needed among the several planning processes affecting the regions—including coastal planning, planning for air and water, and also the comprehensive regional planning that some of the COGs are trying to do. But how these linkages should be established remains a mystery to most observers. . . .[5]

Certain conclusions, however, seem clear. First, voluntary regional organizations have not had the political strength to deal effectively with controversial issues, of which growth and land use are prime examples. Second, as a corollary, whether carried out by regional bodies, state agencies, or local governments in concert, regional land use programs can only be successful if they are sustained by statutory powers. Since the state holds the reins for governmental reorganizations and for the exercise of the police power, it is likely that state legislatures will play an important role in whatever solutions are found for regional organizational problems.

The basic intent of this discussion has been to indicate the breadth and depth of the problems of regional organizations, in the belief that citizens who are aware of these complexities will be in a better position to help try to resolve them.

The remainder of this chapter is devoted to certain specific topics. First, the HUD 701 and the A–95 review process, which have been important stimulants for comprehensive regional planning and project coordination, are reviewed in some detail. Then several innovative regional programs are described as examples of efforts in three different parts of the country—Minnesota, New York, and California—to develop effective mechanisms for dealing with regional problems. In the final section, some suggestions for citizen action are provided.

The HUD 701 Program

The 701 program of the U.S. Department of Housing and Urban Development (HUD) takes its name from the statute which created the program: Section 701 of the Housing Act of 1954.[6] The program provides federal assistance for planning activities to state, local, and regional or areawide agencies. Initially, it was primarily a boost for planning by states and individual municipalities and the handful of existing metropolitan or regional planning commissions, for which financial stability had been a serious problem. But new regional bodies soon appeared to take advantage of the new funding opportunities, as more states passed regional planning enabling legislation.

In 1965 another stimulus for regional planning came from the 701 program when Congress added a provision making COGs in metropolitan areas eligible to receive 701 grants. The main objective of this new provision was to foster broad metropolitan cooperation by encouraging organizations of policy and decision makers representing the various local jurisdictions in an area.[7] These organizations were authorized to receive grants to undertake studies, to collect data, and to develop metropolitan, regional, and district plans and programs.

Throughout the 1960s and 1970s the HUD 701 program has continued to spur planning by regional bodies. In fiscal year 1975, for example, 38.8 percent of all 701 funds went to areawide planning organizations (including COGs), while 22.6 percent was granted to the states for planning activities, 36.3 percent to localities, and 2.3 percent to others, including Indian tribal groups. The 38.8 percent granted for areawide planning was divided into two categories: 28.9 percent went to organizations in metropolitan areas and 9.9 percent went to organizations in nonmetropolitan areas.[8] For fiscal year 1976 HUD's total 701 budget was cut from the $100 million of fiscal year 1975 to $75 million, and the department has been resisting pressure from the Ford Administration to dismantle the program entirely. This means, of course, that less 701 money is now available and that the future of the program is uncertain.

The most important of the planning activities funded under the 701 program is the development of a comprehensive plan through a comprehensive planning process, a requirement which must be met by every recipient of 701 funds. Section 701's very broad statutory definition of comprehensive planning and the program's stringent requirements for citizen participation are quoted in Chapter 14, in the section on municipal planning. In essence, comprehensive plans developed under 701 grants are intended to serve as a guide for rational governmental decision making with respect to "(i) the pattern and intensity of land use, (ii) the provision of public facilities (including transportation facilities) and other government services, and (iii) the effective development and utilization of human and natural resources."[9] Provisions for citizen involvement in the comprehensive planning process must assure not only that citizens are informed about planning developments, but that they also are given the opportunity to help initiate as well as react to proposals.[10]

By August 22, 1977, all comprehensive plans funded under the 701 program must include a housing element and a land use element. HUD intends that the latter should integrate all existing land use policies and functional planning activities affecting land use. It should serve as a guide to governmental decision making "on all matters related to the use of land including, for example, air and water quality concerns, waste disposal, transportation, protection of coastal areas, open space, agricultural food and fiber production, environmental conservation, development and housing."[11]

The A-95 Review Process

The Intergovernmental Cooperation Act of 1968 established a national policy for intergovernmental coordination and cooperation, requiring among other things that "[t]o the maximum extent possible, consistent with national objectives, all Federal aid for development purposes shall be consistent with and further the objectives of State, regional, and local comprehensive planning. . . ."[12] It also included provisions designed to curb the proliferation of single or limited function special districts. In cases where both general and special purpose units of government are eligible to receive grants or loans, it requires that federal administrators give preference to the former, unless there are substantial reasons for acting otherwise.

Circular No. A-95 of the Office of Management and Budget (OMB) of the Executive Office of the President was issued in 1969 as one aspect of the implementation of this act.[13] The circular, which has been revised and amended several times in the ensuing years, has four major parts:

Part I, "The Project Notification and Review System," deals with State and local review of applications for Federal assistance.

Part II, "Direct Federal Development," provides for consultation by Federal agencies with state and local government on direct Federal development.

Part III, "State Plans and Multisource Programs," requires gubernatorial review of federally required State plans and clearinghouse review of plans for activities being funded from several program sources.

Part IV, "Coordination of Planning in Multijurisdictional Areas," promotes coordination of federally assisted planning at the substate regional level.[14]

The Project Notification and Review System established by Part I, largely on the basis of an earlier areawide project review system developed to implement Section 204 of the Demonstration Cities and Metropolitan Development Act of 1966,[15] is the most important part of the A-95 program. It provides for a system under which state and areawide agencies have the opportunity to review and comment on all applications for federal assistance "to projects and activities which have an impact on State, areawide, and local development, including development of natural, economic, and human resources."[16] The process has been described as "an early warning system" through which conflicts and problems can be identified and hopefully resolved before applications for federal assistance are submitted. It is intended to serve as an essential means of promoting coordination among the different levels of government.

Under the A–95 Project Notification and Review System, applicants for federal assistance must notify state and areawide "clearinghouses" of their intent to make such applications and to summarize the project or activity to be proposed. The clearinghouses then examine the applicant's submission to determine whether it involves any conflict with state or areawide plans and programs. They also identify other state or local agencies or jurisdictions which might have an interest in the proposed project and allow them the opportunity to review the proposal. Within thirty days after the receipt of notification from the applicant, the clearinghouses must advise him whether or not they see possible conflicts, and if so arrange a conference to attempt to resolve the issues involved. If this is done or if no problems are identified, then the applicant has fulfilled his obligation and may submit his application to the federal funding agency, unless the clearinghouse states that it wishes to review the completed application, in which case it may have another thirty days to do so. If there are conflicts which cannot be resolved, then the clearinghouse notifies the applicant that it will prepare comments on the application. These must be completed and sent to the applicant within thirty days. He then must submit the comments along with his completed application to the federal funding agency. These comments, which are advisory only, must be reviewed along with the application by the federal agency, which must report to the clearinghouse what action it decides to take on the application.

There are two types of clearinghouses: (1) state clearinghouses, which are designated by the governor and are usually state comprehensive planning agencies; and (2) areawide clearinghouses, which are substate in scale (though there are a number of interstate clearinghouses for metropolitan areas) and are also usually comprehensive planning agencies. OMB and governors have generally cooperated in the selection of areawide clearinghouses, which are often, though not always, the regional planning commission or COG that is receiving funds under HUD's 701 program to develop a comprehensive regional plan for that area. This arrangement is strongly encouraged by the fact that the federal government does not provide specific financial support to help cover the costs of A–95 review, but the HUD 701 program recognizes A–95 review as an eligible item of work for 701 assisted agencies which are also A–95 clearinghouses.

It should be noted, however, that Circular No. A–95 does not require the states to establish clearinghouses, nor does it prescribe the organization of clearinghouses, the procedures and techniques by which they carry out reviews, or whether or not they review any category of projects or activities covered by the circular. In the words of OMB's descriptive booklet, *A–95: What It Is—How It Works,* "A–95 is designed to provide an *opportunity* for governors, mayors, and county officials and other state and local officials, through clearinghouses, to *influence* Federal and federally assisted programs and projects that may affect their own plans and programs."[17]

The opportunity to comment on applications for federal assistance has been a very important power for many A–95 areawide clearinghouses, which generally lack implementation authority. Although their comments are advisory only, the right to evaluate proposed projects has increased the stature of areawide bodies and has given them a new means through which to express their viewpoints and recommendations.

Part IV of Circular No. A–95 encourages, but does not require, each state to establish a system of substate planning and development district organizations for the planning and coordination of federal, state, and local development programs. Where such district organizations have been established, they usually also serve as A–95 areawide clearinghouses. Part IV also encourages federal agencies administering programs assisting or requiring areawide planning to utilize such substate district organizations, where they have been established, to carry out this planning. Applicants other than substate district organizations which seek federal assistance to carry out multijurisdictional planning must submit a memorandum of agreement between the applicant and the substate district organization indicating how the planning activities of both will be coordinated.

The A–95 review system also provides a mechanism for the dissemination of environmental impact statements (EISs) for comments to interested state and local government agencies, as required under the National Environmental Policy Act.[18] In the case of projects located in coastal zones, Circular No. A–95 requires that the state agency responsible for the management of the coastal zone be given the opportunity to review the relationship of proposed federal development projects to the coastal zone management program.[19]

Assessments of the effectiveness of the A–95 project review system show mixed results. On the one hand, the A–95 clearinghouses have established regional review systems which have improved intergovernmental communication and project coordination. This has been done, furthermore, with reasonable efficiency and a minimum of red tape. In addition, the A–95 review process gives localities an opportunity to express to federal agencies environmental objections which they may have to projects proposed for federal assistance.

On the other hand, in practice, A–95 clearinghouses very seldom submit negative comments on project applications, and often there is no responsible comprehensive regional plan against which clearinghouses can judge projects.[20]

Innovative Regional Programs

Among the most significant innovative regional bodies which have been established in particular parts of the country are the Adirondack Park Agency in New York; the Hackensack Meadowlands Development Commission in New Jersey; the District Environmental Commissions in Vermont; California's Regional Coastal Commissions; the San Francisco Bay Conservation and Development Commission; and the Tahoe Regional Planning Agency in California and Nevada.[21] City/county consolidations of government have taken place in Nashville, Jacksonville, and Indianapolis, while important moves to strengthen areawide government have been made in Miami, Minneapolis–St. Paul, and Atlanta.[22] The Minneapolis–St. Paul Metropolitan Council, the Adirondack Park Agency, and the San Francisco Bay Conservation and Development Commission—notable examples of regional programs in which environmental values play a significant role—will be described in this section. Special note should be made that in each case the state legislature has created a regional body with statutory powers to implement its plans.

1. The Minneapolis–St. Paul Metropolitan Council

In 1959 a suburban housewife in the Twin Cities called the state health department to report that a glass of water she had just drawn from the tap had a head on it like a glass of beer.[23] This call promoted the discovery that nearly half of the individual home wells in the area's residential subdivisions were contaminated by sewage from septic tanks. In response to this crisis, efforts began immediately to try to provide central water and sewage systems to approximately 300,000 suburban residents. The problems which were encountered in this process, along with indications that the municipalities of the area were not dealing with their land use problems in an orderly manner and that the Metropolitan Planning Commission was not able to cope with issues in which the interests of its constituent local governments conflicted, led to a growing popular and legislative conception that there should be a strong policy and decision-making regional body to deal with these problems.

In 1967 the Minnesota state legislature created the Twin Cities Metropolitan Council, now a seventeen-member body appointed by the governor on a nonpartisan basis.[24] The council absorbed the responsibilities and staff of the Metropolitan Planning Commission, which was abolished, and was given the authority to (1) review and approve the comprehensive plans of independent functional agencies, boards, and commissions; (2) review the comprehensive plans of municipalities and counties; (3) review applications for federal and state aid; and (4) prepare a Development Guide for the metropolitan region.

The Metropolitan Council's relationships with the independent functional boards and commissions are a critical component of its operation, since the central approach of the council has been to guide growth through the provision of public facilities such as water and sewerage systems, transportation facilities, and parks. This "public infrastructure" is to be extended into what are called Urban Service Areas, where further growth is planned, but will not be provided in

Rural Service Areas. Designations and maps of these areas have been prepared as part of the council's Development Guide, which also includes policy plans for sewers, highways and transit, and parks and open space.

The Metropolitan Council has the strongest control over the Metropolitan Waste Control Commission, formerly known as the Metropolitan Sewer Board. Although the Metropolitan Waste Control Commission is a separate agency, it is effectively controlled by the council, which appoints its members, supervises its budget and financing, and carries out long-range sewer planning. The commission is empowered to hold title to the sewage treatment plants and interceptor lines needed to carry out the council's plans. It may also require local governments to transfer to it the ownership of their sewer facilities, a power which was very important in the initial establishment of a coordinated metropolitan sewerage program. Thus, through its own planning and the execution of these plans by the Metropolitan Waste Control Commission, the Metropolitan Council can determine the location and dimensions of sewage treatment plants and interceptor lines in the entire Twin Cities region. Since, as has been discussed in Chapter 5, sewerage facilities are a prime determinant of residential growth, this is a considerable power.

The Metropolitan Council also has approval power over the plans, programs, and capital budget of the Metropolitan Transit Commission, and over the comprehensive plans of the Metropolitan Airports Commission, the Metropolitan Mosquito Control District, and watershed districts. In these cases, the council does not control membership appointment or, in the latter three bodies, budgets and financing, but its authority with regard to comprehensive plans involves significant leverage. The activities of these functional bodies must be carried out in accordance with a comprehensive plan, and, if the Metropolitan Council finds that a particular plan is inconsistent with its Development Guide or is detrimental to the orderly development of the metropolitan area, it may suspend the plan indefinitely.

Efforts by the Metropolitan Council during the early 1970s to have the state legislature establish strong housing and park boards, similar to the sewer board, under its authority were defeated. Also rejected were proposals to make the council an elected rather than an appointed body. These actions reflected the reluctance of the legislature at that time to increase the powers and political visibility of the council. Among the forces opposing expansion of the council's role were the less developed counties within its seven-county jurisdiction. Some legislators also apparently felt that an elective council might be competitive with the state legislature.

In 1971, however, the state legislature passed a highly significant metropolitan tax-sharing act proposed by the Metropolitan Council. This law requires that after 1971 each local government within the council's jurisdiction must contribute to the council 40 percent of its net growth in commercial-industrial valuation. The council must then redistribute these funds among the local governments, primarily on the basis of population. The purpose of this law is to mitigate the influence of property tax considerations on land use decisions, by spreading the tax benefits of growth throughout the metropolitan area. The constitutionality of the statute has been challenged, but has been upheld by the courts.

More recently, the council has won several important legislative victories. In 1974 it was authorized to spend $40 million for the acquisition of parklands in the metropolitan area. In the compromise process worked out for the implementation of this acquisition program, the council identifies areas desirable as regional parks and provides funding, but the counties are responsible for land appraisal, purchase, and improvement. If a county refuses to take this responsibility, the council may designate a municipality within the county or an adjacent county to become the implementing agency for land acquisition. If no other governmental unit wishes to become the implementing agency, the Metropolitan Council may buy the land itself.

Perhaps even more significant was the legislature's decision in 1976 to require counties and municipalities to prepare comprehensive plans that conform to the Development Guide prepared by the Metropolitan Council. These plans must, moreover, be not only reviewed, but also approved by the Metropolitan Council. This mandate to assure that local and county plans are consistent with the Development Guide should considerably enhance the policy-making power of the Metropolitan Council and its ability to control the way in which the Twin Cities metropolitan area will grow.

2. The Adirondack Park Agency

The program of land use controls developed for the Adirondack Park in New York State is a good example of the establishment of a special agency with powers over a region that is unified by common environmental values or problems. The Adirondack Park, which is a vast region roughly the size of Vermont, contains both private land and extensive state-owned forest preserve lands which have been protected since 1895 by an article of the state constitution which requires that they be kept "forever wild."[25] Regional control of land use within the park has, however, only been instituted during the last few years.

While public and private lands in the park had coexisted happily for many years, by the late 1960s it was becoming apparent that dramatic, large-scale, and rapid changes were likely to take place in undeveloped areas of the Adirondacks. With the completion of an interstate highway from Albany to the Canadian border, the park had suddenly become within a day's drive of some 55 million people. This ease of access, combined with the great surge in demand for second homes, was almost certain to draw to the Adirondacks the kind of subdivision development and chaotic commercial growth that had already swept through other scenic parts of the country.

Thus in 1971, following the report of a study commission on the region, the New York state legislature passed an act establishing an Adirondack Park Agency and charging it to prepare a master plan for the management of all state lands within the park, to develop a land use and development plan for all private lands, and to review all development which might have an adverse effect on the park prior to adoption of these plans.[26]

The Adirondack Park Agency's plan for the regulation of development on private lands was enacted into law by the state legislature in 1973, after a review and revision process that included fifteen public hearings and numerous informal meetings of various local, regional, and state officials.

Essentially, the plan classifies all privately owned land within the Adirondack Park into six different types of land use areas: hamlets, moderate intensity use, low intensity use, rural use, resource management, and industrial use. For each of these areas it specifies an "overall intensity guideline" which defines maximum development in terms of the number of principal buildings per square mile. Primary and secondary compatible uses are specified for each land use area. Primary uses are those which are generally suitable anywhere in a given land use area, as long as they are in keeping with the overall intensity guideline. Secondary uses are those which are suitable only if they are appropriately located.

This division into six land use categories is similar to the typical creation of districts under zoning, but in the Adirondack Park larger projects and particular areas of the region are further subject to a system requiring permits for development. Large-scale or potentially more intrusive or disruptive proposed projects to be located in sensitive areas are called class A regional projects and must be approved by the Adirondack Park Agency. Less critical projects, called class B regional projects, are controlled principally by local governments which have land use programs that have been approved by the park agency. If a local government does not have an approved land use program, then class B projects in its jurisdiction are reviewed by the park agency. Criteria for classifying projects are different for each of the six land use areas, and an enumeration of the particular types of projects which fall into class A or class B in each land use area is included in the plan.

This system of land use control in the Adirondack Park is a thoughtful mix of local and regional management designed to protect a recognized state resource. Careful planning has been done on a regional basis, and the results of the planning analysis have been given force and effect through the state legislature's enactment of the plan into law.

3. The San Francisco Bay Conservation and Development Commission

The San Francisco Bay Conservation and Development Commission (BCDC) is another example of the establishment by a state legislature of a regional authority aimed at controlling the use and development of a single resource—in this case, the San Francisco Bay. However, unlike the Adirondack Park plan which seeks primarily to protect the open space character of the park, BCDC's mandate requires it to take into account the interests of both conservation *and* development—though development is defined in terms of water-related uses to assure that the essential qualities of the bay are preserved. As one early account of BCDC stated, "[t]he basic purpose of the Commission is to insure that the filling and development of the Bay does not destroy its essential value for water-oriented uses (*e.g.,* ports, power plants and airports) or its function as a recreational area, as a breeding ground for fish and wildlife, or as a beneficial influence on the climate and livability of the San Francisco area."[27]

During the 1960s public concern about San Francisco Bay was aroused by the rate at which the bay had been and was continuing to be filled by developers for a wide variety of uses, many of which did not need water access. By 1967 estimates indicated that the bay had been reduced, through filling and diking, by over 240 square miles.[28] This process interfered with the biological productivity of the bay's shallows and wetlands, resulting in adverse effects on the life cycles of fish and birds and on recreation; it restricted navigation; and it threatened water and even air quality. Further, such development was capable of cutting off access to the bay for many members of the public. Studies which indicated that a large portion of the bay was very shallow and thus was so easily capable of being filled that a "San Francisco River" might be the result captured the public imagination and spurred efforts to "Save the Bay."

In response to a very effective citizens' campaign which focused public attention on the future of the bay, the California legislature created BCDC as a temporary commission and charged it to prepare a plan for the regulation of the bay and the land immediately adjacent to it. This plan was completed in 1969 and was subsequently adopted by the California legislature, whose findings cited the San Francisco Bay as "the most valuable single natural resource of an entire region"; pointed out that the bay operates as a delicate physical mechanism in which changes affecting one part may affect all other parts; and declared that it was in the public interest to create a politically responsible process by which the bay and its shoreline could be analyzed, planned, and regulated as a unit.[29]

The legislature established BCDC as a permanent regulatory agency empowered to implement its plan by requiring permits for all development within its jurisdiction, which includes the bay itself and a shoreline band extending one hundred feet landward. Throughout most of this jurisdiction, BCDC may grant permits only where it finds that the proposed project is either "(1) necessary to the health, safety or welfare of the public in the entire bay area, or (2) of such a nature that it will be consistent with the provisions of [the law] and with the provisions of the San Francisco Bay Plan then in effect."[30] However, projects on the shoreline band which do not involve fill and which are located outside established boundaries for "water-oriented priority land uses" may be denied a permit only if they do not provide "maximum feasible public access, consistent with the proposed project, to the bay and its shoreline."[31] BCDC is also authorized by statute to attach conditions or restrictions to any permit granted.

City and county governments are drawn into the permitting

process through a requirement that they review and comment to the commission on any proposal which also needs their approval in order to go forward. These comments must be filed with BCDC within ninety days. When it has received city and/or county comments or the ninety day comment period has lapsed, BCDC must hold a public hearing or hearings on the proposed project.

All state and local government agencies, as well as private developers, must obtain permits for any regulated activities within the commission's jurisdiction. In addition, BCDC has entered into a memorandum of understanding with the U.S. Army Corps of Engineers in which the latter has stated that all of its proposals will be in accordance with the provisions of state law and the San Francisco Bay Plan.

BCDC has been criticized by conservationists as being too accommodating with developers and by developers as being too committed to environmental values. The commission has also been cited as just another example of a single purpose special district. It is probably fair to say that BCDC has been very successful in fulfilling its statutory mandate to restrict stringently all filling in San Francisco Bay and to protect the bay for water-related purposes. Clearly, the commission also served as a forerunner of the Regional Coastal Commissions established under the California Coastal Zone Conservation Act passed in 1972.[32] The special district criticism has been pointedly answered with the following question: Aren't limited plans that work better than comprehensive plans that don't?[33]

The general models provided by both BCDC and the Adirondack Park Agency illustrate important aspects of effective regulation of a major environmental resource which extends beyond local boundaries. First, there must be an identification of the resource and which of its values should be preserved and protected. Public education is a crucial part of this process, since the establishment of effective organs of regional control is only possible when there is broad support for taking action to maintain or enhance areas which will be lost to the public if piecemeal regulation by local government is allowed to run its course. Second, a program of regulation, usually in the form of a plan or a scheme of prescribed land use controls, should be enacted into law by the state legislature so that the program has binding legal force. Third, enforcement of the plan must be worked out, usually incorporating some type of compromise between control by local units of government and the state's regional entity. Review by the regional body or control over the terms on which local governments allow development is essential. The use of a system of permits can be a very effective approach, since it allows a case-by-case analysis of proposed changes in land use.

Citizen Action

In general, citizens should seek to understand the complexities of regional or areawide programs affecting their area and work to bring about the changes which are most needed in the light of particular facts and circumstances. In this effort, they should bear in mind that there are no clear-cut answers to the question of how regional programs should be structured and coordinated both with each other and with state, local, and the federal government. Regional programs which have been developed in individual areas of the country can provide useful information on techniques which work and those which do not, but the unique characteristics of a given region will always be critical factors in determining what is desirable and possible in that region.

The need for effective regional mechanisms to deal with growth and land use decisions, transportation problems, air and water pollution control programs, and other difficult regional questions should be documented and explained in citizen education efforts. Often areas have been willing to mobilize the resources needed to attack regional problems only when a crisis of some type has developed; when, for example:

· Drinking water from individual wells in the Minneapolis–St. Paul area was so polluted that it foamed like beer;
· Large-scale second home subdivisions threatened to compromise the open space character and "forever wild" forest lands in New York's Adirondack Park; and
· The prospect of San Francisco Bay being reduced to a river was seriously discussed.

Hopefully, other areas will be able to profit from the example of these experiences and will address their shared regional problems before they reach crisis proportions.

Certain specific actions that citizens can take within the existing nationwide framework of particular federal programs include the following:

1. Citizens should seek to ensure the fulfillment of the public participation requirements of areawide planning activities funded under the HUD 701 program, as well as under critical federal environmental programs, such as 208 water quality management planning, air quality control planning, and coastal zone management. This means finding out what agencies are responsible for these programs in one's area, getting on mailing lists to receive public information materials and notices of public meetings and hearings, attending these meetings and hearings as well informed as possible, and being willing to grapple with the difficult issues involved.

2. Citizens should work to see that maximum use is made of the potential of the A–95 project review system for bringing to the attention of federal agencies environmental problems involved in projects proposed for federal assistance. Close contacts should be established with the personnel of the A–95 areawide clearinghouse for one's region, so that citizens can provide environmental information on particular projects when this is appropriate and can keep abreast of the clearinghouse's goals and procedures.

NOTES

1. An analysis and historical account of the development of regional planning commissions and councils of governments can be found in an exhaustive multivolume study of substate regionalism prepared by the Advisory Commission on Intergovernmental Relations, a body established by Congress in 1959 to monitor the operation of the American federal system and to prepare recommendations. Advisory Commission on Intergovernmental Relations, *Substate Regionalism and the Federal System* (Washington, D.C.: U.S. Government Printing Office, 1973), Volume I, Chapter III.

2. These topics are also analyzed in Advisory Commission on Intergovernmental Relations, *Substate Regionalism,* Volume I, Chapters II and VI, and Volume II, Chapter V.

3. *Ibid.,* I: 20–21.

4. *Ibid.,* I: 43.

5. Stanley Scott, *Governing California's Coast* (Berkeley, California: Institute of Governmental Studies, 1975), p. 145.

6. 68 Stat. 640 (August 2, 1954); 40 U.S.C. § 461.

7. Advisory Commission on Intergovernmental Relations, *Substate Regionalism,* I: 71.

8. These figures were provided by the office of Lawrence D. Houston, the director of the HUD 701 program.

9. 40 U.S.C. § 461 (m) (4) (A).

10. 40 *Federal Register* 36863 (August 22, 1975); 24 C.F.R. § 600.80 (b) (1).

11. 40 *Federal Register* 36862 (August 22, 1975); 24 C.F.R. § 600.72 (a).

12. Public Law No. 90–577, § 401 (c), 82 Stat. 1103 (October 16, 1968); 42 U.S.C. § 4231 (c).

13. The most recent revision of this circular can be found at 41 *Federal Register* 2052 (January 13, 1976).

14. Office of Management and Budget, *A–95: What It Is—How It Works* (no date), p. 1. Copies of this booklet may be obtained from: Office of Management and Budget, Executive Office Building, Washington, D.C. 20503.

15. Public Law No. 89–754, § 204, 80 Stat. 1262 (November 3, 1966).

16. 41 *Federal Register* 2055 (January 13, 1975).

17. Office of Management and Budget, *A–95,* p. 4.

18. 42 U.S.C. § 4321 *et seq.* See Chapter 3 for a discussion of NEPA.

19. The federal Coastal Zone Management program is the subject of Chapter 6.

20. Advisory Commission on Intergovernmental Relations, *Substate Regionalism,* Volume I, Chapter V, pp. 163–164.

21. All of these organizations except the Regional Coastal Commissions are discussed in Fred Bosselman and David Callies, *The Quiet Revolution in Land Use Control,* prepared for the Council on Environmental Quality (Washington, D.C.: U.S. Government Printing Office, 1971).

22. The Minneapolis–St. Paul Metropolitan Council is discussed in both *ibid.* and Advisory Commission on Intergovernmental Relations, *Substate Regionalism,* Volume II, Chapter IV. Actions taken in the other cities listed are discussed in Volume II of the latter reference.

23. Bosselman and Callies, *Quiet Revolution,* p. 137.

24. Metropolitan Council Act, Minnesota Sessions Laws 1967, Ch. 896.

25. New York State Constitution, Art. XIV, § 1.

26. N.Y. Executive Law, Art. 27, § 800 *et seq.* It should be noted that there is more than one Article 27 under this law and that under one of these there is even another § 800. Anyone wishing to refer to the law should be forewarned of this confusion.

27. Bosselman and Callies, *Quiet Revolution,* p. 109.

28. Note, 55 *Calif. L. Rev.* 728 (1967).

29. Cal. Govt. Code § 66600.

30. Cal. Govt. Code § 66632 (f).

31. Cal. Govt. Code § 66632.4.

32. Cal. Pub. Resources Code § 27000 *et seq.* This act is discussed in Chapter 6.

33. Bosselman and Callies, *Quiet Revolution,* p. 122.

CHAPTER 14

Local Land Use Controls

I N THE PAST virtually all land use decisions involving private land were made at the local level of government. Today, as the states are redefining their responsibilities regarding land use problems and federal legislation increasingly affects such concerns, land use is no longer a strictly local matter—though local governments continue to make the majority of land use decisions and local participation is a vital aspect of most state and federal programs.

In large part, the greater state and federal involvement in land use decision making has developed because local governments have failed to adopt needed controls or to enforce them effectively. Typically, local governments have been parochial in their interests, with little concern for the regional repercussions of their actions. They have encouraged and actively pursued rapid growth, seeking thereby to increase their tax revenues, without taking into full account the negative impact and costs of such growth. In this shortsighted process, local governments have generally not been sensitive to the need to protect natural resources and ecological systems. In addition, the fragmentation of power among different governmental or quasi-governmental bodies, which has been discussed in Chapter 13, often has made it very difficult for even a local government with the best of intentions to come to grips effectively with land-related issues.

Efforts by local governments to deal responsibly with their land use problems have increased in a number of areas as localities have discovered that growth and development often involve greater costs than benefits and as the public has grown more adamant about preventing land abuse. Nonetheless, opposition to the establishment and enforcement of effective land use controls is still very strong in some areas. Since, as has been pointed out, most land use decisions are still made at the local level and the local role in state and federal programs is usually very important, there is a great need for effective citizen action to support sound land use planning and regulation by local and county governments.

Local governments derive their powers to regulate land use from the state. Each state in the union has the power to enact legislation for the promotion of the public health, safety, morals, and general welfare of its citizens. This so-called police power of the state is the authority upon which state and local statutes regulating the use of land are based, but cities, towns, villages, or counties may enact such statutes only where the state has explicitly delegated to them the right to exercise the police power through regulation of the use and development of land. Every state has delegated this power at least to some degree, and in most states control of land use is exercised at some level of local government rather than at the state level. Nevertheless, the powers which local governments exercise can only be those which have been granted to them by the state government.

The specific types of powers which have been delegated to local governments, the ways in which these delegations have been made, and the levels of local government to which the powers are entrusted vary enormously from state to state. Moreover, the delegation of powers from the state usually does not require local governments to exercise the powers they are given. In the typical, traditional pattern, the state has granted powers to local governments which are then free at their discretion to exercise these powers if they so choose. More recently, however, a number of states including California, Florida, Idaho, Nebraska, Nevada, Oregon, and Virginia have passed laws requiring local or county governments to prepare comprehensive plans or land use plans. In California, Idaho, Nebraska, and Oregon these plans must not only be prepared, they must also be implemented.

A wide variety of powers may be delegated by the state to local governments. Among those most frequently in local hands are the authority to establish and enforce a zoning ordinance and the authority to establish a planning board or commission to prepare a plan, usually called a comprehensive plan or a master plan, for the physical development of the jurisdiction. Other powers affecting land use which may have been delegated to localities include the authority to adopt subdivision regulations; official maps; building codes; capital improvement programs; shoreline, floodplain, or wetlands restrictions; and to acquire or preserve special areas such as open space or historical districts. In addition, many localities have the right to adopt drinking water and sewage disposal regulations, which usually must be in accordance with state public health standards. As has been discussed in Chapter 12, many of the new state land use programs which have been instituted during the past few years involve state and local cooperation or arrangements in which counties or localities are authorized to take certain actions, such as developing regulations for a critical area or for shoreline protection, subject to state standards, review, and/or approval.

The legal form in which land planning and regulatory powers are granted to localities and the ways in which local governments can exercise them also vary greatly among the states and even within a particular state, when different organizational options are allowed. Anyone wishing to monitor a particular local government to assure that it is exercising its powers legally and is making use of all the measures available to it to protect the environment must first find out what powers have been delegated to the locality by the state and what procedures are legally required in the execution of these powers.

This chapter offers guidance on where to look for such delegations and on the kinds of powers for which to look. The first section reviews the three ways in which states typically authorize local governments to use the police power. Then attention is turned to a discussion of specific kinds of powers which local governments are frequently granted. Zoning, the oldest and most common means of local land use control, is explained first and in some detail through a review of (1) the standard zoning enabling act which served as a model for most state zoning enabling statutes, (2) innovations which have been developed to make zoning more responsive to contemporary needs, and (3) an example of typical problems in rural areas. Next follow descriptions of powers pertaining to municipal planning, subdivision controls, official maps, building codes, capital improvement programs, and local environmental conservation commissions. A brief discussion of the local real property tax is included and, in the final section, suggestions are made regarding citizen action which might be undertaken.

STATE DELEGATION OF THE POLICE POWER TO LOCAL GOVERNMENTS

There are three basic ways in which states have delegated the police power to local governments. A given state may have used any or all of these means to delegate authority to its subdivisions. First, such delegation may be made in provisions of the state constitution. Some state constitutions directly delegate to localities powers of home rule which have been interpreted by the courts to include powers over land use. For instance, the California constitution provides that any county or city may make and enforce within its area of authority local police, sanitary, and other regulations which are not in conflict with the general laws.[1]

Two points should be noted in connection with such constitutional grants of home rule powers. First, the constitutional language frequently restricts the grant of power by specifying that local actions must not be in conflict with the general laws. This means that when the state legislature passes a law on a particular subject, the state law takes precedence in this area and the local government must exercise its constitutional power within the bounds of the state legislation. Second, the constitutional grants are frequently phrased in terms which are not specific as to powers over land use. Since zoning and other powers which are now constantly exercised over land use frequently were not exercised by governments at the time when these state constitutional provisions were enacted, the question of whether the grants to local governments include or do not include power over land use regulation has been left to the state courts.

The second way in which authority for local controls may be delegated is through state statutes which grant general home rule powers to towns, cities, or other units of local government. These enactments may be general statutes pertaining to all local governments within a certain category, such as "towns" or "cities of more than 100,000," or the delegation of power may be included in the grant of a municipal charter to a specific locality. Like the constitutional grants, these enactments (particularly the charters) are limited by the general laws of the state, and where land use control is not explicitly set forth, interpretation is a matter for the state courts. The state delegation is strictly construed to limit the grant of powers to those areas explicitly set out or necessary to the performance of the functions delegated. This means that even general grants of the police power will not always be read to include, for example, the power to zone, if such power was not likely to have been in the mind of the legislature when the grant was made.[2]

Third, local exercise of the police power can be authorized through enabling acts passed by the state legislature to give localities the power to legislate in particular areas. The best-known model for such an act in the land use field is the Standard State Zoning Enabling Act, which was developed and distributed by the U.S. Department of Commerce in the 1920s.[3] This act was eventually adopted with modifications and variations by most of the fifty states, and, for that reason, will be discussed at greater length in the next section of this chapter. There are also standard enabling acts on planning which have been adopted by many of the states, and a number of other types of enabling acts delegating authority involving or relating to land use control have been adopted across the country.[4] As Table 9 in Chapter 12 indicates, all of the states have enacted some form of enabling legislation delegating land use powers to its municipalities or counties.[5] Like other grants of state power, state enabling acts are usually strictly construed to limit the grant of power to the locality—that is, wherever there is genuine ambiguity regarding whether or not a specific action has been authorized by the state under an enabling statute, courts will generally presume that it has not been delegated.

ZONING

The Standard State Zoning Enabling Act

The Standard State Zoning Enabling Act was prepared by the U.S. Department of Commerce in the 1920s as a model for state legislatures wishing to grant localities the power to zone. The act was widely distributed, and the zoning enabling acts subsequently passed by most states were substantially based upon it. Consequently, it is a good guide to the essentials of traditional zoning in this country, though the reader should not forget that modifications and exceptions do exist in individual states.

The standard act sets out the powers granted to localities and the procedures by which zoning schemes are to be established, changed, reviewed, and enforced. It begins with a statement that the powers granted are for the classic purpose of the state's exercise of the police power: Promoting the health, safety, morals, or general welfare of the community. The powers granted pursuant to that purpose are set out at length and with specificity. The localities may regulate and restrict the following:

1. The height, number of stories, and size of buildings and other structures;
2. The percentage of the lot occupied;
3. The size of yards, courts, and other open spaces;
4. The density of population; and
5. The location and use of buildings, structures, and land for trade, industry, residence, or other purposes.

These are, of course, wide powers to regulate the use of land, and they can only be exercised pursuant to the broad aims of regulation under the police power. The standard act seeks to establish in a more concrete fashion how zoning relates to the public health, safety, morals, and welfare by setting out the ends which zoning regulations adopted under the act will attempt to achieve.[6] These regulations are to be designed to:

1. Lessen congestion in the streets;
2. Secure safety from fire, panic, and other dangers;
3. Provide adequate light and air;
4. Prevent overcrowding of land;
5. Avoid undue concentration of population; and
6. Facilitate the adequate provision of transportation, water, sewerage, schools, parks, and other public requirements.

The basic structure imposed by zoning is the division of the municipality into districts within which particular regulations are applied. These regulations must be imposed uniformly within each district.

Zoning regulations must also be made "in accordance with a comprehensive plan." This requirement appears on its face to hold out more promise of a detailed and comprehensive investigation and statement of goals in the zoning process than has actually been required by courts interpreting the phrase. Usually, the courts review the zoning ordinance or zoning map itself to determine whether it is comprehensive, and do not look beyond that to require that a plan also be in existence which the zoning scheme implements. This result stems partially from the language of the standard act, which sets out careful requirements for the adoption and amendment of zoning districts and regulations, but includes no requirement for the independent adoption of a comprehensive plan to guide or form the basis for the system of zoning which is established. There are some states, such as California and Oregon, which *require* the adoption of a comprehensive plan and *require* that zoning and land use regulations adhere to the goals and principles set out in the plan; but this arrangement is far less common than it should be.

The standard act provides that, subject to important restrictions, the local legislative body is granted the power to decide how the zoning districts and regulations are to be established and changed, and that the legislative body itself must adopt the zoning ordinance. It requires that the original establishment of the ordinance be a two-step process and that public hearings be held at both stages. In the first step the legislative body of the municipality must appoint a zoning commission to prepare a preliminary report setting out proposals for appropriate district boundaries and regulations for each district. The zoning commission must hold a public hearing on this preliminary report. After the hearing, a final report must be drawn up and forwarded to the legislative body. The legislative body, in turn, must hold a public hearing on the final report of the zoning commission.

Variations in these procedures exist in the zoning enabling acts of some states. In the state of Connecticut, for example, the zoning ordinance is adopted not by the local legislative body, but by the zoning board. Further, the adoption of the zoning ordinance is not always required to be a two-step process.

The public hearings which must be held during the development of a zoning ordinance are a very important part of the process of land use control at the local level. Any scheme of zoning clearly offers a municipality a number of choices on such questions as how much land will be required for parks and how much for industry, whether there are vulnerable or significant natural resource systems which will receive special attention, and what provisions will be made for transportation and shopping facilities. Through the public hearing process, citizens have the opportunity to present evidence to the community regarding how these choices should be made. Also, they have the chance to urge and attempt to assure that decisions are made within the context of a comprehensive plan which sets out a pattern for the locality's development that can be used as a framework for future decisions.

The importance of this stage of the zoning process becomes even clearer when one realizes how difficult it can be to win alteration of the ordinance after it has been passed. The courts will generally defer to a properly enacted zoning ordinance unless it falls afoul of one of the basic requirements, discussed in Chapter 2, which must be met if a land use regulation is to be held constitutional. The court will not substitute its judgment for that of the local legislature unless there is this type of patent failure. Thus, a wide range of legislative discretion simply will not be overturned by the courts.

Further, in order to allow reasonable reliance by private parties on the zoning scheme after it has been established, the standard act purposely makes major revision of the zoning ordinance difficult. The act allows the legislative body to change district boundaries and the restrictions within each district on the basis of majority vote after notice and public hearing, but it also provides for a system of protest by those in or near the area being rezoned which can make such revision much harder. Under the act, if the owners of 20 percent of the area included in the change or 20 percent of those owning adjacent or surrounding lots[7] protest the proposed change, it will become effective only if it is approved by three-fourths of all the members of the municipal legislative body. This effectively means that if a small number of those affected by a proposed zoning change are opposed to it and make a formal written protest against the proposal, it can become law only if the overwhelming majority of the municipality's legislative body is in favor of the change. This provision clearly provides stability for the major outlines of the zoning ordinance and where good ordinances are in force, it should be used to resist changes that secure immediate advantage to some property owners but do not serve the interests of the whole community.

The drafters of the standard act recognized, however, that while major changes of the zoning pattern required careful scrutiny and wide backing, it was virtually impossible to enact an ordinance which did not need minor revisions because of special circumstances affecting particular lots. The power to make such refinements and alterations was, therefore, vested in a board of adjustment. The board of adjustment is an administrative body whose most important powers are to grant special exceptions and variances to the zoning ordinance, as well as to hear appeals on actions taken by the local officials who administer the zoning regulations. Special exceptions are generally approvals for uses which are allowed under the zoning ordinance, but only after approval by the board of adjustment. Variances authorize uses or building types which are prohibited by the ordinance.

These discretionary powers of the board of adjustment can be of great importance. The significance of the power to approve special exceptions is largely determined by how much of the ordinance is mandatory. Clearly, the more rigidly the plan of uses and building types is set out in the zoning laws, the fewer discretionary details may be filled in by the board of adjustment. The standard act itself attempts to circumscribe the variance power by stating that a variance can be granted only when it "will not be contrary to the public interest, where, owing to special conditions, a literal enforcement of the provisions of the ordinance will result in unnecessary hardships, and so that the spirit of the ordinance shall be observed and substantial justice done." Many state enabling acts add to this language a requirement that there also be practical difficulties in complying with the terms of the zoning ordinance before a variance can be granted.

Three basic tests have been employed by the courts in reviewing grants of variances, and thus guide boards of adjustment in this area. First, it must be shown that a reasonable return from the property cannot be made without a variance. Second, the conditions involved must be the result of special zoning anomalies and not a general condition either of the land market or of the zoning ordinance. Finally, the new use sought must not be contrary to the essential character of the locality.

The provision for variances may be properly used, for example, to allow the relaxation of setback or sideyard requirements on a lot that would otherwise be too small to allow the construction of a reasonable house. It should clearly not be used to permit the conversion of significant amounts of land in a residential area to commercial development. In fact, some courts have held that such large-scale changes are actually amendments to the zoning ordinance and thus can be made only in accordance with the procedures required for amendments. In communities which have zoning ordinances citizens who are concerned with the problems of land use should carefully follow the proposals for variances that are put forward, to assure that piecemeal and unnoticed change of the zoning ordinance does not occur.

The standard act provides for citizen access to the actions of the zoning board of adjustment by requiring that the board's meetings be public and that records be kept of its actions, including an account of the votes of each member. Nevertheless, one should not be misled into believing that local zoning administrators and boards of adjustment are usually prepared to provide comprehensive and easily available information to the public. As one authority has pungently stated, "[i]t is not uncommon in smaller communities for the single copy of the zoning ordinance, not always amended to date, to be chained to a counter in a clerk's office."[8]

Although the shortcomings of zoning have been the subject of much debate, the framework of the standard act set out more than fifty years ago is an essentially rational one. The powers of zoning are delineated with specificity, but are broadly formulated to cover many land use problems. Provisions are made to assure the opportunity for public review of the zoning ordinance before it is adopted by the local legislative body and for public attendance at the meetings of the zoning board of adjustment. Minor revisions of the ordinance are possible through the administrative zoning board, but major changes by the legislature are possible only if they have wide backing.

The problem of exclusionary zoning has been discussed in Chapter 2 and the need for innovative mechanisms to relieve the lot-by-lot rigidity of traditional zoning is reviewed in the following section. Other problems which need to be addressed by informed citizens in terms of particular facts and circumstances are the possibility of corruption in the administration of a zoning ordinance, the lack of a comprehensive land use plan, and, of course, the failure to adopt zoning and other types of needed land use controls to protect land from uncontrolled development.

Zoning Innovations

Although the zoning framework set forth in the Standard State Zoning Enabling Act included provisions for special exceptions and variances, as well as amendments, to permit some flexibility within the zoning scheme, as time passed the criticism began to arise that traditional zoning was too rigid to deal with the varying needs of individual communities. This dissatisfaction was fed by a growing awareness of the monotony and wastefulness of lot-by-lot grids of residential development, along with desires to preserve open space and to approach large-scale development projects with a more innovative perspective. As a result, modifications such as "floating zones," "cluster zoning," and the "planned unit development"

(PUD) were developed to give communities more flexibility in dealing with their particular needs. In some cases, states have added provisions authorizing the use of such devices to their enabling legislation, while in others such usage has been developed under the general state delegation of the power to zone.

1. Floating Zones

Floating zones are districts with specified purposes which initially are established by the local legislative body without being actually delineated on the zoning map. Later, when an opportunity arises to carry out the intended purposes on a particular tract of land, the legislative body can pass an amendment to the zoning ordinance which establishes the actual boundaries of such a district. For example, a legislative body might wish to establish a district for carefully planned multiple-family dwellings to serve a cross section of income groups, but prefer to leave the location of such a district indeterminate until a developer submits a proposal for a large-scale development of this type.

Since the local legislative body first establishes the desirability of a specific type of floating zone or district and sets up standards which would protect adjacent lands, and then subsequently acts to place a particular district on the zoning map, this innovation has been held to meet the basic requirements of being in accordance with a comprehensive zoning plan and for the promotion of the general welfare. In this way, the floating zone technique avoids the pitfall of "spot zoning," in which a small tract of land is singled out for special treatment that benefits its owner rather than the community at large and is not carried out as part of a comprehensive zoning scheme.

2. Cluster Zoning

Cluster zoning is a means of preserving more open space without compromising the overall density requirements governing a tract of land. It basically entails the relaxation of zoning regulations on lot sizes, setbacks, frontage, sideyards, and other such restrictions in a development where the total population density will be no greater than it would have been had the land been developed on a lot-by-lot basis. (Another name for cluster zoning is "average density zoning.") This permits the clustering of dwelling units on a smaller percentage of the property and the preservation of large areas of open space for use by those living in the dwelling units. In addition to saving open space, facilities and services for this kind of development can be provided much more efficiently and economically. Of particular importance is the fact that in both construction and operation, such housing requires far less energy than conventional residential development.

A local planning board or commission may be empowered by the local legislative body to approve plans for development projects that use clustering techniques and thus to permit the necessary deviations from the zoning restrictions. As pointed out above, no abridgement of density requirements may be made in the approval of such plans.

Important factors in the review of plans for clustering, whether carried out by the planning board or the legislative body itself, are the suitability of the land in question for such development, the need for open space in the area, and the way in which the plan relates to the overall zoning goals and plan of the community.

3. The Planned Unit Development

The planned unit development, or PUD as it is commonly called, is perhaps the most sophisticated zoning innovation in common usage, and borrows from both clustering and floating zone techniques. In essence, a PUD is a floating district in which not only mixed residential uses (such as apartments and single-family houses), but also commercial and even industrial uses may be allowed, often in clustered patterns of location. Such developments are commonly planned only for large tracts of land, which frequently are on the outskirts of urban areas or in new towns.

The floating zone feature requires that the establishment of an actual PUD be a two-step legislative process. First, the legislative body enacts zoning regulations which authorize the formation of a PUD district at some point in the future, outlines the enactment procedure, and prescribes the standards which must be met before such a district may be created. Very likely, the local planning board or commission will be required to review a developer's plan for a PUD and make recommendations to the legislative body. If the legislative body wishes to approve a PUD plan, it must then amend the zoning ordinance, reclassifying the land involved as a PUD district. In so doing, the legislative body may increase the overall density requirements governing the area to be developed as a PUD —a step which cannot be taken by a planning board in approving a development plan which simply uses cluster zoning.

The standards set for the creation of a PUD district may be exacting. They may require a minimum amount of land for any such project and may specify the maximum percentage of land in the tract which may be covered by buildings or structures. They may also detail requirements for any or all of the following: road systems, drainage systems, water and sewage systems, open space, satisfactory lighting, parking facilities, traffic control, and screening, planting, and landscaping to protect surrounding land and retard erosion.

In addition to setting substantive standards, the zoning provisions authorizing the creation of PUD districts also establish procedural safeguards to assure that adequate official review and public scrutiny take place before a PUD is approved by a community. Given the extensive and complex character of a PUD project, it is not likely that a locality which does not have a local planning board or commission will have PUD provisions in its zoning ordinance. Thus, in the typical case, the developer of a proposed PUD works closely with the planning board and its professional staff in the development of a PUD concept and proposal. In its advisory capacity, the planning board then makes recommendations to the local legislative body on the proposed plan. A public hearing must always be held before the legislative body can amend the zoning ordinance, but public involvement in the assessment of PUD plans should be required in open planning board meetings beginning at the earliest stages of consideration of plans or preliminary concepts. In this process the public should be particularly sensitive to the question of population density and aware of the possibility that a developer may be pushing hard to win a greater density allotment than that allowed under the existing zoning ordinance. The capacity of the land and the natural resource system to sustain the population proposed for a project without significant detrimental effects should always be a central topic of consideration.

Problems in Rural Areas

Many towns and localities which have been granted zoning powers by the state have not exercised them. Consequently, there are large areas of the country which are not controlled by zoning restrictions or which are not zoned with the intent of regulating future large-scale development. These are frequently rural and undeveloped areas where there are the greatest pressures from large development projects.

This problem and a typical town response are described graphically in the case of *Steel Hill Development* v. *Sanbornton.*[9] Sanbornton is a small town in the hills of rural New Hampshire which in 1972 had a population of only about one thousand year-round residents. In the 1960s the town had become much more accessible to Boston and the heavily populated areas of New England when an interstate highway was built through the region. This accessibility, coupled with the lakes and skiing opportunities of the area, gave Sanbornton a seasonal second-home population of one thousand additional people.

In 1969 Steel Hill Development, Inc., bought land in the town and began to plan for the construction of about 500 homes there. This development would have dramatically increased the town's existing total of approximately 730 homes (comprised of some 330 primary residences and 400 second homes). The land purchased by Steel Hill was zoned for minimum lots of about three-quarters of an acre, but the developer hoped to win approval of a cluster plan which would require amendment of the zoning ordinance. While this proposed zoning change was under consideration, the town planning board approved a Steel Hill plan to develop thirty-seven conventional lots on its property, despite local opposition to any development by the company.

The townspeople of Sanbornton were opposed to Steel Hill's plans because of the effect the proposed development would have on the character and environment of the town. At a town meeting in 1971 a new zoning ordinance was passed which dramatically changed minimum lot sizes throughout the town. As a result, 70 percent of the land held by Steel Hill was now zoned for six-acre lots and 30 percent was zoned for three-acre lots. The developer subsequently sued the town on a number of grounds, the most important of which was that the zoning regulations did not bear a rational relationship to the health, safety, and general welfare of the community, and thus were beyond the powers granted to the town and were unconstitutional.

The evidence at the trial reviewed soil conditions and topography and the problems of sewage waste disposal, drainage, and erosion. It looked at the proposed development's impact in terms of water pollution, air pollution, and traffic problems, as well as at its possible interference with fish spawning. There was testimony on the town's desire to discourage dense settlement of the land, its fear of premature development, and its effort to provide for orderly development of unspoiled areas in the town.

In reviewing the case the U.S. Court of Appeals for the First

Circuit found that there was no controlling precedent to determine its judgment. It looked at two types of rulings and found that neither fully applied to Sanbornton. The first type was a series of cases involving suburban areas which attempted to avoid "natural" pressures for growth and development by imposing large lot zoning requirements. State courts in Pennsylvania, Virginia, Maryland, and New Jersey have struck down such zoning ordinances on the grounds that they interpret the general welfare too narrowly. The court also distinguished the Sanbornton situation from cases where rural areas have attempted to keep out new permanent residents simply to preserve open space and to fence out "undesirable" business, where there was no showing of damage to the environment. Ordinances such as these have also been struck down by the courts.

The court of appeals set out the bounds of the general welfare in the Sanbornton case as follows:

> We recognize, as within the general welfare, concerns relating to the construction and integration of hundreds of new homes which would have an irreversible effect on the area's ecological balance, destroy scenic values, decrease open space, significantly change the rural character of this small town, pose substantial financial burdens on the town for police, fire, sewer, and road service, and open the way for the tides of weekend "visitors" who would own second homes.[10]

This is a wide definition of the general welfare which allows towns considerable latitude in establishing their zoning restrictions. It is not entirely endorsed by other courts and although it was broad enough to support the Sanbornton zoning requirements, the court of appeals indicated that there were limits to which such zoning could be pushed:

> We cannot think that expansion of population, even a very substantial one, seasonal or permanent, is by itself a legitimate basis for permissible objection. . . . Where there is natural population growth it has to go somewhere, unwelcome as it may be, and in that case we do not think it should be channelled by the happenstance of what town gets its veto in first.[11]

In Sanbornton, the court simply did not see real evidence of natural pressure from "land-deprived and land-seeking outsiders," but rather an attempt by a developer to create demand for land in the town.

The court approved the Sanbornton zoning only as "a legitimate stop-gap measure." This was done primarily because the town had not engaged in professional and scientific analysis which could support a final finding that its zoning scheme was appropriate for the foreseeable future.

The Sanbornton case is instructive in showing the variety of concerns which are related to the general welfare, and also in demonstrating how difficult it often is for small rural towns to cope with large-scale development. Without having established long-range plans and land use controls, such towns may suddenly find themselves faced with the prospect of development which will rapidly and irreversibly transform their community and its environment. Efforts to win time for needed planning and the development of regulations to provide for orderly growth may be met with legal suits by developers. Sanbornton was fortunate enough to win the suit it faced, but such an outcome is by no means assured where circumstances or judicial opinions differ.

One of the major weaknesses of local governments in their confrontations with the problems of land use and development is the shortage of funds and personnel needed to develop the planning base for land use restrictions and to review competently the proposals presented to the locality. This circumstance must be remedied if local governments are to succeed in establishing zoning restrictions and other land use controls on a sound and unassailable basis.

Faced with serious growth problems, a number of localities have now sought to reconcile the competing interests of growth and protection of the environment through the development of regulatory schemes which control the rate of growth and allow development to go forward in an orderly manner. A regulatory system of this type was approved by the state courts in New York in *Golden v. Planning Board of Town of Ramapo,*[12] which is reviewed below under capital improvement programs, as well as in Chapter 2. In Petaluma, California, another such system was initially struck down by the federal district court as interfering with the constitutionally guaranteed right-to-travel.[13] As is discussed in Chapter 2, however, the U.S. Court of Appeals for the Ninth Circuit reversed the lower court's decision and upheld the Petaluma Plan. Since the U.S. Supreme Court has now denied a petition for review of the case, the adoption of growth control systems such as that developed in Petaluma can be expected to increase in other areas. Such ordinances offer an important form of control to localities which must allow growth, but wish to do so by assimilation rather than by inundation.

MUNICIPAL PLANNING

The growth of comprehensive municipal planning in this country followed the establishment of zoning as the most pervasive local land use control. Today, the enabling legislation of most states authorizes or requires the establishment of municipal planning boards or commissions whose major function is the preparation of a plan —usually called a comprehensive plan, a master plan, a development plan, or a general plan—for the future development of the locality. Such planning bodies may also have a wide range of other duties, such as responsibility for developing and administering subdivision regulations, which are discussed in the following section; reviewing proposed changes to the zoning ordinance and making recommendations to the local legislative body; preparing official maps, also discussed below; and preparing other studies, reports, and maps. In some municipalities the enforcement of the zoning ordinance, or the issuance of some special permits, is entrusted to the planning board.

Planning boards and commissions are composed of community residents who generally serve terms of from three to five years and are appointed either by the locality's chief executive or by the legislative body itself. Although patterns of organization vary widely, planning boards or commissions are usually supported by professional staff members or consultants who carry out the technical work involved in planning. Most large cities have planning departments staffed with planning specialists, while some small towns which cannot afford their own planners turn to the state and to county or regional planning boards for technical assistance. In some areas the county plays an important role in coordinating the planning efforts of localities within its boundaries and in seeing that countywide considerations are brought to bear. County planning boards may even have review powers over some local government actions. As is discussed below, some federal aid to support local planning is available through the "701" program of the U.S. Department of Housing and Urban Development (HUD).

The comprehensive plan prepared by the planning board should be a master design for the future growth of a locality. It should be based on a comprehensive and detailed survey of existing physical and human resources and should embody the basic goals sought by the community. In the preparation of the plan, land capabilities, including such factors as soil, slope, elevation, and drainage, should be carefully examined; natural ecological systems should be considered; plans for the provision of utilities and community facilities should be developed; economic needs and projections should be evaluated; estimates of population growth and distribution should be reviewed; and open space needs should be assessed. The result should be a plan which can guide the community through the many difficulties involved in determining how public and private growth and development will take place within its jurisdiction.

Most comprehensive plans are strictly advisory, presenting the planning board's recommendations regarding the most desirable ways of using land but not requiring the local legislative body to follow these recommendations. In short, the plan is usually a guide to community growth rather than an actual instrument of land use control. In some states the planning enabling legislation does authorize the local legislative body officially to adopt the comprehensive plan, an action which generally establishes that no public structures, roads, parks, or other improvements may be made either (1) in conflict with the comprehensive plan, or (2) without the approval of the planning board.

As was pointed out above, in most states localities can adopt and enforce a zoning ordinance without having first prepared a comprehensive plan of the type discussed here. A notable exception to this rule is the state of Oregon, where the state Supreme Court ruled in April 1975 that zoning ordinances must conform to a comprehensive plan, even if the comprehensive plan was adopted subsequent to the zoning ordinance.[14] Although such correspondence is not required in most states, a well-prepared comprehensive plan provides an excellent basis for the regulations of a zoning ordinance, as well as for other types of land use controls. The plan may also include implementation studies describing what legislative actions could or should be taken to carry out the planning board's recommendations.

The HUD 701 Program

As has been noted, federal assistance for local planning is available through HUD's so-called 701 program, which takes its name from the section of the act which established the program in 1954.[15] The budget of this program was cut from $100 million in fiscal year 1975 to $75 million in fiscal year 1976, and the Ford Administration has pushed for the dismantlement of the entire program. In the face of this pressure, strong efforts have been made to demonstrate the program's effectiveness and HUD has adopted the policy of cutting off funding to agencies whose past performance has been poor.

HUD 701 grants, which are available for state, regional, and local planning activities, may be channeled through the state or in the case of large cities, urban counties, Indian tribal groups, or regional bodies, may be made directly from HUD. Under the 701 program HUD may fund up to two-thirds of various planning activities, the most important of which is the development of a comprehensive plan through an "ongoing comprehensive planning process," which is required of each 701 grant recipient. Comprehensive planning is broadly defined by the statute governing the program to include:

(A) preparation, as a guide for governmental policies and action, of general plans with respect to (i) the pattern and intensity of land use, (ii) the provision of public facilities (including transportation facilities) and other government services, and (iii) the effective development and utilization of human and natural resources;

(B) identification and evaluation of area needs (including housing, employment, education, and health) and formulation of specific programs for meeting the needs so identified;

(C) surveys of structures and sites which are determined by the appropriate authorities to be of historic or architectural value;

(D) long-range physical and fiscal plans for such action;

(E) programing of capital improvements and other major expenditures, based on a determination of relative urgency, together with definite financing plans for such expenditures in the earlier years of the program;

(F) coordination of all related plans and activities of the State and local governments and agencies concerned; and

(G) preparation of regulatory and administrative measures in support of the foregoing.[16]

Provisions of the Housing and Community Development Act of 1974 amending the 701 program[17] require that by August 22, 1977, every comprehensive plan funded by HUD must include a housing element and a land use element. The land use element must include an analysis, standards, and implementing procedures for effectively guiding and controlling major decisions concerning where growth will take place. It must also include as a guide for government action and policy, general plans for the pattern and intensity of land use for residential, commercial, industrial, and other activities.

HUD's regulations implementing this part of its program describe a wide-ranging land use analysis in which all land use policies and planning are integrated.[18] The plans developed under the program are to serve as a guide for communities on all matters related to the use of land, including "air and water quality concerns, waste disposal, transportation, protection of coastal areas, open space, agricultural food and fiber production, environmental conservation, development, and housing."[19] If the plans actually produced live up to these requirements they will indeed be comprehensive.

HUD has built the dictates of the National Environmental Policy Act into the 701 program.[20] Wherever it funds the development of land use plans or policies, HUD requires that the planning body prepare an environmental assessment of these plans or policies. The assessments follow the requirements of NEPA environmental impact statements, and must be made available to the public on a timely basis, including availability prior to any public hearings regarding the plan.

HUD's 701 regulations emphasize the importance and necessity of public involvement in the planning process. Each planning body which receives a HUD grant must include in its progress reports to HUD a statement documenting citizen involvement, and stringent criteria have been established by HUD to assure that citizens are not only informed about but actively involved in planning activities:

> Citizens in addition to being informed should have the opportunity to help initiate as well as react to proposals. . . .
>
> The applicant should provide citizens with access to the decision making process. . . .
>
> Information should be provided sufficiently in advance of public decisions to give citizens an adequate opportunity to review and to react to proposals. Applicants should seek to relate technical data and other professional material to the affected citizens so that they understand the impact of public programs, available options, and alternative decisions.[21]

These are fine goals, but their achievement depends very heavily on citizens asserting their rights and being willing to take an active part in the planning process. Often citizens' groups have found that local planning bodies are not sufficiently responsive to HUD regulations and that only through citizen pressure can the high aims of these regulations actually be realized.

SUBDIVISION CONTROL

Many states provide particular powers to units of local government to regulate the development of subdivisions. Such controls seek to assure that basic services are provided and that purchasers are protected against fly-by-night schemes and developers who do not see their plans through to conclusion. Typically, subdivision controls will assure a reasonable system of roads and connections to the road system outside the development; they will insure that drainage and sewerage facilities are provided; they may require the preservation of open space within a subdivision; and occasionally they will require that schools, or land for schools, be provided.

Local statutes generally require that the plat for a subdivision be approved by the local planning board or commission before it is officially filed. In some areas, the sale of subdivided land is prohibited before filing is accepted, and in almost all cases, financing and promotion of a subdivision are extremely difficult without such filing.

The state legislation which enables local units of government to control subdivision development is frequently broadly written, setting out what must be taken into consideration in approving or denying a subdivision application rather than establishing specific standards such as open space requirements or road specifications. Typically, enabling statutes written in general terms state that the planning board or commission must review the subdivider's plans to assure that there is a suitably located park or parks, that there is a convenient and properly constructed road system, that there will be compliance with any existing zoning ordinance, and that the land can be used for building purposes without safety or health hazards. Further, such enabling statutes may also include a broad provision like the following, which is from an influential model municipal planning enabling act that was developed in the 1930s:

> As a condition precedent to the approval of the plat, the [planning] commission may prescribe requirements of the extent to which and the manner in which streets will be graded and improved, and water, sewer, and other utility mains, piping, connections, or other facilities shall be installed.[22]

Municipalities which operate directly under the authority of a broadly worded enabling act may leave wide discretion in the hands of their planning boards regarding what will be required in a particular subdivision scheme. The planning board is, of course, bound by the general requirements of the police power and cannot arbitrarily discriminate between applicants in similar situations, but it can vary its requirements to meet differences in local conditions, taking into account soils, slopes, water tables, and other natural conditions. Some states require, and many local governments voluntarily establish, regulations which regularize the terms on which subdivisions are accepted for filing. Such regulations give both the planning board and citizen groups clear standards by which to measure a proposal presented by a developer.

Other systems of land use control within a town can also provide means of controlling and monitoring subdivision proposals. These are generally of three types: the comprehensive plan, the official map, and the zoning ordinance. As discussed above, most comprehensive plans are advisory, but since they are usually drawn up by the planning board which must approve subdivisions, they are a basic framework for any subdivision plan and one which the board should be slow to abandon. An official map, which is described in the next section, should act as a guide for or control over subdivision plans whenever such a map has been adopted by a locality. Finally, subdivisions usually must conform to a town's zoning scheme, which serves as an additional check on plans for such development.

Enabling acts for subdivision regulations generally require notice to the public and a hearing on proposed subdivision plans. It is important that citizens who are interested in influencing the form subdivisions will take enter the review process as early as possible. Developers frequently begin negotiations with a planning board on the basis of preliminary plans in order to avoid the major expense of developing complete plans before they have an indication of the board's reaction. In some states approval of preliminary plans is required; in others, such as Connecticut, it is prohibited. Particularly where a planning board has extensive discretion in what it can require of a developer, preliminary review can be an important period of negotiation in which the planning board slowly becomes committed to the plan as modifications and proposals for the dedication of land for public uses are hammered out. Citizens should be aware of this process and should press from the beginning for agreements which will require the developer and not the community to shoulder as many of the costs of the subdivision as possible.

There are, of course, limits to what can be demanded of a developer. New York allows towns to require that up to 10 percent of the development area be set aside for parks or open space. The courts have upheld this requirement, but a requirement of 20 to 25 percent might be struck down. Requirements for schools have frequently been found invalid, while reasonable road and sewerage requirements have been upheld as more obviously necessary facilities that are directly related to the subdivision.

The final important controls on subdividers are the measures which are taken to insure that their promises to provide basic services are in fact carried out. Localities often accomplish this by requiring developers to post performance bonds to protect both the municipality and purchasers from any failure to complete the construction of facilities upon which plat approval was based.

OFFICIAL MAPS

About half of the states have enabling legislation which allows local governments to adopt an official map. The official map is a particular type of plan for the area's future development that is distinct from both the zoning map and the comprehensive plan. It sets out in explicit form on a map existing and future streets, sewer systems, and other basic necessities such as the routes of utility systems. It may also include existing and proposed public parks. The obvious intent of the map system is to provide a clear guide for future rational development and to allow private landowners to plan their development within the context of an agreed upon grid of public services.

The official map is generally adopted by the legislative body of a municipality on the basis of a proposed map drawn up by the planning board or commission. Adoption of an official map, like most other schemes of land use control, must usually be preceded by a public notice and hearing.

The official map is a useful basic means of promoting orderly advance planning, and provides a reasonable basis upon which to judge development proposals that are put before a municipality. Its legal force and effect vary among the states, but it should be consulted and its authority considered in those localities where it has been adopted. The following are examples of possible legal consequences of an official map: subdividers may be required to design their plats in accordance with the official map; developers may be denied permits to build in the bed of proposed streets which are on the map; and installation of municipal utilities may be prohibited on streets which are not on the map.[23]

BUILDING CODES

Virtually every local government is empowered to enact building codes and regulations governing construction. Some states have developed a state building code which may be adopted by local governments. Building codes typically establish the types of materials, wiring, and plumbing which must be used in construction or alteration of buildings. The terms of the code may set out specific materials or standards of performance. In themselves, the codes do not contribute much to the control of land use, but they frequently work as the basic mechanism through which compliance with the zoning ordinance is insured. Typically a building permit will not be issued unless there is compliance with both the building code and the zoning ordinance. This may require approval by both a building department and a zoning administrator or only by one authority. Compliance with the terms of the building permit is usually insured through the requirement that a certificate of occupancy be issued before a building may be used.

CAPITAL IMPROVEMENT PROGRAMS

Many local governments plan and control the public aspects of their growth and development through capital improvement programs. These programs set out a plan of projects to be undertaken by the government over a period of time, such as the next five years, along with the estimated costs of the program and the methods proposed for financing the improvements. The improvement projects planned might include, for example, construction of sewage treatment plants and interceptor lines, road construction or improvements, and acquisition of land for parks. Typically, a tentative budget must be prepared each year by a local official and submitted to the local governing body for adoption. This budget indicates the priorities in the program. All legal provisions for public hearings on local tentative budgets and budget adoptions apply to capital improvement programs, which always should be widely discussed in the community.

A capital improvement program can be an excellent, long-term means of implementing improvements recommended in a comprehensive plan prepared by a planning board or commission. Such capital plans and budgets offer to the local government yet another means of approaching its future needs and development in an orderly, responsible manner. The formulation of a long-range program for the provision of improvements can strengthen a community's understanding of its problems and its ability to control the way in which it grows. Once a capital improvement program is established, it becomes much more likely that developers will have to consider the framework of local services, existing and proposed, when they design and propose projects. Pressures for improvements on an ad hoc basis—which are often spurred by special interests—can then also be more easily answered and controlled. In addition, funds for the development and implementation of environmental programs such as an open space program may be provided through a capital improvement program.

It should be pointed out, however, that capital improvement programs can establish a timetable for the provision of improvements which actually attracts or induces new development. This is particularly true when plans appropriate for urban areas are adopted in rural or suburban areas. Citizens should always carefully consider the hypotheses upon which capital improvement programs are based and make sure that goals, explicit or implicit, are appropriate for the locality involved.

In the 1960s the town of Ramapo, New York, which is within commuting distance of New York City, developed a capital improvement program which has received national attention. The town planning board first prepared a comprehensive plan for the town's future growth. The town then enacted a zoning ordinance implementing this plan and established an eighteen-year capital improvement program (involving three six-year capital programs) setting out a schedule for the construction of municipal services. No land in the town could then be developed for residential purposes unless the developer could show that certain capital improvements—whether constructed by the town or by the developer himself—would be available by the time the proposed project was completed. As discussed in Chapter 2, this program of phased growth was challenged in the courts in *Golden* v. *Planning Board of Town of Ramapo* and was upheld by New York State's highest court in 1972.[24]

LOCAL CONSERVATION COMMISSIONS

During the past twenty years the New England states, as well as New York, New Jersey, and Pennsylvania, have passed enabling legislation authorizing local governments to establish conservation commissions through which citizen concern about environmental issues can be expressed to the local legislative body. Composed of from three to nine members, which are generally appointed, these commissions are advisory only in most of the states, but exercise regulatory powers over wetlands in Massachusetts and Connecticut. The major duties usually assigned to conservation commissions include gathering of information and preparation of inventories on open space and natural resources; advising the legislative body on how the resources inventoried can best be protected; reviewing development proposals which involve open space, wetlands, or other critical natural areas; educating the public on environmental issues; and working to coordinate the efforts of all local environmental groups. In Massachusetts conservation commissions became eligible in 1960 for 50 percent state reimbursement of the costs of open space land acquisition.

In general, conservation commissions must rely on local funding and gifts to support their activities, though some states do provide technical and/or financial assistance. In addition, during the early 1970s the Ford Foundation supported the development of the movement through grants to some 350 conservation commissions in Connecticut, Maine, Massachusetts, New Hampshire, New Jersey, New York, and Rhode Island.

The specific activities carried out by particular conservation commissions have had considerable impact on environmental protection in local communities. Among such activities have been the development of floodplain zoning plans and open space plans, monitoring of air and water pollution control programs, review of pesticide use, identification of sanitary landfill sites, organization of recycling programs, research on local property tax structures, purchase of rights-of-way to public beaches, review of highway plans, planting of shade trees, promotion of cluster housing developments, and enforcement of billboard control laws.

Although enabling legislation for local conservation commissions has been enacted only in the Northeast, agencies similar to such commissions exist in local governments in a number of states across the country and there is considerable interest in the concept nationwide.

The degree to which a local environmental conservation commission composed of citizens is able to influence the local government depends on a number of factors. Perhaps the most important of these are the commitment, energy, and political awareness of the commission's members. Those commissions which are most successful are those which are able to evaluate circumstances realistically, to build strong public support for environmental values, and to establish a viable political base from which to win protection for these values.

THE LOCAL REAL PROPERTY TAX

One of the perennial issues that arises at the local level during consideration of land use and development questions is the impact of development on the real property tax. Traditionally it has been assumed that certain land uses have a favorable impact on local property taxes and ought to be sought after. The reasoning has been that commercial or industrial development, resorts, and second homes all increase the assessed value of real estate within the jurisdiction and thereby increase tax revenues without placing corresponding demands on local services, particularly on schools.[25] Since revenues are enhanced without an equivalent increase in expenditures, taxes can be lowered. Intensive development has also been advocated on the grounds that it brings economic well-being to an area. Finally, it has often been assumed that if a jurisdiction has large areas devoted to agricultural or other open space uses, property taxes will necessarily be higher than they would be if the land were developed.

In fact, this kind of reasoning—which is frequently put forward as an unassailable argument for new development—is far too simplistic to account for the many complex factors involved. For example, in the case of second-home development, no consideration is generally given to such complications as the fact that second-home developments, while increasing demands for community services, do not increase the locality's eligibility for most state and federal aid programs, which are usually based on permanent population figures; or that second-home owners from urban areas often make demands for far more local services and much greater efficiency, in such areas as road maintenance and garbage collection, than existing residents of rural areas have traditionally expected.

In addition, prodevelopment rhetoric usually fails to face up to the full costs of development to a community both in terms of all direct new municipal expenditures (such as the costs of increased fire protection, police, and health services) and in terms of indirect costs such as air pollution, water pollution, decreased water supply, traffic congestion, noise, aesthetic blight, loss of open space, and loss of local character, traditions, and values. Such costs as these have traditionally been overlooked when new developments are proposed, but their impact has become much more apparent as more and more communities have experienced serious growth and development problems—and have come to the conclusion that the full costs of development often outweigh the benefits.[26]

It is essential that citizens be aware of the propensity of developers and local politicians to make strong claims about the property tax benefits of new development and that they refuse to take such claims at face value. The documentation of contrary experiences which is growing rapidly, increasingly deflating development euphoria with more realistic assessments, can be used at the least as an argument for full and thoughtful consideration of proposed development.

Another critical facet of the property tax problem is the tax pressure placed on agricultural lands at the suburban fringe. Such lands are generally assessed in terms of their development potential rather than their present use. As a result, farmers are increasingly forced or enticed into selling out to developers. Chapter 12 discusses the attempts made by many of the states to develop effective property tax incentives for the preservation of productive agricultural land.

CITIZEN ACTION

Because local conditions differ so greatly across the country, it is not possible to provide specific advice on how citizens can most effectively influence their local government's decisions on land use and development. It is possible, however, to make some general suggestions.

1. The most important thing a citizen who wants to do something about an environmental problem can do is to find other people who share the problem or who are willing to give support—and organize. One person working alone, no matter how dedicated and persistent, can never hope to be as effective as a well-organized group. A letter written on the letterhead of a group will receive more attention than a letter on plain paper from an individual. Groups may prepare press

releases which newspapers will publish. Government officials will be more willing to meet with a representative from a group than with someone who only wants to discuss his own problems. Defending environmental values is often not an easy job, but many more doors will be opened for an organized group than for a single person working alone. The citizens' group which can serve as an effective vehicle for the expression of the concerns of an aware citizenry can be a very powerful political force.

2. As was pointed out at the beginning of this chapter, citizens need to find out what powers their own local government has to regulate or control the use of land. This information is needed to determine both whether the local government is acting legally in those actions which it is taking and whether it is failing to use powers which it is authorized to carry out. As discussed above, a state may have delegated powers to enact land use controls to units of local government through any or all of the following: (a) the state constitution, (b) statutes granting home rule powers, and (c) enabling legislation dealing with particular subject matter areas. Efforts to track down what delegations have been made in a particular state may begin with a search for all materials that may have been prepared on local planning and land use regulation in the state and with requests for guidance from state agencies concerned with local government problems, planning, or environmental protection. If there is a local conservation commission or other local government agency with strong environmental concerns, it may be able to provide assistance, as may any existing local environmental organization. In their research, citizens should take care to determine what kinds of provisions exist in their state for public involvement in local government deliberations on land use questions, and what possibilities there may be for administrative appeals or legal actions.

3. It is always essential to know when public hearings must or may be held before a decision can be made by an organ of local government. Such hearings give citizens the opportunity to present their views on what action should be taken; well-prepared and well-organized citizen testimony at a public hearing can be a very effective way of clarifying what the concerns of the community are and of indicating the strength of these concerns. In hearings on such issues as the granting of a variance by the zoning board of adjustment or the approval of a subdivision plat by a planning board, such citizen participation can be vital to the determination made. If a final decision is adverse, moreover, strong public sentiment may make it

possible to obtain a rehearing. In some cases, citizens may find themselves opposed to the position taken by the zoning or planning board, while in others they may need to stand forcefully behind a wise position of a board that is being opposed by developers.

If a public hearing is required by law before a particular local government action, this hearing must be held and it must be held in accordance with any specific procedures that are set out by law. For example, it is commonly required that public notice of an impending hearing be given in a newspaper or newspapers of general circulation for a certain number of times, a certain number of days before the hearing. If such legally required procedures are not followed exactly (and it is not unusual for local governments to fail to give proper notice), subsequent actions of the local government will not have legal force and actions may be brought to have them set aside. Here, as in other legal actions discussed below, the assistance of a lawyer will be necessary.

4. The same attention to procedural requirements is also necessary when local governments adopt ordinances and regulations under state enabling legislation. State law may require the formation of certain local entities, such as a zoning commission to draw up the zoning ordinance. It may set restrictions on the membership of such bodies, on the length of terms, and on methods of appointment or removal. Requirements for public involvement, including public hearings, are usually established. In carrying out the powers which the state has delegated to it through enabling legislation, the local government must follow the procedures required by state law. If it does not do so, its actions are subject to legal challenge.

5. When citizens believe that a local ordinance has not been properly adopted or does not promote the health, safety, or general welfare of the community, they may wish to take the question of the ordinance's validity to court. This move is often made through an action for a declaratory judgment in which the plaintiffs ask the court to rule on what their rights are under the law. This type of action seeks neither damages nor an injunction, but rather the opinion of the court on a legal question, such as whether or not a local ordinance is legally binding. However, the action cannot be used merely to obtain an advisory opinion, but must seek judicial settlement of a real controversy through a judgment that is binding on all parties to the suit. For example, if a procedural challenge is being made, the complaint must allege facts constituting a failure by the local government to meet mandatory procedural requirements.

In order to obtain standing the plaintiff (or plaintiffs) in an action for a declaratory judgment must demonstrate that he has a real interest in the controversy concerning which a judgment is sought. He may well have to demonstrate that he has suffered or will suffer pecuniary damage as a result of the ordinance or regulation being challenged. He will very probably have to show that land which he owns or leases will in some way suffer significant adverse effects. Since standing is a very technical legal problem, the requirements for which vary in different states, it is a matter to be carefully discussed with a lawyer.

6. When a problem arises that involves not an ordinance or regulation in itself, but an action or failure to act by a local official charged with carrying out the ordinance, there will probably be administrative channels for complaints or challenges. For example, one of the primary duties of the zoning board of adjustment under the Standard State Zoning Enabling Act is to hear appeals on actions taken by the officer charged with administering the zoning ordinance. Those making such appeals should be careful to follow all procedures set out in local laws and regulations. A public hearing may be required on an appeal, and, if so, should be used as an opportunity to express concerns effectively and to present a show of strength through a large turnout of supporters. Again, the citizen or citizens challenging an officer's action will probably have to demonstrate that they are aggrieved by the action—that is, that property which they own or lease is or will be substantially affected. If there is no formalized avenue of appeal from an action by an officer or official body of the locality, citizens should present complaints to the local legislative body, which is the source of authority for such officers and bodies.

7. If it is not possible to win the relief sought through administrative remedies, citizens may wish to seek judicial review of the action or inaction of a local officer or body. The procedures through which this type of legal action may be taken vary widely in the different states, and an attorney's advice and assistance are essential to guide such an effort. It is important to note, however, that there are usually time limits (often as short as thirty days) set on the initiation of actions for judicial review. Thus, after a final administrative decision or action, citizens should move quickly to obtain legal advice if they believe that the matter should be taken to court.

8. Another very important area of concern is the prevention of uses, development, and construction that are in violation of a zoning

or other local ordinance. Generally, municipalities are authorized by state enabling statutes to initiate an action for an injunction to insure that illegal actions are prevented or stopped. A number of states, however, also provide that taxpayers or residents with substantial interests at stake may bring an action for an injunction to prevent zoning violations. Thus if the municipality does not move to enforce its zoning regulations, individual citizens may be able to shoulder this responsibility themselves.

9. Finally, citizens who want to play an important role in land use decision making at the local level of government should never lose sight of the political realities of their community. They should attempt to assess both their own strength and that of opposing groups and individuals as realistically as possible, and should be willing to work for wider public understanding and backing of the values which they feel must be protected.

NOTES

1. Cal. Const., Art. XI, § 11.

2. See Perry v. County Board of Appeals, 211 Md. 294, 127 A.2d 507 (1956).

3. U.S. Department of Commerce, Advisory Committee on City Planning and Zoning, *A Standard State Zoning Enabling Act* (Washington, D.C.: U.S. Government Printing Office, 1926).

4. As discussed in Chapter 12, the American Law Institute has developed an extensive new model statute called A Model Land Development Code, which seeks both to strengthen the land use planning and regulatory capabilities of local governments and to delineate the role which should be played by the state in land use decision making. The innovative land use legislation enacted by the state of Florida in 1972 was based on the third draft of this model code.

5. The Federal Insurance Administration (FIA) of the U.S. Department of Housing and Urban Development has financed a study called *Statutory Land Use Control Enabling Authority in the Fifty States,* which provides state-by-state summaries of local land use controls, as well as information on home rule delegations and case law. Prepared for use in the FIA's administration of the National Flood Insurance Program, which is discussed in Chapter 7, the study concentrates on flood hazard regulatory authority, but is, nonetheless, an excellent overall research source on zoning, subdivision control, building codes, and planning requirements in the fifty states. For information regarding the availability of the draft or final version of this study contact: Chief, Flood Plain Management Division, Federal Insurance Administration, HUD, Washington, D.C. 20410

6. The American Law Institute's Model Land Development Code sets out a much broader legislative purpose which explicitly acknowledges environmental ends and specifies strong state involvement: "It is the legislative purpose to protect

the land, air, water, natural resources and environment of this State, to encourage their use in a socially and economically desirable manner, and to provide a mechanism by which the state may establish and carry out a state land use policy. . . ." § 1–101.

7. The standard act leaves to local decision the distance from the affected area which comes within the ambit of sufficient proximity to qualify the landowner as a protester.

8. Robert M. Anderson, *American Law of Zoning: Zoning, Planning, Subdivision Control* (Rochester, N.Y.: The Lawyers Cooperative Publishing Co., 1968), § 313–25.

9. 469 F.2d 956, 4 ERC 1746 (1st Cir. 1972).

10. 469 F.2d 961.

11. 469 F.2d 962.

12. 30 N.Y.2d 359, 334 N.Y.S.2d 138, 285 N.E.2d 291, *appeal dismissed*, 409 U.S. 1003 (1972).

13. Construction Industry Association of Sonoma County v. City of Petaluma, 375 F. Supp. 574, 6 ERC 1453 (N.D. Cal. 1974), 522 F.2d 897, 8 ERC 1001 (9th Cir. 1975), *cert. denied*, 96 S.Ct. 1148 (February 23, 1976).

14. Baker v. City of Milwaukie, 533 P.2d 772 (Oregon 1975).

15. 40 U.S.C. § 461.

16. 40 U.S.C. § 461 (m) (4).

17. Public Law No. 93–383, §§ 101 to 118, 88 Stat. 633 to 653 (August 22, 1974).

18. 40 *Federal Register* 36862 (August 22, 1975); 24 C.F.R. § 600.72.

19. *Ibid.*

20. 24 C.F.R. § 600.65.

21. 40 *Federal Register* 36863 (August 22, 1975); 24 C.F.R. § 600.80.

22. Edward M. Bassett, Frank B. Williams, Alfred Bettman, and Robert Whitten, *Model Laws for Planning Cities, Counties, and States* (Cambridge, Mass.: Harvard University Press, 1935), p. 43.

23. Anderson, *American Law of Zoning*, § 20.02.

24. 30 N.Y.2d 359, 334 N.Y.S.2d 138, 285 N.E.2d 291 (1972).

25. Schools have traditionally been the most costly expenditure of local governments. In the past few years, however, state courts in a number of states (including California, Arizona, New Jersey, and Connecticut) have ruled that since local financing of schools through property taxes leads to inequities in educational opportunities, it violates the state constitution. (The U.S. Supreme Court has ruled that such financing does not violate the federal constitution. Rodriguez v. San Antonio Independent School District, 411 U.S. 1 [1973].) As a result of these decisions, states under court orders and others as well have begun to devise new ways of financing schools. At the present, it is too early to tell how widespread this trend will be and what impact it will have on land use considerations.

26. Summaries, analyses, and references to growth studies conducted by various communities can be found in "Nation's Cities Fighting to Stem Growth," *New York Times*, July 28, 1974, page 1; Task Force on Land Use and Urban Growth, *The Use of Land: A Citizen's Policy Guide to Urban Growth*, ed. William K. Reilly, a Task Force report sponsored by the Rockefeller Brothers Fund (New York: Thomas Y. Crowell Company, 1973); and Real Estate Research Corporation, *The Costs of Sprawl: Literature Review and Bibliography* (Washington, D.C.: U.S. Government Printing Office, April 1974). The last reference is a study prepared for the Council

on Environmental Quality, the U.S. Department of Housing and Urban Development, and the U.S. Environmental Protection Agency, which is for sale for $4 by the Superintendent of Documents, U.S. Government Printing Office, Washington, D.C. 20402. It includes (1) an essay on the environmental and economic effects of alternative development patterns, based on both a review of the relevant literature and the background of the research firm conducting the study; (2) a general bibliography of materials reviewed in the literature search; and (3) an annotated bibliography, in which the most important documents in the general bibliography are briefly described.

NOTE ON LEGAL CITATIONS

T HE LEGAL CITATIONS which appear in some of the notes in this
book, while readily understandable to attorneys, may appear
somewhat perplexing to the general reader. The following explana-
tions, therefore, offer some basic clarifying assistance:

1. *Federal Court Cases.* There are three levels of federal courts:
the federal district courts, the circuit courts of appeals, and the U.S.
Supreme Court. The district courts are the courts of first instance;
appeals are taken from the district court to the circuit court of
appeals. The circuit courts also review many decisions of federal
administrative agencies which come to them directly without review
by the district courts. The U.S. Supreme Court has the discretion to
hear such appeals as it chooses from the circuit courts. The request
for an appeal to be heard is made through a petition for a writ of
certiorari. The Supreme Court also has discretion to hear cases
appealed from state courts when the cases raise federal constitutional
questions.

Citations for federal court cases include the name of the case
decided, the series in which the decisions are collected, the court and
the year in which the decision was made, and sometimes the history
of the case. The volume of the series always precedes the abbreviated
title of the entire series cited and the page on which the case begins

always follows the title of the series. This citation system can best be explained through examples:

a. *District Courts:* Bass v. Richardson, 338 F. Supp. 478, 481 (S.D.N.Y. 1971). Bass is the plaintiff in the case and Richardson the defendant. The opinion in the case is found in volume 338 of the *Federal Supplement* ("F. Supp."), which collects the decisions of the district courts. The case begins on page 478 and the particular passage cited is on page 481. The decision was rendered by the U.S. District Court for the Southern District of New York in 1971. There are district courts for each state and the District of Columbia, with many states being divided into more than one district.

b. *Circuit Courts of Appeals:* Gantt v. Mobil Chemical Co., 463 F.2d 691 (5th Cir. 1972). As with all citations, the names of the plaintiff and defendant give the case its title. The decisions of the circuit courts of appeals are collected in the *Federal Reporter,* which is now in the second numbered series ("F.2d"). The "2d" in the abbreviated title indicates the second series, as it does throughout the citation system. The court rendering the decision is indicated just before the date, here the U.S. Court of Appeals for the Fifth Circuit. There are eleven circuit courts of appeals, ten simply numbered and one for the District of Columbia Circuit.

c. *Supreme Court:* Miller v. Schoene, 276 U.S. 272 (1928). The decisions of the Supreme Court are collected in the *United States Reports* ("U.S."). Since this series contains only the decisions of the Supreme Court there is no need to indicate the court of decision before the date in the citation.

In addition to these standard compilations of cases, there are two specialized reporter systems in the environmental field which record cases of federal and state courts. These are the *Environment Reporter Cases* ("ERC") and the *Environmental Law Reporter* ("ELR"). They are cited in the same manner as the official reporters, e.g., Natural Resources Defense Council v. Securities and Exchange Commission, 7 ERC 1199 (D.C. Cir. 1974).

2. *Federal Statutes.* Federal statutes are codified in the *United States Code* ("U.S.C."). In citations, the volume number precedes U.S.C. and the section number of the statute follows. For example, 33 U.S.C. § 1251 *et seq.* (the citation of the Federal Water Pollution Control Act) indicates that the statute can be found at section 1251, and following, in volume 33 of the *United States Code.*

3. *Federal Regulations.* Federal regulations which are adopted pursuant to federal legislation are first published in the *Federal Register,* along with other official notices and information, and are then codified in the *Code of Federal Regulations,* which is cited as "C.F.R." Again, the volume number precedes the abbreviated series title and the part or section number follows.

4. *State Citations.* Citations to state statutes, court cases, and regulations follow much the same format as citations to federal documents, though systems for the codification of statutes and regulations and for the reporting of state court decisions vary from state to state. Decisions of the highest state courts are published in the following regional reporters: the *Atlantic Reporter,* Second Series (A.2d); the *North Eastern Reporter,* Second Series (N.E.2d); the *North Western Reporter,* Second Series (N.W.2d); the *Pacific Reporter,* Second Series (P.2d); the *South Eastern Reporter,* Second Series (S.E.2d); and the *South Western Reporter,* Second Series (S.W.2d).

Further information on citations can be found in the so-called white book, whose actual title is *A Uniform System of Citation* (11th edition, 1967). This reference booklet for lawyers is published and distributed by The Harvard Law Review Association, Gannett House, Cambridge, Massachusetts 02138.

INDEX